D0065312

OPINIONS AND PERSPECTIVES

from

The New York Times Book Review

OPINIONS
AND PERSPECTIVES

from

The New York Times Book Review

EDITED AND WITH AN INTRODUCTION

BY FRANCIS BROWN

HOUGHTON MIFFLIN COMPANY BOSTON

The Riverside Press Cambridge

1964

First Printing   W

Contents

Part III. Reviews and Reappraisals

Part IV. Points of View

Part V. Somewhat Personal

Part VI. The Author's Experience

Part VII. Men and Measures

Introduction

THE OPINIONS and perspectives presented in this collection were first printed in the *New York Times* Book Review. The authors do not speak in a single voice, but with many accents and intonations, and there is no common pattern to their perspectives. Their talk is book talk, good book talk, and what they have to say represents some of the variety of literary experience and expression essential to an appreciation of what men and women during the past decade have been thinking and writing and, yes, reading.

The talk is of our time — in the sense, at least, that when figures of the past, Emerson, for example, are on parade they are not ancient and honorables, but men who have some importance and significance for an existential generation. When Maxwell Geismar asks the question "Was Papa truly a great writer?" and answers yes, with reservations, his answer is shaped by the judgment of today, not yesterday, and similarly when Arthur Mizener attacks the suitability of a Nobel Prize for John Steinbeck, he is speaking as a man of the sixties whose views are very different from those of the thirties when the best of Steinbeck was new and news.

Sometimes the essayists dissent from the modish and the chic, as does Saul Bellow when he warns against the deep thinkers who as critics can read far more into a novel or a poem than can anyone else, including its author. Some are very personal, proving once again, if proof is needed, that writing is indeed a subjective art. Some are reportorial, some are analytical. But there is no point to annotating the table of contents: the essays themselves supply the annotation.

The collection, of course, represents only a very small part of the content of the issues of the Book Review that when assembled and bound at the end of each year make a massive volume. It underscores, however, the fact that while the business of a book review is book reviewing, The *Times* Book Review does not live by reviewing alone. For readers, and editors too, there comes a time every so often when it is wise to halt, to look around, to consider, and thus perhaps to acquire a broader, maybe a deeper, understanding of what is happening in the many worlds of books, and that is why the kind of essay that the Book Review has published and is publishing performs so important a function.

 Sometimes the focus is wide, sometimes quite the contrary. An essay may be concerned with a single work, *Madame Bovary,* say, or with an entire school of writing, or with a major novelist like Henry James. The essayist may be telling of his own experience as an author wrestling alone with his art. Whatever the nature, and however presented, the purpose of course is to furnish perspective, to put in place, to further appreciation, sometimes to challenge the accepted.

Because the collection has drawn upon a decade of the Book Review's essays and reviews, it is extremely selective, and yet, paradoxically perhaps, it is representative. The reviews chosen are those which possess long-time value and make as much of a contribution now as the day they first were printed. By necessity they are concerned with books that in themselves reflect trends or sum up a period or lay down lasting chapters of a man's story. Consider, as an exhibit, Julian Boyd's "Prejudices According to Mencken." He is reviewing H. L. Mencken's *Notebooks,* but he is doing much more, and we can thank him for it: he is recalling the time and tides of Mencken, and the impact thereof on a generation now grown gray. And Alfred Kazin is drawing upon a "lost journal" of Thoreau's as a basis for "One Man's Communion with His World."

The essays, too, have been selected with concern for the persistence of their interest. That has meant leaving out many which, however great their merit when originally published, have lost their pertinence and have become only historical curiosities. There is nothing that tarnishes quicker than the literary essay written to capitalize on the fashion and wit of a fugitive moment.

There is a story, of course, behind each of the essays in *Opinions and Perspectives*. Some are the result of careful editorial planning, one might almost say plotting, in which an idea was born and then presented to the author. James Baldwin's "The Discovery of What It Means to Be American" was such a creation. It came about because a member of the Book Review's staff, not the editor, alas, suggested that Baldwin, who had just returned to America after prolonged residence abroad, ought to have something stimulating, maybe disturbing, to say about his experiences and their effect upon him, and that he ought to say his say in the Book Review. That thesis, somewhat refined, honed, was put to Baldwin, and ultimately out of it came "The Discovery of What It Means to Be American," an essay that on its first appearance attracted a good deal of attention and still does.

Sometimes it was the writer who made the approach. It could be Robert Penn Warren, in a letter from Italy asking if the Book Review would read, with a view to publication, his account of the writing of "Blackberry Winter" — and the answer, obviously, was an enthusiastic yes. Or it could be Saul Bellow at a luncheon table in Sardi's setting forth and discussing the thought and ideas that eventually were to be expressed in "Deep Readers of the World, Beware." Or Alexander Cowie sending his essay on Emerson over the transom as it were, an essay that when it appeared on the first page of the Book Review made clear, as readers bore witness, that Emerson's voice was not as cracked and tired as some critics had supposed.

There have been occasions when an essay grew out of curiosity or friendship or both. Along publishers' row, for example, the story had long been told that Lois Cole, when with The Macmillan Company, had been largely responsible for Macmillan's obtaining that publishing prize *Gone With The Wind.* Despite the fact that she and her family and mine had been friends for many years, the details of her part in the achievement had never been clear to me. What better way to learn them than to ask her to tell the story on the occasion of the twenty-fifth anniversary of *Gone With The Wind,* and that is just what she has done in "Margaret Mitchell Was a Bridge Partner."

The essays are often association items. Germaine Brée, a friend and admirer of Albert Camus, wrote her tribute to him while her grief over his cruel and unnecessary death was still fresh and bitter. Carlos Baker, after a year's living in England, could make his bow as a man of letters in his own right to the English men of letters who had become familiar to us all and to the setting in which they did their work: "This England That Its Writers Know." Often I had talked with Cecil Woodham-Smith about her research for her history of the Irish famines, and her research on the Irish who fled for refuge in this country, and after she had finished *The Great Hunger,* she drew out of the well of her experience the essay "Writing History Is Nervous Work."

Stephen Spender and I once lunched together at that marvelous old London club, the Garrick. Over an excellent bottle of hock, we talked about the London literary life. Tales of its cliques and claques, its friendships, its enmities have always fascinated me. Though the fact is not new to me, I continually find it hard to accept a world in which everybody knows everybody, and the difficulty is greater, I suppose, because of the contrast with the American lack of a literary center, or, in the European sense of the term, a literary life. Spender and I talked a long while, and we talked still more as we walked toward Trafalgar Square afterward; the result, some months later, was "Literary London: A Tight Little Isle." It was even better than I knew it would be.

In selecting the sixty-two pieces for *Opinions and Perspectives* no preconceived scheme was in mind. The only tests were quality and, as I have suggested, some permanence of interest. When assembled, however, they made patterns of their own. One group without any effort marched in step as "American Classics," and another stood together because each of its members was concerned with "The Author's Experience." Still another presented "Points of View," and so with the rest. Each essay had a place, but it was not fixed or determined in advance by any arbitrary dictate.

Nor were the essays written in the first place to fit any pattern, ideological or philosophical. As I said at the beginning, their purpose was, is, to furnish perspective, to further understanding, to challenge, and while the theme of an essay may have been suggested to its author — though many times it was his own — the development of that theme was always his to pursue and his alone.

In these essays the reader shares with the author an exciting journey of intellectual exploration and discovery. From their diversity of subject, of treatment, of points of view, comes a unity of a sort: an appreciation of books and bookmen, of thinkers and thought, and the act of literary creation. That was their purpose from the start.

FRANCIS BROWN

New York
April, 1964

PART I

Consider the Contemporary

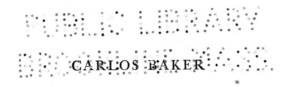

CARLOS BAKER

What Are Critics Good For?

Carlos Baker has something to say on many literary subjects, and the fact that he is a professor of English at Princeton may account for some of his fluency. He has written a couple of novels and many critical essays. He is the author of works on Shelley, Wordsworth, Fielding. He has written Hemingway, The Writer as Artist, *and is now preparing the authorized biography of Hemingway.*

"FINDERS keepers, losers weepers," runs the ancient taunt by which boys justify their acquisitive instincts. Those first two words happen to summarize the whole social duty of the critic: finding and keeping. For if we do not preserve what we already have, we shall not only impoverish ourselves but we shall also lose our grip on those principles by which we measure the perpetual innovations the lively arts thrust upon us. The other half of our duty is to find, among these innovations, all their use and their beauty. Otherwise we may become so stultified among our dusty tomes that our critical progress will amount to nothing but a pretentious parade through terminological changes.

There is no overstating the importance of the critic's obligation as keeper of our ancestral domain, the literary heritage of the Western — to say nothing of the Eastern — tradition. It is the huge plantation to which, individually and collectively, we have fallen heir. We are at once the explorers and the husbandmen. But our first obligation is to preserve. The terrain is crowded with innumerable structures, from the vast temples of Homeric antiquity to the latest split-level novels, and from the Gothic cathedrals of Shakespearean tragedy to the rundown ranch houses of Zane Grey.

Time is the enemy. A hundred foundations that seemed solid in their day have cracked with the frost of centuries; some of the structures have suffered the fateful burial of Herculaneum; others have crumbled into dust and been blown away, round the world. The critic must clear away the verbal rubble, shore up decaying towers, and mend the walls of demarcation which time and human carelessness have allowed to tumble into disrepair. He must rebuild for modern occupancy any structures that deserve it, and repair broken lines of communication between other ages, other lands and other persuasions than our own.

Like any other keeper he must on occasion destroy. He must oppose the meretricious in whatever form it survives — or arrives: the sensational and the trivial, the idle and the puerile, the cheap and the tawdry. He must fell the soft and punklike trees that have shot up to obscure the noble view of distant spires. He must root out the tough old stumps of former errors. It was Thomas Carew's praise of John Donne that he had purged the Muses' garden of pedantic weeds, and thrown away the lazy seeds of servile imitation. But the purge was not permanent; the work of Donne is never really done.

Another part of his task is to determine what is worth keeping. Ralph Waldo Emerson's advice to the American scholar — "defer never to the popular cry" — is as much an indefensible absolute as its opposite: defer always to the unpopular cry. The middle ground of the critic's personal integrity is perhaps the only absolute of this kind that justifies our belief. Wherever his views run counter to received opinion, it is clearly one of his social obligations to stick to his conviction "that a popgun is a popgun," even though "the ancient and honorable of the earth affirm it to be the

crack of doom." And he should be prepared to recognize the accents of thunder in works to which the larger public is obviously
tone-deaf. "The best art of our time," as a critic recently observed, "can easily be missed." It is the critic's social responsibility to see that we miss as little of it as possible, and this he can
never do if he does not remain receptive to innovation.

The task of finding is the second of the critic's social obligations.
It parallels, at one remove, the task of discovery the reputable artist sets himself when he undertakes any significant piece of writing. Matthew Arnold recognized the parallel. Indeed we owe to
him a brilliant simile, one which happens to apply, under the
general rubric of finding, both to the work of the artist and the
work of the critic. He asks us to consider the situation of an Athe-
nian playgoer in attendance at a performance of the *Oresteia.*
"The terrible old mythic story on which the drama was founded,"
says Arnold, can be presumed to have existed at least in bare out-
line within the spectator's mind before he entered the theatre.
"It stood in his memory as a group of statuary, faintly seen, at the
end of a long and dark vista: then came the Poet, embodying out-
lines, developing situations, not a word wasted, not a sentiment
capriciously thrown in: stroke upon stroke, the drama proceeded;
the light deepened upon the group; more and more it revealed itself to the riveted gaze of the spectator: until at last, when the final
words were spoken, it stood before him in broad sunlight, a model
of immortal beauty."

Arnold is here rightly assuming that it is a major office of literature to illumine human experience. Under conditions that
are at least imaginable, however seldom they may be achieved in
practice, the artist causes his three-dimensional statuary to come
fully alive before our eyes. The spectator leaves the theatre, or
the reader lays down his book, in something like total possession
of all that the artist sought to convey. If such an ideal were invariably achieved, the critic as finder would have far less to do. Yet

our experience as readers readily informs us that the artist does not always succeed in the total illumination of his subject. It is perhaps one of the laws of authorship that no one can make his fullest meaning at once intelligible, even to himself. He may even prefer to leave his living statues in some degree of obscurity or ambiguity as a matter of esthetic principle. Even the clearest work of art, while often self-contained, is not necessarily self-explanatory. The multiple relations between its meaning and its form, to take only one example, are ordinarily implicit rather than explicit. The critic as finder would be kept busy enough if his only task were to explore these relations.

Among those who distrust the critic as an intrusive middleman, edging his vast steatopygous bulk between author and audience, it is not uncommon to wish him away, out of the direct line of vision. "It is barely possible," said James Russell Lowell ironically, "that the power of a book resides in the book itself, and that real books somehow compel an audience without extraneous intervention." One wishes that he could believe this wholesome dictum, which was handed down in 1849, a scant two years before a "real book" called *Moby Dick* began its long struggle for the recognition it did not attain until seventy years after publication. The critic's intervention would be needed if only to maintain the reader's receptivity at the highest level of operation. We have merely to consult our own records as readers to recall how frequently the vista between artist and audience can be darkened by extraneous factors. Anything from ignorance to indigestion, or from prejudice to pusillanimity, may, and often does, get in our way.

If, therefore, it is a major office of the artist to illumine human experience, it is assuredly a major office of the critic to illuminate the artist's illumination. As the man of good sense and finer sensibility, he seeks to make the implicit as explicit as possible in any work of art he chooses to explore.

In his function as a finder, the critic may be called the scientist of the unsuspected and the cartographer of the uncircumscribed. He returns from the realms of gold with a relief map of the hills and valleys. He must accept the role of John Keats' Cortez, toiling up the landward slope of some masking range to stand finally upon the peak, seeing for the first time perhaps a broad and heaving expanse whose existence has been known, but whose islands and archipelagos, whose shoals and depths, had not hitherto been adequately charted. He must be prepared for change: what once loomed as a considerable mountain on the horizons of its own epoch may since have been eroded to a minor protuberance by the weathering of successive ages. Like Robert Frost's oven bird, the critic must have some idea of "what to make of a diminished thing." There is also the opposite effect. The tides of time, receding from a former level, may have exposed an island long hidden and unknown. The critic must give it sea room on his charts, taking due account of its relationship to those larger land masses over which critical factions have made war for so many centuries.

Finally, the critic must find power to be fair to the work which engages his attention. Criticism would be of immense social value if it existed for no other reason than the constant exercise it gives to the intellectual morality of the critic himself. In criticism as in religious ethics, there are sins venial and sins deadly.

The seven deadly sins of criticism, if we are to avoid them, and not one of us completely does, require of us a constant reassessment of our motives. There is, for example, the critical sin of covetousness, which may cause the critic to seek fame at the expense of the author whose work he exploits. The closely associated sin of envy leads to the denigration of the work of others for the hidden purpose of self-aggrandizement. To indulge the sin of gluttony is to bite off more than one is prepared to digest, denying others the right to partake. To be lustful is to indulge an inordinate desire for the gratification of one's sense of power. The deadly sin of anger leads to the loss of one's composure and sense of balance during the inevitable exchanges of differing opinion. The deadly sin of sloth is to repeat accepted lies about an author or a body of work because one is too lazy to dig out the truth. The critical sin of pride is to hand down judgments from on high with a godlike assumption of infallibility, and to assume, along with the robes of the judge, the axe of the executioner.

Criticism, in sum, if it is to be socially responsible, ought to begin at home, within the ivory tower of the critic's own cranium, where finding and keeping, if they are to be done at all, must take their origin and prove their worth. And if the finding and the keeping are not done, we shall all be the losers, with every right to weep at the enormity of our loss.

JOSEPH WOOD KRUTCH

American Literature Comes of Age

Joseph Wood Krutch has been a teacher, a drama critic, an essay-
ist, a philosopher. He writes with equal facility about country
life in Connecticut and desert life in Arizona, and he is as much
at home in eighteenth-century drama as in the period he is dis-
cussing in "American Literature Comes of Age." For Measure of
Man, *a philosophical exploration of contemporary thought, he*
was given a National Book Award in 1954.

BETWEEN 1896 and World War II a new American literature was
created. No other half-century of our history saw profounder
changes in the tone, method and subject-matter of its important
books. And in no other half-century did writers exercise so direct
and immediate an influence upon the attitudes of so large a public. Poe, Whitman, Thoreau and Melville were lonely voices
whose influence spread slowly and who were heard by a relatively
small minority of the American people. H. L. Mencken and Sinclair Lewis, to take two examples, were read and cited at every
level of literacy and within a few years helped to change the thinking of a considerable section of the public. Today Hemingway
and Faulkner loom larger in the consciousness of European readers than even the most popular of the earlier American writers
ever did. They may be no more popular than Fenimore Cooper
and Mark Twain once were, but unlike Cooper and Mark Twain,
they have been accepted as part of the literary mainstream and
as models for imitation rather than as curious isolated individuals.

In a certain sense the new American literature has been more important at home and abroad than any previous literature had ever been.

At the turn of the century we were looking back, not forward, and all the major classics of our first flowering had already been written. In fact, if there ever was an age for which the disparaging adjective "genteel" furnishes the most fitting description, it was the period around 1896.

As essayists, critics and editors, Brander Matthews and Richard Watson Gilder represented the prevailing taste. Thoreau had declined into John Burroughs; Henry James had declined into Edith Wharton, who was just publishing her first stories. It is true that Stephen Crane's *The Red Badge of Courage* (1895) was a brief sensation before it was all but forgotten for a generation, and that the decorous William Dean Howells had been for some years mildly irritating many people with his polite realism. Looking back at them we can see or convince ourselves that we can see the beginnings of a new mood. But it hardly seemed such to most readers at the time, and it is not too much to say that few could have guessed what the postwar literary world was going to be like any more than they could guess what the great world would be like socially, politically or economically.

Moderation and respectability seemed to be at last as permanently established in the one as security, peace and that liberty that "slowly broadens down" were established in the other. Continental literature was still commonly regarded as unfortunately marred by bad taste and when Putnam's launched a series to introduce Maupassant, Flaubert and Gautier to American readers, the selection had to be kept so innocuous as to omit the most characteristic works of each. Edwin Markham's "The Man With the Hoe" (1899), was probably the most widely read American poem of a generation, and Elbert Hubbard's *A Message to Garcia,* published the same year, was probably the most popular piece of prose.

Nearly half a generation was to pass before James Huneker, the first influential American critic to attempt to popularize the "dangerous" European writers, began writing. High on the best-seller list for 1896 were Harold Frederic's *The Damnation of Theron Ware*, more or less in the manner of Mrs. Humphry Ward's *Robert Elsmere*, which had created a sensation a few years before, and Charles Sheldon's *In His Steps*, the most phenomenally successful of all the What-would-Christ have done? novels. Five years later Alice Hegan Rice's *Mrs. Wiggs of the Cabbage Patch* was to start the vogue for those "glad girls" who continued to delight a certain class of readers for a whole generation as the treacle flowed from the pens of Mrs. Rice, Kate Douglas Wiggin, Gene Stratton Porter and Eleanor Porter. The last in Mrs. Porter's Pollyanna series appeared the year the *Lusitania* was sunk, taking down with it so much of the prewar world good as well as bad.

It would be easy to overstress this date and take it as the dividing line between the old and the new. Actually Theodore Dreiser, certainly a key figure, had published *Sister Carrie* in 1900 and though it was withdrawn by the publisher as offensive it was reissued in 1907. More significant is the fact that Edgar Lee Master's sensationally successful *Spoon River Anthology* was published in 1915 and that Van Wyck Brooks (who was later to celebrate so successfully our earlier literature but who began as a prophet of the new) published *America's Coming-of-Age* also in the year the *Lusitania* went to the bottom.

On the other hand, it is not possible to doubt that the war had a great deal to do with the public's willingness to accept in literature various attitudes and subject-matter it previously had found irrelevant at best. William Dean Howells' too-often quoted remark that the "smiling aspects" of life were, after all, the most characteristic of America, no longer seemed so obviously true to Americans who already saw a world war facing them. Man and society were not what they had supposed them to be. They were forced to admit that great wickedness and depravity, crime and suffering were not, as they had liked to think, so unusual as to be almost anachronisms. It had certainly become less obvious that the smiling aspects of life were the most characteristic of America or of any other land. Suddenly they had become aware that modern man was still capable of doing, thinking and feeling unspeakable things. Why shouldn't literature treat what it was no longer possible to deny? The genteel tradition was swept away with breath-taking quickness.

A kind of "realism" which would once have been called mere brutality, a kind of "frankness" which would once have been called obscene, and a kind of pessimism which would once have been dismissed as morbidity, were soon spread large over the most widely discussed books. Typical examples were the "frank" *Jurgen* (1919) by James Branch Cabell, the "realistic" *Winesburg, Ohio* (1919) by Sherwood Anderson and the "pessimistic" *Waste Land* (1922) by T. S. Eliot. H. L. Mencken published the first of his *Prejudices* the same year that *Jurgen* appeared and six years later Dreiser, one of Mencken's favorites, reached the height of his reputation with *An American Tragedy,* in which he combined "realism" with a moral nihilism. Even more significant of the change in public taste, for the very reason that they had no literary merit to recommend them, were the celebrations, sometimes frank and sometimes hypocritical, of the exploits of what came to be called, after the title of one of the books, "Flaming Youth."

As is almost inevitable during periods of revolution, both critics and readers were usually violently partisan. Either they rejected the new literature completely or they hailed it indiscriminately, seeing all its protagonists as equally important and all its characteristics as equally admirable. Now it is much easier to discriminate between major and minor figures and, what is even more important, to analyze characteristics and to distinguish limitations from excellences.

Even at the time, unsympathetic critics frequently complained that the new writers were almost wholly "destructive," and that they undermined the existing system of values without having anything to substitute. Defenders brushed this objection aside as no more weighty than the charge of ugliness, brutality and obscenity. Actually, however, it is evident enough that the new literature was largely concerned with rejections. Nearly all of it either implied or made explicit a rejection of gentility, of decorum, of squeamishness, and of the easy assumption that, fundamentally, contemporary life was a good life. It ridiculed provinciality, patriotism, and cultural complacency. As satire or polemic it was vigorously effective. But it certainly was less successful in suggesting what the good life would be.

Some, like Dreiser, seemed to be saying that no such thing as a "good life" is possible. Others like Sinclair Lewis, whose *Main Street* (1920) was the most widely read of all books in the new tradition, seemed to assume that when "culture" had replaced "provinciality," the good life would arise spontaneously — though it was often pointed out even during the heyday of his popularity that Mr. Babbitt was more satisfactory as an example of what Americans should not be than Carol Kennicott was of what a truly cultivated and civilized woman should be. Thus Dreiser and Lewis represented two attitudes whose fundamental difference was inadequately recognized when the new literature was regarded as all of a piece. Radical pessimism on the one hand and a rather easy optimism on the other seemed less irreconcilable than they were because those who were separated by the wide gulf between the two philosophies nevertheless made common cause in their attack upon contemporary American civilization.

If 1915 is only a rather arbitrary date for the beginning of the first phase of modern American literature, 1929 marks much more clearly its end. The sudden collapse of the material prosperity which the *avant garde* of the twenties had despised inevitably shifted attention from the cultural deficiencies of the United

States to economic and political questions. The most immediate, superficial and short-lived consequence was the sudden vogue of the "proletarian" novel, play and poem — "proletarian" usually meaning not merely that the subject was the working class but that the treatment was didactic and more or less orthodox Marxism. During a brief period, a sizable group of writers, most of them unheard of before, engaged the major part of the attention of both critics and the literature-conscious section of the public. But the school did not produce a single work now commonly regarded as of permanent importance, widely read, or, indeed, much remembered.

The depression, however, produced a less obvious yet more profound effect on the whole tone of contemporary literature than increased concern with political and economic questions. During the twenties the intellectual tended to be what we now call "disengaged" and to accept the role of destructive critic. In fact, he often seemed to wash his hands not only of America but of the human race. Mencken's conviction that all men were obscene clowns but that this fact is more evident in the United States than anywhere else clearly represents one aspect of this attitude. The expatriates who fled to Europe because, though a good life might be impossible anywhere, Europe permitted a more acceptable substitute for it than did the United States, represent another. But after 1929 expatriation, literal or symbolic, ceased to be a fashionable response to the contemporary situation — partly perhaps because it was becoming so evident that there was no longer any "better Europe" to which to flee and that, for good or ill, the world was becoming rapidly Americanized and could not be saved from either destruction or itself unless it was saved in the United States. Hence, in one way or another, the writer found himself compelled to be "engaged."

What this means in the case of, say, a John Hersey is obvious enough. Less obvious but no less important was an increased realization of the necessity for examining more closely fundamental premises. Neither Dreiser's rather old-fashioned village-atheist pessimism nor Sinclair Lewis' rather naïve faith in salvation by "culture" would do. The pessimist had to move further into the subtler realm of existentialism, either theistic or atheistic. The optimist had to found his faith on a belief subtler than Lewis' in the dignity, the freedom and perhaps the responsibility of man.

One may get some idea of what this means from John Steinbeck, whose *Grapes of Wrath* (1939) was sometimes wrongly taken as the last and best of the proletarian novels but who has since made it plain that for him the most important of all themes is not economic, political or cultural but the conflict between moral good and moral evil in man himself. An even better insight is possible if one examines the work of Ernest Hemingway and William Faulkner, the two American writers generally regarded both in Europe and at home as best.

Chronologically they are almost exact contemporaries. Yet because one accepted and the other rejected the philosophy of the twenties, they belong to different literary generations. Hemingway, whose *The Sun Also Rises* was published in 1926, was an expatriate of the postwar years. Faulkner, whose first major work, *The Sound and the Fury*, was published in 1929, belonged spiritually to a later period. The two names are often linked as "major novelists," yet they are as dissimilar in style, subject-matter and philosophy as two writers — both of whom deal tragically with what are regarded as "unpleasant subjects" — could be.

Hemingway's simple style, which manages to achieve a classic clarity paradoxically based upon a vocabulary and syntax colloquial almost to the point of seeming illiterate, corresponds perfectly to the simplicity of his convictions. Life is represented as essentially meaningless and essentially valueless. Sometimes, at least, he seeks to be implying that there is no escape from the

realization of overwhelming emptiness except while one is satisfying the two strongest animal instincts — which he seems to
take to be the desire for sexual intercourse and the desire to
kill. Only the soldier, the hunter and the bullfighter have many
opportunities to "live" — not only because they alone have frequent opportunities to kill but because sexual experience is sharp-
est when enjoyed as an interlude in the midst of violent death.

Faulkner is neither so clear nor so simple. He describes horrors
which often seem even more unmitigated and more fantastic.
But he does not celebrate them nor does he accept them as "what
life is really like." And he certainly had Hemingway's literary
generation in mind when, in the Nobel Prize Award Speech of
1950 he said of a type of writer that generation had often professed to admire: "He writes not of life but of lust, of defeats in
which nobody loses anything of value, of victories without hope
and worst of all without pity or compassion . . . He writes not of
the heart but of the glands . . . It is [the writer's] privilege to
help man endure by lifting his heart, by reminding him of the
courage and honor and pride and compassion and pity and sacrifice
which have been the glory of his past. The poet's voice need not
merely be the record of man, it can be one of the props, the pillars
to help him endure and prevail."

Faulkner had only Hemingway as rival for the position of most
esteemed novelist of his generation, perhaps indeed, the most esteemed writer in any form. Would any of the leading writers of
the two preceding generations have regarded his pronouncement
as anything other than "unrealistic" and "sentimental"? If his
credo is compared with Dreiser's rather than Hemingway's, the
contrast is no less striking. Dreiser tirelessly insisted that the
only story to be told of man was the story of his glands, or, as he
usually put it even more vaguely, of "chemistry." And he insisted
no less tirelessly that "naturalism" meant this conviction plus the
further conviction that to write what Faulkner called merely the
record of man is the honest writer's only duty.

H. L. Mencken, to take another example, was a dazzling satirist and the master of a savage comic style — the most original and most effective since Mark Twain. But he, too, professed to believe that the history of mankind is no more than the record of man's rascality and folly and that the task of the writer is to keep this fact constantly before the eyes of his reader.

Recently some commentators have argued that American literature should and will react against the "negative" and "destructive" tone of so much twentieth-century writing by returning to Howells' insistence upon "the smiling aspects" of contemporary American life. They have sometimes proposed the industrialist and the businessman as hero and bid the writer celebrate the triumphs of production and the high standard of living. They have, in a word, bid him be complacent and to tell his readers, not only that the Good Life is possible but that it has already been achieved.

Perhaps their advice will be taken. But is it far from certain that it will. If Faulkner really spoke, as he seemed to speak, for our generation, then the literature of the future will be neither complacent nor despairing. It will again assume that the mind and the heart as well as the glands are valid subjects, that man can be something more than merely the victim of circumstance, and that the writer's business is to remind him of the things he is prone to forget rather than to confirm him in either complacency or despair.

JACQUES BARZUN

Each Age Picks Its Literary Greats

The multifarious duties of an educator have not kept Jacques Barzun from writing some of the most provocative criticism of our contemporary culture (The House of Intellect, *for example, or* Science: The Glorious Entertainment) *and from pursuing his special concerns with music and literature. He has written on Berlioz and edited his letters. He has also edited the writings of that extraordinary prose stylist, the eccentric John Jay Chapman. He is now Provost of Columbia University.*

EVER since the distinction was made, about a century and a half ago, between creative epochs and critical epochs men have worried whether their own time was creative. There always seems to be so much criticism flying about, so little agreement about the worth of the creations to which it refers. Who are *our* creators? Where are they? We are almost angry with them for not making themselves unmistakable.

For we have no doubt that creativeness is a virtue, regardless of the thing it creates; there cannot be too much of it, and we attach the name to whatever we wish to dignify: there is creative interior decoration and creative stockbrokering. No doubt democratic individualism lies behind this honorific usage. Each man being deemed unique, it follows that the deployment of his talents will yield creative work.

In the arts, which are commonly held the realm of creation par excellence, one would suppose that the idea of creativeness would be somewhat better defined and more exactly applied. But all we find is a set of puzzling conventions. Everybody who works in any of the arts (one art alone excepted) is *ipso facto* classed as a creative artist. In literature only is a gulf fixed ahead of time between creative and noncreative according to the genre pursued. To write a novel or a poem is to be creative; to write history, criticism, travels, orations, autobiography, philosophy is to be noncreative. From the grade school to the most fraudulent Learn-to-Write mill for adults, the course in creative writing implies the giving birth to stories or poems. In the other courses are the drones who grind out expository prose.

Now more hangs upon this curious usage than appears at first sight. For what it does by blurring the distinction between a thing attempted and a thing achieved is to blind us to all sorts of literary pleasures, while denying the self-evident proposition that art is art wherever it appears. Some of the forms that art takes may be less profound, less comprehensive, less popular than others. But good writing, as Bernard DeVoto once said, is good writing even in a report of the Geodetic Survey. Should we therefore call it, in that place and form, a creation? Very likely not, though we should not exclude the possibility entirely. What then is a creation if many works, conceded to be art, do not automatically deserve the name?

Before answering the question one must note that the meaning of the original contrast between creative and critical has been distorted. When it was first made by the French social philosopher Saint-Simon, he meant it to mark the difference between the prevailing temper of the eighteenth century, which was to pull things apart, and the spirit he saw dawning in the nineteenth, which was to put things together again. Our mistake is to shift the point of contrast from intellectual result to artistic form. Obviously any piece of writing is put together, composed, and hence a potential creation.

A good example of our error can be found in Saint-Simon's own century. To that century Voltaire was a great creator by virtue of his dozen or more tragedies in verse. He was in fact *the* poet, and if we were consistent we should abide by that estimate or reject him altogether, for his other works were expository and critical. But far from rejecting him, we credit him with one great creation, which is *Candide* — a topical piece of criticism thinly disguised as fiction. Judged strictly as a novel, it lacks verisimilitude and characterization, as well as ascertainable form, since many of the incidents occur without necessity and could be multiplied or removed without much harm to either the thesis or our pleasure. The old warrior of sixty-five tossed off the piece with no awareness that it would stand out as his chef d'oeuvre. And today, enchanted as we are by *Candide,* it would not be perverse to maintain that another of the tales — *Zadig or The Princess of Babylon* — has more concision and hardly less variety. But then only *Candide* has the famous tag line about cultivating our garden, only *Candide* has caught the world's ear and become "a creation."

How this happens is a mystery. Literary immortality, so called, seems to be a variable on the loose: it does not go with perfection, or we would discard the unfinished *Brothers Karamazov.* It does not attach exclusively to invention, or we should exclude Boswell's *Johnson,* the works of Sir Thomas Browne and the Essays of Montaigne. It does not even require consciously artful writing — as witness Pepys' *Diary* and Burton's *Anatomy of Melancholy.*

These and kindred examples suggest the strange conclusion that great creations are made such after the fact, by a retroactive decree of the human spirit. As the Lord looked back upon His creation and saw that it was good, so among mortals a providential critic, coming after a longer or shorter time, falls in love with a certain work and persuades the heedless throng to look back and stare. Until then the creation lacks the very qualities that later make it unique and wonderful. A hundred years ago, all the merits of "Moby Dick" were defects, and Melville was a bungler. And we find it hard now to acknowledge that "Leaves of Grass" was once an obscure and obscene oddity.

The artist puts out his works as a tree its branches, and Creativeness, like a bird, comes and sits on one of them. We rebel against this thought because of our common-sense notion of cause and effect: The cause of the work's greatness, of our later admiration, must first be in the poet. We speak of it as his power, and we dislike the retroactive interpretation all the more because, much as we want to give honor where it is due, we come usually a little late.

It is possible to reconcile the common-sense view and the strange one suggested by history only if we give up the loaded meaning of creative and break it up into categories that really fit the things we are talking about. Let us agree to call creations the elect among works of art, those chosen in the manner just described — not indeed arbitrarily, yet by a special kind of fortune. Then let us call creativity the power that produces great and original works — a far more numerous class than that of creations, although like tuft-hunters we affect a scorn for the second rank. To be sure, the term originality is suspect nowadays because of the fad for invoking Tradition, but the best minds still want original work and are impatient with its opposite. It then follows that we should not call X a creative artist when all he does is turn out novels of the current fashionable cut. Let us rather call him procreative, his forte being reproduction.

Failing these distinctions, we commit ourselves to accepting as creative — appalling thought! — all the bad novels that have ever been written: those billions of indistinguishable words which once came in separate bundles, bound in boards, and advertised in the flimsy pages at the back of Mrs. Humphry Ward's own "creative writing." The advantage of changing our terms is of course that it makes us revise our judgments and let in new delights. We never know how much we exclude by a superstition enshrined in a catchword. In our own world of literary reflection and reference, for example, two of the greatest prose writers America has produced, Lincoln and William James, are generally overlooked. A recent literary history, it is true, accords these two masters a few pages each. The Gettysburg Address is even called "one of the great American poems." But praise is not the point: the treatment of their art is negligible compared with that given to lesser men — say, William Dean Howells. This is obviously because Howells wrote stories, and Lincoln and James did not. They wrote only in the Cinderella genres once courted by Demosthenes and Plato.

And so it comes about that our cult of fiction, which we equate with creation, ends by blinding us to creative power as such, and possibly to creations which the magic bird referred to earlier will yet alight on. For curiously enough, those rare works to which we ascribe intrinsic and universal worth are in fact dreadfully subject to variation. It is among the "unquestioned" masterpieces that the whirligig of taste plays havoc. When we remember what Horace and Cicero meant to the centuries from the Renaissance to the nineteenth, we are aghast to record how little they move us today. Incurable absolutists, we always think our own dictum the last or assume that our estimates go back to the beginning of time.

We forget how recently Shakespeare became the giant we take him to be. We forget the long eclipses of Homer, Virgil, Tacitus, Euripides, Dante, Villon, Ronsard, Rabeleais. And like our predecessors, we can hardly imagine that we are overlooking anybody in our own day: the neglect of Melville and Whitman and Gerard Manley Hopkins argues a stupidity that has been bred out of us. Conversely, we are sure that the names of contemporaries we call great will go ringing down the ages. Yet, where is Abraham Cowley, at his death the unsurpassable master of English poetry? In a corner of an anthology. And where was Donne in Cowley's reign and thereafter until his late rebirth? Not even in an anthology.

The explanation of these changes lies in the nature of art and of human history. Art being a projection of life has the same property of never giving away its meaning, never showing itself wholly or finally to any beholder. Those who form the judgment of an age therefore choose the art they want and subtly alter it by the very fact of wanting it. And they want it for needs which are bound to change with the course of events. We clutch a gloomy Melville to our gloomy breasts. Why should more sanguine times, before or after, take the same delight in him? Nor is there anything fatal to art itself about this fickleness, half conscious and half blind, which it is the task of criticism to make as rational as possible.

But the corollary follows that the creativeness of an age had better be found in the sum of its original constructive efforts, whatever their kind, and not merely in the prime examples of selected genres. If you encounter a St. Augustine or a Rousseau writing his confessions, don't tell him to recast them as a novel of education in the first person. If some unambitious clerk or overworked journalist is producing the equivalent of Lamb or Hazlitt, let him carry on. A critic is not damned by definition and we have poets aplenty. Even the grubbing historian need not be goaded into "the creative field." As Wilde said, anybody can make history but only a great man can write it, and your friend's name might be Gibbon or, alternatively, Thucydides.

SAUL BELLOW

Deep Readers of the World, Beware

It was the picaresque novel, The Adventures of Augie March, *that did it. With the appearance of* Augie *in 1953, Saul Bellow was recognized as the major American novelist that he is, recognition ratified in a sense when with* Augie *he won the National Book Award for fiction. He is also a writer of short stories and of critical essays like those in this collection.*

INTERVIEWED as he was getting on the train for Boston, E. M. Forster was asked how he felt on the eve of his first visit to Harvard. He replied that he had heard that there were some particularly deep readers of his books to be found in Cambridge. He expected to be questioned closely by them, and this worried him. The reason is perfectly understandable.

In this age of ours serious people are more serious than they ever were, and lightness of heart like Mr. Forster's is hard to find. To the serious a novel is a work of art; art has a role to play in the drama of civilized life; civilized life is set upon a grim and dangerous course — and so we may assume if we are truly serious that no good novelist is going to invite us to a picnic merely to eat egg salad and chase butterflies over the English meadows or through the Tuscan woods. Butterflies are gay, all right, but in them lies the secret of metamorphosis. As for eggs, life's mystery hides in the egg. We all know that. So much for butterflies and egg salad.

It would be unjust to say that the responsibility for this sort of

thing belongs entirely to the reader. Often the writer himself is
at fault. He doesn't mind if he *is* a little deeper than average.
Why not?

Nevertheless deep reading has gone very far. It has become
dangerous to literature.

"Why, sir," the student asks, "does Achilles drag the body of
Hector around the walls of Troy?" "That sounds like a stimulating question. Most interesting. I'll bite," says the professor.
"Well, you see, sir, the *Iliad* is full of circles — shields, chariot
wheels and other round figures. And you know what Plato said
about circles. The Greeks were all mad for geometry." "Bless
your crew-cut head," says the professor, "for such a beautiful
thought. You have exquisite sensibility. Your approach is both
deep and serious. Still I always believed that Achilles did it because he was so angry."

It would take an unusual professor to realize that Achilles *was*
angry. To many teachers he would represent much, but he would
not *be* anything in particular. To be is too obvious. Our professor however is a "square," and the bright student is annoyed with
him. Anger! What good is anger? Great literature is subtle, dignified, profound. Homer is as good as Plato anytime; and if Plato
thought, Homer must surely have done so, too, thought just as
beautifully circle for circle.

Things are not what they seem. And anyway, unless they represent something large and worthy, writers will not bother with
them. Any deep reader can tell you that picking up a bus transfer
is the *reisemotif* (journey motif) when it happens in a novel. A
travel folder signifies Death. Coal holes represent the Under-
world. Soda crackers are the Host. Three bottles of beer are —
it's obvious. The busy mind can hardly miss at this game, and
every player is a winner.

Are you a Marxist? Then Herman Melville's Pequod in *Moby
Dick* can be a factory, Ahab the manager, the crew the working

class. Is your point of view religious? The *Pequod* sailed on
Christmas morning, a floating cathedral headed south. Do you
follow Freud or Jung? Then your interpretations may be rich
and multitudinous. I recently had a new explanation of *Moby
Dick* from the young man in charge of an electronic brain. "Once
and for all," he said. "That whale is everybody's mother wallow-
ing in her watery bed. Ahab has the Oedipus complex and wants
to slay the hell out of her."

This is deep reading. But it is only fair to remember that the
best novelists and poets of the century have done much to promote it. When Mairy (in James Joyce's *Ulysses*) loses the pin of
her drawers, she doesn't know what to do to keep them up; the
mind of Bloom goes from grammar to painting, from painting to
religion. It is all accomplished in a few words. Joyce's genius
holds all the elements in balance.

The deep reader, however, is apt to lose his head. He falls
wildly on any particle of philosophy or religion and blows it up
bigger than the Graf Zeppelin. Does Bloom dust Stephen's clothes
and brush off the wood shavings? They are no ordinary shavings
but the shavings from Stephen's cross.

What else? All the little monkish peculiarities at which Robert
Browning poked fun in the "Soliloquy in a Spanish Cloister,"
crossing knife and fork on the platter at the end of a meal and
the rest of it, have become the pillars of the new system.

Are we to attach meaning to whatever is grazed by the writer?
Is modern literature Scripture? Is criticism Talmud, theology?
Deep readers of the world, beware! You had better be sure that
your seriousness is indeed high seriousness and not, God forbid,
low seriousness.

A true symbol is substantial, not accidental. You cannot avoid
it, you cannot remove it. You can't take the handkerchief from
Othello, or the sea from *The Nigger of the Narcissus,* or the dis-
figured feet from *Oedipus Rex.* You can, however, read *Ulysses*

without suspecting that wood shavings have to do with the Cruci-
fixion or that the name Simon refers to the sin of Simony or that
the hunger of the Dubliners at noon parallels that of the Lestri-
gonians. These are purely peripheral matters; fringe benefits, if
you like. The beauty of the book cannot escape you if you are
any sort of reader, and it is better to approach it from the side of
naïveté than from that of culture-idolatry, sophistication and
snobbery. Of course it's hard in our time to be as naïve as one
would like. Information does filter through. It leaks, as we have
taken to saying. Still the knowledge of even the sophisticated is
rather thin, and even the most wised-up devils, stuffed to the ears
with arcana, turned out to be fairly simple.

Perhaps the deepest readers are those who are least sure of
themselves. An even more disturbing suspicion is that they prefer meaning to feeling. What again about the feelings? Yes, it's
too bad. I'm sorry to have to ring in this tiresome subject, but
there's no help for it. The reason why the schoolboy takes refuge in circles is that the wrath of Achilles and the death of
Hector are too much for him. He is doing no more than most
civilized people do when confronted with passion and death.
They contrive somehow to avoid them.

The practice of avoidance is so widespread that it is proably not
fair to single out any group for blame. But if nothing is to be
said or done, we might as well make ready to abandon literature altogether. Novels are being published today which consist
entirely of abstractions, meanings, and while our need for meanings is certainly great our need for concreteness, for particulars, is
even greater. We need to see how human beings act after they
have appropriated or assimilated the meanings. Meanings themselves are a dime a dozen. In literature humankind becomes abstract when we begin to dislike it. And . . .

Interruption by a deep reader: Yes, yes, we know all that. But
just look at the novels of the concrete and the particular, people

opening doors and lighting cigarettes. Aren't they boring? Besides, do you want us to adopt a program to curtail the fear of feeling and to pretend to *like* the creature of flesh and bone?

Certainly not. No programs.

A pretty pass we have come to!

We must leave it to inspiration to redeem the concrete and the particular and to recover the value of flesh and bone. Meanwhile, let Plato have his circles and let the soda crackers be soda crackers and the wood shavings wood shavings. They are mysterious enough as it is.

ELIZABETH JANEWAY

Fiction's Place in a World Awry

When Elizabeth Janeway writes about fiction, she brings to her criticism knowledge that stems from both study and practice. She is the author of short stories, of books for children and of six novels, the most recent of which is Accident.

WILLIAM FAULKNER, talking to students at the University of Virginia, remarked that he had become a novelist because he had failed as a poet. Every writer, talking to an audience instead of addressing himself to a sheet of blank paper, is going to find himself coming out with some observations that bear a stronger relation to hypothesis than to deliberated truth; and I doubt that Faulkner would have contended that his "failure as a poet" during his adolescent years was the sole cause of his career as a novelist. If it was, we should certainly all be thankful that the poems didn't come off, and that instead we got the great Gothic epic of Yoknapatawpha County.

Still, I imagine that we all have some idea of what Faulkner meant. Poetry (at least poetry as we conceive it today) is the most intense and concentrated form of literature. A good poem packs so much meaning into so small a space that its impact on the mind of the reader is like an explosion. The ability to write such a thing is so mysterious that it seems miraculous. Even the novelist, who would not for worlds trade the expanse and the architectural values of his medium, must stand struck dumb with admiration at the poet.

And yet we all know that poets find few readers today and that almost all must support themselves by some compromise means — publishing, the insurance business, the writing of historical novels or teaching. And this is not new, for after the great burst of the Romantic era of poetry, the novelist took over the center of the literary stage and held it for a century. Why was this so? And equally, why does it seem today that the novel is under pressure from that negatively named form of writing known by what it's not, nonfiction?

All art is (among other things) a form of communication and identification. Literature is the way that a society talks to itself about itself. A small, homogeneous, traditional society knows itself pretty well. Its values are more or less common to all, its members agree fairly consistently on what is important, or right, or beautiful. A society like that can talk to itself in poetry. Indeed it must, if it is going to say anything new. Its poems will be elaborations of older beliefs, or juxtapositions of things already known, if never before connected in quite this way. Their meanings will be comprehensible to society in general.

A society can even undergo a certain amount of change and go on talking to itself in poetry, if the change doesn't get down too far. The Elizabethans did (though I believe that the sudden expansion of the drama which took place at the time was a necessary supplement to the older act, serving to explain evolving conditions of life). But too much change forces us into prose. Such a change began in Western Europe with the urbanizing and industrializing of the ancient rural world. With this change came the novel: an event that is impossible to date satisfactorily. Since, however, *Don Quixote* is an isolated mountain peak, and *La Princesse de Clèves* is an equally solitary feat of fiction and since I am writing and you are reading in English, I shall ask the forgiveness of scholars and suggest that we take the arrival of *Robinson Crusoe* in 1719 and *Moll Flanders* in 1722 as a signal for the unmistakable beginning of the change which made the novel the central means of communication in our society.

The novel, you see, as distinct from poetry, is for puzzled people who have lost some of their bearings. Defoe's indomitable hero lost himself completely, and he still came through. Dear Moll had to give up her morals, like so many girls since, and she too managed a quite successful life. If she was shocking, she was also a great comfort. Richardson did not think so, and suggested another set of values in *Clarissa*, and Fielding thought Richardson a romantic ass and poked the first fun at middle-class morality in *Joseph Andrews* and *Tom Jones* — and here is all the new bourgeois society debating and defining its values. Here is the Age of the Novel.

They grew and changed like the sailing ships of the times. They took on new forms, as new segments of society found themselves torn away from their familiar, traditional life, and attempted to discover what had happened to them. As time passed, it became possible (or so it seemed), to write about anything in a novel. More and more people read, so that greater and greater audience was able to take part in the debate over meaning and values via the novel, instead of merely being instructed in them, via the stage. Where is the soul of the nineteenth century to be found if not somewhere within the triangle of Dickens, Flaubert and Dostoevsky? With an American extension bounded by Melville and Henry James?

Then what has happened today to suggest that this wonderful rich instrument has ceased to be our chosen means of conversation? Two things, I think. One of them is discussed in an article by Nathalie Sarraute, written for the (London) *Times Literary Supplement,* and published with others in book form under the title, *The Writer's Dilemma* (Oxford University Press).

There is, she believes, a real and deadly danger for the writer to be found in the great (and overshadowing) works of the past.

"These demand of a writer a difficult type of conduct, a painful, dual effort. For he must at the same time impregnate himself with them, feed upon them, and discard them; be familiar with them and forget them; see with their eyes a universe enriched with all the complexity with which they furnished it, and yet see it intact and new. While studying the admirable implements forged by his predecessors, he must never forget that these implements could only be used by them . . .

"It seems clear to me, therefore, that the real danger for all writers — and I don't believe that I am being paradoxical — is not that of being crushed by mediocrity but rather of being dazzled by genius."

Madame Sarraute, who is herself attempting to find new roads for the novel is honorably qualified to speak of this dizzying, dazzling effect of past triumphs. Why try when so much has been done, a writer may think: I will never match the past. So he descends into being an entertainer instead of a discoverer. And indeed, our times are hard and new roads difficult to find. It is a great deal to ask of a sensitive, serious writer that he subject himself to the struggle. Why should he not turn critic, or teacher, and analyze what we already have, when we have so much?

This is the lesser of the troubles, however. Today some of our puzzled people, at least, have got too lost to be able to talk with the rest of us at all, by way of the novel. They are unable to connect themselves and their lives and their problems to anything so complicated as a fictional plot, to anyone so symbolic as a fictional character. It seems as if the very ability to think in metaphor, which is the whole basis of language, had got lost.

What can a novelist say to an audience that bakes cakes for the birthday of a soap-opera character and mails them to the television station? Nathanael West wrote *about* them, but how can we possibly bring them into the debate, our debate, the eternal and necessary debate over values and right and justice and good sense?

For we must, we need them. These are the people whom Hitler reached when their society ceased to be able to talk to them, and who stand now on street corners in Deep South cities, waiting to beat up "niggers." We cannot live in a society that cannot talk to itself.

So at present we have begun to talk via nonfiction. It is not a very satisfactory medium of communication, for it can deal with nothing but facts and theories. It lacks the ability which fiction inherited from poetry of picking up different facts and compressing them into one truth. It tries to do this, but what it gets from the process isn't truth but either synthesis or sentimentality. Nor can it confine itself to showing life, as good fiction does. It must pause to explain, to point its moral and adorn its tale; and as it does, the magic of immediacy and acceptance drains out of the reader's response.

Well, it is better than nothing. If it holds us together while fiction finds its new roads, it will do enough. And fiction will find such roads, or they will be developed somewhere else in some unlikely medium. For we cannot stop talking to each other; and even if communication breaks down between one section of society and another, the out-groups will still need, and begin, to talk among themselves. The compression of fiction, the swiftness of fiction, its passion and above all its ability to relate one event to another so that they can be seen in context and valued — this is so necessary that it cannot be lost.

Just as, after all, poetry has not been lost. It is waiting for us to grow enough to get back to using it, to find again on a new level the intimate, intricate human fellowship which created it in the first place.

STEPHEN SPENDER

Is There No More Need to Experiment?

Stephen Spender first made a reputation as one of the Oxford group of poets (with W. H. Auden, C. Day Lewis and Louis MacNeice) in the nineteen-thirties. He has gone on from there, and while we still think of him first as a poet, one also has to bear in mind that he has been a literary critic, a short story writer, a translator, an autobiographer. In recent years he has been co-editor of the prestigious magazine Encounter.

IN THE nineteen-fifties, a simplified legend grew up around the young English writers. It arose partly out of a journalistic need for a new movement of young writers for each decade, partly because the plays of John Osborne, Arnold Wesker and Harold Pinter, and the novels of Alan Sillitoe, Kingsley Amis and John Wain seemed to be the result of the mild social revolution initiated by the welfare state. The catch phrase, the Angry Young Men, seemed, at one moment, to cover all these.

A decade later it is clear that, although there was in poetry an amorphous something called The Movement, the fifties were as lacking in a commom direction or tendency as are most decades. It has proved to be a fragmentary decade of different attitudes. One division which might be made is into the defiantly uneducated playwrights, the educated novelists, and the academic teacher poets. Osborne and Wesker seem to represent the will toward a social revolution, whereas Amis and Wain reflect a change in the educational system. The novelists, who are more diverse and varied than either the plebeian playwrights or the academic poets, seem to form a bridge between them. But both novelists and playwrights are more narrowly nationalistic, little-England, than the poets who genuflect to American poetry and whose academicism is more the result of American New Criticism and of residence at American universities, than of the Oxford English school, or the Cambridge of F. R. Leavis.

One generalization which can be fairly safely made is that the postwar generation of English writers does not appear to have read the great writers of the first half of the century in such a way as to have absorbed their influence, still less so as to have been acted upon by it. The poets know Yeats, Eliot and Auden, for instance, but I cannot think of any young poet of distinction who has learned much from them, either in the way of having the same attitudes or aims, or even of using a similar technique. Recently Donald Davy wrote that no poet of his generation could learn anything from T. S. Eliot, though he added that Yeats was a great influence. William Golding is the only contemporary novelist who has clearly been influenced by James Joyce. But to say this is perhaps another way of saying that Mr. Golding is the one postwar English novelist whose books might equally well have appeared in the nineteen-thirties. They have the kind of thoughtful relationship to avant-garde word-laboratory writing, of the kind that appeared in the magazine *transition,* which Henry Green's early novels have to James Joyce.

A characteristic of the other writers I have mentioned here is the apparent innocence with which they seem to be saying no one has written like us before. No one, it would seem, has attempted to write plays about working-class life which use poetic symbols and an expressionistic technique like those of Arnold Wesker. Amis and Wain, who are more sophisticated than Osborne and Wesker, discovered Arnold Bennett some years ago, and defended his kind of realism against the poetic sensibility of Virginia Woolf. But I don't think they thought of themselves as being really influenced by Bennett.

They thought that they were doing something new. They
merely upheld Bennett against Virginia Woolf. The feeling that
there is no need to continue with the experiments made twenty
years ago, and to avoid conventional form and idiom, is surely the
result of a certain confidence that the postwar era has provided a
new society. A generation ago novelists seemed to be writing in
order to make their novels different from other novels. They set
out to conquer new areas of form and language for the novel,
which became a serious competitor with poetry. Probably the
reason why they showed this kind of anxiety (which even D. H.
Lawrence was prey to) was that they did not feel themselves
rooted in a life all around them which was itself new, so that it
would inevitably make their work new also. Some of them were
socialists fighting for a new world, but they did not live in a
welfare state.

Since the war young English novelists have been more preoccupied with keeping up with social change in their work than
with "making it new." The working-class conscious English novelists of today feel rooted in material that is the result of changes
in society. Therefore they do not worry much about form. The
more proletarian their origins and their own material, the less
they seem worried. Thus Alan Sillitoe, who, as James Gindin
points out, in his *Postwar British Fiction,* has directly stated the
need for a working-class perspective in fiction, is very little preoccupied by problems of form and style. Mr. Gindin quotes from an
essay in which Mr. Sillitoe's views are implied: "Working men and
women who read do not have the privilege of seeing themselves
honestly and realistically portrayed in novels. They are familiar
with wish-fulfillment images flashed at them in cliché form on television or in the press, and the novels they read in which they do
figure are written by those novelists of the Right who are quite
prepared to pass on the old values and who . . . delineate only
stock characters."

Here Mr. Sillitoe seems very much of his and Mr. Wesker's generation, in his almost superb disregard for the fact that he is simply dishing up the clichés of the nineteen-thirties. He and Mr. Wesker might argue that the sentiments which were false in the mouths of the bourgeois and pink writers of the thirties are different, being more authentic with them, because they are of and write for and about the working class. But rereading Sillitoe's *The Loneliness of the Long Distance Runner,* I am struck both by its power and by the disturbing question whether novelists of his generation can go on ignoring, in their work the techniques of *Ulysses* and *Women in Love.* The story of "The Loneliness of the Long Distance Runner" is narrated by the runner himself, who has been sent to Borstal, the reform school, after robbing a bakery. The governor of the school and the benefactors who represent established values to the runner wish him to win in order that he may redeem himself in their eyes. This would be a sellout, he thinks, to their values. He deliberately loses the race.

The boy's recital of this story with a theme of Tolstoyan strength is to an imaginary listener. As with all such narrations (one thinks of Joseph Conrad's Marlowe), the device is highly artificial. The artificiality of the device in the nineteen-sixties is bound to make one reflect that a boy who could express himself as well as this would have found a publisher by now! In an age as conscious of idiom as ours, the language he uses seems too fabricated — for example, in a passage quoted by Mr. Gindin:

"So soon as she got the money, Mam took me and my five brothers and sisters out to town and got us dolled-up in new clothes. Then she ordered a twenty-one inch telly, a new carpet because the old one was covered with blood from Dad's dying and wouldn't wash out, and took a taxi home with bags of grub and a new fur coat."

This may, of course, be exactly how such a boy would talk —

but he would not talk so long and so coherently, nor would a purely abstract interlocutor be his audience.

The reader whose memory of modern literature stretches back to the twenties cannot help reflecting that Joyce solved the awkward technical problem of Ancient Mariners — with their glittering eyes and skinny hands, having to transfix impatient wedding guests to listening silence — by fusing narrator, listener and reader into a single state of creative consciousness, and by inventing the artificial but highly convincing interior monologue. This invention may strike one as "dated" today, but it seems odd to revert to the clumsy device of Conrad.

If there were a social revolution creating a working-class audience for novels by working-class writers about the working class, perhaps not to have read Joyce would not matter, and the reading public would accept Mr. Sillitoe's convention as expressing the working-class point of view, just as he would regard Mr. Wesker's cooked-up expressionism as the newest thing that had ever happened. But the problem confronts Mr. Sillitoe and Mr. Wesker that in present-day England they are writing for a middle-class public (though with a difference). The idea of the working-class point of view in fiction and on the stage was a love affair of youth. The writer has to settle down, alas, to marriage with the middle-class reader. A social change transforming the literary situation is the desideratum which seems to have been achieved nowhere, not even in the socialist countries. The subject of a great many English novels remains — and will remain for some time to come — a tantalizing, unresolved social situation in which, altogether there have been great changes in the educational system (and a few in society itself), the structure of English life has not changed correspondingly.

What British writing today reflects is, then, a further breaking up of that fragmentation already present in the nineteen-twenties — most decisively in *The Waste Land*. This fragmentation was

obscured for a few years during the nineteen-thirties by Fascism
— which, in the democratic countries, galvanized literature into
an appearance of anti-Fascist unity. As we have seen it has also
been obscured since the war — partly because of a wish that
there should be a movement corresponding to the supposititious
one of the nineteen-thirties, and partly because sociological and
proletarian novels by Sillitoe, Amis, Wain, Doris Lessing, Colin
McInnes and others seemed a powerful extension into fiction of
the working-class writing which has given vigor to the theater.

The new sociological novelists are in a majority, it is true, but
they do not include some of the best writers — William Golding,
Iris Murdoch and Angus Wilson. If one adds to these Lawrence
Durrell and C. P. Snow they would appear even less truly representative of what is significant in the British novel today.

English writing today is carried on against a background of social change — combined, as it were, with the contradiction of lack
of change. The generations previous to this one expected changes
in the West, and in England. What has happened is that now the
changes have come about they have turned out to be largely an ad-
justment within class structure in most ways unchanged: a stratification of upper and lower, cultured and uncultivated which,
paradoxically, seems more enduring than that of a generation
ago. Mention of the word "Establishment," which today is used
to characterize the top directive layer of the stratification, would,
in the thirties, have seemed like tempting Providence.

The result of all this is a very diverse view of English life in
current fiction; the more one looks the more difficult it seems to
find a common attitude. Under the surface of the supposed movements one finds a collapse of labels: perhaps, what is common
under all the different attitudes is (despite the neglect of French
writing today by English novelists) the Existentialist situation.

There is a left wing of writers like Sillitoe seeking to depict
character from a working-class point of view. There is Angus

Wilson, who seems in some ways the strongest English novelist writing today, perhaps because the problems he poses are fundamentally still those of the liberal conscience. There is William Golding, exploring situations deriving from Christian myths and Christian heresies. There are the novels of Iris Murdoch describing groups of intellectuals in which existentialist situations tend to explode the boundaries of novelistic character. All that one can really find in common among such a diversity of attitudes is an awareness of living in an era which is unprecedented. Perhaps, then, the diversity is an expression of searchings for identity in a world which provides no sensitive person — from whatever part of society — with a place in which he recognizes the reality of his own being.

James Gindin comes to the conclusion that the most significant British novelists are despite their pragmatism, after all, Existentialists: in the work of Sillitoe, Amis and Iris Murdoch, the sensible man must deal with experience concretely, whereas the man who fits experience into an abstract pattern is made ludicrous or vicious. Of these writers, Amis presents perhaps the most pragmatic world. The heroes in Sillitoe, Iris Murdoch, or Angus Wilson do not find the virtue of direct action quite so rewarding. Their worlds are more complex, their facts harder to understand and arrange. Man, for these writers, as for the Existentialists, is caught between his vast potentialities and his still vaster limitations.

CLAUDE MAURIAC

The "New Novel" in France

*Claude Mauriac belongs to the French school of the "new novel"
— le roman nouveau — of which he writes in the following essay.
The Dinner Party and The Marquise Went out at Five introduced him to American readers.*

THE "New Novel" has made a hit in France and is beginning to
be known beyond its frontiers, principally in the United States.
Yet at a recent benefit sale where a group of Parisian writers were
selling their own books, a young man, flanked by his friends,
bought from one of us the least expensive of his works and, refusing the author's proffered inscription, tore the book in two,
saying: "The New Novel? It doesn't exist!"

The joking student was right, of course. From Nathalie Sarraute to Alain Robbe-Grillet, all those whose works the critics
and the public have labeled as being representative of the new
novel — including the present writer — consider themselves no
different from the average writer. Nor do they pretend to be better than writers past or present just because they are trying to do
something different. At most they can be said to have a common
vocation and orientation. Literature as pure entertainment does
not interest them.

As for the novel of classical form, its mold has so long been
familiar in all countries that only a minimum of ability is needed
to use it over again. Not to yield to the easy manner is the point
upon which the writers of the so-called new novel find themselves

unwittingly agreed; they all consider that formulas that have
proved successful in expressing this or that aspect of reality become useless when one is venturing upon the unexplored.

In this sense of the word, it is certainly true that without having
wished or tried to do so we form in effect a school. Nathalie Sarraute, author of *Portrait d'un Inconnu* and *Le Planetarium*,
delves into the still unlit depths of being, at that level where are
formed, but not yet formulated, answers to the queries from
outside. On the other hand, Alain Robbe-Grillet, invading the
geometric outer world in such works as *La Jalousie* and *Le
Labyrinthe*, intentionally stops at the surface of objects, believing
outer description less misleading than the inner one.

Claude Simon as an apprentice-demiurge attempts to capture
an inexhaustible reality by putting together traits and accumulating parentheses, with each detail added to the previous ones and
without any one of them ever being erased. The ambition of
Michel Butor, the author of *La Modification* and *Degrés*, is to
grasp the dual aspect of man, the personal and the social, and the
resulting fusion and fluorescence which time produces.

The author of *Le Diner en Ville* (and of these lines he was so
kindly asked to write) attempts to account for the simultaneous
reality — delusive as it is certain — of things and thoughts, perception and imagination entering on an equal footing into the creation of the inner vision which draws both upon life and desire
(or fear). All of us, following in the footsteps of our forerunners, some of whom, like Samuel Beckett are helping to transmit
directly to us the lessons of Joyce, all of us are possessed by the
same vain hope of being able to understand the universe such as
it appears to us, and to master, not the whole of it — that is unfortunately out of the question — but at least whatever aspects
come under our command with the greatest possible exactitude.

This is nothing new. This has always been the purpose of all
creative literature, of all men who write. Each writer has always

aimed at this unattainable target as well as he could with the
weapons of his time and with whatever precision his talents could
give him. Goethe declared: "The beginning and the end of all
literary activity is the reproduction of the world that surrounds
me by means of the world that is in me, all things being grasped,
related, re-created, molded and reconstructed in a personal form
and an original manner." Thomas Mann annotated this beautiful definition, by adding that each writer must attach his understanding to a form in order to attain exactitude in the realm of
the beautiful. From Goethe to Mann there have been as many
new novels as there have been new novelists. Apart from this,
one can note a slow but sure progress in the writers' appropria-
tion of the field that belongs to them. After Balzac, the vision of
the novelists, of their readers, and even of the public at large
that seemed to absorb it, could not resemble that of Goethe's
time. And we, who come after Dostoevsky, Proust, Kafka, Joyce
and Faulkner, have benefited from their discoveries. Without being unduly hopeful, we are trying to go a little farther still, and
the best among us — for instance, Nathalie Sarraute — are succeeding.

As Michel Butor has explained, a new novelist is a great reader
of novels who in the course of his readings has had the impression and then the certainty "that something is missing, has not
been done. At a certain spot there is, as it were, a hole, a void. If
you are a novelist, you feel an urge to fill this void little by little."
But if what you feel obliged to express is hidden, and therefore
difficult to discern, your approach will be that much more ardu-
ous, and the less chance it will have of immediate recognition.

It is a common and frequent adage to say that creators do not
have the critics they deserve. Only what is already familiar is noticed in their books — for instance, the influence of Virginia
Woolf on Nathalie Sarraute. But what is truly new is guessed
only by a few. These few are not the critics as a rule, but novelists

who, themselves advancing as best they can in the same direction, are better prepared for certain revelations. There was a time not long ago when people smiled at this writer's statement (in a chapter of *The New Literature*) that Nathalie Sarraute went farther than Proust in the limited but virgin area that she had chosen to explore. This fact, which was quite obvious even then, and which only a few of us had recognized, is today quite generally admitted.

Our search — and herein lies perhaps whatever novelty it may hold — brings us closer to the artist than to the traditional writer. We try to convey a vision — both inner and outer — which resembles no other. The apparent subjects of our books are only of secondary importance — a change of residence (*Le Planetarium*), a class in lycée (*Degrés*), a social gathering (*Le Diner en Ville*) — simple traps whereby to catch what cannot be expressed directly. In literature as in painting the anecdote has little value. We are no longer telling a story but depicting a world, our own world. If at times our work becomes too abstract it is because in attempting to express as exactly as possible what reality means to us we must reproduce the distortions and the different forms that appear to us.

Hence the importance of technique in our novel-like essays, techniques which are too frequently and uselessly imitated. Each writer must discover his own language, and the means he uses are very often valid for but a single work. For instance, the narrative and descriptive methods used in *Le Diner en Ville* are linked to the title itself, to which I wished to be faithful. The novel begins in the middle of a sentence when my eight characters sit down for dinner, and it ends in the middle of another sentence when they rise from the table.

I wished to convey a state of reality that unfolded during this meal, on three different levels simultaneously. I therefore had to discover a means of expressing these changes of register, and of suggesting a simultaneity which cannot be reproduced directly in a literary narrative.

There is the first level of harmless, frivolous, ridiculous, sometimes revolting, dialogue typical of a social gathering of people of a certain class. Then there is the second level of the thoughts which are often more serious and contradict the very words that are spoken: the common obsessions with sex, money, sickness, death, but also the giving up of true love.

The third level is more secret still: that of tacit relationships between the characters, from one to another, confronting each other; two guests finding themselves alone despite the presence of the six others, suddenly understand each other without any need for words or even for glances, the bodies themselves being able, in their own way, to express themselves, and also, quite beyond the physical, the hearts, and perhaps the souls, finding a means of communication.

An ambitious goal, and the author does not claim to have attained it, but it could not have been approached even fleetingly had he not perfected a technique long studied. This technique was precisely adapted to its object and will have to change as the subject-matter changes.

KARL SHAPIRO

What's the Matter with Poetry?

When one thinks of Karl Shapiro one thinks of poetry which he has been writing since he was in high school. He has been editor of Poetry: A Magazine of Verse, *has been a teacher, a critic. In 1945, when he was only thirty-one, he received a Pulitzer Prize for* V-Letter and Other Poems.

ALMOST every art in the twentieth century is a flourishing art — except poetry. Painting, music, sculpture, architecture, even the novel and the drama, have contributed richly to the age we live in. Our poetry, on the other hand, can boast only a tangle of subtleties and grotesques and the obscurantism for which it is famous. It is a diseased art.

It is diseased because the standards of poetry, criticism, and the teaching of both are today dictated by the *coup d'état* of Modernism, a minor intellectual program which took the stage more than a full generation ago, about 1915. These standards are enforced rigorously by literary constables ready to haul away any dissenters. Dissenters from what? Who are these literary guardians of the law? And what law must be obeyed? These are strange questions, but I think they can be answered here to some degree.

Poetry, of course, cannot be charted like a history lesson, yet there are moments in literature when the historical demon takes over and guides the progress of letters. A literary junta or gang can seize power as surely as a political gang. Real life, political or literary, goes on outside the "official" life with its maneuvers and diplomatic pronouncements, but history unfortunately takes note mostly of the official view. Yet, in the long run it is usually the artist himself and poetry itself which controvert the dogmas of the culture official and the academician. A poet such as D. H. Lawrence or Dylan Thomas is never recognized by officialdom but by a living audience. This audience, by its very nature, lacks spokesmen and apologists and for all practical purposes is nonexistent. But when true poetry comes along it makes itself felt.

Official poetry, on the other hand, is always thrust before us by its spokesmen. In countries where there are official or governmental academies, literary recognition is a cut-and-dried matter, and the poet may sport a ribbon and a title. It is disturbing to think that something like an academy has been transplanted to the literary soil of the United States in the last several decades, and that this *Académie Américaine,* so to speak, has spread its influence far and wide. When writers nowadays use the term "academic" as a term of abuse, they are referring to this officialdom and not to the presence of writers in the university.

Such terms are very silly but they are anything but meaningless. If we could bear in mind that "academic," "intellectual" "Modern," and what T. S. Eliot calls "Classical," all mean one and the same thing and all refer to a specific type of literature, then we might be able to understand the nature of this official literary movement.

Ours is probably the only poetry in history that has had to be *taught* in its own time. A contemporary art that must be taught to adults before it can be enjoyed is sick. To support and justify this ailing poetry the adherents of Modernism have taken refuge in Criticism. Modern literary criticism is the largest and most formidable body of criticism known. Its authors, amazingly, are often poets themselves, or those poets who have subscribed to the culture program of the "Classical" school. Their obscurantism is as great as that of the poetry it tries to defend.

What we have in our time is not a flourishing poetry but a curious brand of poetry compounded of verse and criticism. It is accurate to call this hybrid "criticism poetry." The person who can understand modern poetry must first be initiated into the vast and arcane criticism of our day. This is why almost every college or university in America must *teach* modern poetry. It is like teaching a foreign language and the key to it is criticism.

Anyone who has taught this "criticism poetry" knows that the student is left cold or horrified, once he is able to see behind it. The only advantage of this situation is that it has provided employment for thousands of college instructors. Needless to say, criticism does not flourish in a time of great or healthy poetry, if it exists at all. Criticism is a branch of philosophy and in rare moments a literary art. In our time it is neither. Modern criticism is a propaganda for a handful of power-hungry writers, many of whom are the authors of the criticism itself.

A criticism-poetry is a mind-centered poetry, an ideological poetry, a poetry of theologies and social theories. Such a poetry prides itself on its "impersonal" character, yet it aims at cultural authority in all realms of value. That poetry of this stripe can become a touchstone is hard to believe, unless we remember that it is both vocal and ambitious, and that it parades "tradition" as its main argument. The holier-than-thou character of modern criticism-poetry arises from its adoration of what is past, conservative, hierarchical, though in practice this literature is full of concealed or open violence and the worst kind of system-mongering. The absolutism of this type of poetry leads it into every conceivable ideological trap, from communism and fascism to Freudianism and theosophy. A contemporary poet without an Ism is considered by the academy to be a kind of rustic. Robert Frost, for instance, was not a Nobel Prize winner, even though he was a far greater poet than most who have been so honored. This is because Frost had no ideology to parade.

The ideological revolution in poetry, if we call it that, was an actual historical event that took place in the decade roughly spanning the years 1915-25. During that brief period certain key works of literature and criticism were published which provided the canon of Modernism. It is this canon which is still referred to when we speak of Modern Poetry. Here is a fair sampling of those works: T. S. Eliot's "Prufrock," *The Waste Land,* and *The Sacred Wood;* Ezra Pound's *Mauberley, A Draft of XVI Cantos;* I. A. Richards' *The Meaning of Meaning;* T. E. Hulme's *Speculations;* Wallace Stevens' *Harmonium;* Marianne Moore's *Observations;* Paul Valéry's *La Jeune Parque;* W. B. Yeats' "The Tower"; James Joyce's *Ulysses;* Ernest Jones' *Essays in Applied Psychoanalysis;* etc.

This is not an arbitrary list, nor is it meant to imply that all the writers in the list met one night in a dark room to form the Modernist Club. Yet it is a list (much abbreviated here) that indicates close allegiances in ideas, in techniques, and in tendencies. T. E. Hulme's book of criticism called *Speculations* (1924) is something like the *Mein Kampf* of modern criticism. In it is laid down almost every precept of modern poetics; the political reactionism, the religious fundamentalism, and the hatred for "romanticism," spontaneity and freedom. The convergence of Hulme's program and that of the Symbolists, with a few other ingredients thrown in, permitted the Eliots and Pounds to establish a philosophy of literature which has become dominant, although only because of a careful and relentless pursuit of their program.

There is, of course, not the slightest divergence of aim between Eliot and Pound at any period of their careers. They are the Dr. Jekyll and Mr. Hyde of modern poetry. If Eliot appears the more savory of the two personalities, that is because of his identification with the British church and state. Pound's statelessness and anti-religious views render him, on the other hand, a rather fearful specter and an embarrassment to Modernism. Yet both writers operate from identical premises and seek a common conclusion to their cause. What is this common cause?

It is first the establishment of a culture orthodoxy. In politics the orthodoxy is anti-democratic, embracing either monarchism or fascism or, among some of our Southern poets, a nostalgia for ante-bellum days. In letters it prescribes anti-romanticism, the annihilation of poets such as Blake, Lawrence and Whitman, as well as all anti-intellectuals and "optimists." In religion it prescribes ritual and dogma, whether on the conventional or the occult level (as in Yeats). With the anti-religious moderns, the ritualism may extend to form, as in Wallace Stevens. And in the case of a poet like Pound, culture can take the place of religion itself. Pound's cultural evangelism shows all the characteristics of a new religion, one which presumably he would have tried out had the corporate state survived.

In education, which the Modernists consider their special province, the orthodoxy is extended to include certain chosen works of poetry which supposedly contain all that is worth saving of the Western tradition (for example, Homer, Dante, the Metaphysical and Symbolist poets). Sociology, ethnology, economics, ethics, and of course esthetics are all taken care of in the Modernist curriculum.

Every college sophomore is dismally aware that criticism has supplanted poetry in the study of literature. He is acquainted with curious textbooks designed to make him understand the most minute and esoteric techniques of poetic style (which even poets are unaware of), without ever being taught who wrote the poem, or when or what its relevance is. The poem is treated as a biological specimen, thoroughly dead and ready for dissection. This kind of pedagogy is derived straight from the precepts of modern criticism and it is partly an attempt to isolate the public from a living poetry. A far-reaching result of such teaching has been to make poets tend to write for the purpose of criticism —

to provide models for the critic to work with. So standardized has this poetry become that dissenting poets such as Dylan Thomas came to associate the American university with bad verse. It is possible that the general public, which refuses to support this de-personalized verse, takes the same view.

The "poetry of ideas" is always a third-rate poetry, and Modern poetry is such. It is not the business of the poet to translate ideol-ogies, philosophies, and psychologies into verse, as we have done for so many years. Nobody knows Shakespeare's "philosophy." All we know is the beauty and the relevance of his perceptions. Shakespeare is not popular with the Modernists; they think of him much as Voltaire did — as a "savage." Voltaire was an ide-ologist.

The revolt against Modernism seems to be gaining ground at long last. New poets are turning away from criticism and the dic-tatorship of the intellectual journals; they are even turning away from the sanctimonious evangelists of the Tradition. They are once again seeking that audience which has for so long been out-lawed by the aristocrats of the Word. They are seeking to regain spontaneity and the use of the human voice, in place of the artifi-cial culture myth and the bleak footnote. They are beginning to use subjective judgment in place of the critical dictum. They are returning to Whitman, the only world-poet America has pro-duced, and to Lawrence and such American contemporaries as William Carlos Williams.

If the new anti-modernist poetry is brutal, illiterate and hys-terical, that is the price we have to pay for the generation-old suppression of poetry by criticism. It appears at long last that the poetry of the textbook will shortly find its way to the library stacks where, in fact, its death-wish has always pointed.

M. L. ROSENTHAL

New Singers and Songs

Poetry is the world of M. L. Rosenthal. He has written it and some of his verse has been brought together in Blue Boy on Skates. *He has written about it in* The Modern Poets: A Critical Introduction. *He has edited it:* Selected Poems of William Butler Yeats. *New York University knows him both as a poet and as a professor of English.*

THE RECENT deaths of Robert Frost and William Carlos Williams remind us forcibly of the slipping away of a wonderful series of generations of American poets. They flourished in the three decades after 1910. In the nineteen-thirties, when Edwin Arlington Robinson died and Hart Crane and Vachel Lindsay committed suicide, the new poetic impulse they represented was in full flood still. Even as late as Edgar Lee Masters' death in 1950 and that of Wallace Stevens in 1955, many of the familiar, famous names continued to be with us. A number, happily, remain present and active. But now, suddenly, in the past two years or so, we have lost not only Frost and Williams but H.D. (Hilda Doolittle), Robinson Jeffers, E. E. Cummings and Kenneth Fearing. A complex of later groups is taking up their "space."

Before looking at the successors, I want to linger a moment over the older group. What was it that these poets, so intransigently individualistic, nevertheless accomplished together for their art and for their country? First, of course, they gave us a body of splendid poems the best of which, for the most part, are to this day unknown even to the educated public. They liberated technique from narrow formalism and imitativeness, while they heightened the sense of relevant tradition and of the need for rigorous artistic self-discipline. They followed Whitman's lead in exploring native motifs and idioms, and on the other hand they opened our poetry to a host of foreign influences. They cultivated psychological and culturally critical frankness, creating a fearless poetry that faced the tragic meanings of the age with candor if sometimes with boisterous mockery. We may quarrel with certain excesses, but that too is a sign of a living, daring body of work. We have an American poetry now, though only the poets and too small a number of readers know it.

Who are the Frosts, the Williamses, the H.D.'s of the future? Impossible to tell when we are dealing with such unique personalities. Longevity, as various wits have remarked, makes something of a difference, and so may the early adversity and neglect that a number of outstanding writers have known. I can conceive of Howard Nemerov's becoming a sort of Frost — or perhaps more accurately, a sort of Frost-plus-Auden — of the future. He has the copiousness, ability to tell a story, wit, wide curiosity and poetic cunning to carry it off, although he is quite unlike Frost in his quick urban intelligence and, especially, in his long, subjectively symbolic sequences. Or we can call Denise Levertov a kind of feminine Williams, spontaneous, personal, open, yet rich in the deployments of her art. Or perhaps Galway Kinnell, with his glad eye for the particular and his way of looking at himself looking at the world, will be our latter-day Williams. But such speculation is tiresome, unjust to all the parties concerned.

Literature is full of meaningful echoes, but no real writer is merely the echo of another. The unexpected and the uncategorizable are the usual thing in poetry. The latest turn in the work of Conrad Aiken, the quiet strengthening over the years (largely unnoticed) in the work of the sixty-six-year-old Horace

Gregory may well mean much more for poetry's future than the easy audacities of last year's vacuum-packed sensation who swept up all the prizes.

My mind staggers when I think of this aspect of my subject: how little attention is paid to the development of poets after their first impact, for instance, and how much excellence without fanfare is destined to be ignored or to be recognized only by near-accident. We have a better soil than climate for poetry. If I should list a few poets in their fifties, or just about to become fifty, who have done a considerable amount of work and have won critical praise and interest, how many would most readers of this piece feel they knew at all well? Here are the names: Richard Eberhart, Karl Shapiro, Winfield Townley Scott, Elizabeth Bishop, Delmore Schwartz, Josephine Miles, Robert Penn Warren, Brother Antoninus, Charles Olson, Stanley Kunitz. It would be easy to triple the list, and in the process to add some names that should be at least as recognizable as those mentioned.

The steadfast effort to sustain moral perspective on Eberhart's part, the intense search for identity of Shapiro, and his trying-on-for-size of many guises in the course of it, the wry astringency of Miles's observations — to select but a few dominant characteristics — are phenomena of revealing importance to us. Scott, whose nostalgic poetry is beautiful and yet abrasive; Brother Antoninus, who shows us what it is to be a religious poet while struggling with daily realities of American life; Olson, who has been trying to crack through the assumptions and expectations both of our modern values and of our modern verse; Kunitz, who has gathered for us in too small a body of writing some of the most wounding motifs of the age — these are all sensibilities at once unique and representative. We ignore them at our own expense, given the fact that each has a language, a style, a way of making poems that is absorbingly suggestive in itself.

The single poet of outstanding power and virtuosity to emerge since the last war is the forty-seven-year-old Robert Lowell. He seems the likeliest heir, in the quality of his genius, to the mantle of Eliot. Our leading "confessional" poet, between his early *Land of Unlikeness* and his 1959 volume, *Life Studies,* he turned more and more to the exploitation of his own private experiences, family background and psychological predicaments as the controlling center of his work. It is a direction indicated not only by his own growth as a poet, but by the whole tendency of serious poetry since the great Romantics and especially since the later Yeats.

Private humiliation and disorientation become in this perspective (as in certain French poets whom Mr. Lowell has studied and translated) the clue to the general human condition. One is tempted to discount the tendency, sometimes, as a type of nasty exhibitionism leading to an aesthetic dead end, particularly as it *is* little more than that in the hands of half-poets. But that is to ignore and to dismiss out of a too-ready squeamishness the profound reorientation of sensibility taking place in our social and personal relationships and reflected in fiction and drama as well as in poetry. In any case, the art of Mr. Lowell is extraordinary in its passion and energy; past the self-degradation, unpoisoned by it and indeed redeeming it, something beautiful comes to birth.

Among the poets we may loosely group with Lowell on the score of either a certain confessional strain or a wildly nervous energy with a self-lacerating backlash to it are the late Theodore Roethke, Delmore Schwartz, W. D. Snodgrass and Anne Sexton. All have written moving poems based on private anguish. Some of Roethke's relatively early poems based on childhood memories of his father's greenhouse are amazingly vivid evocations. His attempts in other work to get deep into the primal psyche are often forced and sub-Joycean (rather than sub-conscious, as intended), but they do catch the pathos of a compulsion to regress and at the same time, curiously, often carry a roaring bawdy humor as well.

Indeed, almost all the dark and depressive poetry I am alluding to now has its paradoxically high-spirited side, sometimes "manic" and hysterical, perhaps, but also expressive of a highly intelligent and humane irony behind what appears the authors' self-indulgence. Roethke's work, again, can be quite simple; he has written some of the most elementally sad poems we have. Recently, he has received a good deal of recognition in England, where among others he has influenced the gifted poet Ted Hughes and his American wife, the late Sylvia Plath. Miss Plath's very last poems, as represented in a recent issue of the *Sunday Observer,* were morbid but brilliant. In the absolute authority of their statement they went beyond Roethke into something like the pure realization of a latter-day Emily Dickinson.

The reader who is unfamiliar with current poetry may feel that he is better off without having to come to terms with such intractable melancholy as I have been describing. And it is true that, take it by and large, our best poetry is often savagely, bitterly, alienated, or at least driven to some extreme of neurotic exacerbation. (See Frost's "A Servant to Servants," among many forerunners that might be named.) Thus, Snodgrass' most successful poem, "Heart's Needle," concerns the suffering he and his small daughter underwent during the ordeal of his divorce and remarriage. As is characteristic of poets writing in this mode, he associated private with public suffering and built into the poem an imagery of cold weather that suggests the wintry state of the human spirit and even the cold war. Anne Sexton's poems deal often with her own mental illness and Delmore Schwartz's with an oppressed psychic condition that is felt as very much a function of the times. (Here I am speaking more of Schwartz's earlier work than his more relaxed recent poetry.)

If proof were needed, then, that this is an age of vast and painful psychological pressures and dislocations, in which the private self feels engulfed by impersonal forces, especially by the recurrence of war and violence and the equally recurrent threat of

more, and worse, to come, then our poetry would certainly provide it. The war poems of Randall Jarrell, and his concern
generally with the vulnerability and pity of innocence, the search
for reconstruction of the fragmented self in Muriel Rukeyser's
poetry, Eberhart's struggle to subdue the active death-consciousness
of his work, the sense of pervasive vileness that permeates Allen
Ginsberg's wailing autobiographical indictments — these and many
other examples amply illustrate the point. One would think our
poets were en masse obsessed with the thought at the beginning
of James Wright's "Saint Judas":

> *When I went out to kill myself, I caught*
> *A pack of hoodlums beating up a man . . .*

To counteract the clear suggestion of unrelieved depression,
anxiety and hostility, we need to recall certain basic principles.
A poem that is well-earned through its mastery of its own language,
voice and structure, is implicitly an assertion of human value no
matter what its explicit theme or viewpoint may be. Their understanding of this principle is one of the things that is so heartening
about the poets whose names are usually associated with Charles
Olson's — Miss Levertov, Robert Duncan, Robert Creeley and
Paul Blackburn.

The actual writing of each of these poets is quite unlike that of
the others, but like Lowell they all understand — as Whitman
long ago taught — that looking hard at one's own realities is the
primary act of courage as well as of sensuous response. They
have (Creeley especially) cultivated a way of presenting emotion-
laden scenes and situations flatly; Creeley so much so that often
he shaves the poetic part of his poem away entirely. Levertov
and Blackburn have too intrinsically lyrical a feeling for their
phrasing and for the presentative life of the poetic image to go to
this extreme.

The feeling that there is more to a successful poem than "mere

poetry" is a dangerous one, but some great poets have had it; in
practice it means that such a pitch of realization has been reached,
or such a desire to break out of given molds, that the poet has a
fierce revulsion against any assumption that what he does is an
esthetic *performance* instead of an exploration of the possibilities
of imaginative projection and emotional discovery. Robert Duncan's work, particularly, reflects this attitude. Despite great un-
evenness, he seems potentially the most challenging poet on our
scene to take up a truly revolutionary artistic direction.

Because of the tendencies I have been emphasizing, I have
neglected a number of fine poets whom we might call, if rather
misleadingly, "moderates." Richard Wilbur's poems, sometimes
of incomparable richness and deftness, stand by themselves in
their own modest perfection. He shares the concerns of the age, of
course, as his poem against the McCarran Act and his "Advice to a
Prophet" — concerning the right way to shock ourselves awake to
the horror of the Bomb — show clearly. A very pure, vivid intimacy with language and the possibilities of traditional form
have made him a poet of almost Classical cast.

One may quarrel, as I have, with this self-limiting quality
against which poets like Duncan strain; and yet, in another mood,
I am sure the quarrel is presumptuous, for one should be grateful
to have what Wallace Stevens called the "noble accents" and the
"lucid, inescapable rhythms" of the true "bawds of euphony."
A neglected poet, James Schevill, has been constructing an interesting body of poetry out of a scholarly sensibility — a unique
ability to catch the special qualities of historical moments, biographical data, particular scenes fraught with contemporary and
traditional significance.

Poets like William Stafford, Gary Snyder and Robert Bly,
very close to the life of their local regions, have been cultivating
a descriptive precision and economy that still allows room for the
play of a sense of strangeness and for a colloquial bite in their

language. The spiraling intensities of W. S. Merwin, closing in on his own location in a spinning or fog-laden world; the gay, knotty, complexly centrifugal flights of Theodore Weiss; the self-discounting, witty, offhand, yet penetrating poetic wisdom of Reed Whittemore — these will suggest how many thriving poets we have, each working in his own way and only tentatively and momentarily, if at all, classifiable.

Do I think them all equally successful and promising for the future? Of course not. But I have tried here less to take sides than to indicate the large number of poets worthy of respect and of far more attention than they presently receive who are now at work. They are the descendants of the great generation that preceded them, who made it possible for serious poetry to thrive on the American scene, and their poetry holds many keys to the subjective meaning of contemporary American life.

PART II

American Classics

ALEXANDER COWIE

Emerson in an Existential Age

Alexander Cowie, who is professor of English at Connecticut's Wesleyan University, is very much at home in American literature. He has written about the American novel, is the author also of American Writers Today.

EMERSON is down; Hawthorne is up. Whitman is down; Melville is up. James is steady. Howells is written off. Mark Twain is "active" but is read less for his humor than for tokens of pessimism, disturbed conscience, signs of a "psychic wound." Poe, always lurking in a shadowed niche, has moved a little more clearly into view. Thus does the age reshuffle the position of the gods in America's literary pantheon. They will be reshuffled again — be sure of that. In the meantime, what is the principle of selection at work in the new alignment?

It would seem to be that in our existentially tormented era we are compulsively drawn toward the darker spirits, choosing Lucifer after the Fall. We are rejecting — for the time — writers believed naïvely innocent of experience and turning toward those who have seen the serpent in Eden, have been initiated into the knowledge of good and evil, especially those who have been probers of guilt and possessors of a "tragic vision."

Emerson doesn't seem to fit in here. He is assessed as naïve. There appears to be no nightmare in him; no anguished search for father or surrogate; no sign of an "unreasonable wound"; no case of inoperable cancerous guilt; no sensitive, lonely homosexually threatened adolescent stumbling toward destruction in an "absurd" world. For us Emerson has come to appear as a pleasant, harmless old codger (a sappy face on a card in the game of authors for children), innocent of experience and suffering, philosophically a virgin, engaged in coining shiny epigrams that could have no conceivable bearing on psychological problems in these "complex" days.

Let him pipe his guileless woodnotes, we say, while elsewhere Whitman straddles America shouting hurrah for the universe and Longfellow croons sugared tunes to a sleepy clutch of kids almost ready for bed. No harm in these old duffers, we say; but as for us, give us the guys with the deep insights.

And they do have insights — Melville and Hawthorne and their present-day existentialist inheritors. Hawthorne and Melville knew some things that Emerson never knew. Yet — and yet — is it necessary to remove Emerson to make room for the others? Is there not space in our pantheon for all? Is it not possible that our present-day salvation and redemption seekers might find aid in Emerson? Or are we too sick to want to be cured?

Ahab, we remember, had to banish the little black boy Pip from his cabin, for, said Ahab: "[Thou art] too curing to my malady." If, on the other hand, we do wish to cure ourselves, it is ironical that we should banish Emerson, for he too had his season in hell, experienced many ills which bedevil the multitude in any generation, including our own. And he cured himself. Perhaps that is the thing that we can't forgive him for: he conquered his woes, learned to transcend suffering, came to terms with the universe.

We have turned Emerson upside down. On the one side he is serene: this side we read and grumble at as superficial. On the other side is the record of his effort to attain to serenity: this side we ignore. It is an additional irony that in an existential age when every man is held responsible for his own fate and, as Sartre said, man is "condemned to be free," we should neglect the writings of a man who faced up to the terror of freedom and survived.

The tangible troubles that attended Emerson's personal life were formidable. As a boy he saw his mother struggle to feed a large family by taking in boarders. Always deficient in physical vitality, Emerson the youth was so disabled by defective vision and symptoms of tuberculosis that his career almost ended before it was well begun. Socially he often felt rejected, lonely. (It may help some of our symptom-conscious brethren to feel a kinship with Emerson if they learn that he had a facial tic — doubtless psychosomatic!)

Death was a frequent visitor in the family, taking the father when Ralph (or Waldo as he was actually called) was nine, two of the younger children in childhood, and two of the brilliant brothers in their young manhood. Stricken by tuberculosis, Edward Emerson (head of his class at Harvard) suddenly became violently insane, and Ralph himself had to help take him in a closed coach to the asylum at Charlestown. Edward died not much later of tuberculosis. Charles Emerson, an almost equally brilliant brother, died soon of the same disease.

Meantime Ralph constantly had the care of still another brother, Bulkley, who remained all his life a mental defective with the mind of a four-year-old and from time to time became completely deranged. Is it any wonder that Emerson's journal at this period of his life contained gloomy entries? He saw, he said, a "huge and disproportionate abundance of evil" on earth which was observable everywhere among the "enslaved, the sick, the disappointed, the poor, the unfortunate, the dying." He was convinced that "few men ever suffered more genuine misery than I have suffered." There was more for him to endure: in 1831 his lovely young wife, Ellen Tucker, died a harrowing death from tuberculosis; Emerson was then twenty-seven years old. Several years later death took his five-year-old son Waldo.

To these concrete instances of suffering and sorrow there must be added the great travail of spirit involved in the professional ordeal he passed through on the occasion of his resigning the pastorate of the Second Church of Boston. It was an ordeal that brought him great agony and that reduced him physically to a shadow. Emerson shielded and insulated against the common griefs of mankind? Unacquainted with evil? It would seem that as a young man, at least, he had a full normal share.

Well, morbid statistics and casualty lists to not add up to a philosophy. Emerson the man knew troubles all right, but as a writer did he ever confront evil and tragedy in a coherent professional manner? The answer must be "no." Emerson has always been the despair and the butt of professional philosophers: he had no "system." He left no extended formal treatment of the subject of evil, only a brief essay on the Tragic Sense; but discursively throughout his writings over a period of fifty years, there is abundant evidence that he did not simply shrug off ontological and teleological matters. With wry humor he reminds us that every man is born to a problem: "It is very unhappy, but too late to be helped, the discovery we have made that we exist. That discovery is called the Fall of Man."

Underneath all Emerson's brave epigrams there lurks an awareness of the eternal battle between the concepts of free will and determinism. He never denied the grip and drag of temperament, heredity, circumstance. He even gave tentative endorsement to modern-seeming explanations of failure and waywardness. Thus he queried: "How shall a man escape from his ancestors, or draw off from his veins the black drop of blood which he drew from his father's or his mother's life." "Men," he once wrote, "are what their mothers made them."

From many of the data turned up by his experience of life, Emerson might well have become a mechanist or a determinist. Nor did he shrink from examining the direst evidence. "No picture of life," he said "can have any veracity that does not admit the odious facts."

Yet somehow Emerson triumphed over his darker intuitions. Nobody quite knows the mode of his victory. Certainly it was not logic that delivered him. In any case success did not come at a particular moment of "conversion"; rather, his liberation was a long-term process, an agenda for a lifetime: "the years teach much which the days never know." Emerson peddled no peace-of-mind pamphlet for a weekend cure of jitters and tensions. The secret of a successful life, he believed, was an endless self-renewal, a constant *becoming*.

Nor could such a victory be attained vicariously. "Nothing can bring you peace but yourself," he said. Nor did Emerson try to "escape" from life; he did not seek to annul reality but to master it, or to transform it. He counseled greater, rather then less, awareness. As a writer he was not a tranquilizer but an energizer. He promises nothing, suggests all. "Man," he said "is a golden impossibility." Empirical knowledge, he knew, could lead to a dead end.

He could not prove freedom of the will, but (like Melville) he came to believe that there is no inherent incompatibility between free will and necessity. "We are sure," he writes in "Fate," "that although we know not how, necessity does comport with liberty." He went so far as to posit the thought that "a part of Fate is the freedom of man." These assumptions put a premium on self-reliance, on effort. They enable one to indulge in hope.

Contemporary readers are often irked by the vagueness of Emerson's faith. His counsel, they find, was to "live in the soul," to confide oneself to the great unnameable Law of all things. They are perhaps looking impatiently for a how-to-do-it manual to be bought at Liggett's; but Emerson, who was a part-time mystic, balks at the demand for definitions and metaphysical security measures. His message must remain general, and the aid he makes possible is finally more psychological than philosophical. He was one of those writers who convince by their presence.

Emerson offered invitation and example, but he never wanted people to imitate him. Each soul has its pattern of salvation, and the self-reliant person will find his own. "Great men," he said, "have been perceivers of the terror of life, and have manned themselves to face it." But there is a paradox here, and perhaps a lesson for our existentially tortured citizenry. Emerson's self-reliance does not mean self-insistence. Indeed pretty much the opposite is the case. It calls for surrender of one's pesky little ego — root of so many of today's anxiety neuroses. Trouble sets in, Emerson knew, when the "individual would be something of himself." It is when a man jettisons his petty ego that he is ready for a voyage of the spirit. It is then that he will stop taking the pulse of his weakness and begin to take the measure of his strength.

He will also learn — what our prosperous pampered times make it so hard to learn — that one must often settle for less than perfection. "I am thankful," wrote Emerson, "for small mercies. I compared notes with one of my friends who expects everything of the universe and is disappointed when anything is less than the best, and I found that I begin at the other extreme, expecting nothing, and am always full of thanks for moderate goods."

This Emerson, this mild-seeming questioner and questor, this serene voyager who yet had looked into almost every abyss designed to terrify men, who stared into the same void we stare into, might well be brought back into our purview. Walt Whitman too. No need to elbow Melville and Hawthorne and Faulkner aside; we need all our great men. Emerson does not answer all questions, and he certainly could not meet modern existential thinkers on their own grounds. And yet it may be that Tolstoy was right in saying that certain great questions are put to mankind not that men should answer them but that they should go on forever trying.

In the meantime there is life to live. Here is where Emerson may be of help to a generation unmanned by existential fears, a generation paradoxically both self-centered and will-less, both morally "emancipated" and guilt-ridden. Perhaps it is better to nurture a degree of hope than to huddle helplessly under a cloud of frightening symbols, picking at the scabs of our psychic wounds. The study of pathological states is instructive and necessary, but something can be learned, too, from health. Emerson was ill and he became whole. Like Robert Frost, he had his own "desert places," and he learned to cope with them. He knew the terror of life and manned himself to face it.

WALDO FRANK

With a Voice as Big as America

Waldo Frank looks back on a long life (he was born in 1889) of literary endeavor. He has been a novelist, an essayist, a playwright. He has been a worker in the cause of inter-American relations, and one has only to witness his reception in a South American city to appreciate the regard in which he is held as a man of letters and a friend.

IN THE CENTURY and more since the first, slim, privately printed volume of *Leaves of Grass* appeared, Walt Whitman has become throughout the world America's most widely read, most deeply discussed poet. But the years have not removed the ambiguities of his place in his own country. He sang for the American people, who remain indifferent. By a consensus of intellectual opinion, he is our greatest poet, yet the fashionable critics and most of the biographers do not understand him, and in many cases actually dislike him.

Whitman's relationship with Lincoln casts some light on this paradox. The two men never met, yet deeply knew each other. When Lincoln was still a lawyer in Springfield, sharing a one-room office with Herndon, he read aloud to his partner from the first edition of the *Leaves*. During the war, on his daily ride with his cavalry guard from his summer residence outside the capital to the White House, Lincoln grew aware of someone gazing at him from the window of a cheap lodging house, and nodded to him. He never identified this man as the maker of the strange songs he admired. And Lincoln was dead before Whitman (who could easily have clasped his hand at one of the open White House receptions) expressed his love for him in "When Lilacs Last in the Dooryard Bloom'd" — one of his noblest poems.

The two men were to be the representative voices of America as the home of human brotherhood. But Lincoln's spirit seemed archaic in the Gilded Age which his death announced and in our Chromium Age which followed; and yet the people nostalgically love him. Whitman's chants are still ignored by the masses, for whom he wrote them, and are reluctantly acknowledged by the poets — yet more and more he is our commanding literary presence.

In Whitman's work there are three master topics: words, religion and self. When he was an old man in Camden, Whitman said to his young friend Horace Traubel: "I sometimes think the 'Leaves' is only an experiment in language." In notes which probably antedate his poems, and which he captioned "The Primer of Words," he jotted down: "Names are magic . . . all lies folded in names . . . A perfect writer would make words sing, dance, kiss, do the male and female act, bear children, weep, bleed, rage, stab, steal, fire cannon, steer ships, sack cities . . ." In an early poem, "A Song of the Rolling Earth," we read:

> Human bodies are words, myriads of words . . .
> Air, soil, water, fire — those are words,
> I myself am a word with them.

Concern with religion saturates Whitman's poems and his prose:

> I say the whole world and all the stars in the sky
>   are for religion's sake.
> Know you, solely to drop in the earth the germs of
>   a greater religion,
> The following chants each for its kind I sing . . .

The centrality of the self in his work is revealed by the one vast unnamed poem, in fifty-two sections, called in later printings "Walt Whitman" and, finally, "Song of Myself," which dominates the ninety-five pages of the first edition of *Leaves of Grass*. And what are the contents of this self? Every one, every thing, present, past, future. "I contain multitudes," Whitman shouts in his "barbaric yawp over the roofs of the world," and tenderly whispers in his great songs of ecstasy.

Words for Whitman are the magic that creates and spells worlds. Religion is the experience that binds each man to man and into the one cosmos. Self is where the miracle takes place, where cosmos is revealed in all its splendor.

This is of course the experience of the mystic. When Whitman was about thirty he had been a teacher in country schools, a printer, editor, amateur politician, a carpenter and a businessman (selling the houses he built with his own hands), a writer of banal tales and verse, a traveler who roved as far afield as New Orleans, a desultory but receptive reader, a lusty loafer. Archetype, one might say, of the American average. Now comes his mystic revelation. Perhaps his Quaker background, perhaps the mounting crisis of the eighteen-fifties, when the country was both booming and plunging toward the abyss of civil war, prepared him for it. Whitman is still "average"; nothing lordly or pretentious, ever, about him. He has simply seen that the average is "divine."

Whitman knew nothing, of course, about the science of myth and linguistics (it hardly existed in his youth), which finds the origin of words in man's primordial impulse to create a mythic world and to communicate his place in it. But Whitman's activity was that of the primitive, myth-making mystic. The romantic notion of America as a "new world" was of course there. Europe had it in the revolutions of 1848. All the Fourth of July orations, all the editorials in the American press, expounded it. Whitman's contemporaries, including such great men as Emerson and Bryant, believed in it and wrote about it. Whitman, with his words, with his life, with his insistence on what America *shall be,* set forth to create it.

At once this meant trouble. When Whitman catalogued the plains and rivers of earth, the occupations and anatomies of men and women, he was expressing his love by naming it. But the reader who did not share the premise of his mystic passion was likely to be bored or horrified. Whitman could chant: "Monongahela . . . how it rolls with venison richness upon the palate!" But to the common citizen the name meant the spot where he had to work and struggle to make a living. If Whitman's world-making words had to be alive, like men and women, the deeds of the men and women must harmonize with the words. And Whitman was far too intelligent not to realize that they did not. By divine right of the poet-prophet, he drafted every man, woman and child in America, every farm, factory, field to tally with *his* vision, to be the word of God he called America. But the men and women were not attentive. They had a job to do. For them the field was making wheat, the factory was making shoes — not Revelation.

Not only was the America with which Whitman insisted on forging the body of his mystic knowledge too busy to hear; Whitman saw from the start that much of the American fact contradicted his creation. A year after the first appearance of *Leaves,* he wrote "Respondez!" — a bitter, angry poem of despair (in his softened old age he tried to suppress it) at the gulf between his American myth and the actual republic. And in the same year (1856) came "The Compost" — one of the most remarkable of poems, which accepts the corruption of the American world but sings the mystery of "the sweet grass rising from it."

O how can it be that the ground itself does not sicken?
How can you be alive you growths of spring? . . .
Is not every continent worked over and over with sour dead? . . .
What chemistry!
That the winds are really not infectious . . .

The corruption takes the shape of war. Whitman wears away his magnificent health nursing the wounded of North and South alike, on the battlefields and in the hospitals of Washington. Then the corruption takes the shape of Reconstruction. In "Democratic Vistas" (1871), Whitman proves how sharp is his touch on the American fact. "Never perhaps was there more hollowness of heart than at present and here in the United States." He fears we may become "a flat and dry Sahara." And where are the bards for his myth? Where are the responders? With the fierce injustice of passionate love, Whitman cries against the literary field: "Do you call these genteel little creatures American poets?"

The pattern is clear. This mystic is not content with the words and figures of the great religions, although he deeply reveres them. He will be, as the Hebrew prophets were, a maker. He will compel the America which he loves with a full, sensuous love to enact the God he finds in it, the God he touches in his self and in all selves. And the American folk can't be bothered. Even as they can't be bothered with the example of Lincoln, finding it easier to make him a hero than to follow him in spirit.

At first the America that reads ignores Walt Whitman. Then it grows irritated. Then it sentimentalizes him away into "a good gray poet." At last the poets and critics will even admit that the old showman somehow managed to write a few great poems. But Whitman insists, like destiny, on being heard. He is still insisting.

How typical that the first appearance of the *Leaves* should have been generously welcomed by Emerson, who soon flinched from them; even omitting Whitman from Parnassus, his 1874 anthology of poetry that he liked. Only from England comes a considerable support. Whitman admits, in his broken old age, that England's sympathy and England's shillings keep him alive. The Old World hailing the maker of the New? Is this also a paradox? It was bound to happen.

Not because England was better or wiser than America. But because it is easier, at a safe romantic distance of three thousand miles, to admire the myth of a new world than to create it, which means to grapple with its crude and crass materials. Europe could more comfortably salute and admire the specific challenge of Whitman, because it was less involved in bringing it into existence. And Europe could more easily understand the poems as aesthetic creations.

For although the energy of Whitman's new world conception was American, the conception itself came from the Old World. In his way, untutored yet strong with the associative powers of genius, Whitman had absorbed Plato and Hegel, the Vedanta and Europe's literary mystics. Under the American surge of his poems, there were ideas and concepts which Tennyson, Ruskin, William Rossetti — and not a few radicals among the British workers — could more readily apply to the common man of remote America than could this man himself or the struggling American artists who had to rub shoulders with him daily.

Soon other countries welcomed Walt Whitman. The religious basis of his work was familiar to their mood; the idealizing of America as the Promised Land was an old tradition with them, which they were invited to appreciate as art, not to meet as a living challenge.

Before his death, Whitman had found lovers and subtle interpreters in France (which had welcomed Poe), in Germany, in Scandinavia and the Hispanic world.* The great Cuban patriot-poet, José Martí, wrote a long study on his work in 1887. Russia came later, although both Tolstoy and Turgenev had been impressed by him and encouraged his translation. By 1920, the Russians were reading him in large editions, and Whitman was the direct source of literary movements in France, Germany,

* See *Walt Whitman Abroad: Critical Essays from Germany, Scandinavia, France, Russia, Italy, Spain, Latin America, Israel, Japan and India.* Edited by Gay Wilson Allen. Syracuse University Press.

America Hispana. Such names as Mayakowski, Jules Romains, Stefan George, Rubén Darío, León-Felipe, Pablo Neruda, reveal the centrality and depth of the currents which Whitman nourished and still sustains.

For Americans, Whitman is the most difficult of poets. The scholars have done well by him; Gay Wilson Allen's biography *The Solitary Singer* is sound because its exhaustive research is directed by an intuitive sympathy for Whitman's central vision. Many writers have picked elements from Whitman's Cosmos. His free-swinging rhythms, his paganism of sex and of the earth, his romantic democratic faith, his imagist vignettes set like gems in the clumsy panoramas, and other fractions of his work, isolate one from another, have found exploiters.

Critics have avidly dissected his errors, which are legion: his want of self-criticism, his frequent poor taste, his pages of prosiness, his failure to confront the reality of evil which at times makes him mawkishly sentimental. They have portrayed him as a "proto-socialist," as an "anarchist," as the champion of free or perverse love, to suit their own myopias. But Whitman cannot be understood without acceptance of the living core and marrow of his work, which is the mystical revelation of God and cosmos within the self, and the active incarnation of this selfhood in the American republic.

This colossal challenge our fashionable writers have disdained, preferring lighter, shallower, predigested diets. It is this fact which prompted the mischievous suggestion of Valéry Larbaud (one of the best of the French commentators) that Whitman was really "a European poet." Whitman knew better. He knew that he embodied, as did Lincoln in another form, the destiny of America. America might ignore or avoid its destiny. The destiny remains. And Whitman remains . . .

JOSEPH WOOD KRUTCH

His Nightmares Go On
for Evermore

[*For some biographical information on Mr. Krutch see page 9.*]

ON OCTOBER 3, 1849, a physician of Baltimore received a note from a printer of the same city informing him that "a gentleman rather the worse for wear" had been picked up at a polling place. "He says that he is acquainted with you, and I assure you that he is in need of immediate assistance." Four days later Edgar Allan Poe died in delirium in a Baltimore hospital.

Almost all of Poe's short adult life had been spent in complicated misery compounded of abject poverty, pathological alcoholism and all the tortures a profound neuroticism could generate. Like the hero of his best-known poem, "The Raven," he was one whom "disaster followed fast and followed faster" — even after death; for he was scarcely in his grave before the false friend, Rufus Griswold, published a memoir in which his character was assassinated.

Ever since then that character has been bitterly disputed by those who would blame and those who would pity him. On the one hand he is as striking a case of genius neglected as the history of literature affords. On the other, there is no doubt that his own weaknesses usually defeated those who tried to help him. Always loyal to his child-wife and the mother-in-law who barely managed to keep the heads of all three above water, he usually struggled pathetically to achieve some sort of stability. Sometimes, on the other hand, he was reckless, insanely arrogant and completely undependable. Literary jobs of various kinds he could often get; keep them for long he never could.

Perhaps it all went back to one of the most unfortunate childhoods any man ever had. Orphaned in infancy when his widowed mother, an actress on tour, died in Richmond, he was taken in but not legally adopted by the wealthy John Allan, who overindulged him as a child, but never gave him any sense of "belonging" and cast him off soon after the first of his youthful escapades. Burning with ambition, proud but insecure, he never fully accepted the position of humble aspirant that was actually his and repeatedly he fled into fantasies of which drink was both symptom and cause.

Most improbably, none the less, he managed somehow to produce a body of prose and poetry which, though insufficient to provide daily bread, established his posthumous reputation as one of the five or six American writers belonging indisputably to permanent world literature. Under his portrait in our own Hall of Fame might well be inscribed Samuel Johnson's couplet: "See nations, slowly wise and meanly just/ To buried merit raise the tardy bust."

It has often been pointed out that, though Whitman sang of the common man and celebrated the optimism and healthy-mindedness supposed to be the essence of the American temperament, he has never been widely read except by conscious intellectuals, whereas Poe, the aristocrat, the esthete and the specialist in morbid melancholy and horror, has been more genuinely popular than any of the other four or five indisputable greats. "The Raven" is unquestionably the best known American poem; certain of his horror tales are among the most often read of short stories. And if "The Gold-Bug" is no longer an outstanding detective story, it and two or three of Poe's other tales created the "thinking-machine" detective re-embodied as Sherlock Holmes and, after him, in dozens of other essentially similar characters.

Poe was not merely a popular writer, and the paradox of his popularity is not so striking as the fact that what might be called his esoteric reputation and influence were as great as his popularity. We are very familiar today with the figure of the *poète maudit,* or poet accursed. Baudelaire's "flowers of evil" and Rimbaud's theory that the poet must strive for a "systematic derangement of the senses" are both long familiar and now enjoying a new vogue. But who would ever have guessed that these concepts would have originated in mid-nineteenth-century America?

Yet Baudelaire, the acknowledged founder of the school (and, incidentally, the translator of Poe into French) loudly insisted that Poe was the first to discover the *frisson nouveaux* or "new shiver," and seriously prayed to him as a saint because, while he himself was still struggling to achieve some method of expression, he came upon some fragments of Poe's writing and "saw with terror and delight not only subjects I had dreamed of, but *sentences* that I had thought of, and that he had written twenty years before." To no other American writer did any important European writer ever acknowledge so inclusive an indebtedness.

Poe's limitations are as indisputable as is his originality when working within them. Death, a nameless melancholy, paralyzing regret over the death of a beautiful woman (which he called the most poetic of all subjects) and fantasies based on terror or torture are the only subjects other than that of the thinking-machine detective he could successfully treat. And it has been suggested that this latter dream of pure rationality was itself merely an attempt to deny himself the extent to which he was dominated by his own irrational fancies. In the two famous essays, "The Rationale of Verse" and "The Philosophy of Composition," he pretended that his effects were deliberately selected in advance and then achieved by deliberate planning. But the unreality of these essays is clearly enough revealed by the fact that even when in desperate need and urged by an editor to supply something less horrible he was unable to "choose" any other effects. The nightmare in which he lived was one from which he could not escape.

The other great defect in his work is a certain crudity and a certain melodramatic tawdriness of which he is often guilty. Emerson referred to him as "the jingle man," and the fact that his verse often is merely jingle may have aided rather than detracted from his popularity with uncultivated readers. Having no formal education beyond one unsuccessful year at the newly opened University of Virginia and no opportunity to educate himself, Poe was not even well read in the best literature of his day.

His models were for the most part second-rate or third-rate writers, whose vulgarities he often imitated for the simple reason that his own taste was very imperfectly cultivated. But it would be a great mistake to make of these crudities more than what they are — blemishes which have led some of his detractors to dismiss him as a mere imitator of the imitators of the German E. T. A. Hoffmann. Poe answered them truly when he insisted that the horrors he described were "not of Germany but of the soul." For him, alas, that was true; and it is the reason why his stories retain their power when the usual horror story of the time has become merely absurd. Poe sometimes borrowed the devices of lesser writers, but he infused them with something peculiarly his own.

It is these crudities rather than the narrow limits of his range that are chiefly reponsible for the fact that though no critic can deny the position in which he is established there have always been some who denied that he really deserves it. Henry James, as one might have anticipated, was among them and he once went so far as to declare that an admiration for Poe's poetry was a sure sign of an undeveloped taste.

Even today some of the very critics who esteem Baudelaire most highly are among the least favorable to the man to whom Baudelaire said he owed almost everything and they are, one sometimes suspects, repelled also by the fact that Poe has been admired so genuinely by non-literary audiences. But it would not be unfair to turn Henry James' opinion around and to say that a contempt for Poe is proof, not of a sound taste, but of a taste so finicky that a few vulgarities prevent it from recognizing originality and power.

What Johnson called "the tardy bust" is no comfort to the man whose genius it honors too late. And one wonders how often, when we honor that genius, our tribute serves the one practical purpose it might serve: by reminding us to wonder what now neglected talents are being left to a still later generation which will be in its turn "meanly just."

Once the pattern of such a life as Poe's has been set any radical help may be impossible. But Poe's fate might at least have been palliated and there are others, less accursed in themselves, whose fate might be entirely different if they were treated by their contemporaries with a little more generosity. We load some with favors, but it is not certain that a century and a half hence our descendants will agree that we chose the right ones. Perhaps, even, it is too much to expect that we should be able to.

ALFRED KAZIN

One Man's Communion
with His World

*Anyone who reads literary criticism is familiar with the percep-
tive, razor-sharp Alfred Kazin. For a generation he has been a
lively critic of letters, and life, too. His books include the autobiographical* A Walker in the City *and a much praised survey
of American literature,* On Native Grounds.

THE GREAT WORK of Henry Thoreau's life — and of his art — is
the *Journal,* published in fourteen volumes. There is no other
work in American literature, perhaps no other writer's journal,
which is quite like it. Although it is entirely a personal document
in appearance, it is a formal literary work, often rewritten from
rough field notes. It is not a "savings bank" for publishable essays, as Emerson called his own journal; even less is it an intimate
confession, on the style of Baudelaire's famous challenge to writers to lay their "hearts bare." It is a highly stylized and endlessly
deliberated work on the stark Romantic-Transcendentalist subject of man's solitary communion with the divinity of the world.

It can be compared, in style and intention, to other works of
the same school — Whitman's "Song of Myself," Wordsworth's
Immortality Ode, Emerson's early essays, the "mystical" sections
of *Moby Dick* which show us the world as seen directly by Ish-
mael the poet. But of course Thoreau's *Journal* contrasts oddly
with such works. For this greatest act of his life Thoreau perfected a particularly disciplined kind of prose and yet celebrates
in his self-portrait the most mulishly solitary character in modern
literature. The *Journal* is a wholly deliberate, plastic and imagi-

native work that became not a reading of life but Thoreau's only life. Without his ceasing to be an artist (except at the very end, when he faltered into imitating the scientist he had never wanted to be), his "Journal" became not only his art, but his mode of existence. He did not merely live for his book, as other great writers have; he lived nowhere else. The box he built of yellow pine to hold the thirty-eight manuscript notebooks was also to serve as his coffin.

It is Thoreau's psychological complexity that has so long kept people from recognizing the artistic grandeur of his *Journal*. Yet there is always the equal temptation: to forget just how peculiar Thoreau's literary lifework is and to read him as a pure visionary. The late Perry Miller, Professor of English at Harvard and author of *The New England Mind, Jonathan Edwards* and other books, took advantage of an unusual editorial opportunity to review the problem of the *Journal* in a more systematic and passionate way than, to my knowledge, has ever been done before. The occasion is the first publication of the so-called "Lost Journal" which is simply the third notebook in a group of six composed during the earliest period of the *Journal,* but of which only five appeared in Volume I of the published journal itself. This "lost" notebook, which covers the period from July 30, 1840, to January 22, 1841, appears to have been mislaid by Harrison Blake, to whom Thoreau's sister Sophia had bequeathed the entire work in the famous pine box. It was Blake who first printed sections of the *Journal* under seasonal titles — a very misleading introduction to the inner mind of Henry Thoreau. The box passed through various hands and eventually went to the Morgan Library, which in 1956 acquired the "Lost Journal" and for the first time in many years was able to fit the whole *Journal* snugly into place.*

* *Consciousness in Concord: The Text of Thoreau's Hitherto "Lost Journal" (1840–1841) Together with Notes and a Commentary* by Perry Miller. Boston: Houghton Mifflin, 1958.

The "Lost Journal" is a characteristic document of Thoreau's early journalizing, before he went to Walden and began to make deliberate literary use of his personal experience. It belongs to the period before Thoreau realized all that he could make of the journal as a form. As Mr. Miller says, it is really an anthology of his previous thoughts, and goes back to the period when Thoreau used the journal as a commonplace book rather than as the labor toward the full revelation of his consciousness that it eventually became. The greatest moments of the *Journal* — they record some unforgettable flights of the solitary mind — are not here. But Mr. Miller has seized the occasion for a thorough analysis of Thoreau's peculiar literary situation. If the book is more Miller than Thoreau, it is because, as the intensity and concern of Mr. Miller's own commentary shows, there is something endlessly frustrating as well as fascinating in Thoreau's double use of the *Journal:* first as art, then as life.

The situation may be summed up this way. Thoreau, a Transcendentalist artist with unlimited faith in the symbolic resources and objective reach of his personal consciousness, conceived of his journal as a "song of myself" which, theoretically, could have had as much objective artistic validity in its daily "nature notes" as other works that have come out of the romantic cult of the imagination. It is not absurd to say that Thoreau's *Journal* has the same broad intention — to show the meeting of the inner and external worlds — that Proust shows in erecting his great symphonic novel on the foundation of introspective analysis. Thoreau's favorite myth — the imagination (or "soul") in the material world is like Apollo condemned to work as a shepherd for King Admetus — was especially dear to Proust, who in the form of a quotation from Emerson used it as the epigraph to his first book, *Pleasures and Days.*

Mr. Miller stresses the resemblance between Thoreau as the hero of his own book to Joyce's Stephen Dedalus. But whether one thinks in terms of Proust or Joyce, it is clear that like all the great twentieth-century writers whose concern with the stream-of-consciousness really starts from the romantic discovery of man's unconscious as a power of divination, Thoreau's whole literary faith is based on the mystic bonds between the private imagination and reality. Our generation is beginning to understand that Thoreau is not a "naturalist," and that the subject of his work is not the external scene, "nature," but the greater world of being with which the imagination claims affinities.

What makes Thoreau so different from the great modern symbolist novelists is that he really had no subject but himself, and so had to strain for an "objectivity" that he could only simulate, not feel. Living in Concord with no real respect for anyone but himself, being a person with a shattering gift for holding his experience down to his image of what it should be, he let nothing grow wildly under his hand, allowed nothing to surprise him. He was always in control — in the *Journal* — and the life he held in such harsh control finally evaporated in his hands. He did not let the world flower under his benevolent gaze, as Whitman did — and Proust; he kept it as *his,* all the time, until there was nothing to possess but the *Journal* itself, which the world rather tends to see as the dead records of his vanished love.

If the essence of the romantic artist's faith in "consciousness" is that he thinks it puts him in touch with the Absolute, the tragedy of Henry Thoreau, as Mr. Miller succinctly names it, is that he tried to be the Absolute himself. The world which Proust was able to *discover* through his personal consciousness, Thoreau lost by trying to assimilate it entirely into his own. At the end of the *Journal,* as Thoreau himself seems to have acknowledged with dismay, he was forced to impersonate the deliberate and "scientific" observer of nature, to limit himself to the artificial "facts" and external shell of things he had always been able — in his rapturous and marvelous flights — to bypass before.

G. STUART DEMAREST

The Voice America Understood

University College, Rutgers, New Jersey, is the address of G. Stuart Demarest. As a professor of English he has been on intimate terms, as he makes clear below, with Longfellow. He is now associate dean of the college.

HENRY WADSWORTH LONGFELLOW is a national poet only by courtesy of a vanished reputation. Although a few scholars and critics are trying to proclaim a revival, little more than a shadow of his former fame is likely to appear. With the ordinarily unpoetic folk to whom he once looked for his ultimate criticism, he is now a name associated with bad puns and some jouncing lines on sentimentalized history. Little has survived of a familiar affection that was almost personal.

In one sense the dismissal of Longfellow is serious. It has deprived the country of one of its best influences, not unlike Chaucer's, for keeping warm a sense of human history, that fourth dimension of reality. The continuity of mankind has received a palpable check, and a large segment of the past has been curtained off from the modern view. Because Longfellow's vast, miscellaneous, essentially personal poetry had animated reality for millions of people, literature gained a national vigor which later writers had cause to be grateful for. But those properties of life he had disclosed are no longer visible.

Today, it is true, he is often mildly puzzling. Swarms of critics once praised his noble sentiments, his high moral tone and his sweetening style — suggestions of which sometimes crept into his work. And in the twenties he went down into oblivion, not without a hastening shove, for precisely these reasons. Yet how did this gentle poet reach the feelings of unimaginative Americans so well? Why, too, have so many ordinarily clear-minded critics, like Lowell, Whitman, Saintsbury, or Canby, felt a curiously uncritical pleasure in his poems?

One bar to a revealing evaluation of Longfellow's poetry has been the narrowed vision from a fixed point in history. The question which true judgment eventually turns upon is very simply: what, after all, does life look and feel like to the thoughtful mind? If Longfellow gave it too much allowance of sentiment and morality for our taste, it is because he granted spirit to reality, largeness of soul to men, and optimism to literature, all now relatively unfashionable and unreal.

On such grounds, nevertheless, must Longfellow's significance be found — or rejected. For in accepting as his poetic mission the finding of ideal meanings in a hitherto rather fixed and untractable world, he opened an almost unexplored cultural wilderness. At his hand were American life and the mellowed, sometimes shabby riches of European art and history. But in himself, with his love of books and his reflective moods, were a simple candor and the inclination to share his intellectual pleasures with a nation of "plain people." By such gentle influences was American literature led out of library and college, without actually forsaking either, to meet American minds at their own hearthsides.

There had been forerunners equally able — in Franklin, Irving, Cooper and Bryant; in John Neal and Charles Brockden Brown — who had summoned America to look to its own life. But they had done more summoning than answering, and although the nation had responded hopefully, it had not yet discovered itself, its mind or its literary character. With an exciting past, a challenging life in town and countryside, and a beckoning future, the nation lacked the artistic instrument for getting at them — an artist who should stand in the dooryards and look out with his mind and America's eyes.

What seems to have carried Longfellow closer to American homes than his predecessors was his quiet conviction that life is, after all, real and not an empty dream or a formal design. This was his main difference from the sentimental classicist. The sturdy anatomy of his poetry was such as to render things, places, customs and people fit for enjoyment by ordinary, healthy American minds. Often he rearranged reality. But the Viking, the Indian, the Pilgrim were at base recognizably human, and so also, for that matter, was the Psalmist. And in drawing as close to his subject as his experience, or his sometimes obtrusive sources, would permit, he sought in his strong, firm style to suggest its human implications. This may explain why, from the time of his first enchantment by Washington Irving, his work began to resemble a poetic Sketch Book of his own tastes. It may also explain how he came onto a rather bleak literary scene with a richness and a directness that both refreshed and heartened.

The record of how he developed his literary character and placed it at the disposal of the American people forms a sort of bibliographical biography. When he graduated from Bowdoin his confidence in his own talents had convinced him that what American literature principally needed was a writer with talents very much resembling his own. But Bowdoin offered him a professorship of modern languages, and literature stepped aside. A preparatory three-year tour of Europe gave him mainly a rather unscholarly delight in taking trips to Europe, and when George Ticknor assisted him to a Harvard professorship six years later, he had to hurry back with his attractive wife for the rest of his scholarly training. The young professor was ready neither to teach nor to write — nor yet to live, as he presently discovered.

When Mary Longfellow died in Rotterdam, Henry faced what

in fact was a choice between consuming himself in a romantic, Werther-like melancholy or becoming a national poet. His later, though temporary, rejection by the talented Frances Appleton of Beacon Street did nothing to make his conflict less bitter. In the misery of a solitary professor's life in Craigie House in Cambridge, his problem had little to do with poetry; it centered squarely on the man. Out of this, as Sir Philip Sidney showed him, came poetry.

His first book of verse, *Voices of the Night*, was for Longfellow his most important, because it contained "A Psalm of Life," that much abused fragment of a man's inner battle. "From the cool cisterns of the midnight air my spirit drank repose," he sighed in "Hymn to the Night." Yet his Yankee temperament became persuaded that life is real and earnest, that the past must bury its dead, and that a man must act in the living present.

From the American public he received a reply in sales and letters that confirmed his resolution. It was, in fact, "A Psalm of Life" that got America its poet. Sidney's admonition to "look in your heart and write" very seldom thereafter meant exhibiting it on the sleeve. The reposeful "midnight" moods became a kind of delightful laboratory, a step in the poetry-making, in which experience could be savored and given shape. After his marriage to Fanny Appleton, he turned his gaze steadily outward for the materials of poetry. Even the moralizing had an external sound.

Ballads like "The Skeleton in Armor" had opened the realm of old stories for him. And in spite of the controversy over an unfamiliar hexameter, "Evangeline" advanced him to the top rank of American poetry. That he understood his talents now was clear when he wrote to his classmate Hawthorne, who had passed along the story: "This success I owe entirely to you, for being willing to forego the pleasure of writing a prose tale which many people would have taken for poetry, that I might write a poem which many people take for prose."

Eleven years after his marriage he was ready to leave Harvard and press for what may be his greatest work. In *Hiawatha,* the Indian was to receive at least poetic justice. Longfellow had known him in Cooper and Chateaubriand, but he had also known him on his very doorstep, and like many other Americans he realized he was not the noble savage of Cooper's pink-ribboned literature.

The scholar knew where to turn. Henry Rowe Schoolcraft and others had reported their firsthand experiences, and the poet needed only a series of sketches which would "weave together their beautiful traditions." In twenty-two cantos of a verse that mildly suggested an Indian trot, he captured a forest life that was peculiarly Indian, ideally human and characteristically Longfellow. In tales, episodes, songs and fables; among tribal rites, village characters, animal personalities and manifold natural symbols, the half primitive, half divine Hiawatha moved through his wilderness life toward the promise of peace in a white man's civilization. For the most part this was a physical world as the Indian might see it. Yet there was a haunting sense of pain and sadness consequent to his being merely mortal.

Longfellow's own happiness had to be maintained, during much of his life, from some sort of inner hearth. In 1861, with a rich career still before him, it was dashed to the rocks in a single evening. His wife, while sealing some locks of her children's hair, set fire to her dress. Longfellow clasped her against his own body and only burned himself. Fanny died next day, and Henry stepped in a moment from his domestic happiness into a lonely, grief-stricken world. The only cry he ever uttered publicly was "The Cross of Snow," published after his death.

In his need to act in the living present, he resumed the translation of Dante, which had often served as relief from creative toil. Translating, he felt, was "like running a plowshare through the soil of one's mind." Still, he added, "it sometimes seems like an excuse for being lazy — like leaning on another man's shoulder." Here, in effect, he was confessing the scholar's habit, which brought Poe's wrath down on him, of forming his poetry out of existing materials. Something that already had a body of its own stimulated his genius for finding meanings. Yet from the companionable business of editing and translating Dante came the famous sonnets on "Divina Commedia."

His creative energies were still active, however. From earliest days he had planned to build some towering masterpiece with Christianity for a theme. Gradually the three-part *Christus,* ideas for which can be traced across forty years, took shape on the themes of hope, faith and charity. But whether because life had taken too much from him or because his countrymen were not ready, the work that had best promised an enduring name dropped quietly out of the public mind and was forgotten. Only the medieval *Golden Legend* was praised. *The Divine Tragedy* may have suffered from having been done better elsewhere. Longfellow was not to compete with the King James Version of the New Testament.

The third part, the twin "New England Tragedies," on the Quaker persecutions and the witchcraft delusions, was particularly disappointing. One of his biographers wryly observed that, "Rather than read of Giles Corey's fate, a generous man would prefer to pass a pleasant afternoon in the morgue. There is no light, no relief, no escape from the fateful march of events."

Such strange criticism of Longfellow suggests that his attachment to the real had at last carried him out of his own day and close to ours. Many of the dramatic speeches were lifted bodily from court records, from old chronicles and histories, as if the poet had discovered "noble meanings" in the living language. This way, of course, lay realism.

In his last ten years he completed the *Tales of a Wayside Inn* (actually another sketch book) and a multitude of other short and long poems. But in "Michael Angelo" Longfellow rounded out the whole. Much he had planned was still unaccomplished, much had disappointed him. And death was now, he said, a constant companion. Yet he had completed for his country a full circle of its poetry — a poetry that had come from the mind, perhaps more than the heart or the soul, but still a man's poetry that had stirred the imagination of an awakening nation.

WALLACE STEGNER

Yarn-Spinner in the American Vein

For years Wallace Stegner has conducted the Creative Writing Center at Stanford University, all the while setting an example for creative writers. He is the author of short stories, novels (The Big Rock Candy Mountain, Shooting Star), and most recently of a somewhat fictionalized memoir of frontier boyhood, Wolf Willow.

On first glance it seems curious that the most natural and fecund storyteller in our literature — and a storyteller moreover who was best at the short haul — should have had to wait until the nineteen-fifties to have had his short stories collected.* But it is not so curious as it seems; he had few short stories to be collected. Charles Neider in his introduction to the collection makes an eloquent apologia for the things he has put in it, and the fact is that he has had to make it largely of sketches, parodies, jokes, anecdotes, yarns, fables, episodes from longer works and occasionally the longer works themselves.

Only by stretching definition past its elastic limits can one call both "A Day at Niagara" and "The Mysterious Stranger" — or either of them — short stories. The one is a piece of frivolous journalism and the other is a novel. And some of the things that may legitimately be called short stories in this collection look alarmingly like old-fashioned pieces of contrivance, more reminis-

---

* *The Complete Short Stories of Mark Twain,* edited with an introduction by Charles Neider. Garden City: Hanover House, 1957.

cent of Fitz-James O'Brien and Frank R. Stockton than suggestive
of the modern short story with its organic structure, its fetish of
compression and its concern with psychological states.

Mr. Neider's anthology offers a convenient basis for reappraisal;
the sixty pieces which are here hospitably called short stories illustrate both the weaknesses and the strengths of Mark Twain as
a writer of fiction. They teach us all over again that Mark was
not a fully conscious artist, that he was a fiction writer more by
accident than by design, that he fell much too frequently into
triviality and improvisation, and that at their best both his materials and his forms are an inheritance from the forming culture of
the Mississippi Valley and the experiences of his boyhood and
youth. In almost nothing was he an innovator: his genius was essentially nostalgic, his forms and techniques most naturally those
he adapted from the journalism, the lecture platforms and the
law-circuit yarning of his time and place. His achievement was to
elevate these shapes of folklore and journalism, and along with
them the vernacular in which they were expressed, into literature.

When he followed the lead of books and other writers he often
went wrong. His bookish vein is represented in this collection by
such respectable fabrications as "The £1,000,000 Bank Note" and
"The $30,000 Bequest," by some sentimentalized and Harte-ian
items such as "The Californian's Tale," and by the pure saccha-
rinity of "A Horse's Tale." His non-bookish vein is more than
sufficiently demonstrated by a dozen or two humorous sketches
that would probably not be preserved if they had been written by
a lesser writer. But his pure native vein, his Mother Lode, is also
represented by some pieces completely inimitable; and though I
should say the proportion of good Twain to bad is actually rather
low in these collected sketches and stories, even one or two of
Mark at his best and truest is enough to redeem the rest.

Mr. Neider is quite right in saying that Mark Twain had no
formal interest in the short story, and quite justified in extracting

from *Roughing It, A Tramp Abroad,* the *Autobiography,* or anywhere else the yarns and fables that Mark scattered through
them. But it would be a mistake to assume that because Mark
gave the formal short story only token attention, he was utterly
indifferent to form in anything. His novels, it is true, are episodic
and his attempts at the literary short story seem contrived. But
the yarns that he scattered through his books, the stories that fall
as naturally from the lips of his characters as they did from his
own, the beast-fables which conceal behind their apparent innocence an irony as alert as a blacksnake — these are not formless.
They have their own aesthetic, they are built to a traditional pattern, which Mark Twain had not so much learned as caught, like
chickenpox, from the air of his youth.

"The Notorious Jumping Frog," the blue jay yarn from *A
Tramp Abroad,* the old ram story from *Roughing It,* are of the
kind that illustrates Mark's talents best. Their lingo even yet
falls upon the ear with the magical rhythms of spoken speech.
Their narrators — those garrulous, innocent, wandering, tedious
old yarners whose very point is their pointlessness — represent
Mark's improvement upon a stock character of the frontier hu-
morists, particularly of Artemus Ward. The stories utilize the
devices of the humorous story, described by Mark himself in
"How to Tell a Story," one of his few ventures into formal aesthetics. And if they are baited for laughter, they catch other and
bigger game: Jim Baker's blue jay yarn is a fable in every way
worthy of Aesop or La Fontaine, and in some ways perhaps beyond them.

So Mark Twain is less a short story writer than a fabulist, satirist, parodist. If he did not write such neatly shaped and pic-
turesquely colored narratives as those of Bret Harte and the other
local colorists, he did better: he embedded in *Roughing It* and
Life on the Mississippi stories with their own deceptive shape and
their casual and incomparable faithfulness to both the fact and

the spirt of the raw societies they mirrored. Modern students of the short story will be going to Henry James, with his impeccable and self-conscious craftsmanship and his subtle modulations, or to Stephen Crane with his precocious impressionism, when they want ancestral models for their own stories. But Mark Twain's fables and yarns, looked at closely, reveal themselves to be just as truly "rendered," just as completely "written," just as fully under the control of an artistic intelligence and an extraordinary artistic sensibility, as their more formal stories.

The writers who seem to derive from Mark Twain are not the advocates of that formal short story that Mr. Neider rather irritably blames on the French. The writers who derive from Mark Twain are the Will Rogerses, the Thurbers, the Whites, the Disneys, the yarners and parodists and satirists and fabulists, workers in another tradition. They need go no farther than Mark in their search for a father; Hemingway was probably right in declaring that in Mark all American writing begins.

He was maimed, a little, like many American artists; his sensibility was more delicate than the instruments his society gave him. He never fully mastered the most sophisticated (and borrowed) elements of his culture. But he brought triumphantly to full usefulness some of the half-developed and subliterary and Beowulfian elements of a stage of American life. He made silk purses from sows' ears, and if — as in the present collection — there are some untransformed ears among the purses, we should not complain. For the virtues and the weaknesses of a writer like Mark Twain are inseparable, sometimes almost interchangeable.

HENRY COMMAGER

Howells: For Fifty Years a Literary Dynamo

In a sense one might say of Henry Commager that the world is his oyster, his interests are so wide-ranging. Trained as a historian, his view of history includes not only battles and leaders, but battles for ideas, and he moves easily from political history and biography to literature, not excluding that for the young.

THE HALF CENTURY after Appomattox was the age of Mark Twain, Henry James and William Dean Howells. Critics seem to have concluded, now, that Mark Twain and James belong to the immortals, and have relegated Howells to the realm of history rather than literature.

It is interesting to recall that James couldn't abide Mark Twain — he thought him commonplace and vulgar, while Mark Twain's comment on James' novel *The Bostonians* — that he would rather be damned to John Bunyan's heaven than have to read the book — is familiar enough. But Howells loved them both and understood and welcomed them both, and both of them cherished Howells as friend and counselor. Howells was the first critic to recognize the genius of James; he published *Roderick Hudson* in *The Atlantic* and offered to give him "half the magazine" every issue. And Howells was Mark Twain's closest literary friend and wrote what is still the most perceptive interpretation of him in our literature.

Van Wyck Brooks has tried to re-create Howells for us, to restore him to his rightful position.* It is a portrait and an interpre-

* *Howells. His Life and Work.* New York: Dutton, 1959.

tation rather than a full-dress biography, and painted with that impressionistic technique of which Brooks remains the acknowledged master. It is warm, sympathetic, penetrating; it catches what was most significant about Howells, and what was most characteristic, too. In a sense, Mr. Brooks has done for Howells what Howells himself did for Mark Twain — he has brought him to life with affection and artistry.

Howells was, indeed, as Mr. Brooks says, "the one writer who was aware of all the others." Never has there been a more perceptive literary critic, or a more catholic and sophisticated one. He opened the pages of *The Atlantic* to all the young writers on both sides of the water; he discovered Ed Howe; he sent Hamlin Garland back to his Wisconsin coulees; he championed Stephen Crane (and read Emily Dickinson to him); he celebrated Frank Norris and Finley Peter Dunne and Thorstein Veblen. He was the first to popularize Bjørnsterne Bjørnson and Palacio Valdés; he embraced Tolstoy and Zola and Ibsen; in his old age he held out the hand of fellowship to Edwin Arlington Robinson and Vachel Lindsay and Robert Frost. He was as national as Mark Twain and as cosmopolitan as Henry James.

He was a distinguished critic, but he was far more than that. For over fifty years he dominated the American literary scene as no one had done before, and none has since. Fresh from Ohio — and Venice — he came to edit *The Atlantic;* when he moved to New York in the eighties to take over Harper's, the literary center of the country moved with him. Earlier, in 1865, Howells had written on European and literary topics for the *New York Times.* "They paid me well and more than well," he recalled. "A personal interview with the editor in chief [Henry J. Raymond] made me feel that I had seldom met so busy a man. He praised some work of mine that he had read in his paper, but I was never recalled to his presence; and now I think he judged rightly that I should not be a lastingly good journalist."

He was pervasive; he was ubiquitous. Turn where you would, there was Howells. He wrote, it sometimes seemed, all the novels. He drew a literary portrait of Boston, and then of New York; he painted the farms and small towns of New England, and the summer resorts; he re-created the Ohio frontier.

He went traveling to Niagara or to Quebec, or abroad; he gave the surest picture not of the expatriate but of the American abroad; he added Utopian novels. But that, like the editing, was merely part of his prodigious fecundity. He was the historian and the interpreter of Italy, of Spain, above all of England; he translated all the more obscure books that Americans should know; he gave us the most extensive of literary autobiographies — an autobiography that became a history of the age; for good measure he added thirty or forty plays.

"Stroke by stroke, and book by book," Henry James wrote him, "your work was to become, for this exquisite notation of our whole democratic light and shade, and give and take, in the highest degree *documentary.*" And not so long ago Lionel Trilling observed much the same thing, that Howells belonged rather to the history of culture than to literature. It is not clear that these things are exclusive; that would rule out of literature a good deal of Dickens and Balzac, of Frank Norris and Theodore Dreiser and Thomas Mann.

Certainly Howells belongs to the history of American culture; he dominated one important chapter of that history. Certainly, too, he provided documentation for much of American life; it is to Howells we turn for much of our understanding of American Victorianism. But many of Howells' novels are quite independent of history and documentation. It is for the moral problem, the analysis of character that we read *The Rise of Silas Lapham* and *A Modern Instance* and *Indian Summer* and *The Undiscovered Country* and half a dozen others. Howells was not only historian and interpreter, he was a moralist and a craftsman.

If the moral problems to which Howells addressed himself seem not so much dated as tame, that is because Howells was so faithful to his own principles of literature, because — as Henry James pointed out — "he adored the real, the natural, the colloquial, the moderate, the optimistic and the democratic," because he disliked everything that was sensational or violent. He knew that very few people are involved in the problems that confronted a Macbeth or a Faust, and he addressed himself to the problems that are commonplace and familiar.

"Ah, poor real life which I love," he said, "can I make others share the delight I find in thy foolish and insipid face?" It is charged against him, too, that he addressed himself to "the more smiling aspects of American life." He did feel that, on balance, American life was more innocent than European, and presented, perhaps, more smiling aspects; after all, most of our major writers have said this, from Crèvecoeur to Robert Frost with his wryly ironic question:

> *How are we to write*
> *The Russian novel in America*
> *As long as life goes on so unterribly?*

It is proper to remember that Howells was the friend and accomplice of the rebels of his generation; that almost alone among the novelists of his time he addressed himself to the problems of labor, to the ruth of the industrial system, to the inhumanity of man to man; that he championed the victims of the Haymarket affair; that he counted himself a Socialist and provided one of the most severe of all literary indictments of American society in *A Traveler From Altruria.*

"After fifty years of optimistic content with civilization and its ability to come out right in the end," wrote Howells, "I now abhor it and feel that it is coming out all wrong in the end." Abhor was a strong word for Howells; his moral sentiments were righteous rather than heroic; his books were subversive but not inflammatory, but he continued, to the end, to encourage those who were inflammatory.

In a sense, it can be said that Howells has been buried beneath the ruins of his own triumph. He vindicated realism, but few now recognize a realism so demure; he transformed literature from a New England to a national affair; he used literature as a vehicle for social protest; he familiarized Americans with the literature of modern Europe — all the things that now seem so dated.

It is eminently so appropriate that Mr. Brooks should have added this study of Howells to his long row of studies of American letters, for he came closer to occupying the position that Howells himself occupied in American criticism than anyone else of our time. And he resembled Howells not only in the catholicity of his learning and the breadth of his sympathies and the depth of his understanding, but in this, too, that for fifty years he *was there* — a familiar and affectionate figure on the literary horizon, guide, interpreter, historian and symbol. Like Howells, too, he was suspicious of the violent and the sensational; he prefered the commonplace, the familiar, the authentic; he had an unfailing appreciation of the intricate pattern of our intellectual and cultural life.

LEON EDEL

The Enduring Fame of Henry James

As a biographer and critic, Leon Edel has made Henry James his life. He has edited James' stories, letters, plays, essays, and he is the author of a biography of the novelist that has now reached three volumes with more to come. For this truly magnum opus he received in 1963 both a National Book Award and a Pulitzer Prize.

THE HENRY JAMES "revival," as it is commonly called, has been under way for the past two decades. Evidence of it is to be found all around us: his works are multiplied in the paperbacks; his first editions are hard to find; his letters are sought after; his novels are endlessly "explicated" in the colleges and the little magazines. Three of his works have furnished the theatre with substantial successes; he has been televised to millions and broadcast around the world. And I am told by bibliographers, who take a competitive as well as statistical view of literary studies, that James is leading in the list of recent writings about American authors: he fills six more pages than Mark Twain.

Virtually untranslated during his lifetime, he is being rendered into many languages, including the Russian. In tribute to his "enduring fame," his publishers, Scribner's, are now reissuing the famous New York Edition of 1907–1909, twenty-four thick volumes long out of print and containing James' "international" and English novels, and fifty-two of his 112 tales. (Two additional volumes, brought out posthumously in 1918, will actually bring the new issue to twenty-six volumes.)

This controversial figure, so recently called "rootless" and "insubstantial," characterized by Vernon L. Parrington as "a self-deceived romantic," patronized and ridiculed by a whole generation of critics, has by the quiet authority of his work, and the gravity of his mind and style — as well as the power and compassion of his vision — imposed himself upon the twentieth century. Few today, I think, would question his right to be considered the greatest American master of the novel-form, and the greatest of all fictional theorists. T. S. Eliot long ago called him "the most intelligent man of his generation."

We have recovered him slowly from that twilight into which his reputation sank after his death in 1916. His very weight and mass forced criticism to deal with him piecemeal. For a long time he remained a partially scaled peak in our literature. Now that he is being climbed and measured, surveyed and explored, we can deliver larger judgments, see him as one of the most civilized Americans of his time and one of the boldest and most dedicated of our artists, who possessed an extraordinary sense of style.

Living a long life and writing for fifty years, he was able to surpass himself many times. Unlike certain promising moderns, who burn themselves out after a book or two, James saw more than one hundred of his volumes — novels, tales, critiques, plays, travel — through the press. And to read some part of him, an early or late novel, a handful of his stories, is a little like visiting a single city on a large continent.

The reasons for his "enduring fame" can now be more readily perceived. I would suggest at least four: the richness, variety and contemporaneity of his subjects and themes; his ability to render them in memorable prose; his searching innovations as a craftsman; and his anticipation of the more subtle findings of modern psychology. He was the first great explorer of the "international" novel. He virtually invented it, and certainly he perfected it. In that sense he was less "parochial," we might say, less national than certain nineteenth-century Europeans: Balzac and Flaubert had their France; Dickens, Thackeray and George Eliot their England; but Henry James had to deal with large transatlantic territories, and with civilizations on both sides of the sea.

As early as 1867, in the aftermath of the Civil War, when he was twenty-four, he recognized this to be his goal as artist. "To be an American is an excellent preparation for culture," he wrote to a Newport friend. "We have exquisite qualities as a race, and it seems to me that we are ahead of the European races in the fact that more than either of them, we can deal freely with forms of civilization not our own, can pick and choose and assimilate and in short claim our property wherever we find it." And he foresaw "a vast intellectual fusion and synthesis of the various national tendencies of the world" and expected "something original and beautiful to disengage itself from our ceaseless fermentation and turmoil."

And so James began to write his tales of Americans confronting Europe and Europeans confronting America. A witty explorer of Anglo-American manners in his earlier phase, he moved ultimately from light ironic comedy to a brooding tragic vision, and by dint of a heroic fertility he explored, long before we were ready to understand what he was doing, the role of the American in the world — not in the passing terms of international struggle, but in the eternal terms of civilization and humanity. No subject could belong more markedly to the twentieth century.

In his time he saw Americans as innocents, freshly emerging from a Garden of Eden by tasting the apple of knowledge — which was Europe — and thereby discovering the evil and corruption of the Old World. His social subjects were the international marriages contracted by Americans (prophetic in that ultimately one would occur between an American "commoner" and a British king), the contrasts between New England rigidities and European laxities, the "American girl," in the plenitude of her freedom, her brashness, her innocence; or in her refined egocentricity and self-made careerism.

His psychological subjects were the evil created by individuals who meddled in other peoples' lives, or who prey on one another; the erosion of loneliness and anxiety, the conflicts of the drive to power. And these themes were rendered in a rich and allusive style, at first of crystal clarity and simplicity, and later of a complex virtuosity to which Max Beerbohm in his time, and James Thurber in ours, paid the tribute of gentle and affectionate parody.

The young James could toss off such pleasing generalities as that "an aristocracy is bad manners organized." He could advise young novelists to "try and be one of the people on whom nothing is lost." His aphorisms were larger, less personal, than Wilde's. "The English are the only people who can do great things without being clever," he once remarked — a line Wilde or Bernard Shaw might have willingly used in a play. James was to say many other things about the English, critical and friendly, and during World War I he was to mint certain phrases which served Winston Churchill (who knew him then) in World War II. "This decent and dauntless people," a phrase which Churchill used to stiffen British morale in the grimmest days of the nineteen-forties, was first uttered by James in an interview he gave to the *New York Times* in 1915. The great sentences of his middle and later period reverberate and echo like the widening circles of sound made by a great and resonant bell. With all the later idiosyncrasies of "manner," James was a master of the summarizing sentence, the diagnostic phrase, the echoing truth.

His rich subject-matter and his style have helped him prevail in a century of slipshod and overworked prose. But I believe that James' zest for literary experiment has given him still another claim on new readers. He was a "difficult" writer in his time; however, a generation nourished on Joyce, Proust, Kafka, Faulkner, can take him in its stride, and usually discovers with surprise the extent to which he foreshadowed the moderns. He used the "camera-eye" before movies were invented; he is the acknowl-

edged forerunner of "stream of consciousness." By piling elaborate sentence on elaborate sentence, he obtained certain effects of
"simultaneity" and montage which Joyce would carry to an extreme in *Finnegans Wake.* James was never tired of exploring
some new way to tell a story.

With this, he was a master psychologist. He understood "inter-
personal relations" long before psychology began to explore them.
He knew how society "conditioned" the individual. Before
Freud he subtly studied, and described, anxiety, fear and guilt in
his tales. This is why such a story as the complex and thickly
spun "The Beast in the Jungle" has been so frequently reprinted.
It explains also why "The Turn of the Screw" continues to be one
of the world's most widely read ghost stories. No mere phan-
toms appear in this tale. They are the ghosts we fashion in our
own minds, the fears with which we frighten ourselves.

In his own time, as with posterity, James had the extraordinary
power of self-renewal. If he made his fame with *Daisy Miller* in
the eighteen-seventies, he won, in the eighteen-eighties, a new
reputation with *The Aspern Papers.* In the eighteen-nineties he
wrote "The Turn of the Screw" and in the new century "The
Beast in the Jungle." These were high watermarks in a constant
production that culminated in the magisterial novels of 1901–
1904: *The Ambassadors, The Wings of the Dove* and *The
Golden Bowl.* As with Yeats, James' power seemed to grow
rather than decline with age. Even his fragment, *The Sense of
the Past,* yielded a memorable play in the nineteen-twenties —
Berkeley Square. He was a writer deeply intellectual and reflective; there is virtually no physical violence in his work; his dramas
are all dramas of the struggle of ego with ego, of "states of mind,"
of the conflict of the individual with his own nature.

The James "revival," which began with the centenary of his
birth in the dark days of 1943, has taken its impulse from a series
of creative forces generated by James himself — his subjects, his

methods, his style, his psychology. The general radiation of his powerful temperament has been aided by the editing and republication of his works, the abundant and continuing critical and biographical writings which have surrounded it, and the popularization of his novels and tales through the theatre and other visual and auditory media. *Washington Square* is better known as *The Heiress* of stage and screen. Michael Redgrave's version of *The Aspern Papers* ran a year in London.

The reissue by Scribner's of the New York Edition — which he named for the city of his birth — creates both publishing and literary history. Who would have dreamed, in an age when we no longer tend to buy the old-fashioned "set," that it would be Henry James' selective edition that would be revived first, rather than the many-volumed Kipling, or Meredith, Hardy or Stevenson? As might be expected in an artist with James' formal sense, he found an organic design for his edition. Having produced on a prodigal scale, he could afford to be extravagant. He demanded a high standard of his past performances. No critic could have been as severe.

He banished from his final canon *Washington Square, The Bostonians, The Europeans;* he disowned *Watch and Ward* as an indiscretion of his youth; and he cast out more than half of his tales. It was clear from his exclusion of his American subjects that these were a category apart; and that the Edition was designed to display the "cosmopolitan" novelist. He led off with *Roderick Hudson* and *The American,* the one dealing with an American artist in Rome, the other with an American businessman in Paris. He followed with *The Portrait of a Lady,* the expatriation of an Albany girl with a fine consciousness and a determined personality. Then came his strictly English novels, such works as *The Princess Casamassima, The Tragic Muse, What Maisie Knew* and others. Finally there were eight volumes of tales.

He not only excluded; he revised and he even rewrote. Such early works as he deemed acceptable had to be tidied up, raised to the level of his maturity. While this testifies to a kind of Flaubertian standard of perfection, it raises certain profound questions. James argued that his revisions were merely the cleaning of old dusty canvases and applications of fresh varnish. Critical readers have replied that the Master also daubed too much color from his late palette on the old paint, and thereby robbed certain of the originals of their early bloom.

There has been no argument, however, about the special prefaces written for the Edition. These are long and subtle; idea folds within idea in luxuriant verbal imagery; they are exquisitely nuanced in their Proust-like mixture of memory and aesthetics. The reissue differs from the original in one respect: the old frontispieces, a series of beautiful photographs by Alvin Langdon Coburn, are not reprinted. This is a pity, since they consisted of symbolic scenes — a bench in Hampstead, a Venetian palace, a London street — which added a distinct atmosphere to each volume.

With its particular features, its controversial revisions, its admirable groupings and structure, the New York Edition stands at the very center of James' work. At the end he said it contained all of his fiction which he felt was worth preserving. But he did not insist on this point. In one of the prefaces he slyly remarks that some of the excluded tales were like "well-nourished and substantial" relatives, left behind at some family function for want of extra carriages. He quite clearly hoped to find further transportation for some of his too obvious omissions. Posterity seems to be providing it. Even his minor writings have been revived: his travel sketches, his art criticisms, his drama reviews, his fugitive journalism. As his work is reprinted and as the legends are dissipated, he emerges more and more as the prototype of the vigorous, active artist, a consummate professional, who insisted on living by his pen alone. The James "revival" is not of the passing moment; it is our discovery in him of those mysterious and self-perpetuating forces by which a writer's work ultimately comes to be known as "classic."

PART III

Reviews and Reappraisals

Madame Bovary:
A Revolution in Letters

1. HARRY LEVIN
—But Unhappy Emma Still Exists

In that useful reference work, Twentieth Century Authors, *Harry Levin says, in writing of himself, "I started with Shakespeare and Elizabethan drama, to which I return as often as I can. But I am conscious of progressively moving toward the modern period, the novel and France." Thus it is that his bibliography spans the years and literary men from Shakespeare and Marlowe to Stendhal, Hawthorne and Melville, and, in a big leap, to James Joyce.*

"SHE HAD ceased to exist." With these cold words, Gustave Flaubert ended the existence of his passionate heroine. Her unhappy story, *Madame Bovary*, has existed for more than a hundred years — has, indeed, been the dominating influence on the fiction of the past century. If, when we speak of classics, we mean works of perfected craftsmanship, then Flaubert's novel was a classic from the very moment of publication. Though it was the first published work of its thirty-six-year-old author, it was the finished product of five long years of painstaking research and strenuous composition. If any other writer ever revised his manuscript so conscientiously, he has not documented his endeavors as Flaubert did, to the extent of 3600 pages. And surely no one else has ever attested, in so detailed and moving a series of letters, what it means to devote one's own existence to what Flaubert lovingly called "the agonies of art."

Today, when we rather casually refer to almost any writer as an artist, we forget that these two terms came to reinforce one another through the struggle of Flaubert's generation. Under the July Monarchy, about which he wrote, and even more under the Second Empire, during which he wrote, the serious practitioners of all the arts had to make common cause against the official forces of bad taste and against those archetypes of meanness and smugness which Flaubert — like Daumier — has immortalized in depicting the bourgeoisie.

Since the world belonged to the rampant bourgeois, and was being reshaped by their crudest scramble for its rewards, Flaubert practiced his calling in semi-retirement. Placing himself under the special protection of St. Anthony, that paragon of resistance, he pursued a literary career as if it were a religious calling. Hence he himself became a patron saint for such later writers as Proust, Valéry and Joyce. For them he set the example as he had preached the doctrine, of artistic detachment.

Now it was the current scandal of the studios, while Flaubert was writing *Madame Bovary,* that the state-controlled Salon had refused to exhibit the paintings of the highly original and radically democratic Gustave Courbet. Courbet staged his own exhibition in 1855, calling it "The Pavilion of Realism." Critics were quick to pick up the new rallying cry, and to use it for and against controversial writers. Flaubert, who was no rallier, did not consider himself a member of the realistic school; nor was he any more willing, when Zola coined a newer slogan, to call himself a naturalist.

None the less the scientific outlook, as it was affecting literature, found its masterwork in *Madame Bovary;* and Sainte-Beuve concluded his review by announcing that the anatomists and physiologists were taking over the field of the novel. It was not for nothing that Flaubert came from a well-established medical family, or that he had grown up in the residential wing of the municipal hospital at Rouen.

Literature comes to terms with art on the one hand and with

science on the other in *Madame Bovary*. That is why it occupies such a unique position in the modern consciousness. It also sustains an equilibrium between the man and his work, which tends in his subsequent writing to be overweighted upon one side or the other. His temperament, which inclined him toward the poetic and the exotic, naturally flowered into books like *Salammbo* and *The Temptation of Saint Anthony*. His recoil from his epoch, in the direction of critical analysis or a more satirical point of view disciplined the shaping of *A Sentimental Education* and *Bouvard and Pécuchet*. His life, as he was well aware, acted out a dialogue between two selves: the lyric poet and the detached observer. But in this respect he was merely dramatizing the typical dilemma of the latter-day writer-as-artist who inherits the accumulated riches of European tradition and must somehow employ them in finding a pattern for the clutter of contemporary experience.

Therefore it was not just the exaggeration of a faithful disciple when Maupassant said, "The appearance of *Madame Bovary* constituted a revolution in letters." It was at least as much of a revolution as that which had taken place in the name of romanticism a brief generation before. The romanticists had made their manifestation at the première of Victor Hugo's *Hernani*. The realists, too, could center their attention on a fairly spectacular public performance: the trial of Flaubert, together with his editor and publisher, on the charge that the novel — even in the passages excerpted and expurgated for magazine publication — had offended against the principles of morality and religion. The prosecutor juggled the usual device of introducing quotations out of context, especially the passage where Emma Bovary receives extreme unction. Counsel for the defense dwelt upon the respectability of Flaubert's connections as well as the purity of his intentions. He was acquitted with a judicial reprimand for having pushed fiction beyond its appointed limits.

The misunderstanding was based, as it usually is in such cases, upon a confusion between the book itself and its subject-matter. To draw a sharp line between them, to maintain an objective attitude toward his material, ironically enough, had been Flaubert's main concern. Perhaps he distinguished too sharply between form and content, since he was so preoccupied with esthetic order and so far removed from social commitment. Baudelaire, who faced the same problem in his poetry, created beauty out of ugliness in *Flowers of Evil;* but *Flowers of Evil* was suppressed by the court that had recently exonerated *Madame Bovary.* Flaubert had indulged the poetic side of his nature in reconstructing the sentimental education of his heroine; he had identified with Emma so closely that, according to one hostile critic, the reader was offered sensations instead of sentiments. But here, precisely, the other side of his divided mind, the clinical approach, enabled him to regain his distance and achieve a kind of psychological catharsis.

Consequently the book abounds in contrasts, pictorially set forth in vivid colors. The rustic abundance of Emma's wedding, which might have been depicted by a Norman Brueghel, is to be contrasted with the ball at a neighboring château, so glitteringly calculated to foster her yearnings for elegant society. The opera, which rekindles her romance with the ineffectual law clerk, Léon, implies a comparison with the operation, the ill-fated surgical project in which her patient and persevering husband loses his professional repute. Most striking of all — because here the conflict of values is comprehended within the double focus of a private scene with a panoramic background — is the famous agricultural show, where the speeches of the prize-givers outside are matched by the propositions of the forceful Rodolphe, beginning his seduction of Emma in the deserted town hall. The real heroine of this complex occasion is the peasant woman Catherine Leroux, who is rewarded for fifty-four years of service with a silver medal and twenty-five francs.

Flaubert has often been regarded as an impassive and impersonal novelist; and some of his theories go halfway to meet that misconception. However, he deeply believes in those stoical virtues which he embodied in the weathered figure of Catherine and which are even more evident in the sympathetic glimpse of Charles Bovary's old teacher, Dr. Larivière — a sketch which is said to be modeled on Flaubert's own father.

Just as the dignity of the peasant woman is a standing rebuke to the restlessness and frivolity of the doctor's wife, so the selfless insight of the older doctor is a devastating comment upon the village busybody, M. Homais, and all he stands for: a bumbling confidence in the material progress of everything and particularly his personal interests. Dr. Bovary dies, the victim of a triple tragedy, maritally betrayed, professionally humiliated and financially ruined; and the novel breaks off on a note of satire. Homais, at all events, is still alive, going from strength to strength, garnering honors and publicity.

Emma stands somewhere between the tragedy and the satire, since she has been victimized by her own illusions. Flaubert, suiting his method to his theme, has rendered the diagnosis of her case history, along with the poem of her self-betrayal. Her malaise did not disappear when she ceased to exist; on the contrary, it has become epidemic. Victims are claimed every day by that mental disease which is termed Bovarism by Flaubert's successors. Teen-agers bovarize when they pattern their fantasies of hope or fear on the movie magazines; so do mature suburbanites when they can be manipulated by the expert bovarizers of advertising and mass communication. We are all bovaristic whenever we let our feelings serve a shallow or tawdry set of ideals. Our eagerness to be taken in is a trait which matches our wariness of being duped. Our novelists have made us realize that starved emotions subsisted along Main Street and that the bourgeois did not change his spots when his name was Babbitt.

Flaubert's great novel has thus renewed its relevance with the passing years; and we may take particular satisfaction at seeing it made available at last in good American English by Francis Steegmuller.* Many of our readers have been dependent, for much too long, on the rather stilted rendering by Karl Marx's daughter, whose fate so unhappily resembled Emma's. The version by Gerald Hopkins is up to date and reasonably accurate; but it interposes a certain Britishness which becomes painful when the peasants speak dialect.

In some ways, our dialect of the English language gets closer to French than do those of the British Isles. We seen to use more Latinisms, for one thing; the passage where Homais discusses the relation between a pharmacist and a chemist is difficult for the English translator, because the term "chemist" ordinarily covers both functions for his readers. The Homais who said of Emma, "She is a woman of parts," was a somewhat different character from the Homais who now says, "She's got class."

This is thoroughly inelegant; but Flaubert frequently made a point of inelegance in his carefully noted conversations and in italicized colloquial phrases. These, of course, are offset by the grace of his more characteristic style, which is generally easier to translate than they are. There is no Flaubert among translators, as Francis Steegmuller reminds us in his modest and sensible introduction; and one might add that it is hard to imagine how Flaubert would write, if his language were English; but the outstanding achievement of Mr. Steegmuller is that, for the most part, he does not sound as if he were translating. His prose has a rhythmic movement of its own, yet nearly always, when we probe the meaning, we find him more exact than his predecessors.

Looking for something to cavil at one might question one or two habits which seem to spring from overconsciousness. Occasionally, with technical expressions, Mr. Steegmuller prefers to leave them in French rather than hazard a rough approximation.

* *Madame Bovary.* New York: Random House, 1957.

Yet again, because he has no footnotes, he slightly modifies his text to explain or avoid a possible obscurity; twice he inserts the name of Rousseau, where Flaubert had "philosopher" at one point and "Confession of a Savoyard Vicar" at the other. But all translations are bridges; and the best are those that start very close to the original and end very close to their readers. That Mr. Steegmuller's *Madame Bovary* measures up to this standard will be no surprise to those who have profited from his study of Flaubert's early career, or enjoyed his selection from Flaubert's correspondence. The pursuit of *le mot juste* is an endless business; but there are pauses for congratulation over what has been already accomplished; and this is one of them.

2. FRANCIS STEEGMULLER

The Translator, Too, Must Search for Le Mot Juste

Translation is only one of the arts practiced by Francis Steegmuller. He is at home in the novel. He has written mysteries. He has edited a selection of Flaubert's letters and (with Norbert Guterman) essays by Sainte-Beuve. He is also a biographer and literary critic. For his most recent book he moved to modern French poetry: Appollinaire: Poet Among the Painters.

"WRITING is a lonely occupation," says the cliché; but it must have been invented by a nonwriter, or else by some novelist or biographer or translator as a joke. For even on days when the persons one is inventing don't get off the ground they seldom abandon one to the point of loneliness; and when one grapples with men and women who have already lived, or who have previously been invented by a master, the hours are full and flying.

During the six months I spent translating *Madame Bovary* there was much time when I was alone with Emma and her fellow beings. Indeed the bulk of the work was done in that kind of "solitude." But every once in a while there arose a puzzle that called for consultation, and the "solitude" would be broken by a phone call, a letter or a visit. I appealed — appealed for information or confirmation; and the response to my appeals would have cured a misanthrope. How delightful everybody was! The following are a few lines of tribute.

Early in *Madame Bovary* Flaubert describes the laden dinner table at a house party in the château of a Norman marquis. Then he adds a brief sentence: "Mme. Bovary remarqua que plusieurs dames n'avaient pas mis leurs gants dans leur verre." Keeping in mind that Emma was much impressed by her surroundings that night, and that the French "remarquer" is sometimes a little stronger than the English "remark" or "notice," and that at such a dinner in France the "verre" probably wasn't a water glass, and that whereas French syntax calls for "verre" in the singular English requires the plural, and that English prose has rhythms different from French rhythms, a fair equivalent for the original seemed to me to be: "Madame Bovary was surprised to notice that several of the ladies had failed to put their gloves in their wine glasses." All very simple — one of the simple sentences in the book to translate — though there remain a few little points both in French and English that specialists could argue about if they wanted to.

That was what Flaubert wrote. But what did Flaubert mean? Why should Emma Bovary have expected all the ladies to put their gloves in their wine glasses? Why was she surprised that some of them didn't?

The full answer was hard to come by. Mademoiselle Gabrielle Leleu, of the Municipal Library at Rouen, who has helped me solve many a Flaubert puzzle, was herself puzzled by this one. "Many ladies drank wine in France at that time," she wrote me. "I don't see why they should have, as you suggest, been expected to put their gloves in their glasses to indicate to the *sommelier* that they wanted none — the equivalent of putting one's hand over one's glass, or turning the glass upside down today."

The first ray of light came from Oberlin, Ohio. "Having read in Sunday's New York Times . . . that you are doing a new translation of 'Madame Bovary,' I am taking the liberty of sending you some notes I had printed for the use of my students . . .": so began a welcome letter I received one day from John C. Lapp, then Professor of French at Oberlin. The "notes" proved to be a veritable *Madame Bovary* dictionary and encyclopedia combined, and here I found a quotation from one of Alfred de Musset's plays, ironically listing the things a young girl of 1836 must do to be in the swim: "Does she put her gloves in her glass when the champagne comes around? . . . If she doesn't know enough to do that, she hasn't learned very much."

And then the road to the complete, fully nuanced solution was shown me one day by Douglas Cooper, the excellent art critic. "Why don't you write to the painter Jean Hugo at his farm in Provence?" he said. "He's full of knowledge of nineteenth-century customs." I followed his advice, and back came a note from Jean Hugo, enclosing one from a friend whom he had consulted, the Vicomte de Noailles:

"A hundred years ago it was generally held that a woman who was *comme il faut* never drank wine. But I think that in respectable provincial society this must have been much more the case than in the more advanced court circles, at the Tuileries, for ex-

ample. Probably among Normandy squireens the most provincial still held to the custom, and Flaubert had been struck by the
fact that in such circles as that of the Princesse Mathilde it had
come to be ignored. Still, even in my own youth I saw the Com-
tesse Murat, who was a bit affected in that she never drank
champagne, put the lace-edged handkerchief she carried in her
hand into the *flûte de champagne* when she sat down to dinner.
Remember: Women didn't have handbags in those days."

So it all became clear. Emma, in expecting all the ladies at
table to put their gloves in their glasses, was following, in her own
genteel, young-lady way, the custom observed by her provincial
though noble hosts, and followed by most of their guests. But
among the company were a few who were more "advanced" —
they had probably come down for the house party from Paris —
and those ladies surprised Emma by their freedom. The party at
the château Flaubert is telling us, even though glamorous to the
provincial Emma, was in itself provincial. It's a good thing to
know the precise meaning of what one translates. And this time
it was good to know that the rendering of "remarqua" by "was
surprised to notice" was justified — indeed, called for — and that
the "verre" was unquestionably, and so very interestingly, a *verre
de vin!*

Later, when I recounted the puzzle of the gloves in the glasses
at Bernard Berenson's villa, near Settignano, a woman who was
present laughed. "You should have come straight to me," she
said. "I could have told you." I assured her that I would the
next time. But if I had, I wouldn't have had the final paragraph
of the Vicomte de Noaille's letter, which I like as much as what
preceded it:

"The wine question is very close to the cheese question. I once
heard Madame de Chevigné say: 'In my youth a woman who was
comme il faut never ate cheese.' "

An enjoyable bit: especially since Madame de Chevigné, Mad-

ame de Noaille's grandmother, was one of Proust's models for
Oriane de Guermantes.

And then there was the question of Madame Bovary's piano.
When she played "with dash," Flaubert says that "les cordes
frisaient." "The strings—": what did they do? The word *friser*
has so many meanings, the most common, of course, being to
curl — frizz — one's hair. Did the strings curl up? Unlikely,
especially since Flaubert goes on to say that the piano could be
heard "to the end of the village." Dilemma. I took it quite braz-
enly to Theodore Steinway, and this time it was he who wrote to
France. His colleague there knew perfectly well what Madame
Bovary's piano did: it jangled. I'm grateful to those two gentlemen, for Mansion's two-volume French dictionary doesn't breathe
the word "jangle" under "friser" (Fr-Eng), or the word "friser"
under "jangle" (Eng-Fr); and in those early days (this phrase,
too, came near the beginning of the novel) I had not yet realized
how many specialized meanings the big Larousse provides. Poor
Emma! Even her piano, one of her great sources of distinction,
was a rattletrap.

And what about Binet, the grotesque bachelor with the passion for making wooden objects on his lathe, whom Madame Bovary calls on in her desperate quest for money? What does Binet
have on the shelves of his room when Mme. Caron and Mme.
Tuvache, the Mayor's wife, spy on the interview from behind
the laundry hung up to dry at a nearby attic window? He is
engaged, they see, in turning out a hideous, nameless object — "a
conglomeration of half-moons and of spheres carved one inside the
other, the whole thing standing erect like an obelisk and perfectly
useless." And on his shelves were "napkin rings, candlesticks,
and *pommes de rampe." Pommes de rampe? Pomme* is apple, potato, almost anything round or roundish. *Rampe* is ramp, or stair
rail. But *pommes de rampe?* The answer seems easy now that I
have it, but I had to seek it on 116th Street.

"Finials," said James Grote Van Derpool, librarian of the Columbia School of Architecture. Thank you again, Mr. Van Derpool. You are certainly right: could Flaubert have imagined anything that lent itself better than the knobs of newel posts to the unimaginable horrors of Binet's creative invention?

There were many such blessed informants. Charles Weatherill, the renowned tailor, who told me exactly what Flaubert meant when he said that the trousers worn by provincial worthies were of *drap non décati;* Dr. Harold W. Rickett, bibliographer of the New York Botanical Garden, who furnished the English equivalent of every plant name I offered him; Norbert Guterman, whose extraordinary sense of verbal equivalents helped me in many a tight spot; anonymous voices at the other end of the telephone, responding to my appeals from harness shops, livery stables, museums.

In "The Isles of Unwisdom" Robert Graves offers as his favorite mistranslation of all time the rendering of "Le peuple ému respondit à Marat" as "The purple emu laid Marat another egg," and it is, of course, to try to avoid laying such spectacular eggs as that that a translator bothers friends, acquaintances and strangers.

Cautionary examples aren't hard to find in translations of *Madame Bovary* alone.

At the mi-carême ball Flaubert tells us, Emma wore "a cocked hat over one ear" ("un lampion sur l'oreille"), but one of the current British versions of the novel has her dancing with "a Chinese lantern dangling from one ear"—a merry picture indeed! And Charles, the medical student, instead of singing songs "at student gatherings" ("aux bienvenues"), is made to sing them "to women who were always welcome."

When Doctor Larivière, at Emma's deathbed, says "C'est bien, c'est bien" ("Yes, yes"), he is merely expressing more or less polite impatience with Doctor Canivet, whose circumstantial narration of the case is pointless now that Emma is beyond help. But I have seen a critical article in a worthy publication that renders the words as "Good, good," and interprets them as expressing Doctor Larivière's satisfaction in Emma's imminent death, a satisfaction reflecting Flaubert's supposed conception of his heroine as a character too sublime for this world.

And I remember with particular pleasure an early British translation of *Madame Bovary* that is embellished with a grandiloquent introductory essay by Henry James. James writes much about "the rich and the rare" in the book, and promises the reader many aesthetic joys. But what do we find in the English text, which James clearly didn't bother to read? For Flaubert's description of one of the wedding guests, "un mareyeur de leurs cousins, qui même avait apporté, comme présent de noces, une paire de soles" ("a fishmonger cousin, who had actually brought a pair of soles as a wedding present"), we find this equivalent: "a practical joker among their cousins, who had even brought a pair of boot soles for a wedding present."

A perilous job, translating! It's enough to make one long to sink one's teeth into a good filet de semelle!

FRANK O'CONNOR

Chekhov: A Writer Who Refused to Pretend

The best way to describe Frank O'Connor is to say that he is the greatest short story writer of contemporary Ireland. He has also written plays (he was once director of the Abbey Theatre), verse, novels, biography. He has taught in many American colleges and universities, and is married to an American.

THERE ARE certain great writers and painters whose reputations pass under a cloud soon after their deaths. In fact, this is true of most good writers, and the better they are the heavier the cloud under which they lie. The cloud is finally scattered only by the patient work of critics and scholars, but even then, the figure that reappears is never that which his contemporaries saw. It would be easy to attribute this to changes of literary fashion, but I suspect that there is rather more to it. Most great writers have a streak of the charlatan in them. Some acquire it in early years as a defense against their sourroundings, others in later years as a means of disposing of their otherwise unsalable wares. They strike a pose; they talk big; they feel they have a message. And then since there is nothing on earth so dead as a dead salesman, they fade from our consciousness. Tolstoy sold himself to his generation as a latter-day saint, Dostoevsky as a mystic, Kipling as the bearer of the white man's burden and Yeats as the vague creature who saw darling little leprechauns in every corner.

There are a few painters who never seem to strike a pose — Toulouse-Lautrec and Degas, for example — but I should be hard

put to name any writer but Chekhov who doesn't. He was born
on January 17, 1860, died on July 2, 1904. In the years since his
death, his reputation has not suffered at all. Instead, it has grown
steadily and quietly, like the man himself, until today there is
scarcely a critic who would not place those brief stories — by a
man who always regarded himself as a minor writer and never attempted to emulate his famous contemporaries in the writing of
long novels — among the major achievements of Russian literature.

I know enough about the business of storytelling to be able
to put my finger on certain devices that maintain the astonishing freshness of these stories. The devices are not unlike those
that Lautrec and Degas used; ultimately, they can all be traced to
the naturalistic theory about describing what you see — the simplest artistic theory in the world until you begin to ask yourself
what you *do* see. As in Degas' "L'Absinthe" the figures are not
placed solidly in the center of the picture and the figure of the
man trails off inexplicably behind the frame, so in Chekhov there
is always a deliberate artlessness of composition — people walk
on and off, and sometimes a fascinating character is described
and then dropped. Men are always being caught buttoning their
trousers and women pulling up their stockings, and their outraged
glances as we catch them at it are always part of the total ironic
effect. But any satirist can demolish a pose in that way, and
nothing fades so fast as satire. There is a great deal more to
Chekhov than his ironic attitude.

What it was we can only learn from life. He began as a
writer of skits for the comic papers and the music halls in the endeavor to support an impossible family while studying to be a
doctor. The music halls of the period play a big part in its literature and art. They were the characteristic minor art of an age
when the major arts had ceased to be representative — an age of
easy money, easy living, easy drunkenness and easy vice, over

which stretched a protecting pall of humbug — hypocrisy in the courts, the churches, the academies and the publishing houses. Hardy wrote its epitaph:

> *Say ye rejoice, though grieving,*
> *Believe, while unbelieving,*
> *Behold, without perceiving.*

Only the comic papers and the music halls admitted the truth about society, and they did so while conniving at the cheat. It was easier to connive. Maupassant, who had begun in the stalls, ended up behind the scenes, conniving with the rest. Chekhov, a poor boy who had begun behind the scenes, ended up in the stalls, refusing to connive and yet refusing also to abandon the vision of life that the music halls had given him. "Don't let's pretend!" he seems to say. "Let's tell the truth outside as we see it in here. Perhaps after all we *are* a little better than the hypocrites outside. We may even build a better world out of our knowledge of the truth."

That conflict in Chekhov was there from the beginning. In a famous letter he described himself in youth, "brought up to fawn on rank, kiss the hands of priests, accept without questioning other people's ideas, express his gratitude for every morsel of bread he eats, a young man who has been frequently whipped, who goes to give lessons without galoshes, engages in street fights, tortures animals, loves to go to his rich relations for dinner, behaves hypocritically toward God and man without the slightest excuse but that he is conscious of his own worthlessness."

His aim was "to squeeze the slave out of himself." We have endured the sponger artist to the limit, but here is one of the great artists of the world whose only desire was to be "dacent" in the good Irish sense of the word, and who was "dacent" to the day he died, still supporting his circus of a family, still making light of the fact that he was a dying man, and sacrificing most of the things a real artist values.

In scores of stories that he wrote when he was emerging from the sense of his own inadequacy we can see his preoccupation with "dacency." It is in one of his most famous stories, "The Chorus Girl." The chorus girl, lounging round half naked with her lover, Kolpakov, opens the door to her lover's wife. Kolpakov has been found out in the theft of $500 from the office, presumably to buy the chorus girl's favors, and Mrs. Kolpakov, to keep him out of jail, has come to demand it back. The little chorus girl has never had anything but candies from her lover, but, embarrassed at the tragic grief and indignation of a real lady, she hands over the few trinkets she owns. When Kolpakov emerges from hiding it is not to express his gratitude to the chorus girl, but to beat his brow at the thought that a great, noble lady like his wife has actually begged from a fallen woman, and he stalks out with a change of heart that turns him from a nonentity into a lout, while the poor little chorus girl bursts into tears of fury and frustration. One of the many curious things about this story is that it is almost a straight crib of an equally famous story, Maupassant's "Boule de Suif" — even though in the previous year Chekhov had told his friend Maria Kiseleva that Russian editors would detect any stealing of Maupassant's subjects. But the contrast is even more interesting than the comparison. Maupassant is only interested in striking down the patriotic pretensions of Boule de Suif's traveling companions. He doesn't really know anything better than the pretensions, but Chekhov does, and is trying to discover it in literature.

Graduating from the world of the music halls into the professional world he admired, it would have been easy for Chekhov to forget what he had learned first, and write books like *Anna Karenina* to prove that a woman who committed adultery must necessarily end up under a railway engine. In fact, Chekhov was greatly attracted by Tolstoy's teaching, and if there is a false note in his work it is when he wrote under Tolstoy's influence, but he soon outgrew it and wrote that "there was more love for humanity

in electricity and central heating than in chastity and abstention
from meat." Dostoevsky had been a poser from birth, but Tolstoy was a bit of a poser too. Women who commit adultery
don't always end up under railway engines. Anyhow, adultery
was neither here nor there. For the young man who was trying
to squeeze the slave out of himself, morality was something infinitely more complex and difficult. There is a very good chance
that the little chorus girl will be saved on the last day because she
has a fundamental sense of decency, but who would bet a nickel
on the chances of Kolpakov and his wife?

If one really wants to understand Chekhov, one must realize
that he was the moralist of the venial sin, the man who laid it
down that a soul is damned not for murder, adultery or embez-
zlement but for the small, unrecognized sins of ill-temper, un-
truthfulness, stinginess and disloyalty. The woman in the "Grass-
hopper" who is unfaithful to her dull doctor husband with a
flashy painter is not going to be damned for adultery; she will be
damned and damned thoroughly for the supercilious way in which
she addressed her husband in company. As in Degas and Lautrec the whole beautiful theory of the art schools is blown sky-
high, so in Chekhov the whole nineteenth-century conception of
morals is blown sky-high. This is not morality as anyone from
Jane Austen to Trollope would have recognized it, though I suspect that an orthodox theologian might have something very
interesting to say about it.

How that effect was achieved in real life is described in Gorky's
great essay on Chekhov, one of the few magnificent descriptions
of one writer by another. Gorky tells us how, during the Russo-
Japanese War, some ladies, full of patriotic fervor, called on
Chekhov to pay their respects and to tell him of their services to
the Motherland. Chekhov endured the patriotic frenzy for a
while, and then asked them their recipe for a standard Russian
dish. At once they became what they normally were — intelli-

gent and civilized people who were authorities on cooking as
Chekhov was on morality.

It is not only that Chekhov realized he must ask himself "What
do I see?" He also asked others "What do *you* see?" and discovered that in practice the majority of human beings are infinitely
wiser than they know themselves to be or than anyone assumes
they are. All one has to do is to get past the lying generalizations,
the pretenses we all put up, to see what they are like at home,
with husband, wife or children.

Mind! I am still not persuaded that the theory of the well-
made painting, the well-made story or the well-made play lacks
substance, as they seem to do when I look at Lautrec or read
Chekhov. I doubt if any great writer has influenced me less. I
once saw a wonderful performance of the *Three Sisters* in Dublin
that almost persuaded me, but not since. When I detect Chekhov's
influence as in Katherine Mansfield or Joyce, it only irritates me.
That too casual composition, that unexplained figure who in their
works apparently comes on merely for a chat, exasperate me as
they do not exasperate me in Chekhov. I can only explain this
by a double paradox. For the benefit of orthodox theologians the
weakness of Chekhov's morality is that it is almost a branch of
aesthetics. Sin to him is ultimately a lack of refinement, the inability to get through a badly cooked meal without a scene. But
at the same time one can say that his aesthetic is moral as Katherine Mansfield's and Joyce's are not. All the casualness is only apparent. When Laevsky in "The Duel" says "The same thing every
day. Why not have cabbage soup?" somebody is in great danger
of being damned for it.

I am not at all certain that the spirit in which I approach
Chekhov is not the spirit in which I used to approach confession in the days before there were mortal sins to tell. "Father, I
was rude to my mother"; "Father, I was mean. I wouldn't give
a fellow a candy"; or "Father, I said a mean thing about a fellow

that was nice to me" — all those miserable petty failings that don't seem to have improved at all with the years and that still wake me at four o'clock in the morning and make me writhe as they did when I was seven, and I am not sure but some orthodox theologians would agree with me that Chekhov was the greatest moralist of them all. I am not even sure that my theologian would make too much fuss about the fact that Chekhov believed that a remark like "The same thing every day" was the outward and visible sign of an inward lack of grace, meaning in Chekhov's sense of the word refinement — Chekhov's notion of the horror that Adam and Eve and the Apple first brought into the world.

To the World of English, He Counseled Perfection

In the British Who's Who, *Eric Partridge lists under his recreations: cricket, reading, persons. It's hard not to believe that playing with words is also one of his recreations, for this New Zealander in Britain has always seemed to be having so much fun in his books about words that he hardly fits his own scholarly label, "etymologist." But an expert on words he is, an expert with a twinkle, a chuckle, sometimes a belly laugh. Look up his* A Dictionary of Slang and Unconventional English.

For the English-speaking world the name of Henry Watson Fowler is inseparably linked with his great work *A Dictionary of Modern English Usage.* When "M.E.U.," as scholars call it, appeared in 1926, I was a very junior lecturer in the University of Manchester, a fact I mention only to show that, surrounded by a university's staff and students, I was in a position to note and enjoy the stir it made. Students and other irreverent persons delighted in Fowler's pillorying both of the London *Times* and other important periodicals and of celebrated writers: "and" — to adapt a passage from "The Song of Songs" — "the voice of the victim was heard in the land."

Fowler decided upon this courageous course not in order to puncture this reputation or that, nor yet to show how clever he was — after all, he possessed so very much more than mere cleverness — but simply to perform a public service. The louder and more numerous were the outcries the more appreciatively did the general public savor the dry wine that was "Modern English Usage."

Henry Watson Fowler (1858–1933) was a very different person from what most of his readers have imagined him. He did not confine himself to the vast field of the English language. He did not, like Goldsmith, adorn every subject he treated. He did better than that: he enriched and illuminated it.

For seventeen years after he left Balliol College, Oxford, he taught in what we English so oddly call a public school. It is true that "once a teacher, always a teacher"; but he was the very best kind of teacher, a notable member of that selfless profession to which we owe so much and which we treat so shabbily.

He possessed exceptional physical and moral courage and that much rarer quality, fortitude. He falsified his age (fifty-seven) by many years in order to serve in France during World War I, not as an officer on a gilded staff but in the ranks and the trenches. He had an inexhaustible sense of fun, a rich sense of humor, a pleasant wit.

Always kindly and considerate to others, he himself lived a simple, indeed a Spartan, life. When, after the war, he settled down to lexicographical work in the service of perhaps the most generous of all publishers, the Oxford University Press offered to provide him with a servant, so that he might be free to enjoy his Somersetshire cottage and carry on his work.

His reply to this offer, at the age of sixty-eight and in the month of November, is famous in English academic circles but little known elsewhere: "My half-hour from 7 to 7:30 this morning was spent in (1) a two-mile run along the road, (2) a swim in my next-door neighbor's pond. . . . That I am still in condition for such freaks I attribute to having had for nearly thirty years no servants to reduce me to sedentary and all-literary existence. And now you seem to say: Let us give you a servant, and the means of slow suicide and quick lexicography."

Everywhere he went he inspired not only respect but affection; not only admiration but liking, whether among scholars and students, as was natural, or among all other sorts and conditions of men and women. He was a great man. He was also, in the best sense and in the best ways, a very good man. This "merely moral man" put most professing Christians to shame.

All his life Fowler worked hard and carefully. He scorned the slipshod and the shoddy alike. He paid his readers a compliment few could have deserved, for he had a first-rate mind and all his work is first-rate. Even as a versifier (he knew that he wasn't a poet) he wrote with clarity and charm. As an essayist he wrote in addition with distinction, although without success.

In the earlier half of his writing life H. W. Fowler mostly collaborated with his brother Francis (1870–1918). Excellent classical scholars, the two brothers in 1905 published the best of all translations of that Greek satirist Lucian, who set the fashion in "dialogues of the dead." A year later they issued a famous work, *The King's English,* revised finally by H. W. alone in 1930 and still used by the older generation of teachers and students and deserving to be used more freely by the younger generation.

The brothers Fowler owed the idea of their astringently corrective book to Dean Henry Alfrod's *A Plea for the Queen's English,* which, published in 1866, had reached its seventh edition in 1888 and was still being used right up to 1906, when *The King's English* — a much better book — killed it stone dead. *The King's English,* although existing and thriving in its own right, has often been regarded as a *ballon d'essai* for *Modern English Usage,* despite the fact that the earlier work, succeeding beyond the authors' hopes, merely gave them the idea for the later and greater work.

Twenty years intervened between the first publication of *The King's English* and that of *Modern English Usage.* Apart from the disruption caused by recruiting, by soldiering, by munitions work, most of that period of H. W. Fowler's life was occupied in lexicography for the Oxford University Press, especially on *The Concise Oxford Dictionary of Current English.*

Appearing in 1911, The Concise Oxford, as it is affectionately known, was initially the work of the two brothers. Revised, it has retained its place, almost immediately won, as the best concise dictionary of English for scholars, students, teachers, authors, journalists and for all others whose tastes are literary and artistic rather than scientific or technological. It combines precision and elegance.

Francis Fowler had no hand in the writing of *Modern English Usage,* but he did help H. W. to plan the work and to get it under way. This world-famous book contains a moving and eloquent memorial dedication to the younger man, a dedication remarkable for the attribution to Francis of "a nimbler wit, a better sense of proportion, and a more open mind, than his twelve-year-older partner."

Even before his death Henry Fowler had become a legend. A legend he has remained. As always happens after a great man's death, and so soon as a decent interval has been allowed to elapse, the jackals and the hyenas first insinuated and then asserted that *Modern English Usage* contains many faults. Of course it does! Every worthwhile book contains many faults, and every worthwhile writer commits them. Look how shockingly incorrect is much of Shakespeare's English!

There does, however, exist one very serious objection to *Modern English Usage.* Even when it appeared, the book was slightly out of date. Let me explain that apparent heresy. In its principles and, with one minor exception, its precepts "M. E. U." is impeccable. Its teachings have proved invaluable; they still are. But Fowler sometimes failed to notice what was happening in postwar English. His theory seemed to rest, in the main, upon the practice of the writers of (roughly) 1890–1914. For instance, the section on "as if" and "as though" is very good, so far as it goes; it doesn't go far enough, for he neglects to mention the distinctions involved.

To me "M. E. U." has always been a grand book to consult; yet it has always impressed me with a sense of unreality. To say that it contains only counsels of perfection would be to exaggerate, yet it does contain very little else. Its slight archaism, its decided perfectionism, its pervasive and disquieting unreality do not prevent it from being the best book of its kind ever written in any European language.

ACCORDING TO FOWLER

These excerpts are from A Dictionary of Modern English Usage, *by H. W. Fowler*

The spread of education adds to the writer's burdens by multiplying that pestilent fellow the critical reader.

.   .   .

Now & then a person may be heard to "confess," in the pride that apes humility, to being "a bit of a purist"; but *purist* & *purism* are for the most part missile words, which we all of us fling at anyone who insults us by finding not good enough for him some manner of speech that is good enough for us.

.   .   .

The English-speaking world may be divided into (1) those who neither know nor care what a split infinitive is; (2) those who do not know, but care very much; (3) those who know & condemn; (4) those who know & approve; & (5) those who know & distinguish.

.   .   .

It need hardly be said that shortness is a merit in words . . . short words are not only handier to use, but more powerful in effect; extra syllables reduce, not increase, vigor. This is partic-

ularly so in English, where the native words are short, & the
long words are foreign.

. . .

The ambition to do better than our neighbors is in many de-
partments of life a virtue; in pronunciation it's a vice.

. . .

Pedantry may be defined . . . as the saying of things in language so learned or so demonstratively accurate as to imply a
slur upon the generality, who are not capable or not desirous of
such displays. The term, then, is obviously a relative one; my
pedantry is your scholarship, his reasonable accuracy, her irreduc-
ible minimum of education, & someone else's ignorance.

. . .

Of course, as the herald of an out-of-the-way fact that one has
just unearthed from a book of reference, is a sad temptation to
journalists.

. . .

If the abnormal, or at least unorthodox, final preposition that
has naturally presented itself sounds comfortable, keep it; if it
does not sound comfortable, still keep it if it has compensating
vigor, or when among awkward possibilities it is the least awkward.

. . .

The assumption that puns are *per se* contemptible betrayed by
the habit of describing every pun not as a *pun,* but as a *bad pun*
or a *feeble pun,* is a sign at once of sheepish docility & desire to
seem superior. Puns are good, bad, & indifferent, & only those
who lack the wit to make them are unaware of the fact.

WALTER ALLEN

The Time and Place of T. S. Eliot

As literary editor of The New Statesman, *Walter Allen had a first-rate observation post from which to survey contemporary writing. Some of what he saw supplied material for his latest book,* The Modern Novel in Britain and the United States. *He is a novelist as well as a critic, and he is a sometime teacher. In 1963–1964 he taught a course in the modern novel at Vassar.*

You don't need to be a great age to remember the days when T. S. Eliot was a literary Bolshevik. Back in 1932, when I was an undergraduate, it was a favorite gambit of my professor of English to goad us with such words as "Mr. T. S. (*sniff*) Eliot, whom some of you young gentlemen profess to (*sniff*) understand and (*sniff*) admire . . ." My professor was no doubt a reactionary even then, but he was a great scholar and the most eminent Wordsworthian of his generation; and he lived long enough to see the triumph of the revolution in poetry and poetic taste for which in Britain Eliot was mainly responsible. What he made of it I don't know: for him, English poetry had ended with Robert Bridges' *The Testament of Beauty*. But I can't believe he ever foresaw Eliot the Nobel Prize winner, much less Eliot the admired playwright of Broadway and the West End.

But there it is. Mr. Eliot is now *the* elder statesman of the British literary establishment; and no one (or almost no one) seriously denies — least of all those who have not read him — that he is the greatest living British poet. He is, moreover, very much a public figure, beloved by the newspaper gossip-writers. He is undisputed monarch, and a whole generation of poets and critics has grown up under his shadow for whom his literary practice and principles were not, as for us, heady with the fumes of revolution, but rather rich with the incense of sacred books.

No doubt about it, by precept and example Eliot altered our whole notion of poetry. He gave the word "tradition" a new meaning. It was no longer something to be passively inherited but something to be obtained "by great labor." It involved the recognition "in the bones" not only of the poetry of our own time but of the simultaneous existence of the whole of European literature from Homer onward. In his own practice as a poet Eliot made the late nineteenth-century French symbolists contemporary, as it were, with Shakespeare, Webster and Donne.

He changed, too, our sense of what was significant in past poetry. Before Eliot, Milton had always been one of the greatest of poets; but for Eliot he was a prime example of what he believed to be the "disassociation of sensibility" that had occurred in the seventeenth century, the split between the intellect and the emotion, the condition of being which was the very opposite of that described by Donne when he wrote of Mistress Elizabeth Drury "that one might almost say, her body thought."

Then, with his doctrine of the "objective correlative," he produced what was tantamount to a definition of poetry as potent and, it seemed, as revealing as Wordsworth's "the spontaneous overflow of powerful feelings," which it flagrantly contradicted. "The only way of expressing emotion in art," he wrote in his essay on "Hamlet," is by finding an " 'objective correlative'; in other words, a set of objects, a situation, a chain of events, which shall be the formula of that *particular* emotion." With this clue in mind, we saw how *The Waste Land* could be translated into an expression of Eliot's own emotions; and it seemed to show, too, why some works of art were successful and others failed.

Like Donne, Dryden and Wordsworth before him, Eliot gave the poets who followed him a whole new range of models, and he gave the critics who came after him a new vocabulary. Small wonder, then, if his writings, poetry and criticism alike, had the authority of sacred books. For the majority of British critics they no doubt still have; yet all the signs now point to the beginnings of a serious reaction against Eliot's work.

In part the reaction was predictable and not particularly honorable. Such things happen, almost as a law of nature. We all know what happened to Aristides: the Athenians became so bored with hearing him constantly called "the Just" that they drove him from their city. Doubtless, too, Mr. Eliot's success in the commercial theatre has worked against his reputation with the more intransigent eggheads. More serious than this, though, is the fact that Eliot appeared in the theatre as the harbinger of a new poetic drama. Apart from Eliot himself, however — and even his warmest admirers found *The Elder Statesman* something of an embarrassment — the poetic drama got nowhere, or at least nowhere beyond Christopher Fry; and the newest drama in England owes absolutely nothing to Eliot. Here he has certainly proved a false prophet.

Yet the symptoms of reaction against Eliot that I wish to consider now are much more serious. They were first widely manifest with the publication in 1957 of *On Poetry and Poets,* and my guess is that they took even those who were reacting against Eliot by surprise. They were, in fact, reacting involuntarily. *On Poetry and Poets* was Eliot's first collection of criticism for years; and while it contained nothing absolutely new, it did gather together lectures and pamphlets that had become difficult to obtain and it gave critics the opportunity of surveying Eliot's criticism as a whole.

The book had a curiously embarrassed press. There was much tipping of the hat toward it on the part of reviewers, but along with that went a note almost of dismay. Was this the Eliot who almost forty years before had wrought a revolution in English literary criticism with *The Sacred Wood?* Then what a very respectable, fuddy-duddy old gentleman, what a pillar of the Establishment, the erstwhile revolutionary had become! This from young men who had imbibed Eliot's principles as poet and critic almost with their mothers' milk.

The youthful T. S. Eliot — and one tends to forget that *The Sacred Wood* was published when he was thirty-two — had with not much more than a single phrase deposed Milton from his place among the great poets, and Eliot had done this so completely that for years in the most influential critical circles Milton's had been a dirty name. And here was the elderly Mr. Eliot apologetically putting him back. Similarly, the young Eliot had summarily disposed of Goethe — and now Goethe was most handsomely restored.

Reading the reviewers on *On Poetry and Poets,* one could hardly escape the impression that Mr. Eliot had finally succumbed to an uncritical and woolly benevolence. Much of its merit, I happen to think, was overlooked in the general astonishment that greeted the performance. But that is by the way; and when one looks back, hindsight reveals that the reaction against Eliot's criticism had already set in. Reaction, let me hasten to say, caused by the best of reasons. At some point, round about 1953 perhaps, it dawned on us that Eliot's criticism was now sufficiently of the past to demand the same order of rigorous examination as other classic criticism, Johnson's or Coleridge's or Arnold's.

I give the date as 1953 because in that year Kathleen Nott published *The Emperor's Clothes* — though one mustn't forget that F. R. Leavis, the most influential academic critic in Britain and for years Eliot's most formidable champion, has also for years been increasingly critical of Eliot's later pronouncements. Kathleen Nott called her book "an attack on the dogmatic orthodoxy of T. S. Eliot, Graham Greene, Dorothy Sayers, C. S. Lewis, and others," but in between the swinging polemics she managed to get in some acute literary criticism, in particular some acute criticism of the famous doctrine of the "dissociation of sensibility" in the English poets that Eliot had told us had set in after the Metaphysicals. In 1957 an attack on the doctrine from a rather more scholarly position was made in *The Romantic Image*, by Frank Kermode, Professor of English at the University of Manchester.

Other of Eliot's critical concepts that have become increasingly challenged are his notion of "the objective correlative" and his whole idea of tradition. No one, of course, is denying Eliot's greatness as a critic. That remains; but the criticism comes to seem much less of an ordered system, much more a piecemeal affair, than it did in the past. It seems, in other words, much more personal to the poet, much more a practitioner's notes on his craft, the product largely of what he himself was trying to do in verse.

So far, Eliot's poetry has not been directly challenged. But it is being "placed," and the placing suggests that a scaling down of its importance is inevitable. In a sense, the placing consists of the discovery that Eliot is an American before he is an English poet. Some years ago, A. Alvarez published *The Shaping Spirit: Studies in Modern English and American Poets* (called, in America, *Stewards of Excellence*). Alvarez, one of the best of the younger British critics, has the advantage over most of them of being equally at home with American as with English poetry. One of the questions at the center of his book is, "Why have the great creative possibilities of modern poetry come, in fact, to so little?" His answer is that " 'modernism' has been predominantly an American concern, a matter of creating, almost from scratch, their own poetic tradition. It has affected English poetry peculiarly little." His admiration for Eliot is great, but against

him he sets Yeats. He sees Eliot as, so to speak, the self-made
poet, the poet who has had to devise his own language, his own
rhythms, whereas "Yeats' poetry is the new flowering of a very
old tree," the tree precisely of English poetry.

A critic who goes even further than Alvarez is Graham Hough,
Fellow of Christ's College, Cambridge, and Lecturer in English
at the university. In his *Image and Experience,* Hough suggests
that what has come to be known as modern poetry (which for
convenience may be summed up in the names of Eliot and Pound,
with Joyce as their analogue in prose) is not the main road of
literature but "a diversion from the main road. Traffic along the
main road has been proceeding all the time, and we do not sufficiently remember this. In talking of modern poetry we ought to
recall more often than we do that Hardy was writing till 1926,
and that among the poets of our century are Robert Frost, Robert
Graves, John Crowe Ransom, Edwin Muir and John Betjeman.
But the detour has been considerable, and most of the heavy
traffic has chosen to travel on it. It is probably time it rejoined
the main highway."

Hough's book was reviewed by Frank Kermode in the *Spectator.* Kermode was bold enough to entitle his review "Counter-
Revolution." By no means an insular critic, Kermode is the most
sizable and persuasive champion of Wallace Stevens in Britain;
but he responded to Hough's book with great sympathy. And
while he ends his review by confessing "to be glad" that "the
days when 'Ulysses' and 'The Waste Land' will be regarded as
curiosities for scholars are presumably still some way ahead," he
can still ask the question (though he does not answer it): "What
if 'The Waste Land' should be, after all, an extremely haphazard
and incoherent poem?"

For all his admiration of Eliot's poetry, Hough plainly believes
that Eliot's work may be so described. The poem is based, he
contends, like Pound's *Cantos* and Joyce's *Ulysses* and *Finne-*

gans Wake, on a faulty poetic rooted in the fallacy that poetry proceeds by "a logic of the imagination," not by "a logic of concepts." The result has been a rejection of much that is traditional to poetry. Such poetry as Eliot's and Pound's Hough sees "as in some sense opposed to the English literary tradition."

And where is that tradition to be found today? Alvarez and Hough alike invoke Yeats, and Hough adds Hardy as well; but both have been dead many years now, and so has Lawrence. There is Robert Graves, the rise in whose reputation has paralleled the decline in Eliot's. Yet there are very few other poets living in Britain now in whom anything like so grand a thing as a tradition can be said to exist. We shall be able to take the displacement of Eliot seriously when the criticism in reaction to him has brought forth its own contemporary poet adequate to be set against him. Until that time, the world outside Britain may very well see the reaction as another sign of current English provincialism.

LAWRANCE THOMPSON

Frost Spoke the Language of the Ordinary Man

As the authorized biographer of Robert Frost, Lawrance Thompson is peculiarly qualified to write an appreciation of the poet. They were friends for many years, and Mr. Thompson has dug deep into the story of the poet's life and work. His essay was to have appeared in the New York Times Book Review *at the time of Frost's death in 1963, but the New York newspaper strike then in progress prevented it. It is now printed for the first time.*

ROBERT FROST made himself a poet of the people by speaking to and for them in a language they understood. He was their witness tree, uttering cautious affirmations in an uncertain age, and though by a world of doubt surrounded. There is no quick way of explaining how he became America's best-known and best-loved poet. But one basic factor in his triumph was his early determination to make his idiom honor the language of the ordinary man, and thus to make his poetry meaningful to the sensibilities of the people.

At the start, he found himself opposed to the overappareled rhetoric then fashionable in poetry. When he wrote and published his first verse, in 1889, the general taste was for sweet musical cadences, prettiness of imagery, and themes of aspiration. Artificial adornment was considered necessary to lift poetry above the language of the ordinary man. In America as well as in England, the mannerisms of Tennyson were still in style: "There is sweet music here that softer falls/ Than petals from blown roses

on the grass." In the United States, the white-bearded Longfellow was the uncrowned poet laureate. Perhaps our Puritan
fiber made general readers cherish as models of good poetry the
moral exhortations of Longfellow, Holmes and Bryant. "Lives
of great men all remind us/ We can make our lives sublime, and,
departing, leave behind us,/ Footprints on the sands of time."

As one might expect, Frost's own apprentice verse rendered at
least brief tribute to these tastes and thus gave support to his
later confession that every poet must start as a cloud of all the
poets he has met. But as soon as he began to discover what was
native to his grain he avoided those musicalities, those conventions of prettiness, and those lofty exhortations.

He was not surprised when his matter-of-fact lyrics, employing
the language of the people, failed to attract immediate attention.
Editors complained that his lines lacked the qualities which made
poetry poetic. While still searching for self, he was warned by one
friend that his verse "sounded too much like talk." Too much?
That quality was precisely what he had been trying to establish.
From wide reading he had convinced himself that even a lyric
should possess those dramatic elements provided by a speaker's
natural and colloquial tones of voice.

Even in the early days, Frost found nothing disparaging in the
epithet colloquial. It implied the blend of imagery, phrase, tone,
which he thought anyone should enjoy in living conversation and
in poetry. More than that, he believed that "the sound of sense"
conveyed through the overtones of everyday discourse could be
compressed and intensified for purposes of endowing flat state-
ments of fact with subtly meaningful enrichments. He wanted to
demonstrate, in his verse, that prose utterances permeated with
voice tones could make valid poetry.

When Frost was twenty-six, a doctor's mistaken diagnosis enabled the poet to extend his theories. The doctor guessed that
the pains in Frost's chest were symptoms of tuberculosis and he

advised his patient to spend more time out of doors, preferably on a farm. With an initial sense of despair, Frost submitted. A background of city life, first in his native San Francisco and then in Lawrence, Massachusetts, had given him inclinations to do little more than play at farming. From boyhood experiences on farms he knew enough to be certain that the drudgery of routine barnyard chores would be repulsive to him. But after he had settled on a small farm in Derry, New Hampshire, with his wife and child, he found many consolations. Among them was the discovery that his stranger-neighbors could show him something more than how to farm. He watched them, studied them, and soon began to admire their stoical cherishing of daily farm rituals: caring for livestock, caring for whatever grew in fields and orchards, caring about the weather (and with good reason), but always intensely caring. Here was something more than a grim acceptance of hardships which earned them a marginal living.

He also listened to his neighbors and noticed that, although their talk was terse and blunt, their briefest utterances were often enriched by subtle inflections. Even their silences conveyed meanings. The more he listened, the more he heard new ways in which "the sound of sense" artistically handled could translate ordinary talk into extraordinary poetry.

Always hoping that he might eventually make his living as man of letters and not as farmer, Frost nevertheless paid his Derry neighbors the high compliment of imitation — for purposes of poetry, not farming. The latter held so little appeal to him as work, even though he continued to enjoy it as play, that from the moment he reached Derry he gave his best energies to his art, surreptitiously. When farm duties interfered, he slighted them. Rising at dawn to milk his one cow became so irksome that he solved the problem in a way which must have amazed his neighbors. He slowly eased the cow around until he was milking her at midnight and at noon, and when she dried up he was glad.

The more he neglected his fields and gardens and livestock, the more he wrote poems about an ordinary New England farmer, somewhere north of Boston. For literary purposes, that fictional role enabled him to illuminate truths discovered in his own maturing experiences. The role also justified his artistic adaptation of the back-country ways of colloquial speech, which he himself had learned to imitate in his own everyday talk. The role further justified his making metaphors out of down-to-earth images and rituals inseparably bound with pains and pleasures of caring and cherishing. It even enabled him to endow those local elements with national and universal significances.

Frost kept telling himself and others that in his poetry he was merely shaping to his needs and tastes a few of the very old ways. His earlier studies of Latin and Greek poets had made him aware that he could find classical models for his purposes in Theocritus, Horace and Virgil. It seemed to him that those ancients had demonstrated, at least in their pastoral verse, that they understood the poetic values of colloquial modes. So they did more for him than merely encourage his making metaphors out of rural images.

As for his chosen ways of renewing poetic diction after it had become stale and artificial, he might have found additional support if he had turned to Wordsworth's Preface to *Lyrical Ballads*. Instead he gained confidence from a source nearer home. Emerson had roamed far enough through the southwest corner of New Hampshire to discover and praise poetic elements he heard in the conversations of the people there. He had said so in his poem entitled "Monadnoc" and Frost liked to quote the following passage from that poem to illustrate his own convictions:

> *Now in sordid weeds they sleep,*
> *In dulness now their secret keep;*
> *Yet, will you learn our ancient speech,*

These the masters who can teach.
Fourscore or a hundred words
All their vocal muse affords;
But they turn them in a fashion
Past clerks' or statesmen's art or passion . . .
Rude poets of the tavern hearth,
Squandering your unquoted mirth,
Which keeps the ground and never soars,
While Jake retorts and Reuben roars;
Scoff of yeomen strong and stark,
Goes like bullet to its mark;
While the solid curse and jeer
Never balk the waiting ear.

After Frost had bettered Emerson in making poetry from the language of the people, he tried to encourage his readers to develop what he liked to call the "audial imagination." He invited them to collaborate with him by noticing and appreciating how his poetry became, as he said, "good speaking caught alive"; how it managed to release to any sensitive ear those undertones and overtones of voice which added subtle extensions to the literal meaning of words.

The thought-felt quality of dialogue soon found its way into all of Frost's best verse, even into his lyrics. In addition, the structural patterns of his ideas, poetically handled, accentuated opposites to such a degree that the colloquial matter of dialogue blended perfectly with his colloquial manner. The converse between order and chaos, in nature and in human nature, always fascinated him. Hence his insistence that the poet's act of giving orderly arrangements in words to slippery and chaotic meanings is a symbol of all human attempts to impose meaningful forms of order on any kinds of chaos: "Every poem is an epitome of the great predicament; a figure of the will braving alien entanglements."

Brave acts of will or of conscious choice form important parts of Frost's preoccupations. But he was aware that tragedy always threatens the trial by existence. He granted that the unforeseen and uncontrollable events of inner and outer life repeatedly reduce even the most heroic endeavors to failure. Personal experience had taught him that, painfully. Born and brought up in an atmosphere of family predicaments, he was further conditioned to failure later by his inability to attract attention to his poetry until he was nearly forty. For these and other reasons he had to adjust his viewpoint to comprehend the dark and tragic possibilities of failure. In such poems as "The Housekeeper," "The Self-seeker," "Design," " 'Out, Out —' " and "Home Burial" he grieved over different forms of darkness, loss and even horror. Nevertheless it is a mistake to characterize Frost as being primarily a "terrifying" poet. He looks at and through the worst primarily to express his optimistic preoccupation with various possibilities for human reconciliation of failure and success, pain and pleasure, despair and hope, horror and ecstasy, denial and affirmation.

Consider for example the colloquial imagery in Frost's narrative dialogue "West-running Brook." The title image is a New England stream which boldly flows westward even though it will eventually be forced eastward into the Atlantic. Standing on opposite sides of the brook, a husband and wife admire its contrary motion. Then they notice something else. The black current of water, catching on a sunken rock, flings a white wave backwards, against the current. "Speaking of contraries," the husband says, "see how the brook in that white wave runs counter to itself." He goes on to interpret that image as a gathering metaphor. To him it represents "time, strength, tone, light, life, and love — / And even substance lapsing unsubstantial; / The universal cataract of death / That spends to nothingness . . ." Yet, he adds, the fact of death is always resisted, and at times successfully resisted, by the creative impulses of human life.

Frost repeatedly honored such contrary resistance. His last book *In the Clearing* justified that superb title by giving climactic emphasis to the same general theme: the bold and triumphant venture of the human spirit into and through and beyond matter. But because he was primarily a poet, not a philosopher, he could and did permit the expressions of his changing moods to illuminate ideas which also ran counter to each other. That typically Frostian habit of mingling thoughts and feelings annoyed and confused the logicians, the academicians and the dogmatists. They complained that Frost was an anti-intellectual, and even a spiritual drifter. They were wrong, and the critical mistakes they made were attempts to measure him with impertinent yardsticks. If they had bothered to notice, they could have found a counter-complaint in one of Frost's doubly colloquial blends of matter and manner:

> *I love to toy with the Platonic notion*
> *That wisdom need not be of Athens Attic,*
> *But well may be Laconic, even Boeotian.*
> *At least I will not have it systematic.*

Another countercomplaint which Frost teasingly made against the dogmatists was that they frequently imprison themselves in a single metaphor. It is the function of a poet, he reminded them, to keep replacing old metaphors with new to provide "a clarification of life — not necessarily a great clarification, such as sects and cults are founded on, but in a momentary stay against confusion." When the same critics attacked him for that statement by complaining further that his poetic clarifications were nothing more than momentary stays against confusion, he taunted them anew. Repeatedly, and in many ways, he asked whether they escaped confusion by possessing an inside pipeline to and from the Truth, the whole Truth, and nothing but the Truth.

The people seem to understand Frost better than the specialists do. His ordinary readers seem to feel, correctly, that his poetic handlings of his own opposed negations and affirmations always tipped the balance meaningfully and sensibly in favor of cautious and sensible affirmations. They further seem to feel, again correctly, that while it might be impossible to pigeonhole Frost into any poetic camp, into any philosophic school, or into any religious sect, his independent position made sense, and continues to make sense. They find that his poetry reveals him to have been a theist who believed that human beings are given enough powers of choice, in most cases, to save themselves or to destroy themselves; a theist who had faith enough to believe in the chances for human survival through and beyond the atomic age.

As for Frost's views concerning the limitations of human knowledge, there is a passage in his "Masque of Reason" where the Biblical Job is permitted to say that, in spite of all his sufferings, he understands all he needs to, about the ultimate mysteries. Then he reviews and answers negating attitudes in these doubly colloquial lines: "We don't know where we are, or who we are. We don't know one another; don't know You; Don't know what time it is. We don't know, don't we? Who says we don't? Who got up these misgivings? Oh, we know well enough to go ahead with. I mean we seem to know enough to act on."

Frost frequently said he hoped he had lodged a few poems so firmly that they would not soon be shaken off. As it happens, many of his lines stick like burrs to our memory. Perhaps there is no better measure of a poet's chances for literary survival than the frequency and ease with which he keeps cropping up in everyday conversation. If the people continue to quote Frost as readily in the future as in the present, it seems probable that his hope will become a fact.

ARTHUR MIZENER

A Classic of the American
Experience

*F. Scott Fitzgerald was a literary hero to Arthur Mizener long be-
fore he wrote* The Far Side of Paradise, *the first full-dress biography of Fitzgerald, and it is not surprising therefore that he has
some important things to say here about Fitzgerald's masterpiece*
The Great Gatsby. *Arthur Mizener is professor of English at
Cornell. His latest collection of essays is titled* The Sense of Life
in the Modern Novel.

THE GREAT GATSBY, IT IS probably safe now to say, is a classic of
twentieth-century American fiction. There is a special irony in
the belated fame of *Gatsby* because Fitzgerald was a man like
Gatsby himself, at least in this, that he had a heroic dream of the
possibilities of life and a need, amounting almost to a sense of
duty, to realize that dream. If the world was for him, as it was
for Gatsby, "material without being real" unless he could live
with that dream, the dream was a mere self-indulgence unless he
could realize it in the actual world.

As one of his friends said when his work became popular again
in the early fifties, *"How* Scott would have loved to know that
people admired and cared for his books!" He would have, and
not out of vanity, but because his sense of achievement, his very
sense of identity, depended on recognition.

Like so many of the feelings that went deepest with him, this
one came out most clearly in the wry jokes and drunken extrava-
gances of his defeated years. About the time he was discovering

that the bookstores no longer carried his books, he wrote himself
a postal card. It said: "Dear Scott — How are you? Have been
meaning to come in and see you. I have [been] living at the Garden of Allah. Yours, Scott Fitzgerald." And whenever he was
drunk, he would insist on telling people who he was and pressing
them to recognize him — "I'm F. Scott Fitzgerald. You've read
my books. You've read *The Great Gatsby,* haven't you? Remember?"

With all the terrible irony of the original speaker, he could
have said, " 'Tis better to be vile than vile esteemed,/ When not
to be receives reproach of being." And indeed, he did say it, in
"Pasting It Together." "If you were dying of starvation outside
my window," he wrote there, "I would . . . give you the smile
and the voice (if no longer the hand) and stick around till somebody raised a nickel to phone for the ambulance, that is if I
thought there would be any copy in it for me."

But when, a little later, he summoned up once again his whole
sense of life for his last hero — Monroe Stahr, the producer in
The Last Tycoon — he imagined a man who, though dying,
fought to control a whole industry in order that he might create
something that was both good and popular. Stahr is deceived
about nothing. When a British novelist he has hired to write
scripts says, "It's this mass production," Stahr answers, "That's the
condition. There's always some lousy condition." Like Stahr,
Fitzgerald always tried to make his work as good as he knew how
to, and, like him, he could not believe in the reality of an unrecognized good.

Since this was his sense of things, there was a special irony for
Fitzgerald in the reception of *The Great Gatsby.* It was an immediate success with professional writers and that curious underground of serious readers in America who have, almost alone,
kept many good books alive when the reviewers and the popular
audience have ignored them, as they did *Gatsby.* At its publica-

tion they thought it skillful light fiction. For the next twenty-five years, on the rare occasions when it was discussed, it was considered a nostalgic period piece with "the sadness and the remote jauntiness of a Gershwin tune," as Peter Quennell said in 1941.

For a man with Fitzgerald's almost renaissance feeling that "if our virtues/ Did not go forth of us, 'twere all alike/ As if we had them not," this reception was unfortunate. Indeed, because he had staked on *Gatsby* his hope of the only life he really cared for, the life of a serious writer, it was disastrous. He made later efforts to achieve that life, but in a very real sense he lost his faith in its possibility for good with *Gatsby*'s failure to achieve recognition.

He had begun to plan the novel in June, 1923, saying to Maxwell Perkins, "I want to write something *new* — something extraordinary and beautiful and simple and intricately patterned." But that summer and fall was devoted to the production of his play, *The Vegetable*. When it failed miserably he discovered he had many debts and had to spend the winter of 1923 working night and day on magazine stories to pay them. The stories were, he said, "all trash and it nearly broke my heart."

It was not until April, 1924, that he could write in his Ledger, "Out of woods at last and starting novel." But very little of it — not more than the first chapter — was on paper before he was interrupted again when he and Zelda decided to move to the Riviera, where a serious crisis in their personal relations developed. By August, however, he was back at work, not to be interrupted again until he sent the manuscript to Maxwell Perkins on October 30.

The exhausting and valueless work of the previous winter, together with his lifelong anxiety about loss of time, sharpened Fitzgerald's feeling that *Gatsby* was the supreme test. He committed all his imaginative resources to it, and despite his anxious joking about it between its completion and publication, he clearly knew it was a good book. The question was whether it would be recognized for what it was. "Write me the opinion you may be pleased to form of my chef-d'oeuvre and others' opinion," he said to John Peale Bishop. *"Please!* I think it's great because it deals with much debauched materials, quick-deciders like [the critic Burton] Rascoe may mistake it for [the then popular novelist Robert W.] Chambers."

Up to the very last possible moment he was busy rushing revisions to Scribner's, including an extensive rewriting of Chapter VI, in which Daisy and Tom Buchanan come to Gatsby's party, and an entirely new version of Chapter VII, which describes the crucial quarrel at the Plaza between Gatsby and Tom. At the same time he refused an offer of $10,000 for the serial rights in order not to delay the book's publication.

By publication day — April 10, 1925 — he was almost beside himself, and within twenty-four hours he was cabling Perkins, ludicrously and touchingly, "Any news?" When the news did come, it was far from what he had hoped for. Good readers, to be sure, saw how fine a book *Gatsby* was, and it meant a great deal to him to get perceptive letters of praise from writers like T. S. Eliot, Edith Wharton and Willa Cather. But this was after all private opinion, and much as he treasured it, what Fitzgerald needed was the public recognition of reviewers and readers.

What really shook him was "that of all the reviews, even the most enthusiastic, not one had the slightest idea what the book was about." They found in it only the bright but trivial talent they had seen in his earlier books. *Gatsby* was, they said, "clever and brilliantly surfaced but . . . not the work of a wise and mature novelist"; it was "a little slack, a little soft, more than a little artificial, [falling] into the class of negligible novels." Mencken said that it was "certainly not to be put on the same shelf with, say, *This Side of Paradise*," and Isabel Paterson that "what has never been alive cannot very well go on living; so this is a book for the season only."

Nor did the sales of *Gatsby* suggest any general recognition of its nature; by October, when the original sale had run its course, it was still short of 20,000. In 1926 Owen Davis' dramatic version had a successful run in New York, and in the same year Paramount issued a sentimentalized movie. Both brought Fitzgerald money that he needed, but they did not bring him what he needed more, the kind of recognition that would make real for him the serious novelist he dreamed of becoming.

In the last year of his life he wrote his daughter, "I wish now I'd *never* relaxed or looked back — but said at the end of 'The Great Gatsby': 'I've found my line — from now on this comes first. This is my immediate duty — without this I am nothing.' " But though without this he was, in his own eyes, almost literally nothing, this is to blame himself for not having acted in a way that, given his nature, was not really possible for him.

For at least a decade after the publication of *Gatsby* the reviewers' estimate continued to be the public opinion of it — if it was thought of at all, as it usually was not. In 1933 Matthew Josephson, in an article on "The Younger Novelists," was pointing an admonitory finger at Fitzgerald and urging him to recognize that "there are ever so many Americans . . . who can't drink champagne from morning to night, or even go to Princeton or Montparnasse" — as if Fitzgerald had not shown in *Gatsby* the deep and meretricious tragedy of their longing to.

A year or so later Harry Hartwick was describing his work as the kind "in which sensuality becomes half flippant and half sentimental and plays the youthful ape to sophistication," a remark that must — if Fitzgerald ever saw it — have reminded him ironically of what he believed to be *Gatsby's* one great defect, its failure to represent the relation between Daisy and Gatsby, a failure he admitted was the result of his own unwillingness to face the "sensuality" of the only relation that was possible for them. In 1934 *Gatsby* was introduced into the Modern Library, but it was dropped in 1939 because it failed to sell.

All through this time, however, the book kept its underground audience. " 'The Great Gatsby,' " says J. D. Salinger's Buddy Glass, "was my 'Tom Sawyer' when I was twelve." (Like Salinger himself, Buddy was twelve in 1931.) Writers like John O'Hara were showing its influence and younger men like Edward New-house and Budd Schulberg, who would presently be deeply af-fected by it, were discovering it. And to their eternal credit, Scribner's kept it in print; they carried the original edition on their trade list until 1946, by which time *Gatsby* was in print in three other forms and the original edition was no longer needed.

By the late thirties faint echoes of this underground opinion were being heard on the surface. In 1935, T. S. Matthews, re-viewing *Taps at Reveille* for the *New Republic,* was saying, "there seems to be a feeling abroad that it would be kinder not to take any critical notice of the goings-on of Fitzgerald [the short story writer], since his better half [the novelist] is such a superior person . . . but there is no real difference." A little later Her-bert Mueller observed with remarkable inconsistency that, though *Gatsby* was "tinged with the flippancy, the hard-boiled sentimentality, and cockeyed idealism of [its] period," it was "on the whole honestly, soberly, brilliantly done."

This was about the state of opinion when Fitzgerald's death late in 1940 and the republication of *Gatsby* in Edmund Wil-son's edition of *The Last Tycoon* in 1941 produced an outburst of comment. Most of it agreed with the judgment, if not the reasoning, of Margaret Marshall, who observed in *The Nation* that Fitzgerald had been a failure, apparently because he could not survive the world's discovery that "the October Revolution was nothing but a heap of Stalinist cinders," but that *Gatsby* was "enduring." But the voices of those who had always admired *Gatsby* were getting louder.

The New Yorker's "Talk of the Town" had a devastating com-ment on the ill-informed obituaries in the New York papers, and *The New Republic* — then under Malcolm Cowley's literary editorship — put together a group of wholly serious tributes to Fitzgerald from writers as diverse as Glenway Wescott and Budd Schulberg. As late as 1944, when Charles Weir published the first full-length article on Fitzgerald, the two judgments of his work were still just about in balance. But by 1945 the opinion that *Gatsby* was merely a period piece had almost entirely disappeared.

In that year *New Directions* published Edmund Wilson's edition of *The Crack-Up,* and a new edition of *Gatsby,* with an introduction by Lionel Trilling which quietly asserted that "Fitzgerald is now beginning to take his place in our literary tradition." In that year, too, *Gatsby* was reprinted in the Viking Portable Fitzgerald and in Bantam Books. There were still faint echoes of the old attitude in the slick magazines. *Time* continued to suppose that in *Gatsby* Fitzgerald was "portraying the hollowness of his racketeering hero's life," and *Newsweek* that "Fitzgerald evaded almost every issue of his time." But most reviewers were now taking the importance of *Gatsby* for granted and trying to explain it.

Malcolm Cowley wrote a brilliant article for *The New Yorker,* and William Troy pointed out that *Gatsby* is "one of the few truly mythological creations in our recent literature." By 1946 full-length articles were developing this view in the *Kenyon* and *Sewanee* reviews, though it is amusing to notice that the final evidence of a book's acceptance as a classic — a rash of M.A. and Ph.D. essays about it — did not begin until after 1951, the year that two full-length books (three if one counts Mr. Schulberg's *The Disenchanted*) were devoted to Fitzgerald.

The obvious values of the book have now been reasonably established, and we are ready to consider the qualities which, though more difficult to deal with, are probably quite as important. One is the book's realization of the fluidity of American lives, the perception behind Tom Buchanan's wistful drifting here and there, "wherever people played polo and were rich together," in Wolfsheim's sentimental longings for the old Metropole, in Nick Carroway's wry feeling that Tom and Daisy were "two old friends I scarcely knew at all," in Gatsby's whole career. Another is the book's voice, "more important," as Lionel Trilling has said, "than [its] shape or its wit of metaphor."

Almost for the first time Fitzgerald created with that voice an image of The Good American of our time in all his complexity of human sympathy, firm moral judgment and ironic self-possession. We can now afford to turn our attention to such things — because, whatever disagreements we may have over Fitzgerald's work as a whole, there remain few doubts of the greatness of *Gatsby* or of its imaginative relevance to American experience.

Was "Papa" Truly a Great Writer?

The American novel, and the men who made it, have been the concern of Maxwell Geismar throughout his literary life. It was apparent in his first critical work: Writers in Crisis (*1942*). *It has been emphasized in* The Last of the Provincials, *in* Rebels and Ancestors, *and most recently in the controversial* Henry James and the Jacobites.

Ernest Hemingway died on July 2, 1961. The testimonials, the encomiums are long since in. The reminiscences have begun, and a full-dress biography is under way. It is not too soon to try to strike a balance between whatever is limited and transient in his writing, whatever durable, memorable.

It is no secret that during Hemingway's later years the more he became a popular symbol of "art" in the United States, the more his serious reputation declined — perhaps because he himself no longer appeared to be serious as an artist. Perhaps this was due to the unfortunate *persona,* or public mask, which Ernest Hemingway chose for himself during his later career: the benign "Papa" of American fiction, who, however benign, brooked little interference and less criticism. He might have done better to remember the aging Walt Whitman who "made much of negatives" and yet cried to his Creator: "Old, poor and paralyzed, I thank Thee." Or again, take the ridiculed and neglected Herman Melville, who on his deathbed, describing life itself as that "oblique, tedious, barren game hardly worth the poor candle burnt out in playing it," still left us the beautiful and immortal *Billy Budd*. Hemingway, by contrast, had very early trapped himself into the stereotype of the romantic and virile literary "man of action," so American in essence, and so little conducive to either intellectual or emotional development.

The magic pen of Hemingway's earlier and authentic talent never deserted him, even in some of the inferior later works. A rereading of his first collection of stories, *In Our Time* (1925), or his early novel, *A Farewell to Arms* (1929), makes it easy to understand the impact upon the post–World War I period of a new style and a singular vision of contemporary experience. The earliest sketches of Hemingway's boyhood in the Michigan woods (his hero was called Nick Adams) were encircled by a boundary of pain, suffering, and human loss. The horrors of World War I confirmed this native bent of Hemingway's dark talent. This was the perfect meeting of a temperament and a time, both equally ridden by convulsive agonies of destruction and death.

For this anatomy of war, all of whose tissues were saturated by pain rather than evil (since Hemingway apparently made no moral judgments; nor was he interested in social or historical "causes" or, let us say, sequences), he evolved his famous flat style: the literal, factual description of the "way things are." "They shot the six cabinet ministers at half-past six in the morning against the wall of a hospital. There were pools of water in the courtyard." What cabinet ministers of what country, for what crime, or for what historical movement, and with what justice, or with what miscarriage of justice, we are never told. Rather as in the case of another earlier American virtuoso, Stephen Crane, these elements were rigorously excluded from the writer's art, in order to intensify the description of pure pain and horror.

It was in these earliest books of Hemingway's, too, that his Nick Adams recorded his decision to make "a separate peace" with the society or the culture which had created such scenes of senseless suffering. In *A Farewell to Arms,* another early Hemingway protagonist, Lieutenant Frederick Henry, is a deserter from the Italian Army after the great defeat at Caporetto. This novel remains one of Hemingway's best works just because of its descriptions of army life, of the marvelous Italian peasants, and of its central, if highly romantic, love affair. But *The Sun Also Rises* (1926), the novel which almost created the Lost Generation of the postwar expatriates, seems less good today; more artificial, brittle and mannered. Just as none of us could live up to the disenchantment of all those attractive, wounded, desolate pleasure-seekers in the Basque country (as I wrote about this book in the early nineteen-forties), few of us managed to be so overwhelmingly ineffectual. Hemingway's postwar generation was frustrated with an intensity and cunning of purpose, with an almost diabolical sense of self-defeat, that was far from being realistic.

In the nineteen-thirties, a period of relative "peace" amid the social anarchy, the revolutionary turmoil, the life-and-death upheavals and convulsions of contemporary history, the mood and tone of Hemingway's work became even darker. He retreated in *Death in the Afternoon* (1932) from the "game of war" (the game of life) to the sport of bullfighting in Spain. This book was bitterly attacked (and with some cause) by the new generation of social critics in the early years of the depression. We realize now that Hemingway had found his "positive," his form of belief, in the primitive virtue of both the matador and the bull. Quite similarly, for a writer who was concerned only with the high moments of life, who scorned all its domestic details and all its prosaic surfaces — a writer who deriving from the suburbs of Oak Park, Illinois, became a great primitive of modern letters — Hemingway found the true drama of animal dignity and courage in the moment of the kill. But the great virtue of this book was that Hemingway's sympathies were still equally divided between the victor and the victim: the matador and the bull were united in the moment of final fusion, the moment of life-in-death.

Well, frankly, even while I state this thesis, I must admit it appears to be an odd diversion for a major artist. Ring Lardner, during the same period, annihilated bullfighting as a "sport" with a few well-chosen pages of poker-faced nonsense. Yet in *The Green Hills of Africa* (1935), Hemingway continued with the same theme, and the same central trinity of the hunter, the hunted and death as the fusion, the synthesis and the climax. Here, too, he celebrated his own divorce from modern civilization more explicitly and even more eloquently. He was through serving time "for society, democracy and the other things." It was easier, he declared, "to keep well in a good country" (that is, Africa) by taking simple precautions than "to pretend that a country which is finished is still good." (And that was, the United States of America.) "Our people went to America because that was the place to go then. It has been a good country, and we had made a bloody mess of it and I would go now somewhere else as we had always had the right to go somewhere else and as we had always gone. You could always come back."

There were curious undertones in such utterances, of course. Who were "our people," and who were the "others" who had come to America because they did not know it was too late? Rather like Henry James, the more Hemingway abandoned his own country, the more right he claimed to sole ownership. Yet nevertheless, such are the ways of genius, the period of the nineteen-thirties was also the period of the great dark short stories of Ernest Hemingway which will remain as his most enduring contribution to world literature. These appeared in a series of volumes from *Men Without Women* (1927) to *Winner Take Nothing* (1933) and the collection called *The Fifth Column and the First Forty-nine Stories*, in 1938. And what stories they are! You may remember the Billy Campbell of "A Pursuit Race," who has shot himself full of dope and retired to bed. (The cool sheets are as soothing as a woman.) "They got a cure for that," says his manager. "No," says Billy, "they haven't got a cure for anything."

There is Frazier's monologue in "The Gambler, the Nun, and the Radio" — this Hemingway protagonist who "avoided thinking," as we are told, "except when he was writing," and who concludes that bread, and not religion, is the opium of the people. (Along with economics, patriotism, sexual intercourse, gambling, ambition, a belief in "any new form of government," so Hemingway declared, and of course drinking, perhaps the best opiate.) There is the famous Spanish "Nada" of "A Clean, Well-Lighted Place." "Hail nothing, full of nothing, nothing is with thee." There is the American businessman's brief "coming of age" in "The Short Happy Life of Francis Macomber," when he loses his lifelong sense of fear and becomes a man — just before his wife takes him out with a well-placed rifle shot. There is the dying and distraught artist-hero of "The Snows of Kilimanjaro" (reputed to be Scott Fitzgerald, but actually closer to Hemingway himself), tracing the ruins of his life and career in a feverish reverie of horror.

These stories, as well as the more famous and highly anthologized tales like "The Killers," are at the core of Hemingway's work; and within their framework they are perfect. No artist who wrote such stories can ever be ignored, or patronized — even though he had reached the end of his own demonic, solitary and obsessed talent. His future direction was uncertain, his later work imperfect.

The novel *To Have and Have Not* (1937) marked, apparently, both Hemingway's return to the United States and to contemporary civilization itself. He had returned, if briefly, to Key West to record a memorable epitaph on the Boom period of the nineteen-twenties. "Some made the long drop from the apartment or the office window; some took it quietly in two-car garages with the motor running; some used the native tradition of the Colt or Smith and Wesson: those well-constructed implements that end insomnia, terminate remorse, cure cancer, avoid bankruptcy." And it was here, in a novel which was itself both desperate and disorgainized, that Hemingway's racketeer-hero, Harry Morgan, also dying, made his famous decision to rejoin the human race. "A man . . . One man alone ain't got . . . No man alone now . . . No matter how a man alone ain't got no bloody . . . chance."

This was the prelude to Hemingway's belated social conversion in the play called *The Fifth Column* and the famous and popular novel of 1940, *For Whom the Bell Tolls* — a novel of the Spanish Civil War which sold close to a million copies. Sometimes called Hemingway's best novel, too, it is a curious mixture of good and bad, of marvelous scenes and chapters which are balanced off by improbable or sentimental or melodramatic passages of adolescent fantasy. For you couldn't always "come back," as Hemingway had declared; or if you did, you paid the price of leaving.

The younger and typical American writer of the depression years, Tom Wolfe, knew the score more accurately in his *You Can't Go Home Again*. Here, like many another fiction writer of the twenties, Hemingway paid the price for the cutting of his native roots. An earlier generation of American realists, from Theodore Dreiser and Sherwood Anderson to Ellen Glasgow, who had never dissociated themselves from their native society even when they appeared most critical of it, continued, like their European counterparts, to develop and grow. Hemingway, by contrast, simply continued to pour the romantic emotions of youth, now somewhat stereotyped and stylized, into his aging later heroes. In this respect *Across the River and Into the Trees* (1950) was probably his worst novel. In a kind of Jungian reversal, all of this artist's prejudices, affections and obsessions, usually contained within the rigid discipline of his craft, were released in this chronicle of a veteran of World War II.

The Old Man and the Sea (1952) was a partial comeback, though again Hemingway celebrated the familiar theme of the solitary individual drifting on a blind and hostile sea of life: a watery Darwinian universe of shark-eat-shark, and winner take nothing. The Nobel Prize awarded for this book was in effect (and as usual) a recognition for earlier, more original and more enduring work.

Yes, it is true that the boundaries of Ernest Hemingway's literary reputation have contracted since the first glowing period of his advent. That was the time when the present reviewer, with many others, believed he was the brightest talent of the modern American epoch. In that sense he is a writer who gets smaller as you grow older. Yet there still lies at the very center of Hemingway's world that perfect cluster of great short stories which are as immune to criticism as they will be impervious to time.

JULIAN F. BOYD

Prejudices According to Mencken

In the field of historical scholarship, Julian Boyd is an awesome figure. He is the editor of The Papers of Thomas Jefferson, *a many-volumed work that has set the standard as to how the papers of public men should be edited. A president of the American Historical Association, he was once the librarian of Princeton, and it was while in that job that he collected and microfilmed something like 11,000 letters of H. L. Mencken.*

ON the evening of January 16, 1899, Henry Mencken, a stripling of eighteen who worked by day in the tobacco firm of Aug. Mencken & Bro., arrayed in his best suit and wearing a high stiff collar with an Ascot tie, presented himself before Max Ways of the old Baltimore *Morning Herald,* seeking employment as a reporter. The spectacle, as he himself later confessed, was hardly one to exhilarate a city editor. He looked frail and smelled of the lamp, having read so omnivorously in his teens as to endanger his health. He was educated only to the extent of having been graduated from Baltimore Polytechnic and exposed at nine to *Huckleberry Finn,* an event he later described as "the most stupendous of my whole life." He was without experience as a reporter, and had published nothing save a verse or two in a rival paper which, under the circumstances, he thought it better not to mention. He knew little of the mysteries of the city room and nothing at all of those of the press room.

Yet Ways gave Mencken the chance to become a newspaperman,

thereby making this a momentous meeting in the history of American journalism, though it is more correct to say that the editor merely recognized the inevitable. At this first interview, he gave the stock answer — no vacancy, come back again — and Mencken did come back, night after night for weeks on end, even when the trolleys were snowbound, until at last he was told to seek a story in an outlying village. He leapt at the chance, and at Govanstown some unknown druggist, one of the few citizens still awake, supplied the local happenings. Late that night Mencken wrote and rewrote his first story:

"A horse, a buggy and several sets of harness, valued in all at about $250, were stolen last night from the stable of Howard Quinlan, near Kingsville. The county police are at work on the case, but so far no trace of either thieves or booty has been found."

This was competent, but scarcely immortal prose. Yet when the exhausted author, up with the milkman to search it out in the morning paper, found it printed exactly as he had written it, he experienced a thrill that ended forever his career as a tobacconist. Thenceforth he was a newspaperman. The handling of words, the probing of their origins and precise meanings, the shaping of a style that belonged to him and to no one else — these were the surest means, as they were also the loneliest and the most agonizing, for meeting his deepest need of expression.

From this fountainhead flowed a great stream of literally millions of words of reporting, editorials, essays, commentary, articles and books, all of it bearing the unmistakable stamp of individuality possessed by a master craftsman who was also a man of honor, of intellectual curiosity, of humanity and of superb wit. He became famous as an editor, first of *The Smart Set* and then of *The American Mercury* and as an author of the Prejudices series, *In Defense of Women, Notes on Democracy, Making a President, Treatise on the Gods,* the mellow reminisences of the *Days* volumes, and the astonishing performance in *The American Language* and its supplements which lifted philology, a subject that generates pedantry almost spontaneously, to the level of popular literature.

In the fall of 1948, when Mencken suffered a stroke, the flow came to a halt. He recovered most of his physical vigor, but there was no new writing under the famous signature. A few months before his death, however, Mencken's secretary discovered the notebooks published in *Minority Report*.* Mencken meant them to be published. He wrote in the preface:

Ever since my earliest attempts as an author I have followed the somewhat banal practice of setting down notions as they came to me . . . and then throwing these notes into a bin. Out of that bin have come a couple of dozen books and pamphlets and an almost innumerable swarm of magazine and newspaper articles, but still the raw materials kept mounting faster than I could work them up, so I am printing herewith some select samples of them . . .

In the twenties, with so many asserting their individuality that the idea of revolt became itself a sort of cult of conformity, Mencken's *American Mercury* was the bible of the undergraduate and his word the alpha and omega of the emancipated. His scorn of the Uplifters, the Yahoos, the Wowsers, the Booboisie — the very words need explanation today — was repeated endlessly by many who did not realize that his fulminations proceeded from a solid foundation of self-discipline, learning and an inborn passion for the decencies embedded in the Bill of Rights. This more or less blind adulation filled him with something akin to contempt, for he knew that, at best, on another day his followers would pant after different gods and, at worst, he himself would occupy the role of one of the "jitney Messiahs" upon whom he directed his withering blasts. Yet in a measure he was trapped, and forced to permit the follies and aberrations of humanity to employ his superb gifts. He was producing brilliant pyrotechnics against stupidity long before the twenties, and continued to do so long

* New York: Alfred Knopf, 1956.

afterward, but, as the event seems to have proved, this is likely to be the most ephemeral part of his work. His more enduring monuments seem to be promised in the incomparable autobiographical and linguistic volumes.

Yet, all of his belaboring of theologians, politicians and pedagogues was in truth a defense of religion, democracy and learning. He was affronted by attempts to explain the unknowable in terms of the not worth knowing. His blast against democracy was aimed at the detractors of the free man and the cheapeners of free institutions. His ridicule of jargon, pedantry, and obscurantism in education was a blow in behalf of the seeker after truth. He was born without envy and, by his own confession, "with no more public spirit than a cat," yet his blows against the reigning potentates in religion, in politics, and in education would scarcely have been delivered with such fury if he had not felt his own beliefs profaned by their actions. His doubts rested on certainty, his pessimism on an ultimate optimism, even when he hid his sensitive nature behind a cosmic guffaw.

The nature of those beliefs is made apparent in *Minority Report,* whose title is more painfully apt today than it would have been in the twenties. This volume of selected observations culled during "long years devoted to the pursuit, anatomizing and embalming of ideas," contains more than four hundred items, running from a line or so to several pages. They cover theology, capitalism, communism, education, philosophy, the Negro, the Jew, love, poetry, universal suffrage, democracy, altruism, fashion, adultery, the clergy, Haeckel's recapitulation theory, ethics, canon law, the female moron, life in Mississippi, and a great many other topics familiar to the seasoned Mencken reader, arranged in no more systematic order.

Some of the familiar landmarks still stand out boldly — that belief in immortality is a vestige of childish egoism; that the scientist "who yields anything to theology, however slight, is yielding to ignorance and false pretenses": that the United

States has not only failed to produce a genuine aristocracy but has also failed to produce an indigenous intelligentsia; that in a democracy "the man who is barely human is treated as if he were the peer of Aristotle; that human life is basically a comedy; that God made a bungling job of the human body, forcing man "to lug around a frame packed with defects, from imperfectly centered eyes to weakly arched feet"; that no other religious system has such troubles with the sex question as Christianity does, and that it is "indeed, the most unhealthy of religions"; that it is impossible for a metaphysician to state his ideas in plain English, most of those ideas being basically nonsensical; that the only part of the Bill of Rights still effective is that prohibiting the quartering of troops on citizens in time of peace.

Further, that democracy, by encouraging the incompetent and envious man, throws its weight against every rational concept of honor, honesty, and common decency; that the proverbial wisdom of the East is "even more blowsy and senseless than the metaphysics of the West"; that the "existence of most human beings is of absolutely no significance to history or to human progress"; that there are some people, "the bibliobibuli," who read too much and are constantly drunk on books, as other men are drunk on whisky or religion; that it "is impossible to imagine the universe run by a wise, just and omnipotent God, but it is quite easy to imagine it run by a board of gods," and if such a board "actually exists it operates precisely like the board of a corporation that is losing money." And so on.

There is no question but that this reflects the minority view, and the faithful Mencken followers will be saddened to consider that it is also a final report. But they will be heartened to know that the Old Master went down with the flag still flying, even snapping more saucily than ever, and they will refuse to believe that the vast bin from which these thoughts were culled has become empty.

GERMAINE BRÉE

Albert Camus: An Essay in Appreciation

Because she was a friend of Albert Camus as well as a close student of his work, Germaine Brée wrote from the heart the appreciation that appears below. She is the author of studies of Camus, of André Gide and Marcel Proust. At present she is a professor at the Institute for Research in the Humanities at the University of Wisconsin.

"IN THE DREAM of life is man who finds his truths and loses them, on death's earth, in order to return through wars, clamor, the passion for justice and love, through suffering too, toward that peaceful land where death itself is a happy silence." Two years after he wrote these words Albert Camus died, at forty-six, in a brutal and senseless accident. Even those who did not know him felt his death as a personal loss. For his friends, it was and would always remain an unbearable, an irreparable catastrophe.

For France, the loss is immeasurable, but not for France alone. Camus, not long before his death spoke to me of his "dialogue" with his American readers and of the inner strength he had drawn from their understanding. He had planned to come back to America when the book he was writing was finished. "No," he wrote me later, "I shall not come to New York for the time being; I am working in seclusion at Lourmarin and I don't wish to be diverted from this interminable labor. Not without regrets for New York and America — but it is only a visit postponed."

Camus died too early, in the full maturing of his work. After

he was awarded the Nobel Prize he had withdrawn to the quiet
village of Lourmarin, in the south of France, where he now lies
buried, there to spend a part of his time. He liked the dry, bare
foothills of the Alps, the small scattered villages, the presence
nearby of his friend, the poet René Char. In the hills around
Lourmarin one encounters silent, isolated houses: the ruins of the
Marquis de Sade's château; a strange Venetian type of fortress,
hidden in a hollow and from which only a slim turret rises toward
the sky, above the curve of the hills; an enclosure of high walls
and locked gates beyond which, in an invisible house, lives another solitary human being. "Three conceptions of solitude,"
commented Camus, half amusedly, half sympathetically, no doubt
comparing them with his own. His own house was set at the
edge of the village.

Camus fully enjoyed too his life as stage director and producer
in Paris. "Why am I active in the theatre? I've often wondered.
The only answer I have found up to now will probably seem to
you discouraging in its banality; simply, the theatre is one of the
places in the world where I am happiest." He was not a recluse.
He had measured the dangers of his spectacular celebrity and had
wished to reserve for himself a zone of tranquillity "rich in
shadow and in works that belong only to me."

Like Camus' visit to America, those works which were to come
out of the solitude of Lourmarin are forever postponed. For us
his death is grievous. How much more grievous for Camus himself, cut off so violently at a time when he felt that there was so
much still to say, that his "work was not begun."

Since 1944, for many of his contemporaries, Camus seemed
more fully present than any other man. His words carried more
weight, perhaps because he never ceased to be, as Sartre once
said, "a real person"; a man complex, vulnerable, generous and
endearing; exact and quiet in speech though sometimes quick to
anger; a man deeply involved and yet strangely detached; a man

modest yet stubborn and occasionally mistaken, but always eventually, scrupulously honest, who struggled to remain, however exceptional the circumstances and whatever the cost, "a man like all men." He was in his early twenties when he began to write. By the time he was twenty-five he had published two small volumes of essays — *L'Envers et l'Endroit* and *Noces* — which today have lost none of their freshness.

From the outset, what Camus had to express was his love of life itself. The natural, sensuous beauty of his native Algeria was a source of joy so deep that it was almost all-sufficient. It nourished a violent hatred of death, that definitive "exile from beauty," which gave the young man an intense and urgent vision of his own enigmatic destiny. "I have always felt," he later wrote, "that I lived on the high seas, menaced, at the heart of a royal happiness."

The menace was real: illness, an illness which never left him, the harrowing life of the Resistance and finally the chance mishap on the road. But Camus was always concerned, not so much with the menace as with the "royal happiness" at its very heart. In *Caligula,* the first play Camus wrote, when the mad emperor decides to incarnate the ironic fate that governs our lives, he is opposed, though understood, by the young poet, in love with life's beauty, and by the man who, knowing life's futility, knows too, unlike Caligula, the value of human happiness. Camus' "passion for justice" was a facet of this exigency of happiness, as was also his unremitting revolt against all that threatens individual freedom.

It was not, however, his personal experience as such that Camus wanted to communicate. It served only as a point of departure. In Camus' eyes no writer in our time can hope to create a valid work of art who has not, in some measure, and to the limits of his power, attempted to rethink the fundamental problems of life common to us all, reliving them first within the concrete context of today's world. He diagnosed as one of the characteristics of our age a divorce — or gap — between our automatic adherence to certain formulae and institutions, the church among others, and the more or less covert intellectual assumptions by which we live. In that gap, between the mask and the reality, lies the fertile realm of our indifference — indifference to life, indifference to death (ours and that of others), indifference to suffering. *The Stranger, The Myth of Sisyphus, Caligula, The Misunderstanding* are all literary explorations of this theme. The collective experience of World War II taxed to the utmost Camus' will to give some form, some unity, to events lived amid disorder and consternation. *The Plague, The Rebel, The Just Assassins,* are the widely known products of that time.

Creation, Camus once said, begins at the limit where thought ends; and again, "a creative period in art can be defined as an order of style applied to the disorder of an age." Camus, in these terms, was essentially an artist. Through thought he attempted to elucidate his own experience, objectifying it; where thought stopped, uncomprehending, creation began. Of necessity, it was limited, welded to the urgent, and, for a time, to the ugly problems of the moment: mass murder, for example, or the dialectics of political assassination. From these there was, for Camus, no escape, if, as an artist, he was to preserve his integrity. To this integrity, which cost him so much in time, in effort, in apparent diversion from his work, he owes his unique position.

Camus was a versatile writer, with a mastery of style almost unique among his contemporaries. "The last of the heirs of Chateaubriand," Sartre called him. His language is rich in imagery and highly controlled. He was a "Latin," it has often been said, though Camus himself felt more closely in sympathy with the Greeks. From the Greeks, from the French classics he inherited his sense of structure, his desire to create balanced, ordered and carefully stylized works, and through them to arrive at an objective expression of his own experience, a new experience valid precisely through its ordering.

"The idea that every writer must of necessity write about himself, is one of the puerile notions we have inherited from romanticism," he wrote. "It is not at all impossible that a writer may be more interested in others, or in his time, or in familiar myths . . . As far as possible I should have liked to be an objective writer. I call objective a writer who sets himself subjects without ever taking himself as an object." Each one of his works, whether literary or political in nature, has that quality.

The characters he creates tend, therefore, to become, in Camus' terms, "mythical"; in our own terms, perhaps, more exactly allegorical. Situations, conflicts and characters give shape and substance to a highly imaginative transfer of emotions and thought. Meursault — the Stranger; the Plague; Clamence — the hero of *The Fall;* Caligula, are embodiment of attitudes, feelings or experiences that Camus felt were latent among us. This is true too of the Promethean image of man, as rebel, which gave its unity to Camus' long meditation on revolt.

The collective experience of the thirties and forties, with which Camus as an artist felt he must in some way come to terms, was marked by brutality, a brutality arising in Camus' eyes from the nihilism extant among us. To describe it directly would have been merely to perpetuate it twice and art, according to Camus, can only be on the side of justice, freedom and beauty against violence, brutality and death. Each of his books therefore is a statement, through art, of the experience explored and at the same time marks a stage in the development of his thought.

Therein, for our generation, lies the great attraction of his work. "If, a few centuries from now," wrote a French critic of *The Stranger,* "only this short tale were left as witness to what man is today, it would be enough to give a fair image of what we are." There is no living writer in France, perhaps even in Europe, who so consistently gave his contemporaries reason to attempt "to serve human dignity by means which remain honorable in the midst of a history which is not honorable."

Slowly, in his last years, the tensions had lessened. *The Fall* and *Exile and the Kingdom* seemed to be exploring new paths. The work accomplished since the first two small volumes published in Algiers is considerable: novels, short stories, plays, essays, articles, prefaces. "I know with certainty that a man's work is nothing but the long journey to recover, through the detours of art, the two or three simple and great images which first gained access to his heart," he wrote in 1957 and, a few years before, "every artist, no doubt, is in quest of his truth. If he is great, each work brings him closer to it, or, at least, gravitates more closely to that central, hidden sun, where all, one day, will be consumed."

THE AUTHOR'S OWN WORDS

There is also a will to live without refusing anything of life which is the virtue that I most admire in this world. — *L'Eté*

. . .

All my horror of dying is contained in my jealous passion for life. I am jealous of those who will continue to live and for whom flowers and the desire of women will give all their flesh and blood meaning. I am jealous because I love life too much not to be an egoist. What is eternity to me? — *Noces*

. . .

The problem is to serve human dignity by means which remain honorable in the midst of a history which is not honorable. — *Actuelles 1*

. . .

From a certain point of view the meaning of tomorrow's history is not what we think it to be. It is contained in the struggle between creativity and inquisition. — *L'Eté*

. . .

Real generosity toward the future consists in giving all to what is present. — *L'Homme révolté*

. . .

My role, I know, is not to transform the world, nor man: for that I have not virtues enough, nor clearsightedness. But it consists, perhaps, in serving, where I can, those few values without which a world, even transformed, is not worth living in, without which a man, even new, would not be worthy of respect. — *Actuelles 1*

. . .

We live with a few familiar ideas. Two or three. In our chance encounters with worlds and men, we polish, we transform them. It takes ten years to have an idea all one's own — about which one can speak. Naturally, it's a little discouraging. — *Noces*

ARTHUR MIZENER

John Steinbeck and His World

[Another reappraisal by Mr. Mizener, and facts about him, are on page 154.]

PROBABLY everyone who was adult in the late thirties has a special, warm spot in his memory for the books John Steinbeck wrote then. It was a time when the consciences of Americans were shocked into an awareness of the suffering imposed on helpless people by unemployment and poverty. We became responsive to even feeble renderings of such suffering and, with the typically impatient idealism of Americans, eager to be offered a course of action that sounded, however superficially, as if it would remedy the situation. As one publisher wryly observed, it was smart to be Marxist then. There was a generous and undiscriminating appetite for even bad proletarian novels in the thirties, not unlike the appetite of a hundred years earlier for abolitionist novels like *Uncle Tom's Cabin*.

It was in this atmosphere that Steinbeck's best novel, *The Grapes of Wrath* (1939) achieved its immense popularity. It was then that his thinly fictionalized though — in itself — stimulating debate on Communist strike tactics, *In Dubious Battle* (1939), had its special success with intellectuals. The response we felt to these books seemed to be wholly justified by Steinbeck's lesser works of the period, in which his strong sympathy for the poor and simple and his deep if sentimental conviction of their purity of heart were displayed in happy, charming books like *Tortilla Flat*

(1935) and in tragedies of the joys and sufferings of the young — whether in fact or in mental development — such as *The Red Pony* (1938) and *Of Mice and Men* (1937).

After *The Grapes of Wrath* at the end of the thirties, most serious readers seem to have ceased to read him. It is a fascinating if somewhat melancholy task to reread these books in the sixties, when our feelings are no longer under the special influences that affected them strongly in the thirties. Steinbeck's novel of the sixties, *The Winter of Our Discontent* (1961), shows considerable intellectual discipline and a good deal of careful planning and execution; it is full of local color and at times is even witty. Even so, there is something unsatisfactory about it, some lifelessness, as if the author's feelings had attached themselves to an abstract idea about New England life or even American life as a whole and the story, for all its painstakingly local color and its careful execution, was merely a mechanically constructed occasion for the display of his idea.

There is a hint here of what is in fact glaringly obvious in Steinbeck's less disciplined novels, a hint of some discontinuity between the narrative surface and the symbolized meaning of the novel. It is his limitation, that is, to care so much for the abstractly formulated moral of his story that, in all his novels to some extent, and in many to an intolerable extent, the moral disorts the story. He is an incurable amateur philosopher of the kind Francis Bacon had in mind when he remarked that this kind of mind "snatches from experience a variety of common instances, neither duly ascertained nor diligently examined and weighed, and leaves all the rest to meditation and agitation of wit."

There is in our time a powerful and fashionable prejudice against "agitation of wit" in the novel, and we ought to be on our guard against it. But there cannot be much question that when such agitation of wit is in itself of bad quality and also causes the novelist to make his representation of the world a mere illustration of it, it is a serious defect. Both these things are true of a great deal of Steinbeck's work. The only clear exceptions are the stories in which he appears to be drawing on personal memories so vivid to him that his impulse to philosophize them is temporarily subdued.

Something like this appears to have happened in *The Red Pony*. In any event, this story of the boy who grew up in the Salinas Valley, in the shadows of "The Great Mountains," has an integrity, a responsibility to experience and a consequent unity of surface and symbol that Steinbeck has never achieved since. We are wholly convinced by Jody's feeling for the life of nature and by its culmination in his love for his red pony and his grief at its death. We accept as natural his feelings about the successful if terrible birth of Nellie's colt — "He tried to be glad because of the colt, but the bloody face, and the haunted, tired eyes of Billy Buck hung in the air ahead of him." We can accept the mysterious Gitano, who comes home to die and eventually rides off into the Gabilan Mountains carrying his beautiful rapier; we can even accept Grandfather, the tiresome old man who had somehow felt the mystical power of the westering people he had led, that "whole bunch of people made into one big crawling beast." "I tell these old stories," Grandfather says, "but they're not what I want to tell. I only know how I want people to feel when I tell them."

There are things in *The Red Pony* that, with hindsight, we probably feel uncomfortable about: the business of the red pony and Nellie's colt has a tendency to turn into a faintly corny fable about "the terrible beauty that death gives life"; Gitano with his rapier and his riding off into the mountains has just a touch of third-rate fiction's stock portentousness. But I think these things would not bother a reader unacquainted with the rest of Steinbeck's fiction. It is only because we know what they have grown into that they bother us.

Apart from *The Red Pony,* Steinbeck has written two kinds of fiction, each of which has had, in his hands, its special limitations. The first kind is the loosely organized collection of stories about a special group of people; the second is the "philosophical" novel, in which the author is primarily concerned with some abstract idea for solving a social problem or explaining human nature. He began writing the first kind of book with *The Pastures of Heaven* (1932). We see Las Pasturas del Cielo first through the eyes of a Spanish corporal, up to the dirty business of enslaving the Indians in the name of the Church. "Holy Mother!" he whispers. "Here are the green pastures of Heaven to which our Lord leadeth us." We see it last, one hundred and fifty years later, through the eyes of a bus driver: "I guess it sounds kind of funny to you folks, but I always like to look down there and think how quiet and easy a man could live on a little place." In this frame, the skillful little stories about the valley become images of Man living happily the simple good life of Nature, and there is in them all the slightly saccharine flavor of the prologue and epilogue.

Steinbeck has been exploiting this vein at odd intervals ever since, most notably — or at least popularly — in *Tortilla Flat,* in which the childlike *paisanos* live a life of divine natural innocence and gaiety. I suppose the sentimental charm of *Tortilla Flat* is harmless enough, as we do not take the conception of life that lies behind it too literally. But Steinbeck's own tendency to do so is clear from his Preface: "when you speak of Danny's house you are understood to mean a unit of which the parts are men, from which came sweetness and joy, philanthropy and, in the end, a mystic sorrow. For Danny's house was not unlike the Round Table, and Danny's friends were not unlike the knights." This "mystic sorrow" is glaringly serious in *Of Mice and Men* and spreads like a cancer through the second kind of book Steinbeck has written.

This second kind, the "philosophical novel," begins with *In Dubious Battle,* a novel of which it can be said that it is slightly superior to Steinbeck's other novels of this kind in so far as the Marxist ideas of its protagonist, Mac, have a certain order and clarity (though Steinbeck's own kind of moony philosophizing leaks into the book through Doc Burton). But if the doctrine of the book has a superior clarity, it also destroys the action of the book nearly completely. The story of *In Dubious Battle,* except for one or two scenes of action, is a sketchy illustration for a sermon. "I don't know why it is," Mac says to Jim, "but every time I talk to you I either end up soap-boxing or giving a lecture." It is all too true.

Moreover, we are again reminded of Steinbeck's future by two rather ominous aspects of the book. One is his preoccupation with the mystical sense of well-being that descends on a man when he becomes part of a group, a preoccupation that reminds us not only of Grandfather in *The Red Pony* but of one of Steinbeck's major subjects for philosophizing in nearly all his later books. The other ominous sign in *In Dubious Battle* is the author's habit of reinterpreting either history, or, more frequently, the Bible, to make them conform to his "philosophy." Thus Jim treats us to a schoolboy summary of the Battle of Salamis in order to explain a piece of strike tactics and is reminded — at painful length — by an anonymous woman combing her hair of an image of the Virgin he has seen in a church — "she had the same kind of a smile, wise and cool and sure."

At the end of *The Moon Is Down* (1942) Socrates turns out to be like Steinbeck's conception of an anti-Nazi mayor, but it is in *East of Eden* (1952) that this habit of reducing experience to "profound" abstractions and then identifying them with some genuinely great image of our experience reaches an appalling climax. In this book the whole absurd "philosophical" point of the story is made analogous to the original account of the expul-

sion: "And the Lord set a mark upon Cain. . . . and Cain went
out from the presence of the Lord and dwelt in the land of Nod
on the east of Eden." This analogy is hammered home over and
over again, to the almost complete destruction of the novel's life,
in endless sermons by innumerable wise men (including an in-
scrutable Oriental who reads us long passages from Marcus Au-
relius.)

"All novels, all poetry, are built on the never-ending contest
in ourselves of good and evil," the narrator of *East of Eden* asserts
with dazzling profundity, and Steinbeck turns all his characters
into monsters of good or evil to prove it. "I believe," his narrator
says elsewhere, "there are monsters born in the world to human
parents"; Steinbeck's heroine is clearly one of them. She is an
exquisitely beautiful woman, a modern Duessa, "Till on a day
. . . I chaunst to see her in her proper hew,/Bathing her selfe
. . ./A filthy, foule old woman I did view,/That ever to have
toucht her, I did deadly rew." Having made Cathy thus implausibly monstrous, Steinbeck then implausibly makes her human, at least to the extent of giving her a conscience in order
that she may be tortured by guilt and commit suicide. A more
unconvincing muddle of effects it is hard to imagine a novelist of
Steinbeck's experience producing, except out of some deeply sin-
cere concern for the wrong kind of thing.

But perhaps the most painful example of the destructive effect
of his love of philosophizing is his most famous novel, *The Grapes
of Wrath,* because here is a book that comes close to making real
all that is best in Steinbeck, his deep feeling for simple people,
especially for their innocent helplessness and their instinctive
courage, his love of the land, his sense of the grandeur man
sometimes achieves when he is "westering" en masse. Much of
the time these feelings get into *The Grapes of Wrath* undistorted,
mostly into the small particulars of the Joads' saga-like journey,
especially those that have to do with their car. But Steinbeck

cannot resist watering down his fine action with a theory that is constantly falsifying it.

When the hard-boiled waitress, Mae, is gruffly moved to sell the proud Joads food at half price, I think we feel a little uncomfortable; and when the truck drivers pay for the food and Mae sighs "reverently," "Truck drivers," I think we are sure that Steinbeck's theory of what human nature ought to be has made him forget all he has observed of what men are. This kind of falsification occurs all too frequently in *The Grapes of Wrath;* the characters are constantly being forced to display in an implausible way Steinbeck's theory about them; "What we got lef' in the world," says Ma. "Nothin' but us. Nothin' but the folks." Just folks, folks.

Perhaps those Europeans who awarded the Nobel Prize in Literature to John Steinbeck in 1962 were simply behind the times and in all sincerity believe that the judgments of the thirties are still the established judgments. This attitude would be re-enforced, from one direction, by the European social democrat's inclination to place a very high value on sentimental humanitarianism, especially when it is displayed about the poor, especially when these poor exist in a society that is supposed by many of them to be the last stronghold of uncontrolled capitalist exploitation. It would be re-enforced, from another direction, by the lingering European dream of America as a "natural," even in some sense primitive, place; the effect of this dream is plain enough in the European popularity of Cooper and Jack London, and once led an otherwise distinguished European intellectual to say — apparently quite without irony — that our greatest writer was Dashiell Hammett.

Perhaps the explanation is even simpler. Perhaps the time had come around for some American to receive the award, and among Europeans Steinbeck turned out to be, for one or another reason, the most widely read American author, just as Sinclair

Lewis was when he received the Nobel Prize in 1930. Neither of these explanations is, I am afraid, very flattering. But it is difficult to find a flattering explanation for awarding this most distinguished of literary prizes to a writer whose real but limited talent is, in his best books, watered down by tenth-rate philosophizing and, in his worst books, is overwhelmed by it.

WILLIAM T. MOYNIHAN

Boily Boy and Bard

William Moynihan is a critic of fiction and verse with special concern for the work of Dylan Thomas. He is assistant professor of English at the University of Connecticut.

I USED to think," Dylan Thomas said, "that once a writer became a man of letters, if only for ten minutes, he was done for." When Thomas died suddenly in 1953, he escaped all the surging forces of chance and criticism that were conspiring to make him a man of letters in his lifetime, but in the years since his death these same forces have shaped him into one of the most distinctive figures of English poetry.

The "explosive bloodbursts of a boily boy" (as he described his early poems) rocked London in 1934, when he was twenty. The poetry of the youth from Swansea, Wales, was hailed as "the most absolute poetry . . . written in our time" and also scorned as "an unconducted tour of Bedlam." Striding, as he wrote, "on two levels" in a "fusion of rose and male motion," "in a wind on fire from green Adam's cradle," he won an ever-widening audience. He became, especially during his American appearances in the early nineteen-fifties, the discoverer of a new public, a large popular audience whose existence had scarcely been realized. The last years of his life were a maelstrom of public adulation, and when he died at the age of thirty-nine, the profession of grief was unprecedented in this century.

In the afterglow of this meteoric rise and blazing extinction, there was a prevalent sense of something having been worked with mirrors, of some sleight of voice. The literary world, as if expecting Thomas's reputation to shrink as rapidly as it had grown, often reduced him to a tree-worshiping romantic who had written one or two remarkable poems. His detractors cited him as an example of a poetic charlatan. An obvious British-American split also developed — the American affinity for the everlasting "yea," for poetry of exultation and affirmation, produced stanch exegetes and defenders, while British critics in general registered greater reservations.

For a time, his admirers remembered him mainly in rumors from the carnival of excess in which he had starred — and in recriminations about responsibility for his death. "One cannot tell the truth," wrote one of his friends. "It would be too harsh, too unbelievable; too rich, too deep, too wild, and too strange." As the grief and scandal subsided, the great public issue became the insinuation that America had killed him — a contention about as credible as the accusation that Blackwood's magazine had caused Keats' death.

Such recriminations, however, brought to painful light John Malcolm Brinnin's "intimate journal" (*Dylan Thomas in America*), which chronicled the poet's irreversible progress in self-destruction. His wife, Caitlin Thomas, seeking a "better truth" than Brinnin's, produced her own even more intimate journal (*Left-Over Life to Kill*), which read as if ghost-written by her husband and told of the grim and wailing life of a relatively young widow.

Whatever the sources of such passional outpourings, they are the stuff of legend. Critical acclaim and youthful death are insufficient in themselves to fashion a legendary literary figure. The death and the acclaim must create an aura of fatality, they must exist in the brilliance and doom of prophetic insight. And the doom is in no way better revealed than in mysterious suffering and scandalous death. Young Sir Philip Sidney died in battle, his contemporary Christopher Marlowe in a barroom brawl; but it is Marlowe's death which has enticed biographers — and undoubtedly much of the fascination lies in Marlowe's "dark" and "blasphemous" reputation. Thomas's life offers similar enticements. The son of a Welsh schoolmaster and the grandson of a minister, Thomas, seeking to bring to light "even more . . . than Freud could realize," was the *enfant terrible* of modern poetry. And his struggle against some inner demon, some ancient chaos of self, climaxing in the tubes and oxygen tent of his hospital ordeal, provokes a melancholy fascination.

Everything clearly autobiographical in his work has had unimaginable public success. Shortly after his death his bawdy and satiric play of a day in a small Welsh town, *Under Milk Wood,* rivaled popular plays on two continents. Emlyn Williams' readings from his autobiographical short stories were an instant hit both in London and on Broadway; his own recording of "A Child's Christmas in Wales" now appears each holiday with the regularity of Dickens' "A Christmas Carol."

"The black spit of the chapel fold . . . dying of women," the drunken man who had been "happy as the grass was green" and "prince of the apple towns," whose final poetry sang of "the sundering ultimate kingdom of genesis' thunder" — this poet has become legendary. Outwardly a Falstaff and inwardly a Faustus, Thomas was a personification not only of the poet but also of the alienation of modern man. A Faust with a bottle of beer instead of Helen and a satiric humor rather than satanic hallucination, a Falstaff babbling ineffable mysteries of man and dreaming of doom and apocalypse, Thomas in many respects summed up his era.

While his life has been fashioned into literary legend, his voice has added a new dimension to literary history. He will surely be remembered as the first in modern literature to be

both a maker and a speaker of poetry. The epic singers, from
Homer to the Welsh bards of the Middle Ages, held their places
as public performers as well as makers, but the art of public
reading had never been preserved, nor in fact much practiced,
after the advent of printing. Modern electronics have changed
that, both by enabling the poet to reach unprecedented hearers
and by preserving his own readings.

The effect of the poet's undying voice must loom large in time.
It is not difficult to imagine the posthumous impact of some
obscure Thomas Campion possessing the supple and haunting
resonance of a Dylan Thomas. A poor performance could have
detrimental effects on the reputation of some poets. But, allowing for the inevitable pendulum of taste, Thomas' pre-eminence
as a reader seems certain. The typical reader who shies away from
the printed complexities of his poems becomes incurably en-
tranced after hearing him recite. No other contemporary poet,
not even Robert Frost, has had quite the same effect.

Yet the tragic, roaring boy genius with the lilting and soaring
voice is only indirectly involved in the poetry. The biographical
catch phrases are only exciting eavesdroppings from backstage
and have little or nothing to do with the poetry — the high
mimesis that was performed upstage. As Yevgeny Yevtushenko
says at the beginning of his own autobiography, "A poet's autobiography is his poetry. Anything else can be only a footnote."
Thus, while general readers have been enthralled "to hear the
golden note turn in a groove," scholars, misled neither by the
legend nor by the voice, have been piecing out the perfections
and imperfections of Thomas' *Collected Poems.*

What does all this critical labor mean? It means that the stay-
ing power of Thomas extends beyond his legend and his elo-
quence. It also suggests a desire on the part of readers to understand the poetry as fully as possible. Though there is some truth
to his own judgment that "the poems most narrowly odd are

among [the] . . . earliest and that the later poems are wider and deeper," criticism has established that all of his poetry, both early and late, is the work of a genius. And, though dissimilar in many respects, his genius now seems comparable to that of Keats.

Though speculation persists as to what Thomas might have achieved if he had lived, there is in retrospect an esthetic completeness to his life and work. He moved surely through surrealistic, and romantic influences, developing and perfecting his poetry at each stage and climaxing his work with incomparable odes, such as his birthday poems, "In Country Sleep," "Over Sir John's Hill," and "In the White Giant's Thigh."

The poems often baffle and exasperate, but their tenor — from the dedication "for the love of man and in praise of God" to the final lines telling of the "Love for ever meridian" — is clear. His is a poetry of intensity and passionate awareness. *Collected Poems* tells each succeeding generation, in Walt Whitman's words, "This is no book, /Who touches this, touches a man."

Touch Thomas' poems wherever one will, there is the madness and the splendor of man. He sought out the truth of sense and imagination and found that "when logics die, /The secret of the soil grows through the eye." The secrets he revealed through unborn embryos and sacerdotal herons are finally the secrets of mankind itself: "Four elements and five Senses, and man a spirit of love."

In the confidence of youth, rebellious and uncompromising, Thomas was the "dark denier." But in the chaos of his "voyage to ruin" he became the celebrator, the psalmist of affirmation, who wrote:

> . . . *the closer I move*
> *To death, one man through his sundered hulks,*
> *The louder the sun blooms*
> *And the tusked, ramshackling sea exults.*

William Faulkner, 1897-1962

I. IRVING HOWE
A Talent of Wild Abundance

Irving Howe, professor of English at Hunter College, has been a prolific writer of essays on politics, cultural history, literature, one could almost say the human condition. Some of these have been collected in his book, A World More Attractive. *"A Talent of Wild Abundance" was written on the occasion of Faulkner's death.*

IT IS a tribute to William Faulkner, to whom death came suddenly on July 6, 1962, that we know so little about his personal life. In an age of publicity, when journalists and even scholars keep searching for "colorful" items of trivia, Faulkner preserved a pleasing aloofness. The American cult of personality repelled him; and if any trouble or pathos darkened his last years, there is a seemliness in the fact that these remained his own trouble, his own pathos, unrecorded by popular columnists or sophisticated magazines. In personal bearing, as in public conduct, Faulkner suggested that aura of independence — less pride than shyness and less shyness than reticence — which he valued so much in his characters.

The lament over wasted gifts and truncated careers that has become familiar in discussions of American literature has very little bearing upon Faulkner. To the limits of his talent and energy, he was a fulfilled writer. His great creative period, a blazing outburst of composition, came between 1929 and 1942, between *The Sound and the Fury* and *Go Down, Moses.* In those years he wrote five or six novels of the first rank, one of them, *The Sound and the Fury,* sustaining comparison with the highest achievements of European modernism; he wrote seven or eight stories that are certain to survive; and there is a good deal of other work frequently arresting and intermittently distinguished. No other American novelist except Henry James can match this record of creative energy.

There was not, to be sure, the kind of culmination in Faulkner's career, the serene and masterful "art of old age," which came so radiantly at the end of James' life. Faulkner's work during the last twenty years has been that of a man unwilling to rest in the security of his fame, searching for new subjects and forms, stumbling into patches of sterility, and strained toward encompassing moral fables beyond the reach of his imagination. Still, one wishes to honor him even for these partial failures: He was never content, nor cautious, nor relaxed. And while his readers naturally wish he had lived on for many years, writing more stories about Yoknapatawpha County and creating more figures like Ratliff, Ike McCaslin, Ditsey and Lena Grove, it is important to stress the profoundly satisfying truth that in its essential contours his work stands complete. His deepest energies, his true vision now live in the printed page. To twist Auden's phrase about Yeats, Faulkner became his writing.

At the moment, what strikes one most of all is the sheer, wild abundance of his talent. Like a good many American writers before him, Faulkner was "a natural," a master of excess. Among American novelists of the present century, only he created a world that is complete in itself: Yoknapatawpha County, an imaginary version of his northern Mississippi homeland. In book after book, that world is evoked with a knowledge so deep and expert as almost to be called ancestral; yet it also provided a fictional landscape in which many of the central modern experiences, far transcending the immediate troubles of the South, are enacted.

The characters kept pouring out, drawn in high bold colors,

vibrating with desire and warmth, driven by the most fundamental and often extreme passions. It is a simple test, a somewhat unfashionable one among contemporary critics, but in my
opinion utterly decisive: which American novelist, again except
James, has provided us with such a rich profusion of figures who
remain alive in memory, to become the abiding company of our
lives? Benjy Compson, the pure and speechless idiot clutching
his flower; Joe Christmas, plunging through the swamps in
quest for a life that would be defined neither by whiteness nor
blackness of skin; Addie Bundren, the poor-white mother clamp-
ing the destinies of her children even as she lay dying; Popeye,
the gruesome archetype of viciousness; Ike McCaslin, the ascetic
hero of Yoknapatawpha returning for the last time to the hunting camp that has become a symbol of lost virtue; Flem Snopes,
comic and terrible, the devil's own man in the back country —
the list could be multiplied several times over and not begin to
exhaust Faulkner's inventiveness.

But for all its power as spectacle, and partly through its power
as spectacle, the Yoknapatawpha saga contains a serious moral
inquiry into the nature of modern existence. Faulkner's work is
almost always problematical, the effort of a troubled mind to
come to terms with and, if necessary, learn to discard the inherited biases of his tradition. In his work, as in the work of all
significant modern writers, questions lead but to other questions.
He begins with fixed assumptions and ends with fluid problems.
A facile concern for public honor soon gives way to a devotion to
private integrity. Conventional Southern attitudes are subjected,
in novel after novel, to an increasingly corrosive examination,
so that in the end Faulkner feels toward his homeland a mixture
of pride and disgust, love and contempt.

Finally, it is the Negro who provides the crux of his moral
development. From the stereotyped Negro figures of his early
books to the tortured rebellion of Joe Christmas and the haughty

irascibility of Lucas Beauchamp, there is a steady progress in humaneness, respect and guilt.

The living memory of Christian faith colored Faulkner's imagination, but Christianity could not be for him an assured answer or ready comfort. Nor could any other system of belief or thought. Faulkner's characters may be provincials, and often ill-educated ones, but they are also thinking men who struggle with the problems of moral life which beset human beings at any time and the problems of a deracinated and discordant culture which particularly beset them in our own time. What matters in Faulkner's world is neither success nor failure, happiness nor misery, but the constant readiness to live out the requirements of a man to exhaust, even destroy himself in the effort to fulfill his sense of humanity. It is a world in which vulnerability, the openness to the most painful of experiences, is regarded by Faulkner as a major virtue; a world in which a man defines himself through his suffering. And that is one reason Faulkner is a novelist of extreme situations: he wishes to see, and to make his readers see, the commanding moments of human choice at their most intense, most dramatic, even most grotesque.

Faulkner is a difficult writer: Let no critic dissuade anyone from that truth. He is often hard on the English language, tyrannizing over it and twisting it, sometimes because he loses control, more often because he wishes so desperately to break into the marrow of an experience. He is a difficult writer because he experiments restlessly, takes high rhetorical chances, rejects the fashionable cult of understatement in favor of a full range of expression. He will use any strategy, any device to shake the reader, be it comedy, melodrama, horror, or confusion; he breaks past the austere containments of the modern "art novel" and demands not merely a maximum of attention but also, at times, a willingness to suspend the conventions of literary decorum. But at his best — in *The Sound and the Fury, As I Lay Dying,* and *Light in August* — he satisfies the standard proposed by Thomas Mann when he remarked that "the highest and profoundest claim to feeling is to a stage of intellectuality and formal strictness."

Tastes change, and predictions of immortality are notoriously dangerous. But insofar as anyone can speak with some assurance on this matter, it now seems certain that William Faulkner will be judged the greatest novelist America produced in the first half of the twentieth century. "Sole and exclusive proprietor of Yoknapatawpha County," as he once playfully called himself, Faulkner has left a body of work that will survive, a gift to ourselves and the future.

2. JOSEPH BLOTNER
The Books He Loved Best

Joseph Blotner is a member of the English faculty at the University of Virginia where William Faulkner, during his last years, was writer in residence. He is at work on the novelist's authorized biography.

A FOREIGN literary critic writing in the thirties commented that William Faulkner suffered from the disadvantage of not being able to test out some of his literary ideas around a café table. That kind of assumption — shared by some native critics who should have known better — rested on the idea of the Mississippi novelist as another untutored genius warbling his native wood notes wild. The comment was made, of course, in safe ignorance of the half year in New Orleans where he spent some of his apprenticeship in the company of Sherwood Anderson and a number of other literary lights of considerable sophistication if lesser candlepower.

Shortly thereafter he saw the cafés of Paris — with customers such as James Joyce patronizing them — even if, characteristically, he did not spend much time or talk in them. The critic was also unaware, however, of another factor that nullified the stereotype. It was the absorbing interest literary technique had always held for him and the enormous amount of reading he had done in studying it. The contents of his library reveal something of the extent of this interest and the richness of the literary background on which he could draw from early childhood.

In a foreword to a late collection of his work he recalled his reading in his grandfather's library. After the grandfather's death, a number of these books went to form the basis of Faulkner's own library. It was expanded not only by purchases the young novelist made and gifts he received, but also by books originally acquired by his grandmother, his father and mother, and his brothers as well. And when he married, a number of books from his wife and her cultivated family were added. Later, as his fame and reputation increased, the mail often brought not just fan letters but unsolicited books from authors and publishers, often inscribed but seldom, apparently, read. At the time of William Faulkner's death last year his library held close to twelve hundred volumes drawn from more than two dozen literatures.

Most of these books were housed in the tall shelves lining the walls of the roomy, comfortable library of Rowan Oak, the Faulkners' handsome, ante-bellum home in Oxford. Some of them filled his study's bookshelves and a few hundred had been collected in Charlottesville, Virginia, where the Faulkners resided part of the time during the last six years of his life. A fond grandfather, as well as a man always intensely imbued with the sense of tradition and family continuity, he was accumulating books for the use of his grandchildren as they grew, as his own grandfather had done more than half a century before.

William Faulkner did not, like many readers, scribble his reactions to his reading on the pages themselves. Neither did he mark words or lines. There is only one reliable sign of esteem for books in this library. Those he cared about he inscribed with his name, the date, and the place. About two hundred and fifty of the books are so marked. And they are, for the most part, the ones to which he publicly gave his allegiance — Shakespeare and the Bible, Keats and Dickens, Conrad, Joyce, Balzac and Flaubert. Scarcely more than half a dozen are dated in the twenties, the years when he was emerging from obscurity and moving quickly towards that period of furious energy near the end of the decade which saw the production of his first masterpieces. But in the thirties, when his stature was beginning to be recognized, he began to acquire more books. In 1932 he inscribed his name in nearly fifty. Although his purchases dropped off thereafter, he signed and dated thirty books in 1938. After the war years his own acquisitions were few until his residence in Charlottesville.

One expects classic works in a great writer's library and is not surprised to find them there. Often revealing and interesting are the other tastes represented. In this library they cover a wide range from flying, boating and hunting to that even more widely shared taste, the detective story. The poetry and fiction of flight are complemented by accounts of the aerial combat of World War I, told by such aces as the R.F.C.'s Victor Yeates. Guides for small-boat handling are buttressed with treatises on navigation.

Among the magazines are rows of *Field and Stream* — a shelf away from a few numbers of *Harper's* and the *Hudson Review*, a copy of *Furioso* and one of *La Nouvelle Revue Française*. William Faulkner was, like his mother, a frequent reader of detective fiction. (The germ of *Intruder in the Dust* first appeared, he once said, as a detective-story-style idea.) The classic cases and sleuths are there in hardcover and paperback. Nero Wolfe and Inspector Maigret appear alongside the works of Carr, Dixon, Hammett, Queen, Rinehart and Sayers. Other books point to other recreations and duties — volumes on saddlery and veterinary medicine.

Although this library is varied, it reflects its owner's regional interests and affinities. The Harrises — George W. and Joel Chandler — are represented. But George W. Harris's Sut Lovingood's yarns are balanced by tomes describing Mississippi's archaeology and transcribing its provincial archives. The fiction of Eudora Welty and Robert Penn Warren, of Carson McCullers and Flannery O'Connor, is ranged beside the massive scholarship of Douglas Southall Freeman in his four volumes on Lee and his three on the general's lieutenants. Concerned as he was with the land, it is not surprising that William Faulkner should have owned ten volumes of the works of Francis Parkman as well as accounts of the rugged geography and ruggeder denizens of that stretch of country known as the Natchez Trace.

The literature of the New World makes up about half of all the books in the library. A volume of Twain from Faulkner's grandfather, Hawthorne from his grandmother, Cooper from his father — to these were later added Emerson, Thoreau, Whitman, Melville, Henry James and Stephen Crane. He also inherited the work of writers more faded by time. His mother put her name in her copy of Winston Churchill's best seller, *The Crisis*. His grandmother wrote at length in a flyleaf of Owen Wister's big success, *The Virginian*. (The characterization was beautiful, she felt, and the protagonist captivating.)

The novelist's own immediate seniors are flanked by his contemporaries and a few of his juniors. The catalogue shows Anderson and Cabell followed by Hemingway and Dos Passos, Cummings and Frost. Besides fellow contributors to the old Double Dealer, which flourished in New Orleans, 1921–26, there are also somewhat younger men — O'Hara and Steinbeck — and then a newer generation: James Baldwin, Truman Capote, Ralph Ellison and John Knowles. Most of his own work, pristine from the publisher, stayed in a special bookcase the novelist never bothered with.

In *The Unvanquished* Granny Millard calls John Sartoris's office "the library" because it contains a small collection including Jeremy Taylor and Flavius Josephus. Both adorn the shelves of Rowan Oak, but the learned Jewish historian's works are preceded by fourteen massive and handsome volumes comprising a limited edition of the King James Bible, each volume bearing the Faulkner name, date and place. Homer, Euripides and Virgil are among the other representatives of antiquity. Dante, Boccaccio and Cervantes are among the great names from the Renaissance.

The titles from English literature (the largest section after the American), read like an alphabetical syllabus for a Great Names course — Austen and Donne through Marlowe and Thackeray. The same is true of the next largest group — books from French literature. From Stendhal to Proust, the great Gallic writers are represented. And if Goethe and Mann are the only German masters to be found, the genius of Russian literature is embodied in the volumes of Gogol, Chekhov, Tolstoy, Turgenev and Dostoevsky.

William Faulkner's special favorites are marked not only by inscriptions but also by multiple copies. And these were his perennial choices — five sets of Shakespeare, three of Keats, two of Dickens, two of Conrad and three *Don Quixotes*. More shelves are filled with a thirty-volume Balzac. These were among the books he read in youth and reread throughout his life, dipping into them for the sake of the characters, he used to say, as one would go into a room to visit with an old friend. Not so favorite but of special interest to the Faulkner specialist is another row. Making up more than half the total number of Irish titles in the collection are seven copies of books by James Joyce, one of them a 1924 edition of *Ulysses,* obtained and dated in 1924.

Stuck away casually in the library shelves are also the signs of the laurels that accumulated over the years — the short story collections and other prize volumes in which his work steadily appeared year after year. And there are the copies of publications that were to William Faulkner, in his maturity, almost as are the trade journals of other professional men — the periodic reports and lists from the American Academy of Arts and Letters, the Legion of Honor and the Nobel Foundation.

In the preface to the collection in which he referred to his grandfather's library, he wrote that he had gotten most of his early education there. But there was also one book in it with a sentence that he recalled nearly fifty years later. It was by Henryk Sienkiewicz. He did not give the title, but he remembered that he had been struck by a passage in which the Polish Nobel Laureate had said that the novel had been written at the expense of considerable effort to uplift men's hearts.

When William Faulkner's turn came to stand upon that same summit in Stockholm, he affirmed in his classic acceptance speech that it was the writer's privilege to help man endure by lifting his heart. One of the books in William Faulkner's library inscribed with the name of his grandfather is Henryk Sienkiewicz's *Pan Michael,* in an edition published in America in the year 1898. There on the last page are the lines he had read as a boy: "Here ends this series of books, written in the course of several years and with no little labor for the strengthening of men's hearts."

Stranger by choice though he may have been to the literary salons and cafés, William Faulkner had the company all his life of great artists who had gone before him and among whom he would take his place. He loved great poetry as he did great fiction. He could quote the enduring poets — Shakespeare, Keats, Yeats — by heart. And he could have said, as Yeats did in "To a Young Beauty" in his affirmation of the service of beauty,

> *Yet praise the winters gone:*
> *There is not a fool can call me friend,*
> *And I may dine at journey's end*
> *With Landor and with Donne.*

It was what he had been doing all his life.

PART IV

Points of View

JAMES BALDWIN

As Much of the Truth as
One Can Bear

*James Baldwin has been the leading intellectual spokesman for
the Negro in the continuing struggle for civil rights. Once his
reputation lay in his novels* (Go Tell It on the Mountain, Gio-
vanni's Room, Another Country). *Now it is the impact of his
polemical essays that has given him influence, and particularly in
the universities.*

AFTER World War II, certain names in recent American literature — Hemingway, Fitzgerald, Dos Passos, Faulkner — acquired
such weight and became so sacrosanct that they have been used as
touchstones to reveal the understandable, but lamentable, inadequacy of the younger literary artists. We still hear complaints,
for example, that World War II failed to produce a literary harvest comparable to that which we garnered from the first. We
will discuss the idiocy of this complaint later.

Let one of us, the younger, attempt to create a restless, unhappy, free-wheeling heroine and we are immediately informed
that Hemingway or Fitzgerald did the same thing better — infinitely better. Should we be rash enough to make any attempt to
link the lives of some men with their time, we are sternly (or
kindly) advised to reread *U.S.A.* It has all, it would seem, been
done, by our betters and our masters. In much the same way, not
so very long ago, it appeared that American poetry was destined
to perish in the chill embrace of T. S. Eliot.

Neither I, nor any of my confrères, are willing to be defined or limited in this way. Not one of us suffers from an excess of modesty, and none of what follows is written in a complaining spirit. And it is certainly not my purpose here to denigrate the achievement of the four men I have named. On the contrary, I am certain that I and that handful of younger writers I have in mind have more genuine respect for this achievement than do most of their unbearably cacaphonous worshipers.

I respected Faulkner enough, for example, to be saddened by his pronouncements on the race question, to have been offended by the soupy rhetoric of his Nobel Prize speech, and to have resented — for *his* sake — the critical obtuseness which accepted (from the man who wrote *Light in August*) such indefensibly muddy work as *Intruder in the Dust,* or *Requiem for a Nun.*

It is useful, furthermore, to remember in the case of Hemingway that his reputation began to be unassailable at the very instant that his work began that decline from which it never recovered — at about the time of *For Whom the Bell Tolls.* Hindsight allows us to say that this boyish and romantic and inflated book marks Hemingway's abdication from the effort to understand the many-sided evil that is in the world. This is exactly the same thing as saying that he somehow gave up the effort to become a great novelist.

I myself believe that this is the effort every novelist must make, in spite of the fact that the odds are ludicrously against him, and that he can never, after all, *know.* In my mind, the effort to become a great novelist simply involves attempting to tell as much of the truth as one can bear, and then a little more. It is an effort which, by its very nature — remembering that men write the books, that time passes and energy flags, and safety beckons — is obviously doomed to failure. Success is an American word which cannot conceivably, unless it is defined in an extremely severe, ironical and painful way, have any place in the vocabulary of any artist.

The example afforded by the later development, if one can call it that, of John Dos Passos is at least equally disturbing. And I suppose that there is no longer anything to say about Fitzgerald, at least not by me, and not now. Each of these men in his own way dramatizes for me the extraordinary hazards an American artist must run. Particularly, I must say, an American artist, whose tool is the common penny of language: who must try to deal with what words hide and what they reveal.

We live in a country in which words are mostly used to cover the sleeper, not to wake him up; and, therefore, it seems to me, the adulation so cruelly proffered our elders has nothing to do with their achievement — which, I repeat, was mighty — but has to do with our impulse to look back on what we now imagine to have been a happier time. It is an adulation which has panic at the root.

I think that it is true, but I am willing to be corrected, that the previously mentioned giants have at least one thing in common: their simplicity. I do not refer to their styles (though indeed, flying in the face of both critic and layman, I might be) but to their way of looking on the world. It is the American way of looking on the world, as a place to be corrected, and in which innocence is inexplicably lost. It is this almost inexpressible pain which lends such force to some of the early Hemingway stories — including "The Killers" and to the marvelous fishing sequence in *The Sun Also Rises;* and it is also the reason that Hemingway's heroines seem so peculiarly sexless and manufactured.

It is the sorrow of Gatsby, who searches for the green light, which continually recedes before him; and he never understands that the green light is there precisely in order to recede. Ben and Charley and Moorehouse and the entire cast of *U.S.A.* are tricked by life in just this way; nor is there any intimation in the book that we have, all, always, lived in a world in which dreams betray, and are betrayed, where love dies, or, more unbearably, fails to

die, and where innocence *must* die, if we are ever to begin that
journey toward the greater innocence called wisdom.

As for the work of Faulkner, which would seem, superficially,
to escape these strictures, one has only to consider his vision, running throughout his work, of the gallant South. Even when he
is most appalled by the crimes of his region by which I do not so
much mean the crimes committed against Negroes as the crimes
his forebears and contemporaries have committed, and do commit, against themselves he is testing it against the vision of a failed
possibility.

One hears, it seems to me, in the work of all American novelists,
even including the mighty Henry James, songs of the plains, the
memory of a virgin continent, mysteriously despoiled; though
all dreams were to have become possible here. This did not happen. And the panic, then, to which I have referred comes out of
the fact that we are now confronting the awful questions of
whether or not all our dreams have failed. How have we managed to become what we have, in fact, become? And if we are, as,
indeed, we seem to be, so empty and so desperate, what are we to
do about it? How shall we put ourselves in touch with reality?

Writers are extremely important people in a country, whether
or not the country knows it. The multiple truths about a people
are revealed by that people's artists — that is what the artists
are for. Whoever, for example, attempts to understand the French
will be forced, sooner or later, to read Balzac. And Balzac himself,
in his own personality, illustrates all those vices, conundrums, delusions, ambitions, joys, all that recklessness, caution, patience,
cunning, and revenge which activate his people. For, of course,
he *is* those people; being French, like them, they operate as his
mirror and he operates as theirs. And this is also entirely true of
American writers, from James Fenimore Cooper to Henry James
to William Faulkner.

Is it not possible to discern, in the features of Faulkner's Lucas,
the lineaments of Fenimore Cooper's Uncas? And does not Lam-

bert Strether of James' *The Ambassadors* come out of the loins of
men who conquered a continent, destroying Uncas and enslaving
Lucas, in order to build a factory which produces "unmention-
able" articles — and which, in the absence of any stronger force,
is now ruled by a strong-minded widow? What *is* the moral dilemma of Lambert Strether if not that, at the midnight hour, he
realizes that he has, somehow, inexplicably, failed his manhood:
that the "masculine sensibility," as James puts it, has failed in
him? This "masculine sensibility" does not refer to erotic activity but to the responsibility that men must take upon themselves
of facing and reordering reality.

Strether's triumph is that he is able to realize this, even though
he knows it is too late for him to act on it. And it is James' perception of this peculiar impossibility which makes him, until today,
the greatest of our novelists. For the question which he raised,
ricocheting it, so to speak, off the backs of his heroines, is the question which so torments us now. The question is this: How is an
American to become a man? And this is precisely the same thing
as asking: How is America to become a nation? By contrast with
him, the giants who came to the fore between the two world wars
merely lamented the necessity.

These two strains in American fiction — nostalgia for the loss
of innocence as opposed to an ironical apprehension of what such
nostalgia means — have been described, not very helpfully, as
the Redskin tradition as opposed to the Paleface. This has never
made any sense to me. I have never read an American writer in
whom the Redskin and the Paleface were not inextricably inter-
twined, usually, to be sure, in dreadful battle. Consider, for example, the tormented career of the author of *Tom Sawyer*. Or,
for that matter, the beautiful ambiguity of the author of *Leaves
of Grass*. And what was Hart Crane attempting to celebrate,
in his indisputably Paleface fashion, in that magnificent failure
which he called *The Bridge?*

It seems to me that the truth about us, as individual men and women, and as a nation, has been, and is being recorded, whether we wish to read it or not. Perhaps we cannot read it now, but the day is coming when we will have nothing else to read. The younger writers, so relentlessly and unfavorably compared to their elders, are, nevertheless, their descendants and are under the obligation to go further than their elders went. It is the only way to keep faith with them. The real difficulty is that those very same questions, that same anguish, must now be expressed in a way that more closely corresponds to our actual condition.

It is inane, for example, to compare the literary harvest of World War II with that of World War I — not only because we do not, after all, fight wars in order to produce literature, but also because the two wars had nothing in common. We did not know, when we fought the first war, what we were forced to discover — though we did not face it, and have not faced it yet — when we fought the second. Between 1917 and 1941, the ocean, inconceivably, had shrunk to the size of a swimming pool.

In 1917, we had no enemies; 1941 marks our reluctant discovery — which, again, we have not faced — that we had enemies everywhere. During World War I, we were able to be angry at the atrocities committed in the name of the Kaiser; but it was scarcely possible in World War II to be *angry* over the systematic slaughter of six million Jews; nor did our performance at Nuremberg do anything but muddy the moral and legal waters. In short, by the time of World War II, evil had entered the American Eden, and it had come to stay.

I am a preacher's son. I beg you to remember the proper name of that troubling tree in Eden: it is "the tree of the knowledge of good and evil." What is meant by the masculine sensibility is the ability to eat the fruit of that tree, and live. What is meant by the "human condition" is that, indeed, one has no choice: eat, or die. And we are slowly discovering that there are many ways to die.

The younger American writers, then, to whom we shall, one day, be most indebted — and I shall name no names, make no prophecies — are precisely those writers who are compelled to take it upon themselves to describe us to ourselves as we now are. The loneliness of those cities described in Dos Passos is greater now than it has ever been before; and these cities are more dangerous now than they were before, and their citizens are yet more unloved. And those panaceas and formulas which have so spectacularly failed Dos Passos have also failed this country, and the world. The trouble is deeper than we wished to think: the trouble is in us. And we will never remake those cities, or conquer our cruel and unbearable human isolation — we will never establish human communities — until we stare our ghastly failure in the face.

We will never understand what motivates Chinese or Cuban peasants until we ask ourselves who *we* are, and what we are doing in this lonely place. Faulkner's South, and grandfather's slaves, have vanished: the sun will never look on them again. The curtain has come down forever on Gatsby's career: there will be no more Gatsbys. And the green hills of Africa have come out of the past, and out of the imagination, into the present, the troubling world.

Societies are never able to examine, to overhaul themselves: this effort must be made by that yeast which every society cunningly and unfailingly secretes. This ferment, this disturbance, is the responsibility, and the necessity, of writers. It is, alas, the truth that to be an American writer today means mounting an unending attack on all that Americans believe themselves to hold sacred. It means fighting an astute and agile guerrilla warfare with that American complacency which so inadequately masks the American panic.

One must be willing, indeed, one must be anxious, to locate, precisely, that American morality of which we boast. And one must be willing to ask one's self what the Indian thinks of this morality, what the Cuban or the Chinese thinks of it, what the Negro thinks of it. Our own record must be read. And, finally, the air of this time and place is so heavy with rhetoric, so thick with soothing lies, that one must really do great violence to language, one must somehow disrupt the comforting beat, in order to be heard. Obviously, one must dismiss any hopes one may ever have had of winning a popularity contest. And one must take upon one's self the right to be entirely wrong — and accept penalties for penalties there will certainly be, even here.

"We work in the dark," said Henry James, "we do what we can, our doubt is our passion and our passion is our task. The rest is the madness of art." This madness, thank Heaven, is still at work among us here, and it will bring, inexorably, to the light at last the truth about our despairing young, our bewildered lovers, our defeated junkies, our demoralized young executives, our psychiatrists, and politicians, cities, towns, suburbs and interracial housing projects. There is a thread which unites them all, and which unites every one of us. We have been both searching and evading the terms of this union for many generations. ⌐We are the generation that must throw everything into the endeavor to remake America into what we say we want it to be. Without this endeavor, we will perish. However immoral or subversive this may sound to some, it is the writer who must always remember that morality, if it is to remain or become morality, must be perpetually examined, cracked, changed, made new. He must remember, however powerful the many who would rather forget, that life is the only touchstone and that life is dangerous, and that without the joyful acceptance of this danger, there can never be any safety for anyone, ever, anywhere.⌐

⌐What the writer is always trying to do is utilize the particular in order to reveal something much larger and heavier than any particular can be.⌐ Thus Dostoevsky, in *The Possessed*, used a

small provincial town in order to dramatize the spiritual state of
Russia. His particulars were not very attractive, but he did not
invent them, he simply used what there was. Our particulars
are not very attractive, either, but we must use them. They will
not go away because we pretend that they are not there.

Not everything that is faced can be changed; but nothing can
be changed until it is faced. The principal fact that we must now
face, and that a handful of writers are trying to dramatize, is that
the time has now come for us to turn our backs forever on the big
two-hearted river.

V. S. PRITCHETT

In Writing Nothing Fails
Like Success

The English have a versatility that is foreign to many of us. Witness V. (for Victor) S. Pritchett. He has been the literary editor of The New Statesman, *and as a critic in his own right has written with wit and perception of many a contemporary book and many a book that has joined the category of classic. A brilliant short story writer, he is also a novelist, and since the English have long made an art of travel writing, it is not surprising that, with the help of* Holiday Magazine, *he has made another mark in telling about where on earth he has been.*

"LITERARY success," Cyril Connolly wrote in a review of a successful English novel, "liberates the tensions of a hostile environment by removing the environment and so prepares the way for literary failure." On this subject the author of *Enemies of Promise* and *The Unquiet Grave,* is, of course, an expert. He is our pathologist of the distress called talent — and something also of its fortuneteller. He has always stood by Flaubert and the ruthless artist and has diagnosed the illnesses that afflict himself and his contemporaries.

Sometimes the sicknesses have been the common influenzas, measles and rheumatisms of the literary life: too much money, too little money, popular journalism, literary journalism, marriage, "the pram in the hall." At other times, Connolly has turned to the sickness of industrial society itself. With Henry James he would probably say that life itself — "life, vulgar life" — is the

first enemy of the artist whose sole duty is to create a masterpiece
and nothing short of it. The statement I have quoted at the beginning of this article is described as "Connolly's Second Law."
Is it true?

I have little use for absolutes in literary criticism. What does
Connolly mean by success? Is it a matter of mode and career? Is
it a manifestation of probity? Is it the lucky conjunction of critical
and public applause? Is Connolly thinking of recognition or of a
writer's inner sense that he has done something that "counts"?
When the elder Disraeli compiled his *Calamities of Authors* for
the Victorian reader, success was the one calamity he omitted. Is
Connolly thinking of success as the characteristic modern disaster
— sudden money, publicity, the rich life and Hollywood before a
writer is out of his twenties?

I suppose the Second Law applies chiefly to novelists. What it
means, I suppose, is that a novelist usually breaks with the hostile
world he was brought up in or lives in; but that once he relieves
his conflicts by putting them into writing, he is in danger of losing his basic material for good. At the second flushed attempt he
will begin to furbish, repeat himself, become flaccid or coarsen.
Unknowingly he will have written himself out of one successful
go.

The provincial university, the dreadful slum, the awful villa,
the unpardonable smart set or whatever it is, in which he has
been brought up, have been anesthetized; and by environment,
I suppose Connolly also refers to emotional, intellectual and
spiritual enclosures. Lucky for Emily Brontë (the Second Law
suggests) that she did not have to go on after *Wuthering Heights;*
disastrous that Thomas Wolfe did go on after *Look Homeward,
Angel.* Once we are well we do not need to write. We lose our
talent until something makes us ill again.

Looking at the law again, one notes the word "hostile," the
vagueness of the word "environment." It is assumed that novel-

ists in general have only one significant environment. Are all environments hostile? Surely not, but we must admit that in every
country in the world at the moment, the talented tend to belong
to a huge uprooted group. The break with upbringing is inevitable and general. Many clever first novels are simply the ca-
thartic protests of a talented man or woman against the ill-educated or falsely educated world they have grown up in or the
world that science, industrialism, politics or war have erased.

It is noticeable that Indian, West Indian and African novelists
soon exhaust themselves, once they have recorded their past and
their break with it. They cease to be artists and become intelligentsia. H. G. Wells became a member of the intelligentsia once
he had exhausted the material of his lower-middle-class comedies.
George Eliot herself, when she had used up her childhood and
youth, failed when she moved into worlds she did not really
know in the second half of *Daniel Deronda* and in *Romola*. She
became a member of an ethical intelligentsia. Usually the intelligentsia are political or indifferent.

Or, take the more difficult case of D. H. Lawrence. His earliest
and best work certainly liberates him from a hostile environment; but one cannot call his later work "literary failure," for he
found hostile, indeed created hostile environments everywhere
and was never spiritually or emotionally liberated. One can say,
then, that success does not always liberate. Henry James liberated
himself from American life but was sufficiently a master of the
generalship of art to enlarge his personal campaign and to take on
"the international situation." Personal liberation has not been
fatal to such artists and, if the workings of Connolly's Second Law
can be seen operating in them, then one can only say it does not
operate absolutely or dramatically.

Not only that: many novelists improve by repetition and all improve when they do not substitute automatic writing, the gliding
gin-smoothed style of success, for labor. And the important novelists *do* labor. *Great Expectations* is better than *David Copper-*

field. The great novelists never liberate themselves. When he was writing *Bouvard et Pécuchet,* Flaubert was still locked in conflict with the bourgeois; Dostoevsky has his tensions for life. Tolstoy, indeed, tried to escape at the time of his conversion but, even so, *Resurrection* contains brilliant scenes and *Hadji-Murād* represents a return to the conflicts that had fertilized him. And that, too, is a point against the Absolute: the novelist can return. He can go through hell again, now armed by accomplishment. Literary failure, in the Connolly sense, is fundamentally a failure of vitality, not a psychological injury inflicted by success upon art.

On the other hand, in *The Summing Up,* Somerset Maugham did have some words to say that support Connolly's Second Law. Maugham saw in his worldly way that as novelists become more prosperous after success they tend to get out of touch with the society they really know. They go up in the world. They leave their poor back rooms and lowly friends for luxury flats, Riviera villas, far away beaches, luxury hotels. Their characters become grander and less real. This certainly happened to John Galsworthy as the Forsytes moved into the smart set.

And so we come back to the word "hostile." The novelists who survive Connolly's Second Law are those who do not find their environment hostile; or rather who, finding it hostile, nevertheless cannot or do not leave it. Does Jane Austen succeed because she did *not* make the break? Did she not accept the values of her society? It was a ruthless society, and she was a ruthless novelist. Does not George Gissing's long and agonizing failure seem to us a kind of success, because he stayed in the depressing world that choked him as a person? Thomas Hardy and Joseph Conrad stayed in their worlds. William Faulkner has stayed in his. We can hope that Miss Ivy Compton-Burnett is personally liberated from the macabre families she describes, but she is fortunately not liberated from the rich obsessions which are the nourishment of the artist.

Their tensions and conflicts have nailed such novelists to where and what they were. If they disliked their environment they came to terms with their evil. The literary failures that Connolly's Second Law suggests occur at the beginnings of a career or on the borderline of the novelist's art. A promising first novel is almost always followed by a disappointing second. An obsession *has* been relieved; it has not had time to form again. There are also novelists who write only one good book simply because they do release a personality that desired no more than personal release. They are now different men or women, in a different place. War novelists are a good example — their books were a piece of personal therapy. They wanted to be rid of an exceptional experience. They had no sense of living with it or using it. Such novels are essentially autobiographies: one can see that Edmund Gosse's *Father and Son* is a therapeutic work.

Where Connolly's Second Law is justified lies in one of the meanings we now give to success when we talk of Big Money, Hollywood and so on. This success offers something to the novelist that he was never offered in the past. He is dragged out of his study and given not only a new way of life — which he might survive — but a fixed, glazed and inescapable personality. A Trollope could make a fortune, but he did not have to change his life or rubber-stamp his character in order to attain it, whereas a Scott Fitzgerald was automatically put through the machine.

The young writer is employed to repeat himself. He must always, in this sense, "succeed." Lucky for the writer who is so dull and so stupid that he cannot be used in this way. Even here I see no absolute law. Graham Greene has inoculated himself against this evil because he understands the fundamental failure of the society that goes in for this success. He knows how to live inside the whale. A few novelists have had this gift of identifying themselves with their environment; they exploit it and ransack it as Dickens, Balzac and, I suppose, Zola did.

Short of such a gift for exploitation, what one might wish for

a novelist is, perhaps at first, the success of a law of esteem —
such as Balzac had when he wrote cheap thrillers or Chekhov had
when, year after year, he turned out hundreds of cheap comic
sketches and revue numbers. Reversing Connolly's law, such failures have led to a return to the fecund, hostile environment. And
there are the failures also of the *succès d'estime:* the failure of
Cervantes, for example, to be anything more than a respectable
highbrow writer of no more than estimable novellas, in the educated taste of his time, until personal disaster chained him and
gave him the chance to write *Don Quixote* and fill it with the experience of a lifetime's failure.

ANGUS WILSON

There's a Tyrant in the
Critic's Corner

*In any listing of Britain's contemporary authors the name of
Angus Wilson has prominent place. He is not one of the younger
writers (he was born in 1913), and he published nothing until he
was well into his thirties. He calls himself a "weekend writer,"
but the record suggests crowded weekends: critical essays, reviews,
short stories, plays, four novels.*

I ENTERED the literary world late in the immediate post-war years
when changes of literary taste and loyalty were already in the air.
The first broadcast I gave was, I remember, an attack upon Virginia Woolf. Her books had nurtured me as an adolescent, and I
was in reaction against her influence. I attacked her feminine hypersensitivity, her overconcern with personal values, which I attributed to a private income and a long tradition of upper-middle-
class security. I also said that in her hostility to plot and story
and in her concern with verbal experimentation she had almost
turned the solid structure of the novel into a second-rate substitute for poetry. They were brash generalizations, but then, if I
was not still young, I was new to the literary world and had much
to get off my chest.

I should not phrase my criticism so today. Indeed I should now
hesitate to attack Virginia Woolf and the Bloomsbury school at
all. The traditional English novel as practiced by the great Victorians — the novel with strong social implications, the novel of
man in the community rather than man in isolation or in coterie,

the novel, above all, of firmly constructed narrative and strong plot rather than of formal and verbal experiment — has made a triumphant return in England in the last ten years. I hope I have played some part in helping this return. Yet I am alarmed to see how quickly this neo-traditional novel threatens to exert a tyranny stronger and socially more potentially dangerous than the coterie dogmatisms of Bloomsbury.

It is well-nigh impossible to read a serious English literary review these days without coming upon the same set of adjectives of approbation — mature, vital, healthy, life-enhancing, adult. On what does this scheme of moral values rest? Are they coherent? And should such purely ethical terms play so large a part in aesthetic criticism? We may be sure that most of the great writers in the nineteen-twenties and -thirties would not have thought so. How has this *volte-face* in literary criticism come about? I feel in a good position to criticize whatever tyranny may be present in these new values, for my own novels are essentially traditional in form and my preoccupation is strongly — too strongly for many critics — a social and moral one.

The world of Bloomsbury, and indeed for that matter, of James Joyce and even of D. H. Lawrence, was primarily a London, cosmopolitan and private one. The new criticism and the new novels that have followed in its wake derive primarily from the English provinces and from the English universities; they are markedly academic and social in implication. Two men of outstanding personality and strong conviction have done most to build up this climate of literary opinion in England. In the critical field F. R. Leavis of Downing College, Cambridge; in the creative field C. P. Snow, the novelist, late of Christ's College, Cambridge. If they would largely agree in their dismissal of the gods of Bloomsbury, Snow would certainly not accept Lawrence as the savior Leavis thinks him, and Leavis treats as beneath contempt Trollope, whose everyday efficiency Snow so much admires.

Yet, though their intentions are so different, their effects strangely combine. In one important point their careers have been similar. F. R. Leavis began his teaching in the early thirties, when the Bloomsbury gods that he and his hero, D. H. Lawrence, so mistrusted were at the height of their influence. He fought against current values consistently amid a good deal of academic cold shouldering and sneering by much lesser men. He founded and carried almost alone the weight of a periodical of the highest quality, *Scrutiny,* in which to put forward his neglected ideas. Now his disciples are in every university and school, putting forward his views as gospel.

In those pre-war days Snow was a lecturer in physics at Cambridge, later he was to be an important scientific administrator. He was also already formulating in his mind his novel series, "Strangers and Brothers" — which the taste of that time would certainly have rejected. His first books were comparatively ignored. Now he has contested with Graham Greene the position of the most serious best seller. Both Leavis and Snow have been in great degree the architects of their own literary age.

No one in England, except perhaps T. S. Eliot, has done more to rescue literary criticism from the vapors and anemia of belle-letrism and dilettantism than Leavis. His fight has been long and uphill, but it must be squarely said that, in the course of fighting, his natural vigor, bluntness and tenacity have hardened too often into aggression and moral violence. The terse vigor of his style has too often become an excuse for proffering personal sensibilities as ethical absolutes. Indeed, little though he would welcome the comparison, the feminine hypersensitivity of a Virginia Woolf has its masculine counterpart in the hedgehog prickliness of Dr. Leavis.

Concerned to re-assert healthy tradition in the novel, he has inevitably had to do a lot of excommunication of the second-rate by bell, book and candle; he has been ardent to see his few heroes

— Jane Austen, George Eliot, Henry James, Joseph Conrad and Lawrence — deified for all time. These Johnsonian quirks are allowable enough in a great critic; in the hands of his disciples, who now proliferate in every English university and secondary school, they have become an inquisition. This literary witch-hunting, this aesthetic Calvinism creates a freezing atmosphere most inclement for the nurturing of new talent; but not only is new creative writing threatened, the literature of the past is being steadily converted into no more than a secondary means of teaching moral duty and sound citizenship.

It is important of course to teach the young to discriminate in their reading. Teachers like Lord David Cecil at Oxford, whom Leavis has always attacked, bent only on inspiring in their students a catholic addiction to reading too often produce a sort of negative "love of literature" that makes great writing into part of a gentleman's equipment for life like a visiting card or evening clothes. Against such trivializing tendencies Leavis has fought with admirable courage. As a corrective to this diffuse enthusiasm Leavis' rejection of Thackeray or Trollope or Fielding to a mere footnote has been invaluable.

Nevertheless, the young are always as much in danger of dogmatic certainty, of narrow particularism, and of self-satisfied Olympian judgments, as they are liable to vague romantic enthusiasms. I have found among the youth attending lectures today too many who, in their pleased certainty with rejecting this or that famous author for not being in "the great tradition," have made literature into no more than a pinpricking critical exercise. Primarily a moral educationalist, Leavis has thought to exalt English literature by making it the touchstone of moral values for the young. Great literature is much more than this, and the truth needs to be reasserted.

It seems sometimes to have been assumed by the disciples of Leavis, as indeed by many of the New Critics in the United

States, that to read a work of literature critically it is necessary only to ask one question — does this work add to the health of society? The question, of course, is based upon the idea that society is sick and needs a cure. I was trained as a historian, and too often it seems to me that this analysis has a false historical foundation, that society is not more sick now than it ever has been, only sick in a different way. For Mr. Eliot it may be a valuable fiction for critical and creative inspiration to place the Fall of Man, the beginning of our cultural sickness, at the time of the English Civil War. Prof. C. S. Lewis used the Reformation as a similar symbol of cultural decay. Allen Tate is sure that for American civilization it came about in the Civil War. Leavis appears to see it in the decline of rural crafts. Such watersheds, as I have said, may be useful constructs for these critics, but they are entirely unhistorical. There is no paradise of "true" values enshrined somewhere in past literature, and we waste our time in urging the young to search for it.

The new literary critics tend then to see the purpose of literature as the reinvigoration of society by moral truths enshrined in various authors who lived before their chosen Falls. The position of C. P. Snow and his disciples is equally didactic and dogmatic, but they come to it from another angle. A scientist and administrator, Snow has many excellent things to say in defense of our times. For him there has been no Fall, rather a constant progress, and he looks with a slightly contemptuous sadness upon the purely literary men who do not understand the progress of our time. Disgusted by the social and political reactionary views of so many of the literary giants of between the wars, he has come to confuse aestheticism and concern with formal experiment with political regressivism, to associate the traditional novel form he likes with sound, progressive social principles. I share his belief in modern English society and his preference for plots and stories, but I am very unhappy with the suggestion that this is the only way in which novels can be written.

The novels of verbal experiment, of feminine sensibility and of complicated personal ethic are, it is now said, immature, over-fantasizing, irresponsible, and not proper food for an adult either as a writer or as a reader. Further, they have a decadent tendency, a romanticism that is morbid rather life-enhancing. Something of this may clearly be seen in Snow's attack in his Rede lecture on the decadent tendencies of the great literary figures between the two wars.

In an interview printed in a literary periodical he further suggested that too great permissiveness in the literary climate is liable to encourage such romantic irresponsibility. It is, he suggested, because this romanticism has no place in the less permissive Soviet Union that the future of the Soviet novel is so bright. William Cowper in an article in *Twentieth Century* stated that such experiment as had been valuable in the works of Joyce, Kafka, etc., was now incorporated in the modern English social novel without the accompanying moral and social irresponsibility that had marked the great writers between the wars.

Since France, and with her most of Western Europe, has persisted in experimental novel writing, all this tends to increase the division between English literary culture and European, to encourage a self-satisfied insular attitude which reaches occasional peaks of clownishness in Kingsley Amis' attacks on "abroad." It was to be seen very clearly when Lawrence Durrell's quartet appeared. On the whole the work received a fierce handling from English critics. In many ways it deserved it. Mr. Durrell's aims are magnificent, but his execution was often slipshod and pretentious, and the language floridly vulgar.

Yet too often the implication of the English critics was that Durrell's novel had failed because it was experimental and therefore out-of-date; what is more, there was a distinct implication that this was bound to happen when a chap becomes expatriate, lives abroad and cuts himself off from the main stream of his country's development. This sort of criticism is illiberal, mistaken and bad. It is the dangerous result of a too-rigid swing of the pendulum.

The conjunction of these two streams — of Leavis' criticism asserting a rigid traditional line and of Snow's novel writing demanding a rigid traditional form — seems to me to have dangerous possibilities both for the writer and for the reader, above all because both make their demands upon similar moral and social grounds. That Leavis' criticism saved the teaching of literature from the decay into which it had fallen, that C. P. Snow writes good traditional novels which have re-established the respectability of narrative and plot — these accomplishments only make the dogmatism founded upon their example by overenthusiastic disciples the more dangerous.

There is in much of the writing of Bloomsbury an immature vision, a child's vision; but so I suggest there is in all great writing. The veneration of maturity leaves out one whole part of the artist's imaginative vision as much as does the Romantic concern with the emotions of adolescence. All the great novelists of the past have sought to find a point of fusion between their childhood vision and their mature judgment — this is the meaning of novel making; this is the Proustian conquest of time. But such symbolic conquests of time are valuable *individual* patterns, not blueprints for remaking society.

Ronald Firbank was irresponsible, adolescent and fantastic; he was utterly unconcerned with the health of society, yet I cannot imagine a novel more in love with life, or indeed more likely to make its reader in love with life than *Prancing Nigger*. In any case, is devotion to the life force to be the hallmark of our judgment of a novel? I find it difficult to accept. It is surely neither romantic nor irresponsible to refuse to care whether the moral force of *Timon* or of *Pericles* or of *The Way of the World* be mature and healthy or not. Shakespeare's most mature work, *The Tempest,* ends in despair; it is certainly not a tonic for a sick society. We are allowing, I fear, academic moralists to take their homemade foot rules to *King Lear* and to *Hamlet*.

All this does not matter too much to the creative writer. He will create his morbid, irresponsible, immature masterpiece if he wishes, however much the climate of opinion is against him. It is a good deal more dangerous to instruct the reader to be looking in creative fiction for the means to save contemporary society, especially in an age when universities are increasingly the sole source of educated opinion. The great danger surely is that, if the Cold War should grow more intense instead of tapering off, the demands upon writers in the West to write mature, responsible social novels that will strengthen our camp may grow as strident as those that have been made in the past upon the Communist writer. It will be up to our side to be even more mature, healthier and more responsible.

I have no doubt, as I have said, that those writers who wish to do so will oppose the demand, but I am a little more doubtful whether they will find any readers, let alone any critics to support them. If the novelist has anything to offer to life, it is that he deals with the rich multiplicity of human individuals in an age when standardization threatens individuality; and that he contributes an individual view of them. If "literary opinion" or influential critics or even the educated reader impose upon the novelist the measure of some social myth, some dramatic view of moral health, then eventually we may be sure that this supposedly life-enhancing myth will destroy the true life in the work of art. And the professional life-loving critics will then have satisfactorily rendered useless the only real gift that the novelist can make to the world.

ELIZABETH BOWEN

Rx for a Story Worth Telling

The critic Gene Baro wrote in the New York Times *Book Review:* "*Elizabeth Bowen's presence, her personal handsomeness, her Anglo-Irish wit, her womanly dignity, the alertness and intelligence that she brings to bear upon experience, above all, her sense of the wholeness of the occasion find their transformed expression in her writing. She is an artist of harmony, and her gift is to reconcile the vagaries and conflicts of the human heart.*" *She has been writing fiction since the twenties. Her latest novel is* The Little Girls.

I CAN imagine no age, however scientific, in which mankind will be contented by plain fact, however impressive, or by direct statement, made with whatever authority. Of fact we say, "That is that, that is so." We accept it. But there is some errant part of us which cries, "What next?" and "What then?" We are insatiable children: "Tell us a story!"

What is the need behind the demand? It may have different facets; it may be complex. For one thing, we require to be transported, to transcend boundaries — not, I think, merely with a view to "escape" but out of a necessity for enlargement. Positive rather than negative, this wish carries us to the portals of a world that is at once "other" and our own, a terrain with potentials we barely sense in the everyday. A story deals in the not-yet-thought-of but always possible.

We have within us a capacity, a desire, to respond. One of the insufficiencies of routine existence is the triviality of the demands it makes on us. Largely unused remain our funds of pity, spontaneous love, unenvious admiration or selfless anger. Into these, a story may drop a depth charge.

We need to marvel. Overhung as we are by the nominal, concrete "marvels" of our century — the triumphs of science, the masterworks of technology — we are creatures of numbed fancy and stunned senses. Or could be, did we not resist and hope. Nothing *is* truly marvelous that is not Man. It is his diversity, his passion, his soaring and his endurance, which stir our amazement. Yet we await, it seems, the storyteller's cry of "Behold!"

Finally, we are born with a thirst for myth, its heroic simplicity, its bright air. A story provides life with an ancient prototype, in which action is fearless, decision swift. Vanished, banished as may be the gods and heroes, they bequeath their mantles. Who is to wear them? We need today illusion's reviving touch.

What are the essentials of a story? To begin with, it need not necessarily be untrue, that is to say, invented. I am not thinking of fiction only. Biography, history, folklore, Biblical narrative and, no less, the happening recounted by friend to friend, the memory given voice, or the flash of gossip: all these are stories. I would say, however, that if a story *be* true, it still cannot take its stand on its truth only. To act on us, it needs to be truth plus art; no small part of a story is in the telling. Conversely, when we have invention (fiction), the telling must impart an air of truth; art is summoned to substitute for veracity. Willing though we are to be moved and held, none of us can be held by the unbelievable. Great novels have an inspired lifelikeness. They *could* have been true; they outrage no real-life law.

In the main, a story does two things. It confers importance: characters in it are given stature, and are moreover spotlit, so that their gestures are not only clearly seen but cast meaningful shadows. Enhanced, the characters seem singled out from ordinary men, yet not wholly, for we perceive ourselves in them. Similarly, the settings of the story (the scenes within it), whether rooms and their furniture, city streets and parks or stretches of land-scape, become endowed with a sort of super-reality, which causes them, often, to surround us more nearly than do our own sur-roundings, and burns them deeply into our memories. Something extra also attaches to words and actions, which have about them a touch of fatefulness, for nothing once in a story can be undone. We have this in mind when we say that some real incident has affected us "like something in a book."

A story moves, advances, and it not only can and does do this, but it must. If it stood still, it would cease to be a story and become a picture. As the story moves along, it gains in significance. What we are being shown is cause and effect. If the chain were broken, if the story's movement were altogether inconsequent or at random we should not read with the eagerness that we do. We encounter crises, situations, out of which something is bound to arise — but what? The degree to which we react to the advance depends upon the powers of the narrator.

Is a story, then, wholly within the narrator's power, circum-scribed (as that would imply) by one individual's outlook, mind, pen or voice? Surely not. It enlists a series of faculties which are, no less, ours. In acting upon us, the story is drawing upon us; our responses contribute; our contributions create. The reli-ance of the narrator upon his audience may or may not be con-scious, but it is immense. The reality (for us) of the story is a matter of how much it has elicited from us. We enter in, and through this entering in know ourselves to be active. We cooper-ate.

Sometimes the cooperation may be unwilling. Then we have an uneasy sense of compulsion. One may feel "against" a story on account of its errors, fatuities, lapses of taste, floutings of judg-ment, distortion of emotions, yet be slow to disengage one's self from its hold. To a point, we incline to lend ourselves; we are loath not to. Once under way, a story sets something going, and that is not only true of a "good" story. We allow our doubts to be stilled, our fancies exploited, as I say, to a point. Past that point cooperation does break down, but this happens wonderfully rarely.

Why so rarely? Let us admit: the story's primary power is through suspense, the lure of "What next?" and "What then?" By literary convention, the suspense story is assumed to be the thriller or mystery. I contend that no story fails to invoke suspense, and compel us by it; the question is, simply, what kind, and on what plane? Straightforward adventure or science fiction restricts itself to physical risk together with the physically spectacular; the more subtle mystery blends in the psychological. The play on emotional suspense throughout a love story does not need comment. Novelists know how to arouse what is more complex by revolving their plots around questions of conscience or of equity (such as race or class issues) or by bringing their characters to peaks (of success, exaltation) from which they seem liable to fall or plunging them into morasses (disaster, obloquy) from which the means of their rescue is uncertain. The psychological novel, outwardly more austere, focuses suspense on the inner conflict: the protagonists are, as it were, battlegrounds — what is to be the outcome of the day?

Suspense may account for the primitive hold on us of a story. But when the end is known, when the suspense evaporates, what then? Were there nothing left, one might speak of the story's magic, its power, even, but not, surely, of its strength. The idea of strength is undivisible from that of endurance: in that sense, strength constitutes an inherent virtue.

So far, we have been discussing the story only within the terms of its first telling. After this telling, what is left? The answer to this query, in every case, is the test.

A story may act on us while it runs its course, and for that time only. It is ephemeral. Another story, when its nominal end is reached, is only at the beginning of its term of life; from now on it will continue to make growth, extend, deepen. Rooted in our imaginations, it induces reflectiveness. In itself an experience, it stays at work within us, affecting experiences we may later have. Take the extreme case, the formative power of stories assimilated in childhood. Of a story we have either read or heard, I think we may legitimately ask: to what degree did it transform the world for us?

Great stories have basic themes; the lesser rely on devices and ingenuities. Basic themes, when one numbers them, are few, their recurrence is proof of their immortality. They are traditional, having a touch of lore and at the same time a father-to-son authority. The wonder is, that having been born knowing these themes, we continue to want them and wonder at them. Recollect, however, that they renovate themselves in their outer guise. In effect they reincarnate, donning the different languages, taking in the ideas, embracing the usages of different generations, different countries. Each time, they take color afresh from time or place. Also they renew their expressive quality; they voice, as, it seems to us, nothing else can, the spirit of a century, or of a society, or of a region. The great story is one that remains true.

Conflicts or rivalries and their resolution, pride and its fate, estrangement and reconciliation, revenge or forgiveness, guests and searches rewarded or unrewarded; abidingness versus change, love and its proof — these are among the constants, the themes of the story. The story is a form of history; nothing we are involved in goes unrecorded. Having by nature shape, it imparts that, thereby lessening our chaos. By perceiving nothing to be un-meaning, it enlightens us. It arrives, by its end, at a harmony that is not impossible. For the story is vision turned upon reason, with nothing to fear from reason: therein lies its strength.

SAUL BELLOW

Facts That Put Fancy
to Flight

[The biographical introduction of Saul Bellow is on page 24.]

I HAVE read somewhere that in the early days of the movies a
miner in Alaska rushed at the screen to batter down the villain
with his shovel. Probably he was drunk, but his action was significant nevertheless. This man had considered it a practical
thing to travel thousands of miles into a frozen wilderness to dig
for buried treasure. Money, land, furs, jewels, champagne, cigars,
silk hats he must have accepted as legitimate objects of the imagination. Yet there was no place in his mind for this new sort
of transaction. It must have seemed to him that if the fellow had
taken the trouble to tie the kicking heroine to the tracks, he must
mean business. His imagination could only conceive of real objects. Thus, with the selfsame shovel he dug for gold and swung
at shadows.

Few people make this error in so primitive a form, but almost
no one is altogether free from it. We understand, of course, that
art does not copy experience but merely borrows it for its own
peculiar purposes. Americans however do not find it always
simple to maintain the distinction. For us the wonder of life is
bound up with the literal fact, and our greatest ingenuity is devoted to the real; and this gives reality itself magical and even sacred properties and makes American realism very different from
the European sort. With us the interest of the reader and often of
the writer, too, is always escaping toward the fact.

The non-factual imagination also returns to the fact. Ask a woman to describe her son, and she is likely to tell you with pride that he is six feet two or three inches and weighs 220 pounds, that his shoes are size 14 and that he eats four eggs at breakfast and two pounds of steak at a sitting. Her love, in short, frequently takes a statistical form. Years ago, in Chicago, I used to listen to a Negro virtuoso, Facts-and-Figures Taylor, who entertained shouting crowds in Washington Park by reciting the statistics he had memorized in the Public Library. "You want to know what the steel industry exported in nineteen and twenty-one? You listen to this now."

"You tell 'em, Facts-and-Figures. Give 'em hell!"

People who are not particularly friendly to art may be reconciled to it by factual interests, by descriptions of the stretching or priming of the canvas, the method of applying the paints or the dollar value of the picture. One thinks more kindly of a painting valued at $10,000, the original factory colors dripped from a six-inch brush, than of one which has not applied to the prevailing form of the imagination for consideration. The theatregoer may be pleased to learn that behind the living room represented on the stage are fully furnished bathrooms or kitchens that will never be seen but are there to give a reassuring sense of completeness or closure. The imitation will be absolutely genuine. Because we have a strong taste for the solid background, for documentation, for accuracy, for likeness, we are often confused about the borders between art and life, between social history and fiction, between gossip and satire, between the journalist's news and the artist's discovery.

The demands, editorial and public, for certified realities in fiction sometimes appear barbarous to the writer. Why this terrible insistence on factual accuracy? "Our readers will want to know," an editor will sometimes say, "whether your information is correct." The research department will then make inquiries. How many stories does the Ansonia Hotel really have; and can one see its television antennae from the corner of West End Avenue and Seventy-second Street? What do drugstores charge for Librium? What sort of mustard is used at Nedick's? Is it squeezed from a plastic bottle or applied with a wooden spoon?

These cranky questions will be asked by readers, compulsively. Publishers know they must expect their errors to be detected. They will hear not only from the lunatic fringe and from pedants but from specialists, from scholars, from people with experience "in the field," from protective organizations and public relations agencies, from people who have taken upon themselves the protection of the purity of facts.

Archaeologists and historians are consulted by movie producers in the making of Roman spectaculars. As long as the chariots are faithful copies, the fire real Greek fire, it seems to make little difference that the dialogue makes you clutch your head, that the religious theme is trumped up with holy music and cunning lights. It presently becomes clear that the protagonist is not Ben Hur, not Spartacus, but Knowhow. Art based on simple illusion is art in one of its cruder forms, and it is this that Hollywood with its technical skill has brought to perfection.

The realistic method made it possible to write with seriousness and dignity about the ordinary, common situations of life. In Balzac and Flaubert and the great Russian masters the realistic externals were intended to lead inward. I suppose one might say that now the two elements, the inward and the external, have come apart.

In what we call the novel of sensibility the intent of the writer is to pull us into an all-sufficient consciousness which he, the writer, governs absolutely. In the realistic novel today the writer is satisfied with an art of externals. Either he assumes that by describing a man's shoes he has told us all that we need to know about his soul, or he is more interested in the shoes than in the

soul. Literalists who write to the editor are rather odd and amusing people who do not need to be taken too seriously, but the attitude of the writer himself toward externals is a serious matter.

The facts may excite a writer deeply, and in America we have
a poetry of fact — the details of labor in Walt Whitman, the
knowledge of navigation in Mark Twain, the descriptions of
process in Hemingway's fishing stories. But in every case it is the
writer's excitement that counts. Without this excitement the facts
are no more interesting than they would be in a manual of river
navigation or a Sears, Roebuck catalogue. What is happening
now is that the intrinsic excitement of the facts themselves has
become intense, and the literary imagination must rival the power
of the real. With us this rarely happens.

The American desire for the real has created a journalistic sort
of novel which has a *thing* excitement, a glamour of *process;* it
specializes in information. It resembles the naturalistic novel of
Zola and the social novel of Dreiser but is without the theoretical
interests of the first and is unlike the second in that it has no concern with justice and no view of fate. It merely satisfies the readers' demand for knowledge. From this standpoint it may sometimes be called an improving or moral sort of book. However, it
seldom has much independent human content, and it is more
akin to popularized science or history than to the fiction of Balzac
or Chekhov. It is not actively challenged by the "novel of sensibility."

The living heirs of Henry James and Virginia Woolf do not do
very well, and I'm afraid that they largely deserve their neglect.
They have receded altogether too far from externals, from observation, in their desire for mental independence and free sensibility. They give us very little information; and after we have
visited them in their tree houses once or twice they lose their
charm.

The novel in America has taken two forms, neither satisfactory.
Those writers who wish to meet the demand for information

have perhaps been successful as social historians, but they have neglected the higher forms of the imagination. The novel of sensibility has failed to represent society and has become totally uninteresting.

It seems hard for the American people to believe that anything can be more exciting than the times themselves and our common life. These modern facts perhaps have thrust imagined forms into the shadow. We are staggeringly rich in facts, in things, and perhaps like the *nouveau riche* of other ages we want our wealth faithfully reproduced by the artist.

By now it is misleading to speak of the facts as if they were soluble, washable, disposable, knowable. The facts themselves are not what they once were and perhaps present themselves to the imagination of the artist in some new way. A. J. Liebling, in an uncommonly good article on Stephen Crane,* wrote, "We have seen in our time that the best writers as they mature become journalists — Sartre, Camus, Mauriac, Hemingway." Are we to suppose therefore that the artistic imagination at its highest development must be drawn back into the world and its realities? Is the challenge of journalism higher than that of art itself in our time?

Some of our novelists can scarcely help being better fact-bringers than artists. They are turning ground that has never been turned before — the Army, the laboratory, the modern corporation, the anarchic sexual life of "free spirits": such phenomena in the raw state are not quickly assimilated into art. Moreover, it's hard for writers to get on with their work if they are convinced that they owe a concrete debt to experience and cannot allow themselves the privilege of ranging freely through social classes and professional specialities. A certain pride in their own experience, perhaps a sense of the property rights of others in *their* experience, holds them back.

The novelist, convinced that the novel is the result of his pas-

* *The New Yorker,* Aug. 5, 1961.

sionate will to suppose that he can know everything about the life of another human being, finds that he must get through the obstacles of the literal to come at his subject. Thus, he is prevented from doing the essential thing. Hard knowledge is demanded of him; to acquire this hard knowledge, he must at least temporarily transform himself into some sort of specialist.

How then is the novelist to write about such questions as power — power which he has never experienced? Evidently he is asked to be reliable about the lower ranges of fact and is not expected to concern himself with the upper. He may be realistic but not about the things that matter, the arrangements that shape our destiny. In this smaller way to stick to the facts limits him to minor schemes of social history, to satire, to muckraking and leveling, or to the penny psychology of private worlds. To this sort of "objectivity" writers give all they've got. Strong, on experience, they are much, much less strong on the truth.

The greatest of the realists always believed that they owed a very special debt to truth. "The hero of my tale, whom I love with all the strength of my soul, whom I have tried to set forth in all his beauty, and who has always been, is, and always will be the most beautiful, is — the truth." So wrote Tolstoy at the conclusion of "Sevastopol in May." And Dostoevsky commenting on *Anna Karenina* tells us that he found the book at times very monotonous and "confined to a certain caste only" and that as long as it was merely a description of life in society it made no great claim to any deeper interest.

Later, he says, "in the very center of that insolent and petty life there appeared a great and eternal living truth, at once illuminating everything. These petty, insignificant and deceitful beings suddenly became genuine and truthful people worthy of being called men."

That is, after all, what the novelist wants, isn't it?

WALTER TELLER

The World and They That
Dwell Therein

*Walter Teller is one of the journal-keepers whom he describes
in the following essay as "observer-philosophers." His own philosophical observations are presented in his* Area Code 215: A Private Line in Bucks County.

FROM time to time a book appears that the world places in the
genre associated with Henry Thoreau. The world is not without
judgment, the genre not without honor; yet this species of literature lacks a name. By and large it consists of books one feels better for having read. Classified under whatever rubric — essay,
personal history, travel, regional, nature, American scene — I call
such books journals of thoughts and days; the men and women
who write them, journal-keepers.

Mark off the journal-keeper of thoughts and days from the
journal-keeper only of days. The former aspires, at bottom, to
wisdom writing. He is the observer-philosopher. The latter, the
observer uncompounded, usually reports on experience in some
characteristic trade. He may be a whaler, farmer, man of letters,
explorer or flower hunter. That both kinds of journal-keepers are
likely, at times, to focus on nature tends to blur an important
distinction. The distinction lies in a passion for philosophizing,
in the good use of the word. One kind of journal-keeper goes to
nature for subject matter, the other to find an environment in
which to try to make sense out of life. One seeks his reality in the
happenings of the external world, the other in the mental con-

structions he makes of them. Kant speaks of "the starry order without and the moral order within."

John Burroughs, dead forty years and due for a literary come-back, wrote, "Man can have but one interest in nature, namely to see himself reflected or interpreted there." The English writer, Cecil Torr, said in *Small Talk at Wreyland,* "I meant to keep to local matters but have gone much further than I meant." Burroughs did not confine his journalizing to nature, nor did Torr restrict himself to events.

Masked in whatever form, a journal of thoughts and days sel-dom results in a book the mass of men will throb to. Recall the reception accorded the archetype. *Walden,* published in 1854, sold 2000 copies during its author's lifetime, nor was it reprinted until after his death eight years later. On the other hand, those who care about this sort of thing — either the writing or the read-ing of it — care deeply, and all down the generations. If the journal of thoughts and days is a style never quite in fashion, neither does it go wholly out. Thus any example of the genre, done right, may prove exceedingly durable.

The good place is important to journal-keepers. Where do they go in search of it? Not to fallout shelters. "I went to the woods," Thoreau wrote, "because I wished to live deliberately, to front only the essential facts of life, and see if I could not learn what it had to teach, and not, when I came to die, discover that I had not lived." Taking to the woods, a certain removal, is a con-stant in these intentionally personal equations. The journal-keeper of thoughts and days requires a space he can mentally compass. The rising tide of men and cities and objects forces him into strategic retreat. No recluse he, however. What he demands is life with flavor and meaning. Though he withdraws from the flow, he does not hide from himself. On the contrary, he tries to place himself where he does not feel lost, where he counts for something, above all in such circumstances that his life does not pass him by unnoticed.

It's the personal life he seeks, not the private muse. History is sad, but the journal-keepers I think of do not despair. "I am sure of this," Emerson wrote in his *Journals,* "that by going much alone a man will get more of a noble courage in thought and word than from all the wisdom that is in books." Life is hard — I don't know how else to say it — yet these writers delight in life. In effect, they say it is also good. If old philosophies finally fail, the journal-keeper of thoughts and days rides on.

Walks on, I should say, in various moods, often with a light heart. Most were great walkers: hoofing it is one of the common elements. "There is no fundamental difference between walking in the city and in the country," Brooks Atkinson wrote in his day-to-day *Once Around the Sun.* "Seeing is the chief virtue of walking everywhere." John Muir, Scots-born nature philosopher and early leader of the forest conservation movement, was, I would guess, the walkingest. He kept a journal while navigating on foot from Indiana to the Gulf of Mexico, also on subsequent excursions.

Henry Beston, born in Quincy, Massachusetts, in 1888, a Harvard man, journalized on the beach. In a two-room cabin, he spent a Thoreau-like year on the outer dunes of Cape Cod. In *The Outermost House,* his record of that time, he wrote, "Eager was I to know this coast and to share its mysterious and elemental life . . . I had no fear of being alone . . . Living in outer nature keeps the senses keen, and living alone stirs in them a certain watchfulness."

The ten by twelve cabin of the *Spray,* the 37-foot, home-built sloop in which he single-handed circled the world, proved the good place for Joshua Slocum. The story of that voyage, *Sailing Alone Around the World,* based on the logbook he kept, has been called the nautical equivalent of Thoreau's account of his life in the hut at Walden. Slabside, the very name, hints at the sort of sanctum John Burroughs chose in the hills on the west shore of the Hudson, eighty or so miles above New York. "A hair may show where a lion is hid," he wrote in *Signs and Seasons*.

Lewis Gannett, a family man earning a livelihood in New York, in his own words no Thoreau, went to northwest Connecticut. "We boast of our skyscrapers," he wrote in *Cream Hill: Discoveries of a Weekend Countryman*, "but we are not at home in them . . . Perhaps that is why so many of us who live our lives in cities feel that we shrink and shrivel . . . unless we sometimes get back to the country."

The Southwest for some years has been Joseph Wood Krutch's Walden — without the pond. Before he took up his abode there, he too found in New England the margin for living Thoreau thought essential. In *The Twelve Seasons*, he wrote, "From another year which I hope will be based in the country . . . I promise myself many advantages. But none of them is more obvious or more inclusive than the privilege of being permitted to be continuously aware that I am indeed alive — for that is a fact which the city makes most people forget . . . Only those within whose consciousness the suns rise and set, the leaves burgeon and wither, can be said to be aware of what living is."

Louis J. Halle, professor and scholar of diplomacy, met those very requirements while at work in the national capital. His book, *Spring in Washington,* an international and ornithological mix, tells of man in nature, specifically in Rock Creek Park. "To snatch the passing moment and examine it for signs of eternity is the noblest of occupations," he wrote.

E. B. White first went to Maine as a child. When almost forty, he returned with wife and young son, went to live on a salt-water farm, stayed five years. Meditating through long Maine winters, writing of small events in the course of his farming, he turned out a series of monthly pieces. Gathered together they appeared as *One Man's Meat.* In a foreword to that collection, he wrote: "Usually when a man quits writing in his journal it is either because things are happening to him that he doesn't want to commit to paper or because he has lost interest in life."

Maine continues to be his magnet. "What happens to me when I cross the Piscataqua?" he asked in a later notational book, *The Points of My Compass*. And answered, "I do not ordinarily spy a partridge in a pear tree, or three French hens, but I do have the sensation of having received a gift from a true love."

A generation and more ago, Gamaliel Bradford, half sick and housebound, posted his journals — more than a million words — in suburban Wellesley Hills. Nan Fairbrother, a young London woman, wrote from an old-country house where she and her two small children found refuge during the war. People have saved themselves by keeping journals. Her book, *An English Year*, is one I liked very much.

Every journal-keeper of thoughts and days says, to all intent and purpose, "this is where I am now." None intends to let life go by the board. Emerson called his journals his savings bank in which he deposited opinions and views to be drawn out as needed. John Burroughs recommended keeping a journal "to preserve the flavor of the passing moment." A journal, he said, "is a sort of deposit account wherein one saves up bits and pieces of his life that would otherwise be lost to him."

When it came to hard cash, most managed with little. Most knew the joys of lean living. Rather different was Gamaliel Bradford. "Spent a considerable part of the day over my ledger," he wrote. "I do love to work on my money . . . It will never play so large a part in my journal as it does in Pepys, but as it is not the least interesting part of his, so it may not be of mine. There is this difference, however . . . that he is dealing with a property which he had made himself, whereas I have seized all mine from somebody else." Bradford makes himself sound like a pirate. More likely he was an enthusiast.

What sort of fellow is the journal-keeper? A person gifted or skilled in judging qualities. Brooks Atkinson wrote in *Once Around the Sun* that, in criticism, there should be a large dash of the amateur. "For the amateur," he said, "is a man of enthusi-

asm who has not settled down and is not habit bound." The same
goes for keeping thoughts and days; it too is a branch of criticism — not in the formal way, but rather in the ripening one of
passing judgment, or reserving it, on the merits of many things.

If the journal-keeper of thoughts and days needs some of the
cosmic sense of the poet, he also requires the common sense of the
carpenter or sailor. Consistency is not a law of life; adaptability
is. Bradford notwithstanding — and this, perhaps, was a weakness — journal-keepers are likely to know the beauty of parsi-
mony, of economy in the use of specific means to an end. Is Henry
Thoreau's "Simplicity, simplicity, simplicity!" the instrument with
which he dissected all questions? Certainly to this class of writer,
simplicity is an organizing principle. The principle, moreover, is
an aesthetic one; no scientific reason for it exists. It amounts to
a search for an artistic presentation of life, unobscured by complexity of detail; or to put it another way, the quest for the clean
and beautiful line.

Like Henry himself, journal-keepers do not remain in the
woods. If they often take off, they as often return, and sometimes
with something of social as well as personal value — such as a
book. Thoreau called pitching his wigwam on the pond shore an
experiment. What he learned from it was this: "If one advances
confidently in the direction of his dreams, and endeavors to live
the life which he has imagined, he will meet with a success unexpected in common hours." In other words, he experienced moments of grace.

To one so inclined, keeping a journal of thoughts and days
brings its own reward; a happiness in the word and in the struggle
to gain knowledge from experience. "It is hard to accept that we
are here for no purpose which we can even vaguely understand,"
Nan Fairbrother wrote near the end of *An English Year.* "We
must manage as best we can," she concluded, finally begging all
questions, perhaps, but bravely and with warmth.

NOTE

*Of the books mentioned by Mr. Tel-
ler, the following are in print in these
editions:*

SMALL TALK AT WREYLAND.
Cecil Torr. (Cambridge. 2 vols.
$6.)

WALDEN. Henry Thoreau. (Nor-
ton, $5.50. Twayne, $5. Peter Pau-
per, $4.95. Dodd, Mead, $3.75.
Holt, Rinehart & Winston, $2.25.
Dutton, $1.95. Dolphin, 95 cents.
Washington Square, 60 cents.)

JOURNALS. Ralph Waldo Emerson.
(Smith, $3.75. Modern Library,
$1.95. Dover, $1.85.)

THE OUTERMOST HOUSE. Henry
Beston. (Holt, Rinehart & Winston,

$3. Viking, $1.45.)

SAILING ALONE AROUND THE
WORLD. Joshua Slocum. (Sheri-
dan, $5. De Graff, $2.95. Grosset,
$1.95. Dover, $1. Collier, 95 cents.)

THE TWELVE SEASONS. Joseph
Wood Krutch. (Sloane, $3. Apollo,
$1.50.)

SPRING IN WASHINGTON. Louis
J. Halle. (Smith, $3.25. Atheneum,
$1.25.)

ONE MAN'S MEAT. E. B. White.
(Harper, $4.50.)

THE POINTS OF MY COMPASS.
E. B. White. (Harper, $4.50.)

AN ENGLISH YEAR. Nan Fairbrother. (Knopf, $4.)

LAWRENCE DURRELL

Landscape with Literary Figures

Lawrence Durrell had to wait for fame. He wrote novels, but no one paid them attention. He wrote poetry, plays, travel books; they were ignored. Then in 1956 appeared his novel Justine, *the first volume of the* Alexandria Quartet, *and thereafter Lawrence Durrell was recognized for what he is: a major writer of our time.*

"YOU WRITE," says a friendly critic in Ohio, "as if the landscape were more important than the character." If not exactly true, this is near enough the mark, for I have evolved a private notion about the importance of landscape, and I willingly admit to seeing characters almost as functions of a landscape. This has only come about in recent years after a good deal of travel — though here again I doubt if this is quite the word, for I am not really a travel writer so much as a "residence writer." My books are always about living in places, not just rushing through them.

As you get to know Europe slowly, tasting the wines, cheeses and characters of the different countries, you begin to realize that the important determinant of any culture is after all the spirit of the place. Just as one particular vineyard will always give you a special wine with discernible characteristics so a Spain, an Italy, a Greece will always give you the same type of culture — will express itself through the human being just as it does through its wild flowers. We tend to see culture as a sort of historic pattern dictated by the human will, but for me this is no longer absolutely true.

I don't believe the British character, for example, or the German has changed a jot since Tacitus first described it; and so long as people keep getting born Greek or French or Italian their culture productions will bear the unmistakable signature of place.

And this, of course, is the target of the travel writer; his task is to isolate the germ in the people which is expressed by their landscape. Strangely enough, one does not necessarily need special knowledge for the job, though, of coure, a knowledge of language is a help. But how few they are those writers! How many can write a *Sea and Sardinia* or a *Twilight in Italy* to match these two gems of D. H. Lawrence? When he wrote them, his Italian was rudimentary. The same applies to Norman Douglas' *Fountain in the Sand* — one of the best portraits of North Africa. We travel really to try to get to grips with this mysterious quality of Greekness or Spanishness; and it is extraordinary how unvarying it remains, true to the recorded picture of it in the native literature: true to the point of platitude.

Greece, for example, cannot have a single real Greek left (in the racial sense) after so many hundreds of years of war and resettlement; the present racial stocks are the fruit of countless invasions. Yet if you want a bit of real live Aristophanes, you have only to listen to the chaffering of the barrowmen and peddlers in the Athens Plaka. It takes less than two years for even a reserved British resident to begin using his fingers in conversation without being aware of the fact. But if there are no original Greeks left, what is the curious constant factor that we discern behind the word "Greekness"? It is surely the enduring faculty of self-expression inhering in landscape. At least I would think so as I recall two books by very different writers which provide an incomparable nature study of the place. One of these is *Mani* by Patrick Leigh Fermor, and the other Henry Miller's *The Colossus of Maroussi*.

I believe you could exterminate the French at a blow and re-

settle the country with Tartars, and within two generations discover, to your astonishment, that the national characteristics were
back at norm — the restless metaphysical curiosity, the tenderness
for good living and the passionate individualism, even though
their noses were now flat.

This is the invisible constant in a place with which the ordinary
tourist can get in touch just by sitting very quietly over a glass
of wine in a Paris *bistro*. He may not be able to formulate it very
clearly to himself in literary terms, but he will taste the unmistakable keen knife-edge of happiness in the air of Paris — the pristine brilliance of a national psyche which knows that art is as important as love or food. He will not be blind either to the hard
metallic rational sense, the irritating *coeur raisonable* of the
men and women.

The great, big nations, like, say, the Chinese or the Americans,
present a superficially homogeneous appearance; but I've noticed
that while we Europeans can hardly tell one American from another, my own American friends will tease each other to death at
the lunch table about the intolerable misfortune of being born in
Ohio or Tennessee — a recognition of the validity of place which
we ourselves accord to the Welshman, Irishman and Scotsman
at home.

It is a pity indeed to travel and not get this essential sense of
landscape values. You do not need a sixth sense for it. It is there
if you just close your eyes and breathe softly through your nose;
you will hear the whispered message, for all landscapes ask the
same question in the same whisper. "I am watching you — are
you watching yourself in me?"

Most travelers hurry too much. But try just for a moment sitting on the great stone omphalos, the navel of the ancient Greek
world, at Delphi. Don't ask mental questions, but just relax and
empty your mind. It lies, this strange amphora-shaped object, in
an overgrown field above the temple. Everything is blue and

smells of sage. The marbles dazzle down below you. There are
two eagles moving softly, softly on the sky, like distant boats row-
ing across an immense violet lake.

Ten minutes of this sort of quiet inner identification will give
you the notion of the Greek landscape that you could not get in
twenty years of studying ancient Greek texts. But having got it,
you will at once get all the rest; the key is there, so to speak, for
you to turn. After that you will not be able to go on a shopping
expedition in Athens without running into Agamemnon or Cly-
temnestra — and often under the same names. And if you happen to go to Eleusis in springtime you will come upon more than
one blind Homer walking the dusty roads.

The secret is identification. If you sit on the top of the Mena
House pyramid at sunset and try the same thing (forgetting the
noise of the donkey boys, and all the filthy litter of other travelers
— old cartons and Coca-Cola bottles), if you sit quite still in the
landscape diviner's pose, why, the whole rhythm of ancient Egypt
rises up from the damp cold sand. You can hear its very pulse
tick.

Nothing is strange to you at such moments: the old temples
with their death cults, the hieroglyphs, the long slow swirl of
the brown Nile among the palm-fringed islets, the crocodiles
and snakes. It is palpably just as it was (its essence) when the
High Priest of Ammon initiated Alexander into the Mysteries. Indeed the Mysteries themselves are still there for those who might
seek initiation — the shreds and shards of the trismegistic lore
still being studied and handed on by small secret sects. Of course,
you cannot arrange to be initiated through a travel agency! You
would have to reside and work your way in through the ancient
crust — a tough one — of daily life.

And how different is the rhythm of Egypt from that of Greece!
One isn't surprised by the story that the High Priest at Thebes
said contemputously: "You Greeks are mere children." He could

not bear the tireless curiosity and sensuality of the Greek character — the passionate desire to conceptualize things metaphysi-
cally. They didn't seem to be able to relax, the blasted Greeks!
Incidentally, it is a remark the French often repeat today about
the Americans, and it is always uttered in the same commiserat-
ing tone of voice as once the High Priest had used.

Yet the culture of Greece (so different from that of Egypt)
springs directly from the Nile valley — I could name a dozen
top Greek thinkers or philosophers who were trained by Egyp-
tians, like Plato, Pythagoras, Anaxagoras, Democritos. And the
"tiresome children" certainly didn't waste their time, for when
they got back home to their own bare islands the pure flower of
Greek culture spread its magnificent wings in flights of pure
magic to astonish and impregnate the Mediterranean. But just
to hand the eternal compliment along, they invented the word
"barbarians" for all those unfortunate savages who lived outside
the magic circle of Greece, deprived of its culture. The barbarians of course were one day to produce Dante, Goethe, Bach,
Shakespeare.

As I say, the clue, then, is identification, for underneath the
purely superficial aspects of apparent change the old tidelines remain.

The dullest travel poster hints at it. The fascinating thing is
that Dickens characters still walk the London streets, that any
game of village cricket will provide clues to the strange ritualistic
mystery of the habits of the British. While if you really want to
intuit the inner mystery of the island, try watching the sun come
up over Stonehenge. It may seem a dull and "touristic" thing to
do, but if you do it in the right spirit you find yourself walking
those secretive hills arm in arm with Druids.

Taken in this way, travel becomes a sort of science of intuitions,
which is of the greatest importance to everyone but most of all to
the artist who is always looking for nourishing soils in which to

put down roots and create. Everyone finds his own "correspond-ences" in this way, landscapes where you suddenly feel bounding with ideas, and others where half your soul falls asleep and the thought of pen and paper brings on nausea. It is here that the travel writer stakes his claim, for writers each seem to have a personal landscape of the heart which beckons them. The whole Arabian world, for example, has never been better painted and framed than in the works of Freya Stark, whose delicate eye and insinuating slow-moving orchestrations of place and evocations of history, have placed her in the front rank of travelers. Could one do better than *The Valleys of the Assassins?*

Another pointer worth thinking about is institutions. Have you ever wondered why Catholicism, for example, can be such a different religion in different places? Ireland, Italy, Spain, Argentina — it is theologically the same, working on the same premises, but in each case it is subtly modified to suit the spirit of place. People have little to do with the matter except inasmuch as they themselves are reflections of their landscape. Of course there are places where you feel that the inhabitants are not really attending to and interpreting their landscape; whole peoples or nations sometimes get mixed up and start living at right angles to the land, so to speak, which gives the traveler a weird sense of alienation.

I think some of the troubles which American artists talk about are not due to industrialization or technocracy but something rather simpler: people not attending to what the land is saying, not conforming to the hidden magnetic fields that the landscape is trying to communicate to the personality.

One last word about the sense of place. I think that not enough attention is paid to it as a purely literary criterion. What makes "big books" is surely as much to do with their site as their characters and incidents. I don't mean the books that are devoted entirely to an elucidation of a given landscape like Thoreau's *Walden.* I mean ordinary novels. When they are well and truly anchored in nature, they usually become classics. One can detect this quality of "bigness" in most books that are so sited, from *Huckleberry Finn* to *The Grapes of Wrath.* They are tuned in to the sense of place. You could not transplant them without totally damaging their ambiance and mood; any more than you could transplant *Typee.* This has nothing I think to do with the manners and habits of the human beings who populate them; for they exist in nature, as a function of place.

PART V

Somewhat Personal

Mostly It's Money That Makes
a Writer Go, Go, Go

*Robert Graves (b. 1895) is one of those men of letters who seem
perennially young. Perhaps it is because he has always tackled
with a young man's zest many themes and forms. He is a novelist with particular concern for reconstructing in modern dress the
stories of antiquity. He has written about crime. He is a poet
who is no stranger to medals and other honors, and many a man
believes that the Nobel Prize Committee should honor itself by
honoring him. That there is fun in him the following essay
makes clear.*

"WHY does he write?" a prudent publisher asks himself whenever a manuscript arrives from an unknown writer. The answer,
duly filed, serves as a useful guide to future business relations, if
any. (I am here discussing only prose, because poetry is an embarrassing subject in the publishing trade and does not lend itself to statistics.)

Convenient groups for filing purposes are these: (1) Money,
(2) Fame, (3) Fun, (4) Escape, (5) Dire Need, (6) Miscellaneous. These groups are by no means interexclusive. In fact,
pure representatives of any particular group are rare. Even well-
heeled and well-placed writers whose main motive is Fame enjoy adding a few thousand dollars to their bank accounts in proof
of Fame's achievement. And even abject hacks, who have sold
their pens for hard cash, cannot divest themselves of all ambition.
Also, at least a modicum of Fun must be assumed in most cases;

otherwise few books would get beyond that critical seventh chapter. As for Escape: everyone in this complex and corrosive age seems to be escaping from someone or something, if only from himself.

So in the rough table of percentages I shall now provide — a device that always commands attention, however phony the figures — it is each writer's dominant motive that places him in his group: Money, 55 percent; Fame, 18 percent; Fun, 15 percent; Escape, 7 percent; Dire Need, 4 percent; Miscellaneous, 1 percent.

Money heads the list. Dr. Johnson called the man a fool who, when talk was free, had any other reason for writing; and he scribbled *Rasselas,* his most admired work, in great haste, only to pay his mother's funeral expenses. Johnson's remark was aimed at his biographer, James Boswell, who wrote largely for Fame; but it serves as a useful reminder that writing for Money is not incompatible with high literary standards.

Johnson had been anticipated by other capable professionals, including Daniel Defoe, who wrote *Robinson Crusoe, Moll Flanders* and *Roxana* as simple get-pennies. Sir Walter Scott and Anthony Trollope were later to do the same: Scott from a pious resolution to pay debts, Trollope because he could not otherwise afford to hunt foxes. There is this to be said for the Money motive: that an eye to the salability of work obliges a writer to take some thought for his readers, and may even help him to cultivate a clear, vigorous, economical style.

Mediating between writer and public, stands the publisher. Many writers hate the publisher, picturing him as an avaricious, surly and opinionated porter on guard at the Gates of Success. I cannot share their prejudice. Having once published in a small way myself and lost a lot of money by my willful idealism, I sympathize with publishers — and even feel apologetic, in retrospect, for their losses on early, ill-written, and now happily suppressed

Gravesiana. In fact I far prefer most publishers to most authors.

The publisher is either a businessman or a fool. If a businessman, he depends for his profits on a careful study of trade journals and reports supplied by his traveling salesmen. And, since obviously unable to read all the manuscripts that pour unsolicited into the office, he must hire professional readers to grade them into "probable," "possible" and "impossible," with brief judgments on the "probables" and "possibles." These judgments help him to decide on a list that does not conflict with the information supplied by the salesmen and trade journals. He may even read some of the "probables" himself. Any realistic young writer-for-Money, who can be bothered to study the market, should have no difficulty in finding his feet, which any publisher will be glad to guide into the right path for him until they kick up big money.

I admire honest hacks, ghosts and pulp writers who make no claim to literary distinction, but are content selflessly to batter out reading matter for the semi-educated millions on an old typewriter, and raise large, happy families on the proceeds. Personally, I lack the required moral fiber, or humility, and have therefore trained myself not to envy those king-size hacks who write for the film industry or TV, and are richer than any independent author can ever hope to become. One such, a friend of mine, earned a cool $100,000 with a costume-picture script which will never, he knows, be used.

Writers for Money, though a main buttress of the trade, account for few best sellers. Best sellers, if not written by someone in the news, about whatever it was that landed him in the news, tend to be accidents. A garrulous, fun-loving young extrovert with good health, a large appetite, and a no more than moderate education, gets loose one summer holiday with a fountain pen and, guided by blind instinct, astonishingly hits the jackpot. But that means becoming entangled at once in the coils of big business, and the Fun evaporates when enormous offers are made for a sequel. Meanwhile, the book's selling points are analyzed by salesmen and trade journals, and the formula gets passed on to the line of waiting hacks. When customers in the bookshops ask: "have you anything like that wonderful . . . I forget the title . . . ?" the bookseller will soon be able to reply: "Yes, lady, here is the very thing!"

Jackpot strikes, however, are always unexpected. Hemingway's *Old Man and the Sea* seemed far too short, and James Gould Cozzens' *By Love Possessed* far too literary, to do the trick; besides both were written by scarred professionals. All that I found in common between them myself was their unreadableness, but fortunately for the publishers neither manuscript had been sent me for an opinion.

The publishers' darlings are certain heaven-sprung naturals who write for Fun and keep it up year after year. Fun, like boredom, is catching. Even when it degenerates into a nervous habit — as it did with P. G. Wodehouse halfway through his career — the mere sight of a funster's name on a title page provokes anticipatory giggles.

The Escape group is a mixed one. Some of its members want to escape from fathers who beat them, or wives who nag them, or bosses who bully them, or Dictators who oppress them. Writing is about the only profession that can be taken up at any age, without license, diploma, union card or other qualification, regardless of age, race, creed, color, sex or sexual proclivity; no wonder so many escapists choose it! The only basic tools needed are a pencil stub and a few sheets of clean packing paper. And if the need to escape is urgent and dramatic enough, the escapist has a theme crying out for literary treatment.

This Escape group merges at one point with the small group who feel a dire need to write some nightmare memory of war or love or childhood out of their systems. But the sense of Dire Need may equally be provoked by religious conversion (e.g., *Pil-*

grim's Progress) or a sensitive social conscience (e.g., *Uncle Tom's Cabin*) or by any obsession you please, crazy or otherwise. Charles Doughty, author of *Arabia Deserta,* told T. E. Lawrence that he had visited Arabia not in any spirit of adventure or geographical interest, but in dire need of a worthy subject for a book "that should redeem the English language from the slough into which it has fallen since the time of Spenser."

A publisher welcomes a few Dire Need books (if not as eccentrically written as Doughty's, the first edition of which remained unsold for twenty years or more) because they give his list a look of urgency; and because the Dire Need men will, as a rule, sign contracts without reading them. But, in the main, he relies on the Fun group for his best sellers, and on the Money group, reinforced by the more amenable members of the Fame group, for the bulk of his list.

The so-called "Universal Writers" of the past seem to have belonged equally to all groups. If some of Shakespeare's plays and of Dickens' novels contain deplorably dull patches, that is because the incentives of Fame and Fun were temporarily in abeyance. *Don Quixote* remains perennially readable, maybe because it was, partly at least, written in jail. An old-fashioned jail where the prisoner is not required to break rocks, pick oakum or sew mailbags, but where the turnkey will provide pen, ink, paper and a writing table — not to mention food — for a small fee, gives all the five main incentives full play.

When Cervantes secured his release, completed *Don Quixote,* and found himself famous, he followed his success with another long novel, called *Persiles and Sigismunda.* This he wrote for no apparent reason at all, except that another book was expected of him by his patron, the Count of Lemnos; and he advertised it in advance as: "Either the best or the worst book ever written in our tongue." And indeed it was so good, or so bad, that no English or American publisher has ever, so far as I know, ventured to publish a popular translation — even with a scarlet band around the wrapper: "New Full-Length Novel by the Author of Award-Winning *Don Quixote!*"

I feel the question coming: "Why do *you* write?" Though, obviously, I have a lot of Fun, even if it may not be catching, please file me under Miscellaneous. I write mainly for curiosity, to clear my mind on some vexed or obscure topic, and never repeat myself if I can avoid it. I first chose to be a literary hobo because this life promised me the security and independence needed for pursuing a secret vice: poetry. That it has done.

Or put it another way: Prose books are the show dogs I breed and sell to support my cat.

AL HINE

Why Does Trash Stick
in Our Minds?

Once in the long ago Al Hine was an editor of the G.I.-read paper,
Yank. He is also a novelist (Birthday Boy, Lord Love a Duck)
and, as his essay testifies, a wide-ranging reader of other men's
novels.

I CAN remember, while I was still a downy-cheeked collegian,
finding in the University Library at Princeton a set of the novels
of Lady Blessington. In a fortnight of springtime euphoria and
indolence I read through the lot, from *Dead Sea Fruit* to *Marma-*
duke Herbert, from *Lottery of Life* to *The Governess.* Lady
Blessington, an educated and more prolific Rona Jaffe of her day,
hammered on a single plot of assaulted yet finally triumphant
virtue through some thirty novels. Their literary merits are nonexistent, but they stick in my mind today more firmly than most of
the impeccably good books I read in the same period.

The Blessingtons fall into the category of what I think of as
"good-bad" books. There are whole Canadian forests felled for
the "bad-bad" books that we read with some pleasure, but that
leave no lasting imprint on our minds. And there are "bad-good"
books — George Meredith's *The Egoist,* say, or *Pendennis* —
which are simply hallowed (and mummified) names. But the
"good-bad" book is something else again. Let me define it as a
work usually of prose fiction (though sometimes including verse,
history or drama) which cannot, save by the most acrobatic critical wrench, be considered a part of any literary canon, but which

still will not relinquish its grip upon our memories and hearts.

Some titles on a "good-bad" booklist would be written in a language bearing as little resemblance to the idiom of Shakespeare and Lancelot Andrewes as Choctaw. Others would be composed in acceptable prose, but would founder from triteness of plot, paucity of thought or invention, or other internal flaws supposed to make even the most lucid writing nugatory in any literary sense.

Why does trash like this stick in our minds?

The cleverest and most popular explanation falls wide of the mark. Blaming the strength and survival of "good-bad" books on a snob estimate of universal bad taste says nothing at all, for it ignores the very pertinent question of why *these* books survive as against all the other rubbish eliminated as swiftly as it is ingested. An honest answer must rest on examination of some of the books themselves; I submit a sample shelf from my own mental attic.

Let's start with *Pilgrim's Progress.* I was brought up in a relatively Fundamentalist Protestant household, and I was exposed early to *Pilgrim's Progress* in a bowdlerized child's version. It was not at the time so important to me as *Tom Swift,* but it left a stronger and continuing impression. Now John Bunyan, put up alongside such giants in his own field and of his own times as John Donne, Sir Thomas Browne or even Jeremy Taylor, must stand revealed as a canting, trite, Puritan pamphleteer. But I remember The Giant Despair, The Slough of Despond, Mr. Worldly Wiseman, Apollyon and poor bumbling Christian himself better than most of the finest images of Sir Thomas Browne and Donne.

Today, *Uncle Tom's Cabin* is barely readable. For a book which helped set a nation on fire, it drags on every page. Yet it has that same inextinguishable life, and once trapped in its turgid paragraphs a reader does not escape, not even after he has finished reading. Uncle Tom, Topsy, the abominable Eva won't go away.

Jules Verne ground out plots both banal and incredible, based on a scientific knowledge as laughable in detail as prescient in aim. It would take a specialist scholar in French literature to identify the outstanding members of the French Academy contemporary with Verne, but nobody has to tell us who Captain Nemo is, or Phileas Fogg, or Michael Strogoff.

We can lump in a convenient Kraft-paper disposal bag the giants of historico-religious *kitsch* from Bulwer-Lytton's *The Last Days of Pompeii* to General Lew Wallace's *Ben Hur* to Henryk Sienkiewicz's *Quo Vadis* all the way through Lloyd C. Douglas. This latter titan of our own time started off with a soap-opera series of novels (*Magnificent Obsession, Green Light*) before he hit the historico-religious trail with *The Robe* and *The Big Fisherman,* whose wooden characters moved in settings of purest papier-mâché, mouthing dialogue never heard on land or sea. Time hasn't weaned readers away from Bulwer or Wallace or Sienkiewicz, and I suspect it will deal just as kindly with Douglas.

Any list must include Ouida. This half-mad, tireless woman, Marie Louise de la Ramée, filled shelves with a fictional output as unconvincing as her own name. The cardinal rule of her writing seems to have been that sheer ignorance of a subject should never excuse one from writing about it at length. It is easy to sneer at Ouida, and it is impossible to forget the gallantry and self-sacrifice of Cigarette, the half-caste camp follower of *Under Two Flags,* or to dismiss the heart-string tugs of *A Dog of Flanders,* which filled movie houses with damp Kleenex in a film version much gentler than the Ouidan original.

Anthony Hope's *The Prisoner of Zenda* is as laughable in the dark evil of its villain (Black Michael, no less: Rudolph Rassendyll was the *hero*) as George Barr McCutcheon's Graustark romances are in the beauty and virtue of their heroines, always as predictably lovely as (to my youthful eyes) the trolley-card placards for Marchand's Golden Hair Rinse, and as impossibly remote. Hope's Balkan-type principality continues to weave a spell, and McCutcheon's Graustark is more real than Yugoslavia (and Princess Yetive *much* more real than Mrs. Tito).

Baroness Orczy came by her title legitimately, so it is easy to understand the political bent by which her Scarlet Pimpernel devoted his efforts to saving oppressed nobles from the French Revolution. What strains credulity is his continuing survival; perhaps the doltish French anti-monarchists might fail to capture him but surely the insufferability of his sissy pose among his British compatriots should have led someone to kill him out of sheer boredom. So logic tells me; but truth, stronger than logic, compels me to admit that the "demmed elusive Pimpernel's" improbable exploits stir me more than true tales of the Underground of World War II.

Of even closer memory is Edgar Rice Burroughs. Aside from a mastery of the mother tongue just one degree short of total incoherence, the bland and glaring errors of simple geography, biology, genetics, astronomy and physics contained in the Tarzan books, in the Mars series, in the Pellucidar cycle, add up to several volumes of their own. Yet Tarzan stalks in my head beside Hamlet; and Thuvia, Maid of Mars, and John Carter, First Warlord of Mars, stalk close behind him.

Daphne du Maurier's *Jamaica Inn* and *Rebecca* may be dismissed as cleverly mechanical resurrections of Sir Walter Scott crossed with hybrid strains of the detective story and the Gothic novel. For all that, I can remember Rebecca's Manderley better than some houses I have lived in, and I recall, as a boy in Pittsburgh, going out of my way to attend a Methodist church simply because its oratorical pastor reminded me of the smuggler priest in *Jamaica Inn*.

I'm afraid I have also to include *Goodbye, Mr. Chips,* James Hilton's masterpiece of treacle. I won't say that Mr. Chips is unbelievable; I will suggest that if you ever met in life such a moth-eaten, self-pitying, mawkish pedagogue, you would shun him as thoroughly as you would his Empire-happy, sob-sister-under-the-skin, Mrs. Miniver. Still, seedy old Chips and bouncy Mrs. Miniver have identities that make them as strong reference points in recollected reading as pi in mathematics.

I have stuck to novels, but "good-bad" literature knows no bounds. What of most of Charles Lamb's Elia essays? What of potted history like Elbert Hubbard's *Message to Garcia?* What of plays like *East Lynne* and *Abie's Irish Rose?* and why, when I hear the first verses of "Horatius at the Bridge" ("Lars Porsena of Clusium by the Nine Gods he swore/ That the great house of Tarquin should suffer wrong no more") do I get at the back of my neck prickles more authentic than anything evoked by Auden, Eliot, Wallace, Stevens or Allen Ginsberg? Why, as I asked at the beginning, does all this trash stick in our minds?

I think the answer lies in the vitality uncovered in every example from the sheer pulp of an Edgar Rice Burroughs to the masterly carelessness of a Dickens. Critics and other guardians of literature are wary of a quality so difficult to pin down. They try either to sweep the good-bad books under the rug by ignoring them, or, when they cannot be ignored, to explain them in terms diffuse enough to conceal their own bewilderment.

The simple fact remains that the characters in our good-bad books do come to life and refuse stubbornly, in some cases even after centuries, to expire. They may be clichés, they may be one-dimensional, but a live character in one dimension stays with us longer than a character of painfully pricked-out complexity who never begins to breathe in the first place.

This vitality, this life, is a quality that defies precise analysis, measurement and assessment. The critics will go on trying, Lord knows, and may their efforts be blessed. For us, the simple readers, it is sufficient to accept and enjoy. And read.

For, if I see any moral in my examination, it is in the form of a plea for free-wheeling, omnivorous reading. Just that. Reading without qualifications, without pretensions, without snobbism, and above all, without guilt.

Given an initial and unashamed love of reading, you will find time to devour the good along with the bad and the good-bad with both. At the end, the best will stick to your ribs without benefit of culture-clutching justifications or windy critical exegesis.

Charles Lamb, that disgracefully unliterary man of letters, can give us a motto. "I can read anything which I call a book," he said, and I'd like to see the sentence blazoned on a banner.

SEAN O'FAOLAIN

The Meaning of Place

*How does one characterize a man like Sean O'Faolain? He was
born and educated in Ireland, but he has an M.A. from Harvard.
His home is in Ireland, but he is well known on American cam-
puses. He is a short story writer of distinction and also a critic of
perception. He has written books of travel, a biography of Cardinal Newman and an autobiography. In an interview he once
said: "Everywhere I go people take me for an Englishman. I wish,
I wish I was an American."*

WHEN I was a boy at school, reading my Latin texts with one finger on the word and one finger in the Notes, I did not get much
fun out of it. Anyway they made us read the wrong sorts of authors, respectable authors like Cicero and Livy and the dull
parts of Virgil. (This was all Arnold of Rugby's fault; he cut out
the juicy, human authors like Catullus and Plautus and Juvenal in
the interests of Victorian morality.) There *were* a few things
that came my way, then and later at the university, that at least
partly justified all the earlier sweat, blood, toil and tears.

There was Pliny's account of the great eruption of Vesuvius;
and there was an amusingly realistic description by Horace of a
journey by canal barge along the Pontine Marshes, and thence by
carriage along the Appian Way. But I always remember with
pleasure a piece by Virgil, in the *Eclogues,* wherein one Meli-
boeus, about to go into exile, envies his old friend Tityrus who
can remain at home on his little farm. It is not much of a farm —

"bare stones and marsh choke every field with reedy mud" — but to them such modest places meant home and fatherland.

Whenever I used to read it I got the same sensation of intimacy, of familiarity, that I used to get when reading Oliver Goldsmith. I used to see the wet, reedy fields of West Limerick, its straggling hedges, its thatched cottages with their blue smoke becoming visible in the sunset all over the level plain, the willows hanging over the wandering streams, the Holy Well, wood pigeons moaning in scanty woods.

The true response to the poetry of place is a comparatively rare thing in literature: Newman throwing his arms around a willow on the Isis as he leaves Oxford forever, saying, "I am like Undine, killing with a kiss"; Proust remembering Balbec; Gide re-creating his old home in Normandy and his father's land of Provence in *La Porte Etroite;* Dylan Thomas' *Under Milk Wood* — men responding, that is, to something much more, and much deeper, than picturesque surface appeal: to old friends, old loves, precious memories, dear associations.

The nature of a man's response to place is a great test of his humanity. We can tell at once if he is pumping up the emotion, faking it, counterfeiting passion. So, when I say that Virgil's poem reminded me in my youth of Oliver Goldsmith, I was certainly not thinking of "The Traveler" but of "The Deserted Village." There, also, is honesty and intimacy and humanity and sincerity: a poem written not in ink but in tears, a rich suffusion of emotion rising up in a grubby room in Grub Street for a grubby little Irish village. It is the first thing ever written in English by an Irishman that shows true feeling for place. Whereas "The Traveler" is the work of a phony tourist if there ever was one, all full of bogus sententiousness and fake moralizing — just the sort of poem Arnold of Rugby would have made his students admire. It is here that Goldsmith, after writing some banal balderdash about the Italians, cries:

My soul, turn from them, turn we to survey
Where rougher climes a nobler race display.

meaning, if you please, what he calls "the bleak Swiss!"

The fact is that for some two hundred years, between about 1720 and 1920, there have been very few travelers who had any real feeling for place. If they were not bemused by a current sententiousness they were bewitched by a fashionable sentimentality. They confused Poetry with the Picturesque, and of all forms of sentimentality the Picturesque has been both the most insidious and the most persistent. And yet, all this word means is a picture-maker's viewpoint, and at that the viewpoint of a particular convention in picture-making, usually associated with the names of Salvator Rosa and Claude Lorrain, and, I regret to say, Italian taste. (It was the Italians who invented the beastly word.)

We all know those sentimental pictures: the tall, graceful umbrella pine on the left balancing a few broken columns on the right; beyond them, on the one side, a classical balustrade, romantically decayed, trailing bougainvillaea, balanced by a reclining gypsy (undressed if the painter wished to be still more graceful and unlikely); and, behind all, a lake, or blue sea, with a white sail set against a peaked mountain which, at worst, will turn out to be Vesuvius or Etna.

Many a rural British hotel and old-time rectory — unless they stick to hunting scenes — still preserve similar mottled watercolors painted by somebody's great-grandaunt on the Grand Tour. But mock them not too readily, good reader. Be sure, first, that there is not on your own wall a tall and graceful chimney balancing a scarlet fire station against which there leans a *pompier* in the dignified posture of a hussar, while in the background there may stretch a stormy sea of oil derricks against the infinite boredom of a Texas sky. The spirit of Claude Lorrain lives on. Many a contemporary painter (especially the Communist ones) could feelingly adapt Wordsworth's "Lucy Gray":

> *Claude is in the grave, but Oh!*
> *It makes no damn difference to me.*

It is fascinating to watch the Grand Tourists gradually developing this sentimental way of softly seeing, worse still of softly feeling. There is not a trace of the sentimental among travelers before 1700. The letters of Renaissance travelers like Isabella D'Este are almost wholly concerned with practical matters, such as people, social occasions, food, the ardors of the journey. Machiavelli's famous description of country life outside Florence is entirely about the simple pleasures of the cultivated humanist. Montaigne, in Rome, talks only about pleasant friends, good conversations, fine gardens, good food. Addison, on the threshold of the eighteenth century, is still entirely practical. The rot sets in with Thomas Gray who, having been moved by a country churchyard, feels it his duty also to be moved by precipices and torrents; but we are in the very middle of the fashionable current when Mrs. Piozzi starts to gush about the "sublimity and beauty" of a raging volcano, and we are under the full flood of sentimentality when Stendahl writes: "As I stood alone in the Colosseum listening to the singing of the birds . . . I could not hold back my tears."

One does not believe a word these poseurs say, least of all Stendhal, in spite of his enthusiastic defense of *"la vraie passion"* (also à propos of the Colosseum) in *Promenades dans Rome;* indeed we must be all the less inclined to believe him because of his *Promenades dans Rome* — that hefty, three-volume journal of his alleged day-by-day excursions through the city, with two friends who have "real" conversations with "real" people; all imaginary, all written in Paris, and mostly "borrowed" from magazines and books; as when (to give one only of many instances) he blandly describes a Papal Conclave he never saw. "I cannot describe for you," he says, "the transports of joy and impatience that stirred us all . . ." No wonder, seeing that he had swiped it all out of the *London Magazine*.

Not that I have any doubt that he did weep in the Colosseum. He was a tenderhearted man; it is one reason why he is one of the greatest of French novelists. But he was not a good traveler, meaning, simply, that his Truth was infinitely less credible than his fiction.

I confess that I never respond to places like the Colosseum, or Pompeii, or the Roman Forum, or the ruins of Ostia or Agrigento, unless my imagination, or some learned and sensitive friend, can first people them for me as they were when they were alive. (It is characteristic of the sentimental delusion that Stendhal felt that the Colosseum is much more impressive now as a ruin than it ever was when it was in actual use. Then, he says, it was only a theatre. "Only" a theatre!)

Indeed the only time I am certain that I am getting the true feel of Rome itself is when I am, let us say, sitting chatting with some dear friend in the Pincio Gardens, watching the lovers and the children and the idlers stroll by; or lunching after on the terrace of the Villa Valadier overlooking Rome's level plain of roofs, and towers and domes, seeing it all as one close weave of present and past, one unity in which the old Rome was not something secluded or insulated from the new but a continuing and creative power that held, and foretold, and compelled the lovers, the children and the idlers, and the Frascati shining on my table, and even me privileged to share one exquisite moment of its unbroken continuum.

This is why I distrust travelers who dislike change and clamor for the preservation of things as they were when they first saw them. I distrust their life-sense. I feel they are interested less in men than in monuments. Carcassonne has been "preserved"

stone by stone with loving devotion; it is literally stone-dead.
Bruges is a stuffed bird. Weimar may be found touching by
moonlight; it does not survive the busy, human morning. But Ra-
venna, where only the mosaics are tended, is palpitating with
the happy come-and-go of present life. That splendidly neglected
town of Aigue-Mortes, south of Nîmes, once a port, now abandoned by the tide, is attractive not for its age but as a pleasant
oasis of present-day Provençal life.

Where past and present mingle like this, enriching one another, informing one another, we have the best of both worlds.
Paris and Rome are the royal examples. One can, to be sure, be
sentimental in Paris, go about taking photographs of "picturesque
bits"; but not for long. In Rome even Stendhal occasionally
came to the surface; as when, unguardedly, forgetting fashion,
he admitted that the ideal time to appraise the Colosseum is
"after midnight, with an attractive woman."

It is one of the most difficult things in the world to be natural.
There is always some fashionable way of seeing and feeling. The
modern fashion is the Social Conscience, which is infinitely
more boring than the Sentimental Eye. The number of young
Americans I have talked to in Europe who see nothing at all but
statistics, underemployment, bad finance, political chaos, moral
turpitude, underproduction and the devil knows what other social
abstraction! The only possible thing to say to these sad young
people is that the best way to see any city at all is "after midnight,
with an attractive young woman" — and then, by Heaven, I
swear they would sit in the Colosseum reading a Senate report by
the light of the moon.

C. S. LEWIS

A Bubbling in the
Author's Mind

Probably the late C. S. Lewis will be remembered most clearly as the author of The Screwtape Letters, *a dazzling satire in which, as one British critic said, he made "righteousness readable." But this Oxford don wrote of many things: literary history, novels akin to science fiction, Christian apologetics, and, yes, books for children.*

IN THE sixteenth century when everyone was saying that poets (by which they meant all imaginative writers) ought "to please and instruct," Tasso made a valuable distinction. He said that the poet, as poet, was concerned solely with pleasing. But then every poet was also a man and a citizen; in that capacity he ought to, and would wish to, make his work edifying as well as pleasing.

Now I do not want to stick very close to the Renaissance ideas of "pleasing" and "instructing." Before I could accept either term it might need so much redefining that what was left of it at the end would not be worth retaining. All I want to use is the distinction between the author as author and the author as man, citizen, or Christian. What this comes to for me is that there are usually two reasons for writing an imaginative work, which may be called Author's reason and the Man's. If only one of these is present, then, so far as I am concerned, the book will not be written. If the first is lacking, it can't; if the second is lacking, it shouldn't.

In the Author's mind there bubbles up every now and then the material for a story. For me it invariably begins with mental pictures. This ferment leads to nothing unless it is accompanied with the longing for a Form: verse or prose, short story, novel, play or what not. When these two things click you have the Author's impulse complete. It is now a thing inside him pawing to get out. He longs to see that bubbling stuff pouring into that Form as the housewife longs to see the new jam pouring into the clean jam jar. This nags him all day long and gets in the way of his work and his sleep and his meals. It's like being in love.

While the Author is in this state, the Man will of course have to criticize the proposed book from quite a different point of view. He will ask how the gratification of this impulse will fit in with all the other things he wants, and ought to do or be. Perhaps the whole thing is too frivolous and trivial (from the Man's point of view, not the Author's) to justify the time and pains it would involve. Perhaps it would be unedifying when it was done. Or else perhaps (at this point the Author cheers up) it looks like being "good," not in a merely literary sense, but "good" all around.

This may sound rather complicated but it is really very like what happens about other things. You are attracted by a girl; but is she the sort of girl you'd be wise, or right, to marry? You would like to have lobster for lunch; but does it agree with you and is it wicked to spend that amount of money on a meal? The Author's impulse is a desire (it is very like an itch) and, of course, like every other desire, needs to be criticized by the whole Man.

Let me now apply this to my own fairy tales. Some people seem to think that I began by asking myself how I could say something about Christianity to children; then fixed on the fairy tale as an instrument; then collected information about child psychology and decided what age group I'd write for; then drew up a list of basic Christian truths and hammered out "allegories" to embody them. This is all pure moonshine. I couldn't write in that way at all. Everything began with images; a faun carrying an umbrella, a queen on a sledge, a magnificent lion. At first there wasn't even anything Christian about them; that element pushed itself in of its own accord. It was part of the bubbling.

Then came the Form. As these images sorted themselves into events (i.e., became a story) they seemed to demand no love interest and no close psychology. But the Form which excludes these things is the fairy tale. And the moment I thought of that I fell in love with the Form itself: its brevity, its severe restraints on description, its flexible traditionalism, its inflexible hostility to all analysis, digression, reflections and "gas." I was now enamored of it. Its very limitations of vocabulary became an attraction; as the hardness of the stone pleases the sculptor or the difficulty of the sonnet delights the sonneteer.

On that side (as Author) I wrote fairy tales because the Fairy Tale seemed the ideal Form for the stuff I had to say.

Then of course the Man in me began to have his turn. I thought I saw how stories of this kind could steal past a certain inhibition which had paralyzed much of my own religion in childhood. Why did one find it so hard to feel as one was told one ought to feel about God or about the sufferings of Christ? I thought the chief reason was that one was told one ought to. An obligation to feel can freeze feelings. And reverence itself did harm. The whole subject was associated with lowered voices; almost as if it were something medical. But supposing that by casting all these things into an imaginary world, stripping them of their stained-glass and Sunday school associations, one could make them for the first time appear in their real potency? Could one not thus steal past those watchful dragons? I thought one could.

That was the Man's motive. But of course he could have done nothing if the Author had not been on the boil first.

You will notice that I have throughout spoken of Fairy Tales, not "children's stories." Prof. J. R. R. Tolkien in *The Lord of the Rings* showed that the connection between Fairy Tales and children is not nearly so close as publishers and educationalists think. Many children don't like them and many adults do. The truth is, as he says, that they are now associated with children because they are out of fashion with adults; have in fact retired to the nursery as old furniture used to retire there, not because the children had begun to like it but because their elders had ceased to like it.

I was therefore writing "for children" only in the sense that I excluded what I thought they would not like or understand; not in the sense of writing what I intended to be below adult attention. I may of course have been deceived, but the principle at least saves one from being patronizing. I never wrote down to anyone; and whether the opinion condemns or acquits my own work, it certainly is my opinion that a book worth reading only in childhood is not worth reading even then. The inhibitions which I hoped my stories would overcome in a child's mind may exist in a grownup's mind too, and may perhaps be overcome by the same means.

The Fantastic or Mythical is a Mode available at all ages for some readers; for others, at none. At all ages, if it is well used by the author and meets the right reader, it has the same power: to generalize while remaining concrete, to present in palpable form not concepts or even experiences but whole classes of experience, and to throw off irrelevancies. But at its best it can do more; it can give us experiences we have never had and thus, instead of "commenting on life," can add to it. I am speaking, of course, about the thing itself, not my own attempts at it.

"Juveniles," indeed! Am I to patronize sleep because children sleep sound! Or honey because children like it?

KINGSLEY AMIS

What We Need Is Savage Laughter

It was with Lucky Jim *in 1954 that Kingsley Amis made his bow as a novelist, and critics recognized immediately the appearance of an author with unusual talent for satire and social comedy. His most recent novel is* One Fat Englishman.

WE ARE in for a golden age of satire, in my opinion, and if this is so we will be fortunate indeed. Satire offers a social and moral contribution. A culture without satire is a culture without self-criticism and thus, ultimately, without humanity. A society such as ours, in which the forms of power are changing and multiplying, needs above all the restraining influences of savage laughter. Even if that influence at times seems negligible, the satirist's laughter is valid as a gesture — a gesture on the side of reason.

Satire in its modern forms I take to be fiction that attacks vice and folly as manifested in the individual. It is, then, a more limited affair than the great age of English satire understood it to be. Men like Dryden, Butler and Pope turned personal abuse into poetry and made it the expression of a mature and coherent view of life; Swift and Fielding took human institutions, human society and (in *Gulliver's Travels* at any rate) man's very condition as the field of their attack. Faced with that comparison our Evelyn Waughs and Mary McCarthys are likely to seem rather small fry.

It is true that the disappearance of satirical verse is an impover-

ishment to literature, and that the relegation to the propagandist
novel of attacks on social and institutional abuses has meant a
loss to satire. But the modern satirist has two important weapons
which potentially recover for him all the ground he has lost: humor and realism. To imply that these weapons are newcomers
in this field may seem less paradoxical if we recall how little real
laughter emerges alongside Dryden's grandiose anger or Pope's
soaring ingenuity, how little contact with life in detail, life as it
actually unfolds itself, can be salvaged from the airy fantasies of
Butler or the tortured nightmares of Swift. The single exception — a most relevant one — is Fielding, whose realism two
hundred years have not dimmed and whose humor is closer to our
own than that of any writer before the present century.

Postwar England has seen what it would not be excessive to call
a Fielding revival. This has been manifested not merely in a renewed critical interest but in a changing attitude toward the
novel in general. John Wain and Iris Murdoch, for instance, are
two young writers who, though far too often compared and in
most ways poles apart, are alike in their evident feeling that the
novel of a consistent tone, moving through a recognized and restricted cycle of emotional keys, was outmoded.

Without having to picture such writers going through a eureka-
routine with a copy of *Tom Jones,* one can still detect in them
some kind of affinity with its author. Their attempt has been to
combine the violent and the absurd, the grotesque and the romantic, the farcical and the horrific within a single novel. A
possible parallel with Dickens, whose example might admittedly
have suggested the horrific element in the brew, is less immediate. Read alongside Fielding, it is the Victorian who seems remote, naïve, almost primitive, certainly anti-realist and the virtuoso of a mode of humor that stifles action.

Whatever its roots, I think we have something new here, new
in terms of our century anyhow, and of potential importance.

There has certainly been an almost explicit rejection of pre-war satiric modes as exemplified by Aldous Huxley and Evelyn Waugh. Both these writers, indeed, came to reject satire, the one in favor of mysticism and belles-lettres, the other in order to devote himself to threnodies upon the decline and fall of the English aristocracy. Seen in retrospect their earlier work appears uneven, Huxley's brilliance marred by poverty of emotion and incident and by a sort of baroque inlay of erudition, Waugh's humor, wonderfully sure and inventive though it is, streaked with cruelty and partly vitiated by the snobbery that was to erupt with a roar in *Brideshead Revisited.* In more than one sense it can be said of these writers that their world is not our world.

Postwar changes have been quick to reflect themselves in satire, which next to caricature has always proved the most socially sensitive of the arts. The welfare democracy, with its internal shifts in the balance of power, is a satirical arena far vaster and richer than the stratified democracy which is now yielding place to it. Old-established forms of privilege are on the defensive, although far from being on the retreat: at this stage aristocratic posturings are at their most vapid and most vulnerable.

New kinds of privileges are in the ascendant, each battling for mastery: at this stage the vices and follies of the social climb and the economic rat-race offer themselves for deflation. Until the new society is simplified and stabilized, which may not be for decades, we are in for what I have called a golden age of satire. It will be inferior in wit and urbanity to the modes which have preceded it, but in humor, vigor and breadth of scope it is likely to prove superior.

The foregoing sociological homily makes more sense in a British context than in an American one, although I believe that the similarity between their lines of development, is on the increase. In literary terms this is already noticeable. American critics have shown themselves aware of the relevance of English postwar satire to their own environment. I can certainly testify that it is the more satirical of American writers who strike the readiest and fullest response in England, who seem in a sense most familiar. The work of Hemingway and Faulkner — and this must not be read as implying any denigration — appears alien, strongly and essentially non-European, and I connect this with their characteristic indifference to humor and satire. American literature at its most American may be powerfully, even violently, concerned with social matters, but it is the concern of the propagandist, not the satirist, and its irony and indignation are those of Swift, not those of Fielding.

The other side of the picture emerges if the novels and stories of such writers as Louis Auchincloss, Jerome Weidman and John Cheever are carefully studied, and if the work of Mary McCarthy and Peter de Vries is read at all. The last two are thoroughgoing satirists in a mode that, without having any necessary connection with English prototypes, is immediately recognizable to the English reader. Miss McCarthy in fact has at times stood higher in English esteem than any other American writer of her generation. There are many excellent reasons for this, and it cannot be denied that her astringency comes like a draught of cold water after the tepid and messy cocktails averagely purveyed, but that very coldness easily becomes chilling. The satirist's occupational disease is intellectualism, a detachment so poised that it slides into a withdrawn superiority. In this connection, as in others, humor is the satirist's lifebelt.

Nobody could accuse Peter de Vries of not being funny enough: I would rate him the funniest serious writer to be found either side of the Atlantic. I have heard the complaint that he is really too funny, that there is no respite from the constant din of firecrackers. This mistake arises, as it usually does when accusations of frivolity are leveled, from an inability to appreciate just how funny, and hence how serious, the stuff is. De Vries would probably disavow the slightest pretension, but the fizzing hilarities of *Tunnel of Love* and *Comfort Me with Apples* are aimed in deadly earnest. Affectation and irresponsibility, self-dramatization and self-pity are his targets, and the gaiety of the whole performance evinces a rare skill and integrity. This is what the satirist works toward and seldom achieves.

STEPHEN SPENDER

Literary London: A Tight
Little Isle

[*Mr. Spender made his first appearance in this collection on
page 34.*]

A REASON once given by W. H. Auden for leaving England is that
he would not remain in a country where it was impossible to be
alone. England is the country where the writers meet all the time,
know each other completely and never escape from mutual in-
grown self-awareness.

There are a good many reasons why this should be so. The
most obvious of them is London. London is a center as nowhere
else is. Not an intellectual center, like Paris, where ideas are
endlessly discussed, for the English do not like discussing ideas,
and consider it bad form to talk shop. Nor a center where business is done and writers become successes, like New York. For in
London success is considered not only vulgar but also superfluous,
since, essentially, in England the only success that really counts is
joining a "club," getting to know the people you want to know,
and, from this point of view, success is unsociable and boring.
Literary London might be defined as a place where writers
know each other. It is a consciousness, above all a consciousness
of everyone else's affairs. There is a kind of shared tolerance
about it which is certainly decent and civilized, but there is also a
distrust of anything which goes beyond the personal, that makes
nearly all standards conversational, and which is discouraging of
superhuman effort.

In the early part of this century the attitude of literary London to men like D. H. Lawrence and Ezra Pound, who took writing, and life, too seriously, was that they were "bores," and rather embarrassing. Conversation should not be too serious, no one should attempt to monopolize it, and it should not deal with subjects such as foreign countries, illness, heaven or hell, which are not generally accepted topics. It should be concerned above all with personalities; and those who permit their personalities to be discussed, however ruthlessly, soon endear themselves and become accepted.

Of course, every writer does not come to London, and there are a few who, all their lives, manage to remain provincial and regional. But for most writers London is where they meet their colleagues, and it provides their means of livelihood, most of which belongs to a no man's land between literature and the universities, broadcasting and reviewing. But it is the London life that really provides the tone in which the academic and literary meet.

The English writer is not, like the American poet, drawn into the university and made the representative of the Eastern or Midwestern university, speaking for his district, in the parliament of letters. On the contrary, in England it is far more likely that the academic gets drawn into the London world, even without leaving his university. In their capacity as broadcasters and writers in the reviews, the Oxford and Cambridge dons, who write articles and broadcast — Hugh Trevor-Roper, A. J. Ayer, A. J. P. Taylor, Noel Annan, and others — belong much more to the world of literary London than to their senior common rooms.

This is true even of the ex-Angry Young Men of the red brick universities. No one outside Swansea thinks of Kingsley Amis as a onetime don at a Welsh university. To the English reader he is someone whose books are reviewed, and who reviews books, in various journals. Similarly John Wain is not remembered as the

young don from Reading University. He is someone whose books
are reviewed and who reviews books in *The Observer.*

Visitors to London are sometimes surprised to discover how
little sense many English writers seem to have of a public
outside their literary family, how free they are in telling stories
about each other, and how wide a gap there often is between their
privately spoken and their publicly expressed views. An American editor told me recently how shocked he was to hear English
reviewers speak with frivolous disrespect of a novel by a well-
known colleague which, in their reviews, they had discussed at
length and seriously.

The reviewers, if challenged, would probably say that the
novel was not so bad as to be worth attacking, that they liked the
author and met him frequently, and to be nice to him in private
and publicly nasty would seem uncalled for. If the American
editor protested that in this case it was surely disloyal to attack his
novel in private conversation, they would have said, no, not at
all, because within the magic circle of those who really knew, one
can say what one thinks without fear of it getting back to the
author; and, besides, life would be intolerable if one could never
say what one thought.

There is in England a long tradition of discreet indiscretion,
which is perhaps the virtue, or polite corruption, passed on by
an upper class long used to revealing, and covering over, the mis-
demeanors of royal persons. At any rate, there is no country in
which there is a finer sense of what can be said, and by whom, and
to whom.

Gossip in London may seem deadlier than that in New York
because it is based often on more intimate knowledge, and is
therefore more accurate. On the other hand, those who fight with
rapiers may be effectively protected from serious wounds if they
wear masks of wire gauze. And this is true of London gossip,
which hardly extends beyond the small circle of the initiated,

who are agreed, at one and the same time, to indulge in it and ignore it. The gossipers know very well that they are also the gossiped about; but they also know that they live in a small community where few offenses are regarded really seriously — the English literary belong as it were to a league of anti-puritanism joined by common consent — and where the outside world is singularly little interested in the lives of writers, anyway.

When it comes to reviewing each other's books — and there is no one but the other writers to review them — the conflict between the private code of discreet indiscretion and literary values which demand that the reviewer be honest is often extremely painful. There is, I think, comparatively little logrolling, but in the case of "established" writers — who are established not just by their books but by being for long among colleagues — efforts are made to avoid pressing a public obligation to tell the truth which might offend against the invisible laws of personal relations. The novels of the late Charles Morgan are a case in point. His last two or three novels were received with almost the same praise as his earlier ones. It was only apparent when he died, from the obituaries, how the bottom had quietly fallen out of his reputation. It is, indeed, extremely painful to write just what you think about your contemporaries, when you are meeting them every day at the club, or at some party. Where personal relations are so involved, it is almost impossible to be impartial, because being disagreeably "fair" about the work of a friend does give one a feeling of betrayal. Sooner or later one decides never to review the works of one's friends. But this decision may not be so clear cut as it sounds. An older writer is on friendly terms with most other writers, so it may mean having to review the young, the new and outsiders. One decides after all to review a friend's work when one can "objectively" admire it.

Complications of this kind leave their mark on the English weeklies. One notices, for example, that two of the most frequent

reviewers, Raymond Mortimer and Cyril Connolly, seem to devote a disproportionate amount of their attention to reviewing
books of memoirs of royalty, and books about the smaller mam-
mals or the larger spiders. The reviews in the Sunday newspapers scarcely give the impression that the senior reviewers give
their lively attention to the newest developments in literature,
either to praise or to attack these. Obviously a good deal of their
reviewing is evasive tactics.

Of course, some reviewers are insistently outspoken. That they
get the reputation for being so merely transfers the responsibility
for their hostile opinions from the writer to the editor. An entirely honest and greatly respected editor once said to me: "I realize that to employ X to write a review is a hostile act, and I feel
unhappy whenever I ask him to deal with a book by one of my
friends."

I heard recently that an English lady novelist had pointed out
that when writing a novel she was aware of the name of every
single fellow writer who would be going to review it. This lady
is a bit calculating, but her calculations are probably right, because novel reviews are nearly always signed, and, in most papers, usually written by the same person. I suppose the lady
might be tempted to be extra friendly to her reviewing colleagues, meeting them at parties, before her publisher's act of
parturition.

Just as the Japanese are allowed to behave more or less as they
please when they are drunk, English writers are given exceptional latitude when they are young. The young writer is expected to be rude about the works of his elders, but very soon he
gets to know better, that is to say, he gets to know them. They are
no longer the "corrupt bogies" he imagined when he was in the
sixth form. They inquire solicitously about the progress of his
second novel, hinting what a difficult hurdle to take is this one,
and his reviews appear in columns side by side with theirs. The

young writer soon finds that the talk about cliques was nonsense; there is only one clique, and he is in it.

The idea that the Leftist writers of the thirties or the Angry Young Men of the fifties were going to overthrow the Old Gang proved absurd. They had only to raise their voices and the Old Gang instantly surrendered, or seemed to do so. What actually happened was that the New Young Writers were admitted into the ranks of the Old Gang which, for a few months, took on a new look, after which it appeared to be strangely the same. By the time this happened the New Young Writers were all well over thirty.

The English literary scene does not resemble so much a battle-field, or a brothel, as a conspiracy. It has the essential quality which gives strength to conspiracies: the discovery of all parties, however opposed they may seem, that, after all, they are in the same boat. The climatic conditions force upon them the same measures and the same conclusions, and drive them all far away from the land of big operations, big money and big banks, and of an almost totally indifferent public.

Here they are then, making their living out of broadcasting, literary journalism in the weeklies, and hoarding time for what each secretly regards as his "real work." After a time, the young discover the older writers, whom formerly they regarded as corrupted, are merely the spiritually defeated — those who have been too preoccupied with making a living to concentrate on their "real work."

The danger of such a conspiracy is not the extremes of cut-throat rivalry, on the one hand, excesses of mutual admiration, on the other, nor even of corruption. The real danger is that the self-awareness of the London group as a group becomes more significant than anything else for its members. After all, we col-leagues understand each other very well; we are intelligent, and have generated a great deal of tepid mutual esteem and affection;

we have managed to subsist on an audience, and yet to retain our private faces — do we really have to bother too much at acting as if each of us thought he was better than the other, before a hypothetical intelligent public? This is rather the mood. It is comforting to think that E. M. Forster has not written a novel since 1924, and that the excellence of *The Waste Land,* which was also written a long, long time ago, justifies us in not having to attack *The Confidential Clerk,* and the young writers can be anesthetized with short doses of overpraise, followed by long spells of neglect.

So the real English danger is of forming a society of mutual noncompetitiveness among those who are agreed that no one should raise his voice too loud. The society does maintain standards of a very high average. No one is expected to sink below these and no one is loved for rising too far above them.

They verge on being social standards rather than literary ones. They are maintained by general agreement as to the amount of literary and general education which a writer should show in his writing, and as to the measures to be taken if he falls below these. When a young writer, who has mistakenly been accepted, fails to make the grade, he is savagely treated, as happened with Colin Wilson, whose first book was overpraised, his second attacked with fury by those who felt he let the side down.

In such a community, it is still possible to be gracefully accomplished, even to do serious work, and there are many things to be said in its favor. I think the London literary family is fortified today by the feeling that it is more civilized than most of the world, and that we are living in times when to contain an unprecedented situation in a work of the imagination would make such demands on a writer that perhaps it is best to have no such pretensions.

At any rate, to be a rebel in literary London is exceedingly difficult. The simplest way of doing so is to separate oneself from it altogether and become an outsider. This is what Lawrence did, simply by shaking the dust of London off his feet, in a scene described in "Women in Love." His admirer, F. R. Leavis, from his anti-Cambridge foothold in Cambridge, likewise uncompromisingly rejects the London-Oxford-Cambridge circle.

In the long run, however, the rejectors of their culture, even when they claim that they belong to an "alternate tradition," seem to have a good deal to lose from their outposts, and they spice their denunciations with impossible solutions, like Leavis' idea of the "organic community" or Lawrence's Lady Chatterley and her lover.

The most hopeful symptoms in England are contained in the work of writers who do not denounce or make outsiders of themselves, but who, though within the literary family, yet somehow have a stolidity of critical attitude, an independent subject-matter, more rooted values, which resist it. The criticism of V. S. Pritchett and Frank Kermode, the interesting social ideas of Richard Hoggart, and the novels of Alan Sillitoe and Colin MacInnes, seem to have this kind of resistant independent strength. Add to these the theatre of Arnold Wesker — insistently concerned with working-class life, and craftsmanly yet not "literary" — and there is hope that after all the Welfare State will produce a new culture with wider roots in society.

CARLOS BAKER

This England That Its Writers Know

[Mr. Baker has been introduced on page 3.]

POETRY, said Robert Frost on one occasion, is what gets lost in translation. The same might be said of any national culture. Much that belongs to the essence of a nation's common life seems to drop silently out of a novel, a play, or a poem when it moves out of its native land into foreign climes. It is almost literally the buried life of a nation, present and vital as a heartbeat, but just as invisible.

We like to say that the writing and reading of literature is an international enterprise, like rockets and atomic fission. Yet this is true only within certain limits. Is Albert Camus' *The Plague,* for example, the same book to an Algerian or an American that it is to a native of France? Can Gogol's *Dead Souls,* however faithful the translation, be actually translated in the fullest sense across the cultural and temporal borderland behind which it was composed? Can *Huckleberry Finn* speak to the Finnish national as it can to the latter-day Missourian? What will a modern Hungarian student make of *Tom Brown's School Days?*

A significant part of any culture never becomes fully explicit in its literature. Even the best writers tend to take it for granted. Of course it lurks there implicitly between the lines, and the truly initiated in the life of the nation can point it out. But we can probably never discover it for ourselves unless we have lived long and open-mindedly among the people by whom and for whom the literature was produced. Then only can we get the feel of the land, the sense of its unwritten mores, its ethical geography, the values its people tacitly accept. To hear this heartbeat we need the stethoscope of lived experience.

The American reader in England soon finds this out. He may bow to none in his reverence for Chaucer, Shakespeare and Milton. He may regard himself as an inveterate Dickensian and a true Trollopian, an enthusiast in the poetry of Wordsworth and Browning, Dylan Thomas or C. Day Lewis. He may know Waugh and Cary, Kingsley Amis and Colin Wilson like the back of his hand. The common Anglo-American cultural heritage of language and literature, law and religion may elicit his fraternal reflections. But he has not been long in England before the suspicion gradually dawns: there is more to this people than their literature overtly shows. To find it out he must live, as intensively as possible, the actual everyday life of these English people.

Take, for example, the persistent rurality of England. Overwhelmed, as he often is at home, by the inexorable spread of suburbia, the American in the British Isles is surprised to encounter a way of life which he had thought was buried forever in the familiar quatrains of Gray's elegy. The flash of three-dimensional revelation comes upon him as he watches a twentieth-century plowman in mud-caked boots plodding homeward down a puddled lane in springtime twilight. The cotter's Saturday night, the village pub shows, is not much different from what Burns misrepresented with a pretty sentimentality. On the downs of Wessex the moral equivalents of Hardy's shepherds still endure the slings and arrows that mutton is heir to. Daffodils spring as redundantly as they did for Wordsworth beside the plashy shores of Ullswater in the Lake District.

"All seasons," predicted Coleridge, "shall be sweet to thee." He was speaking of his son, but he might have meant the English people, most of whom love their land intensely. The American must learn this love. His heart skips a pleasurable beat the first time he sees a thatched roof in the Quantocks, snowladen, steaming in the sunthaw. As in the days of Milton, tanned haycocks bebutton the meads and smoke ascends busily from cottage chimneys among oak trees. Under the benison of frequent rain, Wordsworth's hedgerows spring as sportively as ever they did a century ago. Keats' redbreast yet whistles in the springtime garden croft, and at the other end of the calendar the darkling thrush with wind-beruffled plume still hurls his valiant song into the teeth of autumnal gales.

The literature of no other people is quite so weather-conscious. Consider the British winter. Readers from more thermotic regions may well speculate on the fact that in none of the five hundred winters between 1380 and 1880 was English literature composed but by men and women whose knee joints had congealed to rigidity and whose pen-holding fingers were pink or blue with cold. A brisk January morning in Southwark or Tintagel, Banbury or Saffron Walden confirms the truth of Hogarth's winter pictures. Coleridge's "Frost at Midnight" takes on additional overtones for any who have lingered before a smoldering peat fire while the environing cold creeps up the stairs of their vertebrae in the dead vast and bottom of an English winter.

Who can truly comprehend *Wuthering Heights* if he has not heard the awesome wuther of the wind across a Yorkshire moorland? Who knows the imagistic emphases of Keats' "Eve of St. Agnes" unless he has cowered beside the frozen effigies of medieval knights and ladies in an unheated English antechapel? What ailed that wretched wight in "La Belle Dame Sans Merci"? Was it really enchantress-trouble or was it simply the consequence of a night's sleep on that damp cold hillside?

Mr. T. S. Eliot, American-born British subject, once listed what he called "the characteristic activities and interests" of the Briton at home. He included "Derby Day, Henley Regatta, Cowes, the twelfth of August, a cup final, the dog races, the pin table, the dart board, Wensleydale cheese, boiled cabbage cut into sections, beetroot in vinegar, nineteenth-century Gothic churches, and the music of Elgar." So far as I can tell, not a single item on this list plays any visible part in English literature, even in Eliot's own poems. The reason is clear: authors simply accept the gray anonymity of overboiled cabbage or the sour tang of pickled beets as something too familiar, or vulgar, or both, to be worth mentioning.

One could easily make, as Mr. Eliot invites the reader to do, other lists equally characteristic, of which the same thing might be said. Broad beans and roast potatoes for instance, ginger wine on Christmas Eve, bicarbonate of soda on Boxing Day, bread fried in bacon drippings, cloth caps, motorcycles, fish and chips in squares of newspaper, the love of quasi-military uniforms, yellow brick, tile roofs and dirty raincoats.

None of this gets into literature, unless perhaps in a short story by William Sansom or a blast by Kenneth Tynan. Yet the American reader, having discovered it, adds it to his store of information about England, knowing that it will illuminate, in all sorts of subtle ways, his future reading of English literature. Whether Thackeray said so or not, Becky Sharp was probably rolling a sweet on her prettily pointed tongue when she first stepped into *Vanity Fair*. In imagining the appearance of every major British heroine from Fielding's Amelia to Meredith's Diana, it is well for the foreign reader to recall the dietetic ubiquity of the potato.

Shaw's remark that the Englishman thinks he is being virtuous when he is only being uncomfortable was an outlander's satirical rapier thrust. The trouble with it is, not that it is untrue, but that it understresses the immense — sometimes even overpowering — virtue of the English people. That inbred spartanism, for instance, which commences in babyhood, reaches incredible heights in the rugger matches of adolescence, is carried like a banner along all the roads and in all the houses and culminates in a determined longevity. One finds a hint or two of it in Maggie Tulliver; it forms an unstressed element in the ordeal of Richard Feverel; it is accepted without complaint by persons as various as Jane Eyre, Dickens' Joe Gargery, Hardy's Gabriel Oak, Soames Forsyte and Mrs. Miniver.

If one has seen in the flesh the British capacity to endure, he is the better prepared for sympathetic appreciation of every English literary hero from Beowulf on down. So with the plucky resilience, the hatred of waste, the carefulness with money (of which there is on the whole so little) ; the persistent policy of bolted gates, high walls, locked doors; the willingness to settle for less in a culture which is learning only very slowly that it is possible to ask for more; the fierce respect for property; the strain of latter-day puritanism that is seemingly so anxious to set one right, to assume the role of governess or nanny in the moral direction of the world.

All these qualities can be located between the lines of English literature if the reader's sensibilities have been sufficiently alerted by a personal experience of island life. But the Englishman, content enough to wear his bowler on his head, wise enough to carry his umbrella in his hand, was never one to display his heart upon his sleeve. Whoever wishes truly to find his buried life in his literature must dig for it among the tacit assumptions on which his culture is based.

LAWRENCE CLARK POWELL

Books That Weren't in My Baggage

*If "a bookman" can be defined as "a lover of books," then Law-
rence Clark Powell is the pure quill. He has spent his life with
them, as a teacher, a librarian, and once upon a time as a ship-
ping clerk in a bookstore. He has collected books and manuscripts, has written about books and their authors, and always
he has communicated to readers — and listeners when he was on
the platform — his enthusiasm of what a book can mean in the
life of a man.*

"Aren't you taking any books?" my wife asked, as I began to pack
my suitcase for our trip abroad. "Hundreds," I replied, and went
on putting in shirts and socks. "They're all in my head."

I had remembered an encounter during the war with the late
Isaac Foot, Lord Mayor of Plymouth, who had come on a mission
to America with six suitcases of books and one dispatch case of
clothes. He told me the selection of the books had upset him for
a week, and even then he lacked the ones he really wanted.
"Next time," he had said, "I'll keep it to two books — the dictionary and *Lorna Doone."*

Yet early the next morning, as my wife and I were descending
through overcast for the landing at Zurich and had a vision of
snowy fields and villages and shining Alps, I suddenly found myself wanting a certain book — John Russell's *Switzerland,* in the
British Batsford series, a civilized view of a civilized country I
had read by chance the year before. And it occurred to me that

airlines on the international runs might well arrange for paper-back printings of characteristic books — to give their passengers more lasting fare than the ephemera they now dispense so lavishly: newspapers and magazines, toiletries and toys, food and liquor.

What would we offer on flights to the United States?

At a concert in the Tonhalle, pleased with the early hour and the exclusion of latecomers, I recalled another good book by John Russell — his monograph on Erich Kleiber, the conductor, who died at Zurich on the 200th anniversary of Mozart's birth, a model work of biographical criticism by the art critic of the London *Sunday Times*.

And then there were the works of James Joyce, of course, there in the city where he toiled on *Ulysses* and where he died and is buried — the great novel and the single poem, "Bahnhofstrasse," and Frank Budgen's *James Joyce and the Making of Ulysses,* a Zuricher's reminiscence of those years before fame. In a bookshop in the Bahnhofstrasse, I admired their stock of Joyce and Joyceana, but I didn't need to open a single book; I had them all in mind.

In Salzburg at last, I found Mozartiana new to me and sent home several parcels of books for later reading. There and in Zurich I was impressed by the knowledge and taste of the employees, even the youngest ones, accounted for by the apprentice system followed in the European book trade whereby to be a bookseller calls for a course of work and study similar to that required of librarians.

I did weaken and bought one book for my baggage: a paper-back translation of Annette Kolb's *Mozart,* published in 1939, an impassioned biography with scathing judgments on those who failed Mozart the most, including the Archbishop Colloredo, Baron Grimm, Mozart's wife, Constanze, and the Viennese public.

It was March in Salzburg, and we were ahead of the festival throngs. The museum of Mozart's birthplace was nearly deserted, and it was also unlighted and unheated, which seemed to me exactly right. Wrong, however, is the statue of him in the Mozartplatz, a travesty of his likeness which should be pulled down and melted. The nearby Papageno statue, and the Mozart-brunnen in St. Gilgen, depicting the boy Mozart with his violin, are beautiful.

Entering Austria over the Arlberg Pass, on the one day the ribbon road was open without chains being imperative was less harrowing than leaving Austria over the Brenner Pass. Although the latter is lower and more of a plateau route through the Alps to Italy, it carries enormous trucking traffic, is two-lane, and it was snowing all the way.

The Brenner was the very route Mozart and his father followed on their first trip to Italy in 1770 — Innsbruck, Brennero, Bolzano, Trento, Verona, Mantova, Bologna and Florence; and it must have been the way that Goethe went, when he first felt Italy's hot breath.

> *Kennst du das Land, wo die Zitronen bluehn,*
> *Im dunkeln Laub die Gold-Orangen gluehn,*
> *Ein sanfter Wind vom blauen Himmel weht,*
> *Die Myrte still und hoch der Lorbeer steht?*

No lemons or oranges were to be seen in the snowy Dolomites as we funneled down to the Lombardy plain; only a million fruit and nut trees in bloom, and the stuccoed-over stone houses painted in pastels, proved we were on the sunny southern side of the Alpine wall. After a crossing of the flood-stage Po, on a temporary bridge made of planks on boats lashed together, we got onto the Autostrada del Sole, and stayed there all the way through the Apennines into Tuscany.

Robert Browning remains my favorite "Italian" poet, and I

found myself wanting my volume of his collected poems, if only to recall the correct text of "De Gustibus," whose only remembered lines were:

*What I like best in all the world
Is a castle precipice-encurled
In a gash of the wind-grieved Apennine.*

In Florence for the first time in thirty years, I found myself pleased with the reconstruction of the Ponte Santa Trinita. We stood outside the Casa Guidi and paid homage to the Brownings.

The Mediterranean shore, was like a library of remembered readings — Trelawney's *Last Days of Shelley and Byron,* Ezra Pound's *Pisan Cantos* and, in Genoa, Richard Altick's *The Cowden Clarkes.*

Traveling without guidebooks and without cameras to fuss with and to come between eyes and the world makes for a fresh vision of all that passes, in which landscape is seen for what it is and not for what someone has said it is. The time to read is later. Besides, driving on today's Continental roads requires unbookish attention; and bedded down at night, the newspaper is best for unwinding the nerve-ends. (Let me enter a diatribe here against the wattage of European hotel lamps.)

So I bought no books in San Remo, Nice, Arles or Montpellier. In the latter town I did recall, however, that it was here that Rabelais took his M.D.; and that made me wish I had with me my copy of Albert Jay Nock's *A Journey into Rabelais's France,* to my taste one of the best travel books ever written, in which Nock went over Rabelais's trail from Chinon to Montpellier and the Isles of Hyères, to Paris and Metz, relating literature and history to landscape and lore. I wish that Nock, one of our most civilized writers, had done a series of such philosophical travel books on, for example, Petrarch and Erasmus and Goethe, Europeans who transcended frontiers.

Rolling toward the Spanish border below Perpignan, the road led through Sète, and I was struck by the town's welcoming sign with a quotation from Paul Valéry — "île singulière"; and then I realized that it was the Sailors' Cemetery that inspired Valéry's most famous poem, "Le Cimetière Marin." And there it was, on the hill above the sea.

On our first visit to Spain, a whole library of books avalanched over me, and I reeled under the impact of Cervantes, Ortega y Gasset, Unamuno, Somerset Maugham and Roy Campbell. The latter's *Portugal* is in the Nock vein — philosophical, opinionated, crusty, passionate. I had read it only a year ago, and it was fresh in mind. Yes, I know, it is about Portugal, not Spain, but I discovered the single fact of life which determines the nature and character of the entire Iberian peninsula and is common to both countries: the Pyrenees.

I intend to go home and reread *Highway into Spain,* an account by the Australian geographer, Marcel Aurousseau of a walking trip from Paris to Madrid. As much as I appreciate Sacheverell Sitwell's *Spain* and his other travel books, I miss in them what is present in Aurousseau — a sense of landscape, of those physical features of earth which have determined character, art, literature.

Northbound from Madrid — Zaragoza to Huesca to Jaca — threading foothills, following river courses and encountering only sheep, shepherds and dogs, a sudden sight of the Pyrenees across the valley of the Río Aragón was perhaps the noblest moment of the entire trip. High over the white battlements, I saw the figure of the medieval hero, Roland, and heard the dying fall of his horn.

Earlier, at Toledo on Good Friday, in the cathedral jammed with worshipers and refugees from the cold rain, we had seen a roomful of El Grecos canceled out by a single Goya in their midst: "Christ Taken Prisoner," a heartbreaking revelation that

made Goya and Rembrandt blood brothers. I would like to
have reread Max White's novel *In the Blazing Light,* which I
remembered as deeply understanding of Goya. What has become of this California writer? How few writers ever reach or
remain in the public mind.

Sheep are the dominant animals of Castile and Aragon, and
I shall never forget the sight of one great flock, as we switch-
backed down *cuestas de contreras* to a crossing of the Río Cabriel
and saw a thousand sheep flowing through rocky underbrush
made up entirely of rosemary in bloom and heard the din of
their bells. French, not Spanish, is a book I read before we left
home: Marcel Moyal's *On the Road to Pastures New,* the account
of a sheep trek from Arles two hundred miles northeast to the
summer uplands of the Savoy Alps.

Following the Garonne from Pau to Toulouse, and then the
Tarn to Albi, and finally keeping a rendezvous with my old Dijon
professor, Georges Connes, high in the chestnut forest of the
Rouergue, we found ourselves in the river country so beautifully
described by Freda White in *Three Rivers of France,* the Tarn,
the Lot and the Dordogne.

We were planning to go up the west side of the Massif Central,
France's volcanic backbone, when a chance note in *Figaro Lit-
téraire* changed our route: Lascaux had been closed the day
after Easter. Green organisms were appearing on the walls, threatening to obliterate the paintings. André Malraux was coming
with a team of parasitologists to see if the invaders could be repelled.

So we went due north into the wintry Haute-Auvergne to Rodez,
St. Flour, Aigues-Chaudes, Clermont-Ferrand; and I admitted to
wanting a copy of Robert L. Stevenson's *Travels in the Cevennes,*
the country to the east; and of Philip Oyler's *The Generous
Earth,* a book about the farm life of the river people to the west
beyond Mont-Doré, the source of the Dordogne.

Destination Vézelay, the hill village in northwestern Bur-
gundy, site of the Basilique de la Madeleine, the Romanesque
church from whence St. Bernard preached two crusades, and the
place to which Romain Rolland returned from Swiss exile and
died. I had seen him once, years before, reading in his garden,
an old man "au-dessus de la mêlée."

A pity Henry Adams did not also do for Vézelay what he did
for Mont St. Michel and Chartres. There are still a few books to
be written. All that's needed is leisure, learning, love.

If I found myself wanting a single book in Paris, it was John
Russell's *Paris,* published three years ago. I did buy Jean-
Victor Hocquard's *Mozart,* cast in the form of a dialogue between "Le Mozartien Fervent" and "L'Amateur Eclairé," an admirable potpourri of words and pictures in a format pioneered
by Rowohlt of Hamburg.

In Paris I saw another of my old teachers, C. F. MacIntyre, poet
and translator, bedridden since a stroke several years ago. His are
among the best translations ever made of Baudelaire, Verlaine,
Mallarmé, Corbière, Rilke and Stefan Georg. And a book of his
own poems, *Cafés and Cathedrals,* published by Oxford in 1940,
remains a model of European travel poetry. Belonging to no
clique and having no claque, MacIntyre is the perennial maverick. I wished for *Cafés and Cathedrals* in my baggage; it weighs
so little, reads so well.

After six weeks on the road in search of spring, it was a great
moment when we wheeled onto the wharf at the Gare Maritime
in Boulogne, albeit in a cold rain, drove onto the Channel ship,
Maid of Kent, and had our first cups of strong English tea with
bread and butter. We slept that night in Dover, at the foot of the
white cliffs, to the sounds of gulls and foghorns. Only one thing
was lacking, and neither the hotel library nor my memory
could supply it: the text of Matthew Arnold's "Dover Beach," a
poem to give the lie to those who say the Victorians were incapable

of passionate utterance. As I lay awake trying to get its lines in order I decided that a copy of the *Oxford Book of English Verse* would not have overloaded my baggage.

So you're going abroad this summer and want to know what books to take? None — and all.

PART VI

The Author's Experience

ROBERT PENN WARREN

How a Story Was Born and How, Bit by Bit, It Grew

Like many another American author, Robert Penn Warren has combined writing with the teaching of it, and most recently at Yale. He has the unparalleled distinction of having received a Pulitzer Prize for fiction (All the King's Men) *and another for poetry* (Promises: Poems 1954–1956); *and for the same collection of verse he was also given a National Book Award.*

I ONCE wrote a story called "Blackberry Winter." It has the form of a recollection, many years after the events narrated, by a fictional first person. On a June morning, a young boy on a farm in Tennessee is being prevented by his mother from going barefoot because a gully-washer the night before makes the morning unseasonably cold. As they argue, they see a tramp, a citified tramp, coming up the lane, and wonder how he ever got back there in the river woods. The mother gives the tramp some work. The boy goes off to explore the damage and excitement of the storm, and then to play with the son of Dellie, the cook, who is sick in one of the tenant cabins. In a moment of annoyance Dellie, ordinarily a loving mother, savagely cuffs her son. The boy, disturbed, goes to hunt Old Jebb (Dellie's common-law husband) who says this isn't merely blackberry winter — that the earth maybe is tired the way Dellie is, and won't produce any more. The boy goes back to the house and sees his father firing the tramp. The tramp is about to resent the firing, but the father overawes him, and the tramp goes off, the boy following until the tramp turns and snarls at him. Then there is a little summary of what had happened to the boy's family and Dellie's family in later years. Then:

"That is what has happened since the morning when the tramp leaned his face down at me and showed his teeth and said: "Stop following me. You don't stop following me and I cut yore throat, you little son-of-a-bitch.' That was what he said, for me not to follow him. But I did follow him, all the years."

I remember with peculiar distinctness the writing of the story, especially the tension between a sense of being trapped in a compulsive process, and the flashes of self-consciousness and self-criticism. I suppose that most attempts at writing have some such tension, but here the distinction between the two poles of the process was peculiarly marked, between the ease and the difficulty, the elation and, I am tempted to say, the pain.

The vividness with which I remember this may come from the time and situation in which the story was written. It was the winter of 1945-46, just after the war, and even if one had had no hand in the blood-letting, there was the sense that one's personal world would never be the same. I was then reading Melville's poetry, and remember being profoundly impressed by "The Conflict of Convictions," a poem about the American Civil War. Whatever the rights and wrongs, the war, Melville said, would show the "slimed foundations" of the world. There was the sense in 1945 that we had seen the slimed foundations, and now as I write this, the image that comes to mind is the homely one from my story — the trash washed out from under Dellie's cabin to foul her pridefully clean yard. So Melville, it seems, belongs in the package.

For less remote background, I had just finished two long pieces of work, a novel called *All the King's Men* and a study of Coleridge's "The Ancient Mariner." Both of these things were impersonal, that is, about as impersonal as the work of a man's hand may be. At the same time I was living in a cramped apartment over a garage in a big, modern, blizzard-bit Northern city. So the circumstances of my life and the work that had held me for so long were far from the rural world of my childhood. As for my state of mind, I suppose I was living in some anxiety about my forthcoming pieces of work, and in the unspoken, even denied conviction that, with my fortieth birthday lately passed, I was approaching some watershed of experience.

Out of this situation the story began, but by a kind of accident. Some years earlier I had written a story about a Tennessee share-cropper, a bad story that had never been published; now I thought I saw a way to improve it. So with that story I began to turn my feelings back into an earlier time. I can't say whether I began writing "Blackberry Winter" before I rewrote the other story. It doesn't really matter much. What mattered was that I was going back. I was fleeing, if you wish. Hunting old bear-ings and benchmarks, if you wish. Trying to make a fresh start, if you wish. Whatever people do in their doubleness of living in a present and a past.

I recollect the particular thread that led me back into the past: the feeling you have when, after vacation begins, you are al-lowed to go barefoot. Not that I ever particularly liked to go barefoot. But the privilege was important, an escape from the tyranny of winter, school, and, even, family. It was like what the anthropologists call rite of passage. But it had another significance; it carried you over into a dream of nature, the woods, not the house, was now your natural habitat, the stream not the street. Looking out into the snow-banked alley of that iron latitude, I had a vague nostalgic feeling and wondered if spring would ever come. It finally came — and then on May 5 there was again snow, and the heavy-headed blooms of lilac were beautiful with their hoods of snow and beards of ice.

With the recollection of going barefoot came another, which

had been recurrent over the years: the childhood feeling of betrayal when early summer gets turned upside down and all its
promises are revoked by the cold spell, the gully-washer. So by
putting those two recollections together, I got the story started.
I had no idea where it was going, if anywhere. Sitting at the typewriter was merely a way of indulging nostalgia. But something
has to happen in a story, if there is to be more than a dreary lyric
poem posing as a story to promote the cause of universal boredom and deliquescent prose. Something had to happen, and
the simplest thing ever to have happen is to say: *"Enter, mysterious stranger."* And so he did.

The tramp who thus walked into the story to cut short the argument between mother and son had been waiting a long time in
the wings of my imagination — an image based, no doubt, on a
dozen unremembered episodes from childhood, the city bum
turned country tramp, suspicious, resentful, contemptuous of hick
dumbness, bringing his own brand of violence into a world where
he half expected to find another kind, enough unlike his own to
make him look over his shoulder down the empty lane as dusk
came on, a creature altogether lost and pitiful, a dim image of
what, in one perspective, our human condition is. But then, at
that moment, I was thinking, merely of the impingement of his
loose-footedness and lostness on a stable and love-defined world of
childhood.

Before the tramp actually appeared, however, I had known he
was coming, and without planning I began to write the fourth
paragraph of the story, about the difference between what time
is when we grow up and what it was when we stood on what, in
my fancy phrase in the story, I called the glistening auroral
beach of the world — a phrase which belonged to a boy who had
never seen a beach but whose dreams were of the sea. Now the
tramp came up, not merely out of the woods, but out of the dark-
ening grown-up world of time.

The boy, seeing the tramp, tries to think of him coming up through the woods. He sees the image of the tramp blundering along, not like a boy who might stand in absolute quiet, almost taking root and growing moss on himself, trying to feel himself into that deep vegetative life. This passage, too, was written on impulse, but as soon as it began I knew its import; I was following my nose, trusting, for better or worse, my powers of association in relation to an emerging pattern of contrasts. It was natural, therefore, after a little about the tramp's out-of-waterness, to set over against him the brisk self-sufficiency of the mother at the time of the incident, and then over against that portrait a thought of the time later when she would be dead and only a memory — though back then in the changeless world of childhood, as the narrator says, it had never crossed the boy's mind that "she would ever be dead."

In the instant I wrote that clause I knew now how the story would end, for I was still writing by guess and by God, but on what perspective of feeling it would end. I knew that it would end with a kind of detached summary of the work of time, some hint of the adult's grim orientation toward that fact. From now on, the items that came on the natural wash of recollection came not only with their, to me, nostalgic quality, but also with the freighting of the grimmer possibilities of change — the flood, which to the boy is only an exciting spectacle but which will mean hunger to some, the boy's unconscious contempt for poor white trash like Milt Alley (the squatter who lived up the hill), the recollection of hunger by the old man who had ridden with Nathan Bedford Forrest, Dellie suffering her "woman mizry." But before I had got to Dellie, I already had Old Jebb firmly in mind with some faint sense of the irony of having his name remind one — or at least, me — of the dashing Confederate cavalryman killed at Yellow Tavern.

Perhaps what I did with Dellie had, in fact, stemmed from the name I gave Old Jebb. Even if the boy would see no irony in that echo of J. E. B. Stuart's fame, he would get a shock when Dellie slapped her beloved son, and would sense that that blow was, in some deep way, a blow at him. I knew this, for I knew the inside of that prideful cabin, and the shock of early realization that beneath mutual kindliness and regard a dark, tragic, unresolved thing lurked. And with that scene with Dellie I felt I was forecasting the role of the tramp in the story. The story, to put it another way, was now shifting emphasis from the lyricism of nostalgia to a concern with the jags and injustices of human relationships. What had earlier come in unconsciously, reportorially, in regard to Milt Alley, now got a conscious formulation.

I have said the end was by now envisaged as a kind of summary of the work of time on the human relationships. But it could not be a mere summary; I wanted some feeling for the boy's family and Jebb's family to shine through the flat surface. Now it struck me that I might build the summary with Jebb as a kind of pilot for the feeling I wanted to get; that is, by accepting, in implication at least something of Jebb's feeling about his own life, we might become aware of our human communion. I wanted the story to give some notion that out of change and loss a human recognition may be redeemed, more precious for being no longer innocent. So I wrote the summary.

When I had finished the next to the last paragraph I still did not know what to do with my tramp. He had already snarled at the boy, and gone, but I sensed in the pattern of things that his meaning would have to coalesce now with the meaning I hoped to convey in the summary about the characters. Then, for better or worse, there it was. In his last anger and frustration, the tramp had said to the boy: "You don't stop following me, and I cut yore throat, you little son-of-a-bitch."

Had the boy stopped or not? Yes, of course, literally, in the muddy lane. But at another level — no. In so far as later he had grown up, had really learned something of the meaning of life, he had followed the tramp all his years, in the imaginative recognition, with all the responsibility which such a recognition entails, of this lost, mean, defeated, cowardly, worthless, bitter being as somehow a man.

So what had started out as an escape into the simplicities of childhood from the complications of the present had turned, as it always must if we accept the logic of our lives, into an attempt, however bumbling, to bring something meaningfully out of that simple past into the complication of the present. And now, much later, I see that this story, and the novel then lately finished, and my reading of Coleridge's poem all bore on the same end.

I should give a false impression if I imply that this story is autobiographical. It is not. I never knew these particular people. And no tramp ever leaned down at me and said for me to stop following him or he would cut my throat. But if one had, I hope that I would have been able to follow him anyway, in the way the boy in the story does.

ALEC WAUGH

A Novelist in Search of
Plots That Thicken

Alec Waugh has made a business of writing since 1917, when he made a literary splash in London with The Loom of Youth, *a novel debunking the English public school. Many books and several decades later, he recalled that early success (and others) in an autobiography,* The Early Years Of Alec Waugh.

"WHAT are you working on now?" a friend asked me recently, "I'm hunting for a plot," I told him. It is a familiar predicament for me. It is, I imagine, for most novelists.

Some years ago I was in the same position. I had finished a long novel that was in the press. I had no idea what its successor would be like. I started for the Far East with an open mind. I had not been there for nearly thirty years. I had then, on the first lap of a round-the-world tour, spent ten weeks in Malaya, making a month's journey through the teak forests of northern Siam. I had found plots for two short stories.

A longer stay would, I felt, yield more. I planned to return the following year. But on my last day in Singapore I bought Somerset Maugham's *The Casuarina Tree* which had just been published. It contained six magnificent stories about Malaya. I recognized at once that there was no room for a minor writer in a territory which a major one had made his special province.

That was in 1926. Now in 1955 Malaya was a very different place; politically independent, brought by the airplane within easy reach of London. A new way of life had been established with new situations and new plots; I planned to compare Maugham's Malaya with today's.

Traveling by air, I made a detour to take in Aden. Across the water from this outpost of the Empire, British Petroleum has built an oil refinery, set on a bleak stretch of desert. I was taken there on a visit of inspection. It was a self-sufficient, self-contained community, supplying all its own needs, its recreation and entertainment. Aden itself was only a fifty-minute drive away. But as far as the residents of the refinery were concerned, it might have existed in another universe. They lived within the perimeter of their camp.

The married couples had small air-conditioned bungalows. I was taken into one of them. It was one of the biggest shocks I have ever received. I mean "shock" literally. I was shaken, surprised, startled and delighted. Outside was the heat and dust of the desert, the air heavy with the sickly-sweet smell of gasoline. A door opened and I was being welcomed into an air-conditioned room prettily furnished by a charming young woman, a bride of seven months, who had in her cotton frock and smooth make-up the cool, fresh crispness of a salad. The contrast was complete; I saw the life of the oil man from another angle. It was a dream package deal. An air-conditioned bungalow with every modern gadget and an exquisite young wife to go with it.

My first thought was that oil might be the best profession for my younger son. But as I sat talking I looked at the other side of the picture. An air-conditioned bungalow might provide a halcyon honeymoon for a bride who was wholeheartedly in love, but how would it be for a girl who had married mainly "to get away from mother?" I imagined the boredom and monotony of her life. Her husband would leave the bungalow every morning at five minutes to seven. He would not return till eleven-thirty. He would leave after lunch, shortly before one. He would not return till four. For seven and a half hours she would be alone in a house which required the minimum of chores and for whose accomplishment she would have the assistance of a local servant.

When a young wife is bored, she is likely to start a flirtation and there could be no worse place than an oil camp for that remedy. Privacy is impossible, yet she would be seeking the object of her affections every day, at the swimming pool, at the club, on the golf course, at cocktail parties. Under such circumstances what might have been a tepid preference would be lashed into a frenzied passion — out of which might spring crime or suicide.

Here were the ingredients of melodrama; and as I thought of this, I realized that I had found within fifteen minutes the plot that I was seeking. My next novel would be set in an oil camp, with a discontented wife as the central character. It was published as *Fuel for the Flame*.

That is the way that all my plots have come to me, in a flash, but between the plot as it first occurs and the manuscript that is eventually delivered to a publisher there is much difference. I do not know whether many novelists work the way that I do. I know very little about the way in which other writers work. I would like to take a college course in creative writing and learn from a professor of literature how novelists achieve their effects.

Aldous Huxley, writing of *Lady Chatterley's Lover,* said that D. H. Lawrence wrote his novels straight ahead, without a pause. If he was dissatisfied, he would start again at the beginning and write the whole thing out again. He never had the recourse to scissors and paste on which most novelists rely. This remark of Huxley's makes me suspect that the majority of novelists get their books written through a process of trial and error.

Myself, I know that I invariably make a number of false starts. I get a dramatic idea; I work on it. It may develop into a novel, maybe into a short story; or sometimes it will founder, to await rescue in some other setting. Though I had found in Aden the setting for a novel and a central character, I knew that I should only find the sequence of events I needed after several attempted openings — if indeed I ever found it. I do not always.

In 1946, when I returned to writing after six years in the army, I began a novel with a Baghdad background to be called "Murder at the Alwiyah Club." It aimed to describe the mental and emotional turmoil of a woman who has killed someone by mistake and, feeling that no one can connect her with the death, does not tell the police. The situation I had devised was this: A divorced man in his middle forties, employed by the Iraq Petroleum Company, marries a girl of twenty-two. His seventeen-year-old daughter visits him in Baghdad. There is a conflict between the stepmother and the daughter.

A local bachelor with a reputation for facile conquests takes an interest in the daughter. The stepmother forbids him to go on seeing her. There is a scene between the two in which the Lothario taunts the mother with interfering only because she wants to send the daughter back to England quickly. If the daughter becomes involved in a love affair, she will want to linger in Baghdad. The quarrel becomes intense. The woman strikes at the man. As he steps back his foot slips on a mat, he falls, strikes his head against a chair and that is that.

I started the story with enthusiasm. I wrote 25,000 words; then the story stopped, as a car does when it is out of gas. There was nothing to be done but put the manuscript away, knowing from past experience that I should be able to make use of it some day. Seven years later when I was working on a novel about the West Indies, I realized how well the situation of an unintended and unreported manslaughter would fit into the pattern of my plot — only this time it was a man who did the killing.

An essential section of *Island in the Sun* (as the West Indies novel came to be titled) was a rewriting of "Murder at the Alwiyah Club," and when I began to work on *Fuel for the Flame* I soon realized how effectively I could use the situation of the young wife of a divorced man having to cope with a step-daughter only a year or so younger than herself.

I wonder if many novelists have their desks as full as mine is of — I will not say rejected manuscripts because no editor has had the opportunity of rejecting them; abandoned efforts would be a better word — for which I confidently expect to find a use some day. In a way the separate pieces are well enough: the characters are real, the situations grow out of characters, the narrative moves quickly, the stuff is readable, but it will stay meaningless until it has been woven into the pattern of a plot that can give it significance.

Forty years ago I wrote a novel called *Kept* — my first book to have any luck in the U.S.A. It began as the story of a kept woman. I wrote about thirty thousand words — and again had the familiar feeling I was running out of gas. The story was not about anything. I was very near to putting it away when a friend asked me if I had a title for my new novel. "A Kept Woman," I told her. She pursed her lips. "I don't like that. Why not call it 'Kept'?"

I instantly had the idea for quite a different book. I would have a number of characters, each of whom was "kept" in a different way. There would be a painter living on his past reputation. The daughter of an earl married to a rich industrialist for her title's sake, a soldier who had won high honors in the war, a young man who had found promotion in his career through a rich woman's interest. Finally there would be England herself living on her past glories, on the wealth and prestige earned by the Empire builders of the eighteenth and nineteenth centuries.

I saw myself writing in a final speech: "We are all kept, aren't we, in one way or another?" The story of the kept woman that I had originally planned to tell would now acquire significance because it was a window opening onto other lives and ways of life.

G. B. Stern once said to me, "Characters and incidents are like beads scattered on a table; they only become a necklace when you have a thread on which to string them." That is what I mean when I say that I am searching for a plot. I am looking for a theme, a setting, a twist of narrative that will give coherence to the stories that I weave out of the day-to-day experiences of living. A novelist is always telling himself stories about the people he is meeting, imagining how they would behave in this and the other situation, but those dream stories only become a novel when they have been set within the pattern of a plot.

That is what I am looking for now, as I plan my travels. I hope to find a story in Australia. I have also an idea that I may find in Beirut (where I spent many weeks during World War II) a parallel for the Tangier where I have spent many months and which has now lost, with its international status, its scope for drama. That is my rough scheme. But just as I found a plot unexpectedly in little Aden, I may find one in a place I have scarcely heard of and never felt inquisitive about — or again, I may find absolutely nothing. That is what makes novel writing such an endlessly fascinating game. It is a gamble and an adventure for me still, though I have written more than forty books.

JAMES BALDWIN

The Discovery of What It Means
to Be an American

[*For facts about Mr. Baldwin, look back to the note on page 207.*]

"It is a complex fate to be an American," Henry James observed, and the principal discovery an American writer makes in Europe is just how complex this fate is. America's history, her aspirations, her peculiar triumphs, her even more peculiar defeats, and her position in the world — yesterday and today — are all so profoundly and stubbornly unique that the very word "America" remains a new, almost completely undefined and extremely controversial proper noun. No one in the world seems to know exactly what it describes, not even we motley millions who call ourselves Americans.

I left America because I doubted my ability to survive the fury of the color problem here. (Sometimes I still do.) I wanted to prevent myself from becoming *merely* a Negro; or, even, merely a Negro writer. I wanted to find out in what way the *specialness* of my experience could be made to connect me with other people instead of dividing me from them. (I was as isolated from Negroes as I was from whites, which is what happens when a Negro begins, at bottom, to believe what white people say about him.)

In my necessity to find the terms on which my experience could be related to that of others, Negroes and whites, writers and nonwriters, I proved, to my astonishment, to be as American as any Texas G.I. And I found my experience was shared by every

American writer I knew in Paris. Like me, they had been divorced from their origins, and it turned out to make very little
difference that the origins of white Americans were European
and mine were African — they were no more at home in Europe
than I was.

The fact that I was the son of a slave and they were the sons of
free men meant less, by the time we confronted each other on
European soil, than the fact that we were both searching for
our separate identities. When we had found these, we seemed to
be saying, why, then, we would no longer need to cling to the
shame and bitterness which had divided us so long.

It became terribly clear in Europe, as it never had been here,
that we knew more about each other than any European ever
could. And it also became clear that, no matter where our fathers
had been born, or what they had endured, the fact of Europe had
formed us both, was part of our identity and part of our inheritance.

I had been in Paris a couple of years before any of this became
clear to me. When it did, I, like many a writer before me upon
the discovery that his props have all been knocked out from under
him, suffered a species of breakdown and was carried off to the
mountains of Switzerland. There, in that absolutely alabaster
landscape, armed with two Bessie Smith records and a typewriter,
I began to try to re-create the life that I had first known as a child
and from which I had spent so many years in flight.

It was Bessie Smith, through her tone and her cadence, who
helped me to dig back to the way I myself must have spoken
when I was a pickaninny, and to remember the things I had
heard and seen and felt. I had buried them very deep. I had
never listened to Bessie Smith in America (in the same way that,
for years, I would not touch watermelon), but in Europe she
helped to reconcile me to being a "nigger."

I do not think that I could have made this reconciliation here.

Once I was able to accept my role — as distinguished, I must say, from my "place" — in the extraordinary drama which is America, I was released from the illusion that I hated America.

The story of what can happen to an American Negro writer in Europe simply illustrates, in some relief, what can happen to any American writer there. It is not meant, of course, to imply that it happens to them all, for Europe can be very crippling, too; and, anyway, a writer, when he has made his first break-through, has simply won a crucial skirmish in a dangerous, unending and unpredictable battle. Still, the breakthrough is important, and the point is that an American writer, in order to achieve it, very often has to leave this country.

The American writer, in Europe, is released, first of all, from the necessity of apologizing for himself. It is not until he *is* released from the habit of flexing his muscles and proving that he is just a "regular guy" that he realizes how crippling this habit has been. It is not necessary for him, there, to pretend to be something he is not, for the artist does not encounter in Europe the same suspicion he encounters here. Whatever the Europeans may actually think of artists, they have killed enough of them off by now to know that they are as real — and as persistent — as rain, snow, taxes or businessmen.

Of course, the reason for Europe's comparative clarity concerning the different functions of men in society is that European society has always been divided into classes in a way that American society never has been. A European writer considers himself to be part of an old and honorable tradition — of intellectual activity, of letters — and his choice of a vocation does not cause him any uneasy wonder as to whether or not it will cost him all his friends. But this tradition does not exist in America.

On the contrary, we have a very deep-seated distrust of real intellectual effort (probably because we suspect that it will destroy, as I hope it does, that myth of America to which we cling so desperately). An American writer fights his way to one of the lowest rungs on the American social ladder by means of pure bull-headedness and an indescribable series of odd jobs. He probably *has* been a "regular fellow" for much of his adult life, and it is not easy for him to step out of that lukewarm bath.

We must, however, consider a rather serious paradox: though American society is more mobile than Europe's, it is easier to cut across social and occupational lines there than it is here. This has something to do, I think, with the problem of status in American life. Where everyone has status, it is also perfectly possible, after all, that no one has. It seems inevitable, in any case, that a man may become uneasy as to just what his status is.

But Europeans have lived with the idea of status for a long time. A man can be as proud of being a good waiter as of being a good actor, and, in neither case, feel threatened. And this means that the actor and the waiter can have a freer and more genuinely friendly relationship in Europe than they are likely to have here. The waiter does not feel, with obscure resentment, that the actor has "made it," and the actor is not tormented by the fear that he may find himself, tomorrow, once again, a waiter.

This lack of what may roughly be called social paranoia causes the American writer in Europe to feel — almost certainly for the first time in his life — that he can reach out to everyone, that he is accessible to everyone and open to everything. This is an extraordinary feeling. He feels, so to speak, his own weight, his own value.

It is as though he suddenly came out of a dark tunnel and found himself beneath the open sky. And, in fact, in Paris, I began to see the sky for what seemed to be the first time. It was borne in on me — and it did not make me feel melancholy — that this sky had been there before I was born and would be there when I was dead. And it was up to me, therefore, to make of my brief opportunity the most that could be made.

I was born in New York, but have only lived in pockets of it. In Paris, I lived in all parts of the city — on the Right Bank and the Left, among the bourgeoisie and among *les misérables,* and knew all kinds of people, from pimps and prostitutes in Pigalle to Egyptian bankers in Neuilly. This may sound extremely un-principled or even obscurely immoral; I found it healthy. I love to talk to people, all kinds of people, and almost everyone, as I hope we still know, loves a man who loves to listen.

This perpetual dealing with people very different from myself caused a shattering in me of preconceptions I scarcely knew I held. The writer is meeting in Europe people who are not American, whose sense of reality is entirely different from his own. They may love or hate or admire or fear or envy this country — they see it, in any case, from another point of view, and this forces the writer to reconsider many things he had al-ways taken for granted. This reassessment, which can be very painful, is also very valuable.

This freedom, like all freedom, has its dangers and its respon-sibilities. One day it begins to be borne in on the writer, and with great force, that he is living in Europe as an American. If he were living there as a European, he would be living on a different and far less attractive continent.

This crucial day might be the day on which an Algerian taxi driver told him how it felt to be an Algerian in Paris. It might be the day on which he passed a café terrace and caught a glimpse of the tense, intelligent and troubled face of Albert Camus. Or, it might be the day on which someone asked him to explain Little Rock and he began to feel that it would be simpler — and, corny as the words may sound, more honorable — to *go* to Little Rock than sit in Europe, on an American passport, trying to explain it.

This is a personal day, a terrible day, the day to which his en-tire sojourn has been tending. It is the day he realizes that there are no untroubled countries in this fearfully troubled world;

that if he has been preparing himself for anything in Europe, he has been preparing himself — for America. In short, the freedom that the American writer finds in Europe brings him, full circle, back to himself, with the responsibility for his development where it always was: in his own hands.

Even the most incorrigible maverick has to be born somewhere. He may leave the group that produced him — he may be forced to — but nothing will efface his origins, the marks of which he carries with him everywhere. I think it is important to know this and even find it a matter for rejoicing, as the strongest people do, regardless of their station. On this acceptance, literally, the life of a writer depends.

The charge has often been made against American writers that they do not describe society, and have no interest in it. They only describe individuals in opposition to it, or isolated from it. Of course, what the American writer is describing is his own situation. But what is *Anna Karenina* describing if not the tragic fate of the isolated individual, at odds with her time and place?

The real difference is that Tolstoy was describing an old and dense society in which everything seemed — to the people in it, though not to Tolstoy — to be fixed forever. And the book is a masterpiece because Tolstoy was able to fathom, and make us see, the hidden laws which really governed this society and made Anna's doom inevitable.

American writers do not have a fixed society to describe. The only society they know is one in which nothing is fixed and in which the individual must fight for his identity. This is a rich confusion, indeed, and it creates for the American writer unprecedented opportunties.

That the tensions of American life, as well as the possibilities, are tremendous is certainly not even a question. But these are dealt with in contemporary literature mainly conpulsively; that is, the book is more likely to be a symptom of our tension than an examination of it. The time has come, God knows, for us to examine ourselves, but we can only do this if we are willing to free ourselves of the myth of America and try to find out what is really happening here.

Every society is really governed by hidden laws, by unspoken but profound assumptions on the part of the people, and ours is no exception. It is up to the American writer to find out what these laws and assumptions are. In a society much given to smashing taboos without thereby managing to be liberated from them, it will be no easy matter.

It is no wonder, in the meantime, that the American writer keeps running off to Europe. He needs sustenance for his journey and the best models he can find. Europe has what we do not have yet, a sense of the mysterious and inexorable limits of life, a sense, in a word, of tragedy. And we have what they sorely need: a new sense of life's possibilities.

In this endeavor to wed the vision of the Old World with that of the New, it is the writer, not the statesman, who is our strongest arm. Though we do not wholly believe it yet, the interior life is a real life, and the intangible dreams of people have a tangible effect on the world.

MACKINLAY KANTOR

The Author Was a Haunted Man

For Andersonville, *a block-buster of a novel, MacKinlay Kantor was given a Pulitzer Prize in 1956. Some of the spirit present in that book is suggested by his essay on this page. MacKinlay Kantor is one of those authors who gets around. He's been a war correspondent, a Hollywood writer and producer, a technical consultant to the U.S. Air Force, and he's been writing short stories, juveniles and novels for more than three decades.*

THE NEW motel at Americus was clean and comfortable, the bed smooth; still I could not sleep. Too many forces would not let me sleep. Again I looked at my watch: a little after 4 A.M., so it would be hours before the February sun appeared. I got up and dressed. I drove into northeast blackness along that road grown so familiar — Georgia State Highway Number 49. The road brought me, eleven miles away, into a dark unpopulated valley where water trickled from a certain storied spring.

For a time I parked near that spring. Frogs were singing like birds along a tiny watercourse where new grasses tufted fresh as salad leaves. There was the thought of monuments looming, thought of a bareheaded boy made of bronze who stands, cap in hand and eternally youthful face uplifted, amid a low forest of white marble slabs. But the graves were yonder, to the north. Now I did not wish to go there — I was heartily afraid to go, although I had gone many times before in daylight, and on occasion illegally in darkness. Regulations declare that a United

States Military Cemetery may not be visited at night; yet on occasion I had sinned so, and had not felt myself a sinner; I'd felt
that I belonged there. Almost I might wish to lie there eventually, could it be permitted. I felt that I was nearer to those
dead than I was near to a breathing, sleeping world of mortal
men and women.

About five o'clock I drove up the south slope of this valley and
parked near the summit. Barely in gloom could I make out the
few naked markers which approximate the position of the old
Andersonville stockade. Actually I stood within the stockade
area — the South Gate would have been over here, to the left;
the gallows directly ahead, the raiders' pavilion ahead to the
right. Still that constant spurting symphony of frog voices cried
in the pretty ravine, the ravine I could scarcely distinguish in its
mystery.

Clouds were thick, oppressive, blocking the light of even a single star. An owl spoke among underbrush masking the ancient
Island. All fifty-odd thousand of you, I thought. Where do you
drift now? Guards and prisoners alike — Henry Wirz with the
rope mark on your dusty neck — sniveling child and hulking
bully, serene martyr and master-of-the-hounds . . . I thought (in
that intense awareness of one's own dream, the egoistic concentration which impels one to tell the story which he feels must be
told) — men and boys, I am here, waiting. Where have you
gone?

I heard them coming. They twitched in a whispering rank
from woods at the north, they rose up beyond statues and the
superintendent's house; they came walking, massed and steady.
Gently, gently they traveled through and over and under distant
trees, came out into open ground where little circular fences
protected the wells and tunnels they had dug — black pits drilled
down through colored layers of clay. The marchers passed the
fences easily, pacing nearer and nearer. There would be no resisting them.

I turned in panic, and stumbled back to my car, I flung myself
into the front seat, heard the frightened slam of the car door go
banging off through haunted distance. It was no illusion — I
heard those soft-footed thousands walking ever closer. Now their
phalanx was pressing down the opposite slope, passing Providence Spring. I had summoned them, their reply was in their im-
placable approach.

Why was I afraid — I, who had called them brothers for so
long in my mind, who dared to feel that I belonged in their
misty column? It was not solely a fear of ghosts, a quailing away
from the Dead. I had been close to death on a number of occasions in two wars, had walked within Buchenwald, had climbed
into trucks loaded with dead, had tripped across their stiff out-
flung arms when they lay upon the ground. It was something
more. In the next moment, as that unseen soft-treading horde
pressed over the crest of the Sweetwater branch, I recognized the
answer.

They had come to tell me that there must be no compromise.
I had invoked their name and thought for nearly twenty-five
years; they were thronging at last to force me to the task.

I was crying. I had not cried in many years, but now I was
crying. Get out of the car, I said. You must show them that you
have fear no longer, that you are ready to accept orders.

My feet were on the grass, the door clicked shut behind me.
I stood waiting. The wide rustling rank moved fairly in my
face. Then they were touching me, they were all around me,
brushing my face and hands, the hair of my head.

Rain.

A thin, slow-speaking, slow-stepping rain had formed somewhere among miles and ages of darkness before dawn. So it
had moved on many small feet from the direction of the cemetery, had walked open glades, put its coolness on monuments,
now it was touching me. I was glad to be brushed by it, glad to
feel it on my lips.

At this time I had written perhaps twenty-five thousand words on *Andersonville,* and knew that I must write at least three hundred thousand more. Often the recollection of that rain walking the late hours of a Georgia night came to prod or sustain me. The next fifteen months were a strange confusion from which only the book itself emerged in clarity. I worked here, there, everywhere. There were several very good reasons why I must be abroad a great share of this time; but never was the country or the place or the room where I sat of first importance. A great deal of the time I worked near our Spanish home in Andalusia, alone in mountain foothills. I had secret hideaways carefully surveyed: the promontory where I rolled stones to free a path for my cart — another hill near the road to a lonely village called Benilmadena, where I was free from the incursions of herdsmen and gypsies alike. For several years I'd worked habitually in the car, with portable typewriter set up on a folding chair for a table; it was my peripatetic office, complete with books, briefcase — a basket of bread, cheese, olives and sausage, a bottle of thin country wine. It didn't matter where we went or what we did; I was working each day from the 16th of December, 1953, until the 25th of May, 1955. I mean working each day.

Nights were frequently the worst part of the whole business. It is a mean experience to labor within the stockade all day — say alongside Father Peter Whelan — and then to have Veronica Claffey stalking into her tomb, and you going with her, through all the remembered hours of exhausted sleep.

They say that Carcassone is fabulous, that the Cité crusted on its little mountain is a sculptured wonderland. I do not know. I have been there, and my wife and my dog went walking and exploring and painting for days (Irene did the painting, Lobo the exploring), but my memory of Carcassone is of a double-door where wind rattled across a balcony, and where I sat with that same gray typewriter before me, and where I was writing about — was it

Willie Mann in Missouri, Judah Hansom up in York State? Oh, no — that was in the Hyde Park Hotel in London, and what a noise the buses made outside. . . . No, it was Naz Stricker and Coral Tebbs. No, that was in Copenhagen. . . . Oh, yes. No, no! It was in mid-Atlantic — Laurel Tebbs and Sergeant Sinkfield — and the smoking room is cold and deserted at six in the morning, and for hours afterward; and you keep your typewriter and the smallest of the several portable bookcases in the steward's locker, and sometimes there is a storm, and you have to hold your typewriter fast to the table with one hand while you type with the other — was it the *Empress of Australia* or the *Mauretania?* Why, it was both. (Folks tell me that a transatlantic voyage is a good way to take a rest cure. Interesting, indeed. I must try it some time.)

I should not on these pages attempt to set down what I feel or felt or believe about Andersonville. If I have not told such things in the novel itself, then the book is valueless and should remain unread. But let me say this: that only once before have I felt so many people breathing down my neck while I was at work, no matter where I worked — and that was when I was writing *Glory for Me* which in time came before the world as a motion picture which told the story of war veterans — *The Best Years of Our Lives.* And the breath of these Andersonville people was especially compulsive; it came cooled by the ice of ninety years, ninety years to the minute.

The book was not written chronologically — few books of such scope could be written chronologically. Nevertheless, it was begun ninety years from the month when the stockade was first reared; and Providence Spring burst forth exactly ninety years from the week when Providence Spring did burst forth; and the last tattered relics were conveyed from the pen in May, 1865; and the last word of this novel was written in May, 1955, and strangely the last word happened to be *Andersonville.*

LOIS DWIGHT COLE

Margaret Mitchell Was a Bridge Partner

The joy of discovery is one of the most exciting an editor in a publishing house can experience, and Lois Cole shares some of this excitement in her account of the discovery of Gone With the Wind. *She is now an editor with William Morrow & Company and is the pseudonymous author of several juveniles.*

THE FIRST TIME I met Margaret Mitchell was at a luncheon bridge, not long after I moved to Georgia to run the office end of the Atlanta branch of The Macmillan Company's trade department. In the flutter of hurried introductions, no names stayed in my mind and no individual stood out clearly. After luncheon, when we drew for bridge tables, I found my partner's name was Margaret Mitchell. She turned out to be a small, rather plump person with reddish brown hair, very blue eyes, and a few freckles across a slightly uptilted nose.

As the cards were dealt I asked, as one did, "Do you follow any particular conventions, partner?" Our opponents stared, and my partner said solemnly, "Conventions? I don't know any. I just lead from fright. What do you lead from?" "Necessity," I told her, at which she gave a sudden grin.

On the first hand our opponents bid four spades. My partner held six; I had two and two aces, and we set them five; whereupon we rose, solemnly if improperly, and shook hands across the table.

As there was more conversation than bridge, it was soon established that I was the Yankee who had come down to work for Macmillan (everyone knew but it was manners to ask) and that I had gone to Smith, where Miss Mitchell had been for a year. During refreshments she edged around to me and asked if I would come to supper the following Wednesday with her and her husband, John Marsh.

In those days the Marshes lived in a small, dilapidated, two-story apartment house known as "The Dump" on a narrow street once known as "Tightsqueezes" behind Peachtree Street at Tenth. To the delighted and never-ending shock of Atlanta there were two cards tacked to the front door. One said "Margaret Munnerlyn Mitchell" and the other "John R. Marsh." The apartment consisted of two, small square rooms and a tiny kitchen.

Over fried chicken and hot biscuits I discovered that evening that Peggy was one of the best conversationalists and storytellers one could find. Not that she monopolized the talk; she was, as she said, "a good ear," as genuinely interested in what other people had to say as she was skillful in luring them to talk.

Since "The Dump" was situated between the Macmillan office and the house where I boarded, I fell into the habit of stopping by after work once or twice a week for tea. Sometimes other friends would be there; sometimes Peggy and I would be alone and would happily compare opinions on books and people. There was a bay with tiny high windows in the living room and beneath it an old-fashioned sewing table that held a portable typewriter and stacks of paper.

Once, when I came in with a friend, Peggy, in shorts, blouse and eyeshade, was at the typewriter. She got up and threw a bath towel over the table. "Well, Peggy," said the friend, "how's the great American novel coming along?" "It stinks," Peggy said with a half-laugh, "and I don't know why I bother with it, but I've got to do something with my time." "When's it going to be done?" I asked. "Macmillan would love to see it." "At this rate it won't ever get done, and no one's going to want to see it."

It is difficult to put Peggy on paper, to convey her gaiety, her interest in and profound knowledge of people, her range of interests and reading, her devotion to her friends, and the verve and enchantment of her talk. Many Southerners are born storytellers, but Peggy told her tales with such fun and skill that a whole roomful would stay quiet all evening to listen to her.

During my years in Atlanta we saw a great deal of each other and became good friends. These were depression times, and sometimes, while our husbands were working late, we would have supper together. We both loathed sewing, and sewed badly; but it was easier to turn the collars on our husbands' shirts if we were discussing books, poetry, history, and people past and present.

Her friends knew, vaguely, that the book she was writing had something to do with the Civil War and Atlanta, for she would complain that the bound copies of the old newspapers in the basement of the Carnegie Library were so heavy she couldn't throw them around or hold them, and the only way she could read them was to lie on the floor and prop them on her stomach, which wore out her stomach.

When Macmillan closed the branch offices of its trade department, I was offered a place as associate editor in New York. In December, 1933, I wrote Margaret Mitchell a formal letter saying that Macmillan would like very much to see ner novel, either when it was finished or in its present condition. She wrote me, just as formally, that the book was not finished, that she doubted if it ever would be, or be worth seeing — but that if she ever did bring herself to show it to a publisher, Macmillan would have first look. Aside from that, our correspondence was informal.

Then, in the spring of 1935, Harold Latham, the editor-in-chief of the Macmillan trade department made his first scouting trip to the South. I wrote to Peggy and to Medora Field Perkerson, of the *Atlanta Journal,* asking them to do what they could to make his stay pleasant and turn up manuscripts. I told Mr. Latham about Peggy's book — that no one had read it except her husband John, but that if she wrote as she talked it would be a honey.

In Atlanta, Peggy and Medora took Mr. Latham to lunch, for a drive, and to a Georgia Writers' Club tea at Rich's Department Store. When he reached Charleston, he wrote to me thanking me for what my friends had done for him and went on to say that Mrs. Marsh had delivered to him the rough draft of an incomplete manuscript that she felt was in need of rewriting. She wished to know if it was worth working on more. The manuscript was so large he could not carry it with him across the country. He was sending it to me to read, so I could talk with him about it when he returned to New York.

Some eight months later Peggy wrote me telling how and why she had given him the manuscript. I had revealed to a mutual friend, who was being catty about Peggy's never-finished novel, that she had been given a contract. This I had confessed to Peggy, since she wished no one to know until the revision was finished. She wrote that she understood, adding that friends and acquaintances had kept her from finishing the book long ago. She told how she had seen one friend "through three psychiatrists and a couple of neurologists, a divorce and a happy new marriage." Later, at a party, when the book was mentioned, the happy bride had said, "Book, pooh! Peggy will never finish it. She's too fond of playing."

Peggy went on: "I've gone through deaths and handled funerals and the very people who call on me for these things are the very ones who say, in all affection, 'Isn't it a shame that somebody with a mind like Peggy's hasn't any ambition?' It never made me especially mad — till the last straw came. After all, when you give your friends something, be it money, love, time, encouragement, work, you either give it as a free gift, with no after remarks, or you don't give it at all. And, having given, I had no particular regrets. But this very same situation was what really made me turn over the manuscript to Mr. Latham. He'd asked for it, and I'd felt very flattered that he even considered me. But I'd refused, knowing in what poor shape the thing was. And that day he was here, I'd called up various and sundry hopeful young authors and would-be authors and jackassed them (that is a friend's phrase) about in the car and gotten them to the tea where they could actually meet a live publisher in the flesh.

"One of them was a child who had nearly driven me crazy about her book. I'd no more than get settled at my own work than here she was, bellowing that she had gone stale or that she couldn't write love scenes and couldn't I write them for her? Or she was on the phone picking my brains for historical facts that had taken me weeks to run down. As twilight eve was drawing on and I was riding her and some of her adoring girl friends home from the tea, somebody asked me when I expected to get my book finished and why hadn't I given it to Mr. Latham.

"Then this child cried, 'Why, are you writing a book, Peggy? How strange you've never said anything about it. Why didn't you give it to Mr. Latham?' I said I hadn't because it was so lousy I was ashamed of it. To which she remarked — and did not mean it cattily — 'Well, I daresay. Really, I wouldn't take you for the type who would write a successful book. You know you don't take life seriously enough to be a novelist. And you've never even had it refused by a publisher? How strange! *I've* been refused by the very best publishers. But my book is grand. Everybody says it'll win the Pulitzer Prize. But, Peggy, I think you are wasting your time trying. You really aren't the type.'

"Well, suddenly, I got so mad that I began to laugh, and I had to stop the car because I laughed so hard. And that confirmed their opinion of my lack of seriousness. And when I got home I was so mad still that I grabbed up what manuscript I could lay hands on, forgetting entirely that I hadn't included the envelopes that were under the bed or the ones in the pot-and-pan closet, and I posted down to the hotel and caught Mr. Latham just as he was about to catch the train. My idea was that at least I could brag that I had been refused by the very best publisher. And no sooner had I done this and Mr. L. was out of town than I was appalled both by my temper and by my acting on impulse and by my giving him the stuff when it was in such sloppy shape and minus so many chapters."

The manuscript arrived, and I spent evenings reading it, breaking off late and reluctantly. It was, physically, one of the worst manuscripts I have ever seen. There was no first chapter (Peggy had tried six or seven and liked none), but Chapter Two was neatly typed on white paper. So was Chapter Three. Then came pages and pages of yellow paper, written over in pencil, and often three or four different versions of one scene. Then came more final chapters, then some would be missing entirely. There were two entirely different accounts of Frank's death. The last chapter was in final form, for that, she told me later, was written first. (When Peggy was on the staff of the *Atlanta Journal* magazine, she was famous for writing her stories backward, starting with the last paragraph and working forward.) In spite of the difficulties of reading the manuscript, I knew it was one of the most fascinating novels of all time.

Mr. Latham read it on his return, and so did Professor Charles Everitt of Columbia, who occasionally advised us about novels. Our enthusiasm carried the Editorial Council, and Macmillan offered Peggy a contract. Here is how she received my wire.

"Lois, your telegram just came and I am overwhelmed! It came at a grand time for I was just limping home from Grady hospital to lick my wounds, having been scragged by a young in-tern whom *I* have scragged several times in the course of Bessie's illness. [Bessie was her cook.] Do you really mean they like it? You wouldn't fox an old friend, would you? I don't see how any-one made heads or tails of it. I am very twittery about your wire and, having phoned John and read it to him, he said, 'You'd better sit down quietly so you'll have less distance to fall when the realization comes over you that someone besides me likes the damn thing.' Well, John was right. I think I had better sit down quietly. I shall fall down in another minute. You are a lamb to send me such a swell telegram and I shall frame it."

In the manuscript the name of the heroine was Pansy, and the title was "Tomorrow Is Another Day." Macmillan asked Peggy to change the heroine's name and the title, for there were thirteen books in print with titles beginning "Tomorrow . . ." She offered "Scarlett" for "Pansy" and sent me a list of twenty-two possible titles. Number 14 was starred. It was "Gone With the Wind," with the source and a penciled note saying, "I'll agree to any one of these you like, but I like this the best." So did we.

Peggy Mitchell never felt that her book deserved all the praise it received, and never, or for a long time, had any confidence it would sell. "I wrote it for fun, for my own amusement. If enough people want to spend $3 so that Macmillan won't lose the money they've paid me, that will be fine."

When she saw an advance copy of our spring announcement list, she wrote:

"Lois, I was overwhelmed when I saw the catalogue, my position in it and my distinguished company. And seeing the opus listed as one of 'four great novels' got me into a proper state. I know it's all due to you, and I'm torn between gratitude and a sense of guilt that I certainly shouldn't be rubbing shoulders with Charles Morgan and Phyllis Bentley. Good God, this book isn't good enough to be there. I know you know your business — but I hope you haven't made an error in judgment because of a kind and loving heart."

Even after the book was taken by the Book-of-the-Month Club and sold to David Selznick for the highest price ever paid up to that time for an unpublished first novel, she still had no faith it would sell.

One of the best things about Margaret Mitchell was that to her true friends she never changed. She resented the multitudinous attempts to invade her privacy, to make use of her, and she was annoyed by the myths circulated about her and by sudden claims of hitherto nonexistent friendship. But to her friends she was always the Peggy we had known when she lived in "The Dump" and covered the stacks of manuscript with a bath towel.

Two years after publication of "G. W. T. W.," when my son was born, Peggy came North to see him since she was his godmother. One afternoon during that visit I was giving her another fight talk about writing another book — anyone who had given so many people so much pleasure had a duty, etc. Peggy said she probably would some day, when the fan mail had fallen off (she answered every letter and thanked every reviewer) and the foreign editions were all published and if her family and friends stayed well.

Then a faraway look came into her blue eyes. "You know, I always liked the book I wrote before *Gone With the Wind* better." I took a firm clutch on the arm of the sofa and said as calmly as I could. "How nice. And where is the manuscript now?" "Oh I burned it up when it was finished. I just wrote it for fun. I never thought of having it published."

AILEEN PIPPETT

The Art of Leading
a Double Life

Aileen Pippett, a critic and biographer, is the author of The
Moth and the Star, *a life and appreciation of Virginia Woolf.*
Some of her experience in telling the story of this famous mem-
ber of the Bloomsbury group is set down in "The Art of Leading
a Double Life."

"MY KIND of writing is a species of mediumship," Virginia
Woolf noted in her diary when she was asked for a personal
tribute to a dying friend. She knew that, as she said, she had to
be "flooded with the idea," to "become the person" — to lead a
double life.

This is true, in varying degrees, of all kinds of creative writing.
Novelists must not only believe in their characters, they must
share their lives before the reader can. They must, like medi-
ums, be willing to submit to domination.

This is neither a dignified nor a comfortable situation for the
writer. First, he has to retreat to some quiet place, not only for
his own sake but to spare his family the embarrassment of knowing what goes on while he is writing. Then, if he has succeeded in
giving life to his characters, they march out and take all the glory
or make a public mock of him by refusing to do as they are told.

Dickens wept over the fate of Little Nell until his face was
swollen to twice its natural size, but she insisted on dying,
whereas Sherlock Holmes would not stay dead, though Conan
Doyle did his utmost to kill him off and wished he had never

heard of him. Don Quixote and Sancho Panza are more real in the mind than Cervantes, Tom Jones than Fielding, Becky Sharp than Thackeray, Soames Forsyte than Galsworthy, and when one thinks of the tremendous characters Shakespeare let loose on the world it is no wonder that the personality of the poet himself is nebulous and enigmatic.

Since fiction, if it is to be memorable, leaves the novelist anything but a free agent, the writer is tempted to turn to something less schizoid, and biography suggests itself. Here your character cannot change his nature in the second chapter or destroy your plot in the third. You do not need to invent; the beginning, the middle and the end of your story are already known. All you have to do is to tell the truth.

Having selected your character, you begin your research. Many surprises await you, whether your study sends you traveling or keeps you confined to a library. Things have changed since you were at school, when a fact was a fact, and no argument about it. Controversy rages, experts swarm, interpretations multiply. Records are incomplete, either lost or still inaccessible. Evidence is frequently dubious, witnesses are often unreliable and contradictory. Hopeful clues lead to fresh mystifications.

But you plod on. Your notebooks bulge with miscellaneous pieces of information that refuse to fit into any orderly file, or with instructions to yourself which are very clear and imperative when issued but often meaningless when next consulted. Your common sense rebels, you are assailed by doubts. Are you even sure you have chosen the right subject?

And then, without any warning, when you are in the depths of bored discouragement with the whole project, something very strange happens. The character you have been studying with decreasing enthusiasm suddenly comes alive in your mind.

It may occur anywhere or at any time, but everyone agrees that some kind of crystallization takes place. Nature makes one of her mysterious jumps; quantity of information becomes quality of understanding. Now you know where previously you had noted. You have acquired some standard by which you can distinguish the true from the false or the less true. You can write with assurance about the character and motives of the person you are describing, instead of laboriously recording the outer circumstances and events of his life. These crucial moments of illumination, when you feel you have been in some strange way in living contact with the past, are often accompanied by some illusion, recognized as such by the rational mind but none the less constituting a genuine experience.

You go into into a great man's room and there he is in his accustomed chair; you look through his window and see with his eyes. You catch him making some habitual, unconscious gesture which a portrait painter recorded long ago. You may feel his fatigue in your bones or be refreshed in spirit by the intensity of his purpose. The illusion will fade, but the conviction that what you glimpsed was real will persist.

The message you receive, however, may be not a welcome but a warning, an indication that your subject has no intention of talking to you frankly. This happened to me in the case of Galileo. He muttered and grumbled about his rheumatism and the bad manners of university students, but I could never get him to come to the point about his trial for heresy. He found me, I felt, ignorant and boring. I also suspect that what is wrong with *Elizabeth and Essex* has nothing to do with the facts but is simply that the queen could not be bothered with Lytton Strachey; he was not her type.

Another time I had a distinct, though indirect, warning that Julius Caesar was not the kind of company I should keep. Intent on hearing from him about the crossing of the Rubicon, I first consulted all manner of historians, geographers, military experts and poets. I visualized the scene very clearly. I heard the wind in the trees, the river flowing over its red pebbles, the movement of the horses hobbled by the ford, the challenge of the sentries as the cloaked leader walked through the camp that historic night. But he himself never spoke.

Suddenly Plutarch jogged my elbow, reminding me of the occasion when Caesar told a man who dared oppose him in the Senate that if he said another word he'd have his head. "And you know," Caesar added, "it hurts me much more to say that than it would to do it." I laughed: but I fled.

My invitation from Virginia Woolf to persevere was also indirect. Two remarks about her collided in my mind. Elizabeth Bowen said, "I heard her laugh before I saw her," and instantly I was edging my way through a crowd at a garden party, determined to meet the woman who laughed. In the very same fraction of a second, William Plomer was describing her as she hurried past the fig tree and the zinnias to her workroom in the orchard at Rodmell, and I was crying, "Wait for me, Virginia!" She didn't wait, of course, but ever since I have been trying to get in front of her and see exactly how she looked when, her mind on her day's work, she sought the haven of that room of her own. She was completely real to me at that moment: and she didn't say, "Stop bothering me, stranger."

All illusions of this sort are sheer midsummer madness; at best a kind of dramatic summary of what has been occupying the mind for months, a waking dream. They have a rational explanation. But what often follows remains inexplicable.

Proofs of what you have long suspected begin to arrive, and from the most unlikely sources. Some may be too late for inclusion in your book — it was not until 1954 that Dr. Carl Weber received the last scrap of evidence supporting a conclusion he reached when he was working on his biography of Thomas Hardy in 1937 — but some will reach you, astonishingly, in the very nick of time. A scientist using the same material you have been study-

ing may reach a conclusion identical with yours by a totally different route; which is in itself not so odd as that you and he hear
about one another's work.

New discoveries are made which show the historian footprints
on the sands of time, and when they are widely reported your
technique for picking up useful clues comes into play. But they
also crop up in quite unexpected places, lying in wait for you in
dentists' waiting rooms in magazines you do not normally read.
Friends knowing your interests will direct information your way;
and so will complete strangers.

Have you become magnetized in some way, that so many of
these fragments of the past come winging to you? The coinci-
dences are uncanny. The chance meetings with people who drop
clues enabling you to fix a date or confirm a theory, the peculiar
way books fly open at the right page or forgotten notes appear on
the top of a heap and suddenly have meaning so that you posi-
tively stumble over a needle that has fallen from a haystack, the
bells that ring in your memory about something you did not know
you knew, the blank walls that reveal doors opening on unsuspected gardens — all this is so astonishing that it is hard to resist the impression that the person you are writing about is, if not
actually writing your book, actively cooperating with you, using
you to tell somebody something.

True, this feeling is by no means continuous, is in fact less frequent than the feeling that you have been chasing a will-o'-the-
wisp and have a long, dreary trudge before you get home. But
when you do have this conviction of being in contact with another mind, it is as irresistible as it is irrational.

You have been haunted by ghosts, though you don't believe in
ghosts. You have been possessed by demons, though demonic
possession is long out of date. Time has slithered like a snake in
the grass, centuries have jostled one another, though chronology
has been your watchword and you have worked with a watch on

your desk and knew you had a deadline to meet. In fact, you have been as mad as a hatter. Surely no one was ever so crazy before?

And just as you ask yourself this question you hear a story or see a sight you know would have pleased the incubus you imagine you are thankful to have shaken off, and you want to share your delight with the companion from whom you have now parted. Or you find that your feeling of identification with another personality is not singular, that others have freely confessed to even more complicated intimations than yours. When you hear, for instance, Walter de la Mare summing up his memories of Thomas Hardy as suggesting that "sharing Hardy's mind and imagination and his living voice had been to me, as it were, a transmutation of myself into a character in one of his novels," then you know you are not alone, that you need not be ashamed to admit you have been leading a double life.

MARK SCHORER

My Life and Nine-Year Captivity
with Sinclair Lewis

In the spring of 1952 the author-critic Mark Schorer, then a visiting professor at Harvard, was asked by McGraw-Hill if he would care to write a biography of a "recently dead well-known novelist." Mr. Schorer did not immediately recognize who was meant but agreed when he learned it was Sinclair Lewis. What he let himself in for is described in his essay.

"WHO is Sinclair Lewis," Elizabeth Bowen asked me a few years ago, "to have taken seven years out of your life?" He took nine finally.

The question seems to have its point, for during those nine years it was asked of me in one form or another by many of my friends and colleagues of a certain kind. We thought your writers, these would say in effect, were William Blake and Henry James and Jane Austen and D. H. Lawrence. What connection has Lewis, that literary roughneck, with any of these?

Or what, it has sometimes been wordily implied, is the interest of a professor of the humanities in that raw, barbarous figure out of a raw Minnesota who became the noisy critic of our culture at its most barbarous, and the protector as well of some of our grossest sentimentalities? Between the humanities, shall we say, and the creator of those dehumanized centers of human activity, Gopher Prairie and Zenith, or of such nearly nonhuman characters as Elmer Gantry?

Is it only a connection in reverse? Not quite. As a young man

Harry Sinclair Lewis respected professors, or, at least, his professors at Yale, and especially William Lyon Phelps. And what a
curious linkage that is! Phelps, a vastly popular professor in the
genteel tradition, who communicated to generations of students
an impression of the glamour of literature and of the literary
life; and Lewis, a vastly popular novelist, whose life communicates
to us rather its frequent grimness.

It is a linkage of the genial professor who, through the ease of
his learning and all the gestures of his charm, persuaded his students of the value of the literary life and who was the adored object of hundreds of them; and of the acrid novelist, generally contemptuous of professors and academic values, whose life, for all
his millions of readers, is an allegory of uneasy, hapless waste, a
life which, long before his death, had become the object of the
world's pity and contempt.

Let us not, I have sometimes said, forget Sinclair Lewis' side of
it. Certainly there were times when I was made uneasy by the
thought of the shade of that man, outraged in its distant circle
(a circle in whose reality he did not believe) — outraged and raging that its helpless life in the world, now out of its hands, should
have fallen into the hands of a professor, and one not entirely un-
tainted by the "genteel."

Yet there was a brief time when even Lewis thought that he
wished to become a professor. At Yale, and more and more seriously in his senior year, he contemplated returning there to take
the Ph.D. in English and then to move permanently into the ivied
ivory tower in the grove. Could he have submitted to the routines
that prevail in that supposedly pastoral place, he would not, I
think, have been a distinguished professor, but he would have
been at least an irascible one. Without ever quite overcoming his
impulse to be a teacher, he did not put himself finally to that test.
At the very end of his last year at Yale he decided that he would
become, as soon as possible, a writer alone. At the front of the

last of his New Haven diaries he recorded the decision: "Humanity outweighs the humanities."

Had I known him, was I a friend of his? This might explain my interest. But no — I met him just once, and our connections were of the slightest.

One connection was provided by the accident of my having been born in a Midwest village not unlike his and named after the same Indians: Sauk City, Wisconsin, instead of Sauk Centre, Minnesota, one with more Germans than Scandinavians, and the other with more Scandinavians than Germans, but each with its Main Street and all that Main Street implies.

We had one other, perhaps more personal connection. When I was in my twenties, I published a windy novel that dealt with Midwest pioneering and small-town Midwesterners. A year or two later when Lewis was addressing teachers in Milwaukee, he took occasion to belabor his audience for its ignorance of native writers, and hailed all the young Wisconsin writers, including me, who had come to his attention. Fifteen years later, I examined his library in Williamstown, Massachusetts, and I was touched to find that first novel among perhaps a dozen novels that he kept in his study, which was given over almost entirely to works of reference. I was amused by his notes in the book, some of which did not find their way into his Milwaukee observations. Among others was the impatiently scribbled, "Cut the subjectivism!"

When, a few years after the Milwaukee address, I published a second novel, which was meant to be stylish rather than folksy, and my publishers sent a copy to Lewis for possible comment, the response was silence. It was the sort of novel most calculated to annoy him. Then, shortly after publication when I was dining with the publisher, Bennett Cerf, and his wife, at Sardi's, Lewis entered the restaurant with a young woman just as we were about to leave. There were introductions. Lewis, scowling, to Schorer: "You made a bad mistake when you left that small town."

Schorer, beaming, not saying to Lewis: "Ever see anything like Sardi's in Sauk Centre, man?" This was the only occasion on which we met, and neither of us, of course, had any reason to suppose that at some later time his life would be messed up by the other.

Still, all the time that I was re-creating Lewis' boyhood in Sauk Centre, I had the curious feeling that I had never left Sauk City. To have experienced so nearly the same social and cultural situation and to have been raised within its limitations, to have known a similar landscape and to have explored its potentialities in pastime and instruction, to have had a comparable initiation into the normal brutalities and the lax amenities of middle-border village life — all this was conceivably a support to the imagination that found itself reconstructing the atmosphere of Lewis' background. There were differences, of course; among others, I, the town fool, nevertheless had two friends in Sauk City; in Sauk Centre, Lewis, that town's fool, had exactly one.

So I have written the life of a man who came from my kind of town. If I had been able to choose (and I was not so much the chooser as the chosen), I would then have preferred to write about a background less bleak, about a man whose riches were older and who carried them more easily. Yet, thinking in terms of about 350 pages and three years at the outside, I agreed to write the biography of Sinclair Lewis.

Having seen the Williamstown house before it was unfurnished, I went on at once to Sauk Centre. Sinclair Lewis was born in 1885 and the memories of his contemporaries were no longer quite trustworthy. Every reminiscence had to be checked, for memory becomes confused with fictitious images drawn from both extremes — of the goofy boy, as the town thought, who grew up there, and of the Great Reputation that never repudiated its origins. The goofy boy is made goofier for having disproved every village supposition by becoming great, at the same time that the

Great Reputation is discovered to have had its obvious roots in Our Town. I found myself involved at once in the complications of myth — and so it was all the way to January, 1951, and even later, when reminiscences began to appear in print.

That this dilemma can be charming is demonstrated by my correspondence with a kindly gentleman who was graduated from Sauk Centre High School in Harry Lewis' class of 1902; he told me that Lewis had been the valedictorian of their class and had delivered a fine graduating address. It was not necessary to ask about the subject of that address because I already knew that on this occasion Harry Lewis had been silent, knew, from the Graduation Program that young Lewis had preserved and from his own account of the exercises as written for and published in the Sauk Centre Herald (and also preserved), that it was my correspondent himself who had delivered the graduation address on the subject of "The Westward March of Empire," and that Harry, one of a class of only nine, with three places of honor open to it, was graduated with no honors at all, and wrote in his diary, not now in his usual code but in German, as if to persuade himself that at least he knew a foreign language, *"Ach dasz ich als* Freshman *und* Sophomore *gearbeitet hätte."*

When I agreed to write the book, I had already arranged for quite other reasons to be in Italy in the following year, so from the beginnings in Sauk Centre I swung to the last years in Florence and Rome. My situation there proved to be not essentially different, but the problem of treacherous memory was complicated, I now discovered, by human vanity. Most people whom I approached were eager to help me, but most people, too, and quite naturally, like to appear at their best. (In these nine years, only four people, each with his own good reasons, declined to help me, and I could understand why; but I still resent that one of them who, after I'd plied him with martinis, fed him his lunch, and for an hour deferentially lit his cigarettes while he told me nothing, walked off with my Zippo lighter!)

There was always the problem then, a problem for any scholar, of getting the fact out of the fiction, or, more usually, the fact out of the semi-fact. Fortunately, the Lewis private papers are so extensive that on most occasions I could check at the primary source. But very soon I became aware of a problem that is probably peculiar to any man's first biographer, his peculiar and weighty responsibility. Suddenly it struck me that I had not taken upon myself just another literary task but that what I was in fact doing was to establish, to fix the image of a life. This was the way that Sinclair Lewis was going to be, and probably for quite a long time. Some notorious examples in the literary past warned me to be more than ever cautious, alert, complete.

And so the three years began to stretch into nine, the 350-page book into a typescript of 1500 pages, the casual commitment into the compulsion, the obsession. Despair. At one point my wife, who has a little money, offered to buy me out of my contract. But I was too far in. Helpless. He had me.

The compulsion is to know everything, even the most trivial details. I have not computed the miles I traveled in following this appallingly restless man to all the places where he lived and worked and disported himself, but the mileage must run well up in six figures. I have not counted the number of people to whom I talked about Sinclair Lewis, but they must number well over a thousand. Nor have I counted the letters I wrote and received, the interviews I recorded on a portable Sound-Scriber, the four-by-six cards in their rows of ruthlessly chronological arrangement from 1885 to 1951 — from before that, of course, and on after.

The danger was the loss of all perspective. A given detail was true enough, but was it important? And if it was not important in itself, might it not serve as a link, a bridge, to something that would prove to be important much later in the book? Or, trivial as it seemed in itself, a clue to a mystery later? So one hoards, and later, perhaps, removes.

A biographer's fortune, finally, becomes this enormous hoard of fact, and whether or not he uses it all, it exists. I know more about the life of Sinclair Lewis, day by day, sometimes hour by hour, than he himself could possibly have known or than I know of my own past. We do not live our lives in the deliberate and conscious way that one pursues biographical research. We forget much, in our necessary indifference and anxiety, that a biographer spends days in reconstructing from the ruins of memory and time. And the result is a little eerie. Inside my life is this alien life; inside my skin, so to speak, is the other man's history. It possesses me at least as much as I possess it.

So the answer to your question, dear Elizabeth, is still a question and one that I must go on asking for some time to come: "Who is Sinclair Lewis to have taken *me?*"

PAMELA HANSFORD JOHNSON

It's Easy to Get Americans All Wrong

In some words about herself, Pamela Hansford Johnson recalled that "at twenty-two I had completed my first novel, This Bed Thy Center *and decided to make literature a career." Over the years she has done just that, writing critical studies (*Thomas Wolfe, I. Compton-Burnett*), plays, and most of all, novels. She is part of a literary household: her husband is the novelist Sir Charles Snow.*

THE DIFFICULTIES of writing about a country not one's own are hideously frustrating. I should love to write about America. Here is this stimulating scene, bright, new, different, but not so different that the visitor can't grasp its essence; yet I dare not, for the moment, anyway, touch it. It is maddening.

I have visited the United States many times, for periods ranging from a fortnight to several months. This has given me just sufficient confidence to put a solitary tourist American into my novel, *The Unspeakable Skipton,* where he occupies about a page and a half, and to set one scene of the novel I am now writing in New York. And believe me, I had the *Skipton* American checked by an American, and I am going to have my new scene checked in the same way. It is so easy, so distressfully easy, to get Americans all wrong.

The problem isn't really one of differing social attitudes, anyway, not in the broad sense. A reasonably experienced observer of human beings has only to spend a month here during a Presidential campaign to get an insight into those, though there are special areas, in the field, say, of education, or of the position of the American professional woman, where the observer can go hopelessly wrong.

To take an example. After my first three visits here, I hugged to my bosom two cardinal beliefs: one, that the U.S.A. was the most comfortable country in the world to live in; two, that the lot of the American woman with a career was bliss unmitgated. I now see the paradox that the more luxurious a country becomes (yours, and to a lesser degree, mine), so it becomes less and less comfortable. The washing machine and the deep freeze are poor substitutes for hired help in the kitchen; Belgium, the Nether- lands, Switzerland, are much more comfortable places. I also see that the professional woman who wants to combine home and job comes up against almost as much hostility, both overt and hid- den, as she does in England, and that if a woman wants to get the top job, she still has to be at least five times as good as the com- peting male. These are not particularly important factors in the sum of things, but a novelist who didn't understand them would get his books subtly and disquietingly wrong.

The chief problem, however, is less that of social manners than of language. I don't subscribe to the silly joke that Americans and British speak different tongues. Fortunately for us both, we speak the same one, with minor variations, but those variations can be devastating pitfalls. American speech rhythms are just a little different from ours; sometimes there is quite a marked dif- ference in the order of words in sentences. We use fewer preposi- tions than you do. We elaborate less than you do. We don't say, "visit with," we just say, "visit." We don't, unless we are Ameri- canized, say, "Why don't you call him up?" "Call him" will do. An English writer doesn't say he is "working on" a novel (a phrase which to me implies a sort of sweating labor, like hacking at a block of wood), he says he is writing one. Small things, but if you are introducing an American into your books, you will ignore them at your peril.

Then there is the problem of slang, of the vernacular. It seems easy enough to learn the slang, but not to appreciate at which point it became outmoded. Few things are sadder than to hear an English adolescent, dull of ear, trying to talk the argot of the Beatnik. Few English writers have any historical appreciation of the fluctuations of American slang, few Americans have any of the fluctuations of English. We all know how terrible the fictional Englishman can be in nervous American hands. He says, "Jolly good." He says, "Old boy." He says, "Awfully, frightfully good." For this, to some extent, one is tempted to blame P. G. Wodehouse, though it is really not his fault. In the heyday of Bertie Wooster, it was quite possible to hear these phrases spoken in England, but not so often; and certainly you won't hear them now.

I said — "You won't hear them now," but in fact I realize, to my consternation, that I have used a few of them even on my most recent visit to this country. I have heard myself do it. The reason is that though I should not normally use words such as "jolly," and "awfully," I don't know what their equivalents are in America, and I feel that my phrases will at least be understood within the convention of the "stage Englishman." My own normal usage would, of course, be rather more profane. But I am a guest among hospitable strangers, and on formal occasions I should not naturally use even a mild profanity. All right then. With what words *does* the American qualify "good," if he is not using "damn good," or "bloody good"? If my ear were finer, I should know. But it isn't, and I don't.

Then there are social nuances I do not find it easy to grasp. Is it the custom in this country uniformly to refer to one's wife, or husband, in talking to people like one's self, as "Mrs. Smith," or "Mr. Smith"? I don't know. The English would invariably say, "my wife," "my husband," or even refer to them simply, if they were known however slightly to the persons addressed, by their first names. My feeling is that the American custom, though practically universal, is not *wholly* so.

Again, what about academic titles? In England, a professor is invariably introduced by that title, and you call him "Professor" until such time as you can relax, use his surname (which we still use a bit more than you do), or better, call him George. In America, the usage seems to vary from campus to campus. On some, "Professor," or "Doctor," gives way to the over-all "Mister." On others, the title is used, and is expected to be used. How shall a foreigner who wants to write, say a story about campus life, get these things right? By making errors in such small matters as these, a writer can jolt his entire book out of the true.

There is also the matter of nomenclature, which is not quite as simple as it seems. I think that, for various reasons, it is easier for English writers to find correct-sounding American names than it is vice versa. Though I read Upton Sinclair's *World's End* series with considerable glee (what *would* Lanny be up to next?) I was constantly bothered by Alfie, an English aristocrat.

Now it is quite impossible for an English aristocrat to be called "Alfie," though he can be called (indeed, the Duke of Norfolk *is* called) "Bert." The name "Alfred" presents some special difficulties. Let us assume that an upper-class Englishman desires to shorten it. "Alf" is impossible: "Alf" is a name used for burglars. "Alfie" is impossible; it suggests a cockney tatterdemalion screeching for her young down a gray street littered with orange peel and old newspapers. "Al" is purely American. "Alfred," in its Saxon entirety, tends to sound a trifle lofty. What is this Englishman going to be called by his family and friends? Almost certainly "Freddie," which retains the right Wodehouse ring and aura of St. James' Street.

The failure of instinct, of ear, of social observation, can drop a blot on a book so conspicuous to the expert (i.e., the affronted national) that the whole book seems one big blot. In *Advise and Consent*, the British Ambassador and his wife are so hopelessly wrong, in every possible way, in speech, in behavior, in social manners, that the English reader finds his disbelief in this respect coloring his attitude toward the entire novel. Unfair, maybe; but only too true.

So long as a visiting foreigner has consciously to observe and to think about the place in which he is and the people surrounding him, he is too raw to attempt to write about them. D. H. Lawrence's *Kangaroo* is often cited as an example of how quickly a country can be absorbed into the imagination. My own feeling is that Lawrence's wonderful visual sense and threatening verbal authority hypnotize the reader into thinking he has succeeded completely. I am sure Lawrence saw correctly, but I don't believe he heard correctly. I don't believe a "dinkum-die Aussie," if that is the unfortunate phrase, would feel it might have been written by a native son. I may be wrong; if so, Lawrence is the exception which proves the rule.

It is one of the common fallacies that travel is of pragmatic value to the novelist. "Traveling Awards," in which money is heaped on young writers to enable them to carry on with their work in Venice or the south of France, seem to me among the most futile of well-meant schemes. Travel is pleasant for the writer; it broadens his mind (I suppose); it gives him a literal idea that there *is* no place like home, and makes him consider, perhaps for the first time, the proposition that all truths may not reside there.

However, it does cut him off from his roots, isolate him from a comprehensible society at the very time he needs to learn about that society if his work is going to be anything but solipsist in character. As a source of "copy," except "copy" of a most marginal nature, it is quite useless. I am quite remorseless in suggesting that the money would be better spent in giving him a year's university course in one of the sciences, applied, physical, medical, social, or even in teaching him a useful trade. At least, this would give him something to write about.

For my part, I think the writer must get to a point where the land of his temporary adoption can be as thoughtlessly accepted as the land of his birth. Trying to write a novel and at the same time conducting a checking process, pausing at every other line to ponder whether an image is right, a phrase of dialogue is right, inhibits the creative imagination. People who don't know how novels are written are always asking if one "goes out and searches for copy," rather as if the writer were buckling on his snowboots and going resolutely out into the Arctic wastes.

A serious novelist does not, or should not, be searching for "copy" in the way that a journalist must; "copy" should, as it were, come to him. It is something he finds he has the good fortune to possess, without having taken any conscious steps to glean it. And then there is the coy, half terrified, half hopeful query, "Are you always studying people so you can put them into your books?" Again, the answer is, "No." One does put people into one's books, either straight, or as composites, but they are invariably people one has come to know rather than sought to know.

As I say, it is frustrating; it is maddening. I know that many, indeed, most serious American novelists feel the size of their country and the social and political chaos of their times so unhandleable that they tend to contract out, retreat into private worlds and write almost entirely about themselves. I can understand the difficulty of the challenge they are asked to face. The English writer lives in so small a society that it is not particularly hard to grasp the whole of it; that is why English regional novels have been so few.

Yet I have often envied American and Russian writers because their challenge *is* such an enormous one. I should like the chance to tackle it myself, even if I failed miserably in the process; but it will be years and years before I shall have anything like the qualifications to make the attempt. I am not going to dismay my American friends by presenting them or their country in any work of fiction, until I can be certain that I shall strike no wrong notes. Nor until, when they read what I've written, they read it without even a passing reflection that I have done the job quite remarkably well for a Britisher. I don't want them to have to think about it at all.

Should one take the risk and attempt the job? I don't think so, not in the light of the demands of modern criticism. Dickens could just get away with his ridiculous Frenchmen, Rigaud and Blandois; Balzac with his absurd English noblewomen. However, if either were written today, he would bring the critical roof down on his head. We are demanding from all writers who are realist or neo-realist the maximum of social, psychological and semantic accuracy. The reading public is not only more sophisticated, but less sweet-tempered than it used to be. This is not to say that I think any living writer can hold a candle to Dickens or Balzac; but they had a more liberal aesthetic convention on their side, which permitted them to indulge in a good many tomfooleries. I am always staggered by the introduction into Balzac's *A Woman of Thirty,* probably the most profound essay into female psychology ever written, of a pirate who kept a grand piano on his ship, loaded with gold doubloons.

I am not going to risk that pirate slinking aboard any ship of mine, even in the form of an American whose prepositions are in the wrong place, whose slang is slightly but queasily out of date, whose *curriculum vitae* is just faintly askew, and who fills any real American asked to contemplate him with a mixture of pity, exasperation and distrust.

AUTHOR'S CORRECTION:

There are times when fate makes an ass of one. Shortly after writing this minatory essay, a compulsion came upon me to write an American novel. The compulsion was irresistible, so, setting my teeth against possible derision (after all my brave words), I wrote Night and Silence, Who Is Here? *I did, however, proceed with some caution. My America was seen through the eyes of an agreeable, but self-indulgent Englishman; and I had every line of American speech vetted, not by one American, but by three. Even so, I am told that a few verbal slips appear. If this is the case, blame these Americans, and not me.*

CECIL WOODHAM-SMITH

Writing History Is Nervous Work

"To make the past live again, to find out the truth and make it real" — that Cecil Woodham-Smith has defined as the task of the historian. She has gone about doing it painstakingly, and with superb literary style. Her Florence Nightingale *is biography at its best. The* Reason Why, *a story of the Crimean War, is a classic. Her latest book,* The Great Hunger, *rousingly re-creates the horrors and stupidities of the Irish famines of the mid-nineteenth century.*

WRITING history is nervous work, thanks to the vigilance of other historians. What Sir Steven Runciman — whose *History of the Crusades* is one of the major works of our century — calls "the watchful severity of his colleagues" is perpetually on the historian's mind; he is a haunted man, haunted by the fear of being caught out in a mistake. Novelists, dramatists, essayists, poets, fear failure, but how much more humiliating is exposure; and historical critics dedicated to historical truth are tireless in pursuit of error. Indeed it has been said that some, on receiving a new book, will sit up all night until a mistake is detected and their mission is fulfilled.

No such exacting standard is required from other writers. Recently the admirable dramatist Jean Anouilh wrote a play round the celebrated conflict between Thomas à Becket and Henry II in which the conflict was made more poignant by the fact that Becket was represented as being a Saxon, one of the race who

had previously ruled England and been conquered, dispossessed
and enslaved by the Normans, while Henry II was the Norman
King. When it was pointed out to Anouilh that this dramatic
clash of nationality had no existence in reality since Becket in
fact was a Norman, he is reported merely to have observed, "I
must have read the wrong history book."

From the historian however, accuracy is required before anything else, and accuracy is the criterion by which his work will be
judged. The historian has assumed a responsibility beyond good
writing. He has put himself forward as the man who states the
truth, who has found out what really happened. But with the
best intentions accuracy is hard to achieve. Assiduity will go far,
especially when working in the comparative safety of printed authorities, but when new ground is broken and original material
used, then the historian finds that facts are not always what they
seem.

When I was working on the biography of Florence Nightingale, I read through a large bundle of letters endorsed Lord Napier. At that time the mass of papers left by Miss Nightingale at
her death had not yet been properly sorted: however letters from
the same correspondent had generally been tied together. Lord
Napier was in India, an ardent worker for Indian welfare, a passionate advocate of irrigation and devoted to Miss Nightingale to
whom he wrote frequently and at length, always mentioning irrigation. Irrigation was to be the salvation of India; he wrote of
crops — and irrigation, medical services — and irrigation, education — and irrigation. He was a very nice man.

Presently it began to strike me that considering his period —
about the middle of the nineteenth century — he was getting
about rather quickly. He was in Madras one day and the Punjab
the next, Calcutta on Monday and Bombay on Tuesday, finally
he appeared to get from Madras to Abyssinia in twenty-four hours.
He was not one man but two, there must have been two Lord

Napiers serving in India. And so there were. Both were passionately interested in irrigation, both worked for the welfare of India, both were devoted to Miss Nightingale. One Lord Napier led the expedition to Abyssinia, was a member of the Viceroy's Council and built the famous Bari Doab canal, now in Pakistan. The other was Governor of Madras and did invaluable work to irrigate Madras Province.

Letters are strewn with pitfalls. Our nineteenth-century ancestors had a confusing practice of omitting to date their letters, heading them merely with the day of the week, Monday, or Friday, not even the year. Important people and officials often employed an amanuensis, therefore did not write in their own hand. It was also a common practice to sign letters with initials instead of names and frequently two people have the same initials. In a country house in Wales, I came on a number of letters signed F.N., the signature generally used by Miss Nightingale when writing to her family and friends. The letters were undated except for the day of the week, were written in a flowing rounded hand, very like Miss Nightingale's as a girl. All handwriting of Victorian women, especially well brought-up young women, has a resemblance.

These were in any case difficult to read because according to the fashion of the time the lines were written first one way across the paper and then the other — "crisscrossed." Each letter began with an endearment and was couched in the language of affection and if Miss Nightingale had been the writer how interesting they would have been. Unfortunately the writer was Miss Nightingale's mother, Fanny Nightingale, who also signed her letters F.N., and never dated them, and the letters were addressed to her husband, Miss Nightingale's father, William Edward Nightingale.

In my book *The Great Hunger* I had to deal with the desperate, almost panic-stricken, emigration from Ireland to North

America produced by the famine. I knew nothing about emigration, and by a stroke of luck I thought I would begin by reading some of the official correspondence. I like to read some original material before consulting authorities. It was a stroke of luck because in the history of North American emigration there is a pitfall, supplied by one Alexander Carlisle Buchanan, British emigration officer at Quebec. After working for some months I was given an introduction to a well-known historian who could, if he thought me worthy, give a great deal of help. His first question when we met was, "What do you know about Alexander Carlisle Buchanan?" I answered, "He was two people," and he said, "You'll do."

Appointed emigration agent at Quebec in 1825, Alexander Carlisle Buchanan retired ten years later. He was succeeded by his nephew and namesake, Alexander Carlisle Buchanan the younger. During the emigration disaster which followed the flight from Ireland in the great famine and the official inquiries and recriminations which took place afterwards, Alexander Carlisle Buchanan the younger, the nephew not the uncle, was in charge. This is a point of a kind dear to historians which several eminent professors have failed to detect. Even official reference books omit to mention the nephew, implying that Alexander Carlisle Buchanan the uncle held the appointment as emigration agent until his death in 1868. The facts are in a file of official correspondence at the Public Record Office, London, entitled C.O. (Colonial Office) 42.

Titles in the British peerage are tricky subjects to deal with owing to what are called "second creations." What happens is this: for want of a male heir there is no one to succeed to a title and it becomes extinct. Then someone who is either going to receive a title for the first time or is going to be "elevated," that is gain a step in rank, chooses the title. He may be a connection and he may not, and he becomes the first baron, earl or marquis of the second creation.

For instance a famous character in English history was Edward Hyde, the devoted adherent of Charles I and author of the celebrated *History of the Great Rebellion,* created first Earl of Clarendon in 1661. However, in 1753 the earldom of Clarendon became extinct, and in 1776 Thomas Villiers, who had married the granddaughter of the fourth and last Earl, was made first Earl of Clarendon of the second creation. Therefore though there are still Earls of Clarendon, and the family maintains its distinction, the title dates from the eighteenth not the seventeenth century, and their name is not Hyde, it is Villiers.

Of smaller pitfalls there is no end. To describe the course of the famine in Ireland I had to identify and locate a number of small villages and towns, mentioned in documents and correspondence only by name. But I found that place names were repeated over and over again in nineteenth-century Ireland. In the *Index to the Townlands and Towns of Ireland* published in 1871, there are twenty-seven places in different parts of the country called Clare, twenty-seven called Ballagh, thirty-four called Acres. There is a Ballina in Mayo, Sligo and Tipperary, a Rathdrum in Cork and Wexford; there are four Clashmores, one in Clare, one in the east Riding of Cork, one in the west Riding of Cork, and one in Waterford. I got the wrong Clashmore.

Even a capital letter can make all the difference. When Sir Robert Peel and his contemporaries write repeal with a small "r," they mean the repeal of the Corn Laws, which protected the price of English home-grown corn; when Repeal is written with a capital "R," it means Repeal of the Act of Ireland. Be sure before you note contemporary comments on one that the other is not intended.

The historian can be certain that no error will pass unnoticed. There is always someone who knows. Armies of old gentlemen buried in remote country places spend their lives delving into subjects one might imagine could interest no human being. Give the minor branch of a family supposed to be extinct wrong precedence and angry representatives start from the ground to put you right; fail to give an obscure colonel his correct rank on the very day he was promoted more than a century ago and his great-grandchildren will demand an apology. When this vigilance is added to the watchful severity of historical colleagues, there is no cause for wonder that writing history should be nervous work.

JOHN KNOWLES

Where Does a Young Writer Find His Real Friends?

For A Separate Peace *John Knowles became the first winner of the William Faulkner Foundation's award for a "notable first novel," and he was also given an award by the National Institute of Arts and Letters.*

THE YOUNG writer today has quite a few friends out there in literaryland and innumerable enemies. Within himself there are both. There is, as always, only one way for him to find out which side will win: keep on writing, and see.

Education, which had rather gone out of style in the literary world, is coming back. Most of the young writers today have more formal education than, say, Hemingway or Faulkner ever had, and is that an enemy or a friend?

It seems to be both. General information about the world is always useful to a writer, and he can even be taught certain skills used in writing itself. He can sometimes be taught to clear up his style to the point where he begins to reveal to his teacher and himself whether he really knows and feels anything important or not. An elementary principle of art can also be taught to him: that the artist, the novelist, does not tell his reader very much, does not explain things to his reader. He does not instruct or preach at him either. Why go through the exhuasting labor of creating characters and a place and time and so on if you are then going to destroy their effect by *telling* the reader much about them?

The young student novelist can learn that he is not going to explain his characters and what happens to them to the reader, but instead re-create as strongly as possible within the reader what his characters are like and what they are going through, so that the reader is led to feel his way, as though he were living it himself, to the novel's conclusion. It will be unforgettable for him if he is made to do this. Experience really is the best teacher. The best novels are experiences which happen to the reader. He may not fully understand them any more than he understands other experiences he has had, but he has experienced them; they are a part of him; he will not forget them.

My second novel, *Morning in Antibes,* was, unhappily, published, to the accompaniment of lots of praise and lots of blame. Naturally I don't like the book — does any novelist by the time his work is published? — because I didn't go far enough in the direction it was tending, because I recounted too much and didn't re-create enough. Others think I went much too far in that direction. They want to be told things, lots of things, lots of facts and circumstances, and most of all they want background. Where did this weak young man fumbling on the Riviera in 1958 over his broken marriage come from? That promiscuous wife of his: what's her background? Those decayed French aristocrats and beach people and those trapped Algerians around them, why aren't they "fully developed"? We've got to know more, they complain, or else we can't care about these characters. Also, this novel happens to lack a beginning; what's even worse, it hasn't got an end. (But does experience have a beginning really, or an end?)

I console myself that these criticisms at least are not as serious as if they had said, "Give us less!" Still, there they are. My problem is that I can't write a novel in which all the stages of the characters' pasts and all the circumstances of their present lives are dutifully recorded. I don't think most of that matters. What they are saying and doing and feeling now, provided *now* is a crucial period in their lives, seems to me enough. Both the past and the future are contained in that now.

I think readers should work more; I don't want to imagine everything for them. If I did so, then there would be nothing in my novel except a neatly rectangular picture of life at which readers could stare for a while until finally their eyes begin to glaze over, and then forget. Readers should participate; a novel should be an experience.

The French "anti-novelist" Alain Robbe-Grillet has carried this principle much further and contents himself with describing in detail the rooms his characters are in, the textures of the wood and cloth there, the angles which the sunlight forms, the arrangement of chairs, the layout of the gardens outside and so on, interrupting these lists now and then to insert scrappy passages of dialogue. But he seems to be carrying a good thing much too far. He gives the impression, not surprising in a Frenchman, of having been deeply influenced by painting. His novels are more like paintings than novels, still-life paintings, very still life.

Yet if education is a friend up to a point, it can also be an enemy, as I myself learned the hard way. Several years after graduation from Yale I decided the time had come to write a novel. So I withdrew to the island of Ischia and began to work out the symbolic pattern of my book, and naturally the metaphysical paradoxes, the underlying myth and the levels. At last I paused for a moment to decide what to put on the surface. Anything would do, so I chose Ischia itself. Why not? After all, there it was all around me. I knew nothing about it, couldn't speak ten words of Italian, knew no one there, but with my brilliant substructure any surface fabric would do.

I actually completed this work, and called it "Descent to Proselito," my name for Ischia. The best critics would detect the word "proselyte" concealed there and so get their first clue to all the meanings. I sailed proudly back to America with the manuscript and laid it before Thornton Wilder, who had been very kindly reading and criticizing my work. "Knowles," his comment ran, "I'm on page 151 and I can't go on. You're not interested in this."

Interested, interested? Did I have to be interested?

Slowly, in the weeks of convalescence which followed, I came to realize that I had been urgently interested in being a renowned novelist on the highest level, but not interested, not really, in Ischia, not even really interested in the Italians in my book, despite their marvelous metaphysical grasp of reality, the grasp only Italians in novels by young Americans possess. So I withdrew "Descent to Proselito" from the publisher, who rather reluctantly thought he might bring it out, and began to write about things which interested me, and involved not just my observation and my mind but my temperament and my feelings. I had failed because I had received more education than I could digest. I needed to go back to an earlier and simpler approach, where I knew how to function.

I now began to write another novel called "A Separate Peace," and if anything as I wrote tempted me to insert artificial complexities, I ignored it. If anything appeared which looked suspiciously like a symbol, I left it on its own. I thought that if I wrote truly and deeply enough about certain specific people in a certain place at a particular time having certain specific experiences, then the result would be relevant for many other kinds of people and places and times and experiences. I knew that if I began with symbols, I would end with nothing; if I began with specific individuals, I might end by creating symbols. Yet they were not my concern.

For the young writer, the rising standard of living has brought another enemy and friend into greater prominence: money. There's a good deal of it lying around the literary field these days, and as the young writer emerges a little from obscurity some of this money begins to edge toward him. It comes not just from books but from the whole machine for communication, the biggest ever, which has been created in America, and which has to have words, words, words.

It can't ever fall silent, because such a huge number of people support themselves by servicing it — from editing a poetry magazine to photographing Jack Paar to putting up a new building for a picture magazine — and millions of other people rely on it to fill an important part of their lives. Into it are tossed masterpieces, trash and everything between which serves its purposes. And so the emergent young writer finds an odd procession of checks from the machine, usually small ones, dropping into his hands.

I find it impossible to describe money as an enemy. For the young writer, it becomes one only if he follows it, because it will lead him into a blind alley. Yet if money follows him, if he writes ahead as he wishes to do and the checks, small or large, drop in his wake, then money becomes an extremely useful friend. The writer can thank the machine for making it somewhat easier to support himself and so concentrate on his writing; he can be very glad if the machine wants to, needs to, must publish and anthologize and translate and adapt and pictorialize what he has written. Unless he is Tennessee Williams he had better live fairly simply always, because the kind of work he wants to do and does best may not always appeal to the machine and a sudden large check may be followed by a very small one, or no check at all.

The other "rewards" of public success as a writer are all enemies (the publicity and the interviews and the lecturing and becoming a "celebrity") because they compromise not the artist's life but his work. Ideally, no one should know anything about a novelist. His books should not even be signed.

If this total anonymity prevailed, then the reader would have nothing to distract him from full attention to the book itself. Turning a page, he would not murmur to himself such irrelevancies as, "There's Waugh's snobbery popping up again"; instead he would think: This author believes in the old traditions and the old families. He would not think: If only Graham Greene weren't a convert, he wouldn't be obsessed with Catholic guilt; he would instead notice and absorb an unsuual point of view about religion.

Novels are artifice; it isn't proper that the reader is allowed to look behind the façade, allowed to probe the surface personality of the author, to link the facts of the novelist's life to the features of his art. Salinger is right to immure himself, because the less we know about him the stronger the impact of his books on us is likely to be. We won't be able to say, "He's writing this because of that emotional problem of his that I know all about," or "Poor Salinger never was the prep-school type." Bits of gossip about the author floating in the reader's head can't help draining vitality from the book he is reading.

Salinger is right, but has few imitators. I can't claim to be one, because if I were I wouldn't be writing this essay. Most of us are too vain or too egotistical or too restless or simply too cheerful and gregarious for such austerity.

At the other extreme from Salinger are a few writers who set out to become public personalities and use all facets of themselves to hold and intrigue the public eye. They lead lives which form a counterpoint to their work.

Success, that is, critical or public recognition, gives one gift of great price to the young writer: people begin to listen to him at last. Until now he may have been pointing out and disagreeing and warring and arguing endlessly, but people couldn't get around to paying attention.

Success has been branded, wrongly, an enemy of the young American writer for so long that we are in danger of forgetting how bad for him failure is. Failure, that is lack of critical or public recognition, is not inspiring; bitterness is not a good atmosphere for writing; poverty is not broadening. Then there is the terrible lack of outlet, like a speech impediment, which torments the failure. He cannot say much, publish much, no one is listening to him; he cannot advance, cannot evolve, because his first feelings and views have not been successfully communicated.

Experimenting with drugs has come back into style again with a small section of the young writing group, mostly among the would-be's. They say that they are imitating Rimbaud, who sought through drugs to achieve a "systematic disordering of the senses" and wrote an extraordinary body of poetry. Yet the genius of Rimbaud was not in drugs, and imitating him, while fun for a while, is no more likely to result in producing another Rimbaud than contracting tuberculosis will produce another Keats. Nobody is ever tempted to try the latter, I notice. Nothing in a drug can compensate for the one price it will surely exact: loss of energy.

Energy is the writer's firmest friend. I don't think any writer is ever "written out." It seems to me that the dullest-seeming life in the world provides material for masterpiece after masterpiece. What fails isn't material or experience but energy, the imaginative energy to dig down deeply into your subject, where the truth about it lies, the artistic energy to form what you find there as it should be formed, and finally the brute physical energy, the same kind used in scrubbing floors, to put it in words on paper.

A good ear is also a friend, an ear and a gift for the shape and shades and pace of the English language. And finally a sense of play somewhere in his approach to his work is a friend of the writer. There should be an element of almost physical enjoyment of writing somewhere in even the most haunted writer. This thin, persistent, streak of joy will free his imagination to do the writing, and put his willpower in its proper subordinate place.

Where does he find these real friends? Within himself. The writer must be his own best friend. He already is, it goes without saying, his own worst enemy.

PART VII

Men and Measures

ALLAN NEVINS

The Telling of a Nation's
Story

*Among the American historians of our time, none looms larger
than Allan Nevins. He was a teacher of English, a journalist,
who came late to history and then made up for lost time. At
Columbia over the years he raised scores of historians and sent
them forth, and in the midst of teaching wrote historical studies
and biographies that brought him two Pulitzer prizes and more
medals and other prizes than he cares to list. His monument is
likely to be his many-volumed history of the United States from
the war with Mexico to the period of Reconstruction.*

THE BUSINESS of the historian is booming. Demand is high and
almost outruns the abundant supply. Why? In the large view,
this is so, no doubt, mainly because the unprecedented events in
the last generation have stimulated an appetite for parallels, contrasts and interpretations. People who watched Franklin Roosevelt and Churchill wish to know more about Washington and
Pitt. Those who lived through Tobruk, Normandy and Leyte
Gulf have a keener appreciation of Marathon, Trafalgar and
Gettysburg. Froissart's assertion that "the most profitable thing
in the world for the understanding of human life is history" is
most readily accepted by intelligent men and women who have
watched bewildered as nations passed through terrible storms
and tribulations.

Agnes Repplier, who wrote history as well as essays, once heard
Henry James say that the only reading of which he never tired

was history: "The least significant footnote of history stirs me more than the most thrilling and passionate fiction." This is a tribute worth remembering on two accounts. It stands to the credit of Henry James' thirst for reality — the Henry James who, H. G. Wells said, turned his back on the greatest drama of the nineteenth century, the rise of the United States, to chronicle the gossip of English drawing rooms. It stands also to the credit of history, which is too often cheaply maligned. No form of literature is nobler, more instructive or more moving than a history of great events greatly related. History sometimes stumbles, but it offers the only sure key we shall ever find to the complex world, the surest guide to judgment and the soundest set of standards.

At this point someone asks, What is history? And this query brings us to the most remarkable fact of the current historical boom: its catholicity. Only those who study the recent annexations to the domain of history know how much amplitude it has gained. The concentration of effort on historical themes in America has become tremendous. Hundreds of universities and colleges, libraries and institutes, and societies local and national urge it on; thousands of workers, professional and amateur, participate. They rule out no subject and no approach. This vast democratic attempt to revive the past and analyze its meaning is as variegated as it is earnest. All roads to truth are kept open.

An ever-increasing wealth of content in history is matched by an ever-widening fertility in points of view. Only two centuries ago the canvas was narrow enough. It was fairly restricted to the great corporate bodies that constituted or bulwarked the state: to the government, the church and the armed forces. One epochal enlargement came with the French Revolution, which brought the common people into view. Another lesson was taught to students of the past by Walter Scott's historical novels; and Macaulay could write that the ideal history would combine the statecraft of Hume's dignified page with Scott's picture of the Covenanters in the glen, the crofter in the cabin and the stage-coach postilion winding his horn. We have long since passed the stage when John Richard Green and John Bach McMaster scandalized conservatives by arguing that full space be given the tradesman, the revival preacher, the journalist, the poet, the architect and the engineer. But still the broadening goes on.

So insatiable is now the historian's curiosity that nothing is neglected. An Indian painting by George Catlin or a Western scene by Alfred J. Miller is as eagerly seized as the old Norse sword, axe and metal bar allegedly discovered near Lake Nipigon in 1930. A university press brings out in five handsome volumes, *The Frank C. Brown Collection of North Carolina Folklore,* edited by an eminent literary scholar, Newman Ivey White; while two other handsome volumes are consecrated to a catalogue-history of dime novels, and a devoted student puts twenty years of research into his book *Showboats: The Development of an American Institution.*

Libraries groan with collections on business history, illuminating manufactures, railroads, great mercantile enterprises and retail business, including the old country store, and the Business Historical Society cheers on innumerable delvers into the area. Herbert Eugene Bolton, who did so much important work on the Southwest and edited such valuable explorations as the five-volume record of Anza's California expeditions, insisted that field-work is a cardinal part of the historian's function — even to the pack mule and lariat.

Meanwhile the volume of mere printed materials becomes overawing and presents staggering if not insoluble problems. Those issued in the conventional politico-military field alone, the stronghold of the old history, are dismaying enough.

American scholars are now producing magnificent new complete editions of the writings of Thomas Jefferson, Benjamin

Franklin, Henry Clay, John C. Calhoun and Alexander Hamilton. These follow the multi-volume edition of Washington's writings by John C. Fitzpatrick and the edition of Lincoln's writings so admirably edited by Roy Basler. They will be succeeded by other series for which the National Historical Publications Commission paves the way, for the commission is surveying appropriate bodies of papers, seeking the advice of scholars, and considering means of financing its recommendations. These sets are national monuments. President Truman fittingly delivered an acceptance address at the Library of Congress on the completion of the first volume of Jefferson's works. Such is the energy of our scholarship that it has assumed certain British tasks, notably complete editions of James Boswell and Horace Walpole. "Only America in a period of great prosperity could afford such studies as these," said the London *Times* Literary Supplement.

The published materials, even including such compilations in the field of letters as the complete edition of Emerson's letters and the never-ending documentary flood from the state historical societies, are insignificant compared with the vast collections of unpublished papers. When the Massachusetts Historical Society was founded in Washington's first Administration, we had no papers. Today they stretch before the historian as a dim, unchartable sea.

The University of Rochester recently announced that its body of Seward papers contains more than 100,000 documents. This is a mere trifle. The original body of Franklin D. Roosevelt papers transferred to Hyde Park was said to number some 5,000,-000 pieces. Subsequent acquisitions of the Morgenthau and other papers have raised the total at this Hudson River branch of the National Archives far above the original level. The historian who pauses at such figures is still only at the beginning. In 1922 the British Government stated that it had accumulated about 25,000,000 documents and 90,000 maps on the field operations alone of World War I. Nobody would dare hazard a guess at the number of manuscripts, many still classified, on field operations of World War II now housed in Washington and its suburbs. They run to hundreds of millions. The Army alone, which has a near-hundred-volume history well advanced, may possess that number.

In the accumulation of data we now take for granted catholicity, energy, lavish expenditure and growing specialization. We regard as a matter of course such depositories as the Hoover Institution on War, Revolution and Peace or the John Crerar scientific and technical library or the William Robertson Coe Collection of Western Manuscripts at Yale — though any one of them would have amazed John Fiske's generation. But has comparable progress been made in the interpretation of all this data?

This much at least is clear: the wealth of content available is matched by an enrichment of the implements for penetrating and explaining it. All the social studies — anthropology, psychology, economics, sociology, political science, social geography (to use a better term than human geography) — have been made handmaidens of history. When one of the groups that cooperated to establish the magazine *American Heritage,* itself one of the remarkable achievements of our time in the historical field, made tests of public taste, it laid before a large body of potential readers a choice among three emphases. Would they prefer narrative and descriptive articles interesting simply for color, drama and suspense? Or articles presenting history with an implied application to present-day events, like "The Arab World in Early American Diplomacy"? Or articles that dealt with important forces and events as reinterpreted by use of various social studies? — say "Battle Fatigue in the Civil War" as viewed by an expert psychologist. The largest vote was for the third category. Even average readers wanted the latest ideas of experts applied to the past.

Such reinterpretation is extremely difficult. It is seldom that the historian is so highly proficient in economics, psychology or any other technically abstruse subject that he can apply its ideas expertly. Service on a local government unit is likely to do the historian more good than hasty immersion in tomes of politics, as a commission in the Hampshire militia gave Gibbon his best grasp of military art. Most men will get a better comprehension of human nature from Shakespeare or Thackeray than from gobbling Freud. But increasingly since Walter Bagehot wrote his "Physics and Politics" the new implements have been used and used well.

Anyone who follows current publications is aware of the fact. Kenneth Stampp's book on the history of slavery, for example, has a solid anthropological basis its predecessors lacked. A long list of volumes, from Marion L. Starkey's *The Devil in Massachusetts,* a fine study in abnormal thought and behavior, to Catherine Drinker Bowen's *The Lion and the Throne,* embody the latest scientific approaches to psychology. Nobody without a considerable grounding in economics could have written such a book as Louis Hartz's *Economic Policy and Democratic Thought: Pennsylvania, 1776–1860,* which proves that government in America more distinctly repudiated *laissez-faire* and more daringly embarked on economic functions in the eighteen-forties than in the nineteen-fifties. The books of T. J. Wertenbaker on the founding of American civilization in the various colonies, as broad as life itself, employ principles from the social studies on a gamut stretching from Indian relations to the two styles of Jacobean architecture.

No nation can say to itself, "Go to, I will have great historians," any more than it can say to itself, "I will have great poets." The best it can do is to create conditions favorable to a great school of history. The direct results of the energy and catholicity of our historical effort are clear enough. Some of the indirect consequences, however, are in the long run likely to be more important. The important provision is not so much a huge accumulation of bricks, stones and timbers for future edifices as a challenging atmosphere. The accumulations in themselves help create this atmosphere. The new modes of interpretation help create it. But the historians still have to do the most important part of the work of creation. They have to supply the clash of ideas, the breadth of view, the earnestness and the literary power.

With his present-day advantages and consciousness of responsibilities, the historian must first of all feel greater humility than his predecessors. The more he has to learn, the greater his sense of inadequacy. This is what Arnold J. Toynbee had in mind when he wrote: "The broadening of the historian's field of inquiry and the multiplication of his sources and the raising of his standards of technique have made it impossible for him to shut his eyes as to his own ignorance. They have also taught him that this ignorance is incurable because it is infinite." Another British scholar, H. Hale Bellot, surveying our historians five years ago, concluded that "most of the American history that was published before 1910 has been outmoded." A hard saying, open to question as regards political history, but a statement conducing to humility.

Of equal importance is tolerance. Historians used to be highly dogmatic about the aims of their pursuit. Some believed in presenting "the past for its own sake." Some held, like George Bancroft and Heinrich von Treitschke, that history should be used to mold the future. Some granted it a cosmic function, religious and philosophical; it was a search for light on the character and destiny of humanity. Catholicity of themes, materials and methods, however, is hostile to exclusive definitions. All truth seekers may be admitted. And American historians have special reason for feeling that their pursuit should be democratic and competitive. Truth is favored by controversy and debate; the hotter they are, the less the danger of stagnation. Controversy may be yoked with tolerance — tolerance as to method and aims, controversy as to fact and deduction. History in democratic lands knows no despot and accepts no limitations of inquiry or statement.

Underneath the increased humility and tolerance lies a new understanding of the complexity of psychological factors in both the making and the writing of history. In the era before James, Freud and Ivan Pavlov, biographers and historians alike had to be content with far simpler explanations of mind, conduct and habit than are acceptable today. We can no longer deal with the characters of Cromwell and Frederick in the confident fashion in which Carlyle treated them. While almost nobody has the insights of Carlyle, nearly every well-equipped writer has a more scientific comprehension of the roots of human action. Social psychology, meanwhile, has advanced far beyond the days when Gustave Le Bon taught us our first lessons in crowd behavior and Graham Wallas analyzed the nonrational elements in mass decisions. Aspects of social psychology once entirely ignored — such as consciousness of status, which is just now being terribly overworked — receive the amplest attention.

Still more is the historian affected by a recognition of the pervasive coloration that his own psychology, and that of his time, give to his writing. This sense of the relativism of historical works to mind, period and place has been overdone. Emphasis on it has been used to excuse much grossly tendentious writing. Up to a certain point, however, it makes for a healthy caution and modesty. We recall with wry amusement that the country's leading literary historian, Charles F. Richardson, said in 1892 that George Bancroft's books were *final*. Actually, they were an expendable beginning. Bancroft thought he was impartial, but we know that he was governed by a dozen personal prepossessions and prejudices. He thought the ideas of his time rational and objective; we know that many of them were irrational and highly subjective. In fact, many would read Bancroft today less for a true history of the Revolution than for an accurate though unconscious image of the mind of Jacksonian America.

The richer his materials and the broader his range, the easier it should be for the historian to be interesting and to achieve lofty literary effects. The reader who comes to the impeachment of Andrew Johnson in James Ford Rhodes or to Stonewall Jackson's secret flank march at Chancellorsville in Douglas Freeman resents an interruption. "Don't tell me how it comes out!" he cries fiercely to anybody who halts him. History is above all to be read. An awareness of the literary requirement in this great field, once ignored, has now become — thank Heaven! — general. In hands of adequate power, history still holds its great function. Its authority as the guide and teacher of nations is perdurable. When Lincoln told Congress and the country that "we cannot escape history," he meant written history; and the more stupendous the events through which a people passes, the greater the responsibilities in world affairs which it assumes, the more compelling is its need for historical light.

GEORGE F. KENNAN

It's History but Is It Literature?

Some years ago George Kennan, a diplomat and a scholar, wrote Russia Leaves the War, *a prize-winning book if there ever was one: National Book Award, Bancroft Prize, Francis Parkman Prize, Pulitzer Prize. He has written others that involve Russia since then, most recently* On Dealing with the Communist World. *He is a former United States Ambassador to the Soviet Union and to Yugoslavia. His essay is based on a talk given before the P.E.N. Club in New York.*

WHEN historians want really to condemn a fellow historian — really to put him beyond the pale — they can think of nothing worse than to charge that what he writes is "pure fiction," "fairy tales," "inventions," "legends." To the poet or novelist, on the other hand, the historian obviously appears as a very pedestrian sort of fellow, a bird without wings, a creature destined to crawl, in fact, laboriously on his belly through the husks and litter of documented fact which past generations have left behind them on the sands of time.

Whatever truth there may be in these observations, it is not the whole truth about the relationship between history and literature. There are ways, I am persuaded, in which they have a close kinship. Not only do they sometimes approach each other in the problems of technical execution but their tasks are kindred tasks.

There is, it is true, a great body of historical material that does not lend itself to literary development. It consists only of the

recitation of bald fact — of what one of my friends calls "lists."
This was, in fact, the earliest form of purely scientific historical
material. There are other historical works which could perfectly
well have been written in a literary way, but just weren't. The
authors either did not care to give them literary form or they
were incapable of it. Still it is history. On the other hand, the
shelves of any historical library are full of works to which the
quality of literature obviously could not for an instant be denied.
Theodor Mommsen and Winston Churchill were both given the
Nobel Prize for Literature, though the writing that earned it
was historical.

Does this mean that there is one portion of history which is
purely science, and therefore dull and unpleasant to read,
whereas another portion is art, embracing only, or primarily,
aesthetic rather than scientific values? Not exactly, for it is at
once apparent that the two overlap — that a great deal of that
portion of history which has greatest merit as a science also falls
into that category which has the greatest merit as art. Both good
history and bad history can be written in a literary way or in a
nonliterary way, depending on the tastes and the talents of the
writer, but there is apt to be — not always, but generally — a
connection between good history and good writing.

The discipline of attempting to say something gracefully and
effectively and in such a way as to bring out the deeper and more
subtle tones seems to be helpful to the scientific essence of history, refining, rather than corrupting, the scientific conscience.
Good history can exist, apart from good language and style. La-
borious and graceless but conscientious, it can deserve the name of
"worthy." It can command the respect of colleagues. Its authors
can be respected members of historical associations. People can
even be grateful to them for their patient industry and erudition.
But their words tend to die in the libraries. They are perhaps
used for reference, but not for much more. It is history as sci-

ence *and* literature, not history as science alone, which reaches beyond the specialized reader, contributes to public understanding of the past, and lives in historical memory.

Is this quality — of being possibly and preferably literature, but not necessarily so — something that sets history apart from other forms of scientific writing? Again, the answer seems to be "no." Other forms of scientific writing — or at least those pertaining to the nature and behavior of living beings — can likewise either have literary merit or not have it, without ceasing in either case to be science. Charles Darwin demonstrated that. So, for that matter, has Rachel Carson, with *The Sea Around Us.* Literary merit is, then, a possible attribute, not essential but also not wholly casual, of any nonfictional writing.

But isn't this also true of what goes more strictly by the name of literature itself: of such things as fiction and poetry and dramaturgy? Here, too, unfortunately, not all that is written is really literature. There is trash; there is pedantry; there is plodding, pedestrian effort, without grace.

There have been novels made up in large parts of what might be called inventories of folklore. Even great writers have sometimes leaned in the direction of pure antiquarianism. A friend of mine, in a recent article on the subject of literary criticism, charged Emile Zola with "trying to make an index of the world." There are passages in Shakespeare that would come into this category. Alexander Pushkin, in *Eugene Onegin,* had a chapter that was largely folklore in substance.

If historians sometimes write literature, what forms of literature do they write? In this day and age, of course, only prose. There was a time, long, long ago, when a considerable portion of such historical knowledge as did exist was recorded in verse. But those were the days when history and literature were indistinguishable in the sense that no one cared about facts for their own sake — the days when fact and fancy were thoroughly mingled in the saga or the epic legend. In modern times, historians seldom burst into song, and if they did, nobody would be fooled.

Poets, of course, sometimes use their medium to write what purports to be history: think of Shakespeare's tragedies, or Tennyson's "Charge of the Light Brigade," or Longfellow's "Paul Revere's Ride." But this, while sometimes poetry, is rarely history. And the converse would certainly be true. Even Aristotle recognized this: "Put Herodotus into verse," he said, "and he would remain a historian, not a poet."

The kind of prose the literary historian writes is very much the same kind that the strictly literary person does. Sometimes it is straight expository material: the expression of thought or analysis. Much of this is of the highest literary quality. Think only of Gibbon's magnificent cadences, of Macauley or Trevelyan.

Next, there is atmosphere. Here, the historian has to be careful. He wasn't there; he didn't see it with his own eyes; or if he was and did, he isn't strictly speaking a historian — he is a writer of memoirs, which is a different thing. But perhaps, if it was a natural scene, he is himself a keen observer of nature; or if it was a human scene, perhaps it was one which he had known at a different time and in different circumstances. Perhaps his imagination could easily and reliably fill in the difference. The historian, like the novelist, could be aided by his own powers of observation.

Take this passage from Francis Parkman:

> More than eight months had passed since the catastrophe of St. Joseph. The winter was over, and that dreariest of seasons had come, the churlish forerunner of spring. Around Ste. Marie the forests were gray and bare, and, in the cornfields the oozy, half-thawed soil, studded with the sodden stalks of the last autumn's harvest, showed itself in patches through the melting snow.

Is this a legitimate use of atmosphere in a work of history? Unquestionably it is. Parkman was a man who had long observed the slow and depressing break-up of the New England winter. He needed no documentary sources to tell him that this was the way it was.

In yet another type of literary prose which is to be found in history, straight narrative, the historian's task is more complicated. He can, of course, relate what occurred, in so far as the documents reveal it. He can, if he knows the subject matter well and if it lends itself to literary development, give to his presentation a sustained tension and cadence similar to that of good fictional narrative. But the material must be adequate to the treatment. The historian may not force it or stretch it. He may not supplement it.

The essence of good literary narrative is, surely, a mixture of roundedness and simplification. Enough must be there to make the point; and what is redundant must be skillfully excluded. But the historian's narrative can be no more rounded than the historical evidence permits; nor can he simplify except where the sources, as sometimes happens, do it for him.

Above all, he is seldom at liberty to use dialogue with good conscience. Rarely do the actual recorded words of people, as distinct from hearsay and indirect attribution, emerge from the historical record in so unambiguous and authoritative a manner as to permit their confident use by the historian; and when they do so emerge, they seldom serve the uses of literary narrative as tidily and effectively as do those of fictional creation. Anyone who has had occasion to plow back through the documentary sources to run down the true wording of things famous people are said to have said so aptly on famous occasions, will know how seldom fact corresponds to legend, and how much the creative imagination of the raconteur has added to the tantalizing inadequacy of the historical record.

The historian finds himself, of course, constantly under temptation to move, in his narrative, from the bleak realm of what is known to have been to the more exciting and colorful world of what might very well have been and probably was. May he do so? In minor matters, and when the probability is very strong, I think he sometimes may.

In this connection I must make a confession. On the last page of the second volume of my study on the early period of Soviet-American relations, I described the departure of one of the last semi-official Americans from Soviet territory in 1918. He and his companion, as it happened, found themselves locked for a time on a railroad bridge spanning the border stream between Finland and Russia, with the gates at each end of the bridge closed against them. About this incident I wrote the following:

> For an hour and a half Wardwell and Davidson sat forlornly on the railway ties of the little bridge (from which the tracks had now been removed), confined between the two strife-torn worlds of thought and feeling which no one had been able to hold together. . . . The sky was leaden; a cold wind blew from the northwest. The wooden shelter on the Finnish side was deserted. Above, on the Soviet side, the figure of a Red Guard, rifle slung on shoulder, great-coat collar turned up against the wind, was silhouetted against the low scudding clouds. The little stream, hurrying to the Gulf of Finland, swirled past the wooden pilings and carried its eddies swiftly and silently away into the swamps below. Along the Soviet bank a tethered nanny goat, indifferent to all the ruin and all the tragedy, nibbled patiently at the sparse dying foliage.

I must confess that if you asked me whether I can prove that the goat was there, the answer is: I cannot. But I never saw such a scene in Russia without a goat. Also, I passed through the same border region at the end of the last world war, in similar conditions of autumnal desolation, and I did see a goat. It was the last of a thousand pages on this subject, and perhaps the chafing of three years of academic restraint had inclined me to a brief fling of indiscipline. I am, in any case, unrepentant.

But these are the limits beyond which the historian has no right to go. It is precisely in resisting the temptation to go further that his quality as a historian, as distinct from a literary person pure and simple, is most basically expressed. The true mark of his trade is the fact that he accepts a set of rules far more rigorous and confining than those which govern the novelist or the poet. He cannot create the pieces of his puzzle; he must attempt to put it together from those that he finds lying around. Not only that, but having found a few pieces, he cannot even order them to his heart's desire. They are ordered for him chronologically in advance by that most imperious of all historical masters, the documented date, and before this authority he must bow his head in unquestioning obedience; otherwise he is no historian.

Above all, he cannot fashion out of his raw material nice clean beginnings and endings to frame the burden of his tale. He can only cut in for a time, on the endlessly moving stream of human affairs. The points that he selects to enter it and to leave it are invariably arbitrary, and his work always suffers to some degree from this arbitrariness. No work of history ever begins soon enough or ends late enough to be wholly rounded.

For these reasons, the unities of the drama are seldom for the historian. His art, when it is an art at all, is an epic one, not dramatic. He can turn his little spotlight, for one period or another, on a small portion of a great and never-ending procession, but he cannot hope to define its origin or its destination.

It is these rules of the game which lead us to the deepest difference between the historian and the literary man; and this difference lies in the plane of reality to which, in the main, each addresses himself. It is with the intimate undercurrent of men's lives that the true literary artist is permitted to deal, and does deal, in his greatest moments — with the inner souls of men rather than with what Freud has called their personae. It is precisely in stripping men of the external façade of personality, in showing them in all their shivering moral nakedness and helplessness, in their secret world of instincts and loves and fears and feelings, lost in the mad company of their personal demons and protecting angels — it is in this that the poet or the novelist finds his true mission.

From all this, the historian is normally barred. The materials to which he is restricted seldom shed light on it, or lend themselves to its description. He comes nearest to it, perhaps, when he is writing pure biography; and indeed biography, with its accent on the doings of the individual as distinct from the doings of masses of individuals, is the point at which literature and history come closest to merging completely. But in other forms of history, it is normally the *external* personality with which the writer is necessarily concerned.

Of those of us who try to write history as literature there are few, I am sure, who do not sometimes peek longingly through the curtain into that more mysterious and more exciting and more dangerous world in which the others are privileged to operate. Still, the historian cannot accept the view that the plane of reality to which he is confined is without interest or importance. What he writes has, if he is a good historian, the virtue of being as close to what actually occurred as human industry and conscience can make it. This record of what is known as distinct from what is felt is an essential and indispensable component of all understanding of the human predicament. It is one of the ingredients from which even the novelist and the poet must distill their insights.

The writing of history may lack the glamour and excitement of fiction, but it is a labor on which the greatest purity and integrity of purpose are never wasted. What is done in this quiet and disciplined realm can have, when it is done with honesty and insight and devotion, a dignity second to that of no other branch of writing.

If history and literature are divided in the plane of reality to which they address themselves, they are united in the fact that for both of them the central purpose is the elicitation of truth. This is the mission of literature no less than of history. That the detail of what is stated in a purely literary work may never have actually occurred, does not in any way controvert this fact.

Let me take an example from my own experience. In writing about Russia in the period of the Russian civil war of 1918 to 1920, I have known my share of anguish in the effort to be faithful to the true fabric of life — to describe things as they were, at whatever cost to my preconceived opinions or to the natural wish of every historian that he could discover some great guiding line or lesson in what he finds. But in reading Boris Pasternak's *Doctor Zhivago,* which dealt with the same period, I was struck by the realization that he was put to an anguish in no way less than my own in precisely this effort to be scrupulously true — true to his period, true to the nature of the human beings that populated it.

As a historian, I was concerned with what can be proved to have occurred to men in the broader aspects of their political and social dealings with one another. Pasternak was concerned to reveal, out of the workings of the artist's sensitivity and intuition, as well as out of his own memories, the sort of thing that could and did happen to individuals in their intimate reactions to these events. His was a vastly greater contribution than mine, but that gives me no sense of shame or inadequacy. There is room for all kinds of workers in this particular vineyard, and if their devotion is to the eliciting of truth, they supplement each other. The literary artist needs the historian to keep him close to the known and the possible. The historian needs the poet as a reminder of the inner world of his own clients — as an admonishment never to forget that he is dealing with real people, with phenomena whose true sources are individual, with impulses which are only outward reflections of the wonder, the anarchy, the tenderness and the brutality of the individual human soul.

C. VANN WOODWARD

Our Past Isn't What It
Used to Be

The South and aspects of its history have been the chief concerns of C. Vann Woodward, who won a Bancroft Prize not so many years ago for his Origins of the New South. *His academic honors have been many, not forgetting the Harmsworth chair of American history at Oxford. He is at present Sterling professor of history at Yale.*

A DECADE or two is a brief span of time as history goes, but in the interpretation of history it can make a difference. Those who "learned" their American history before World War II or in the years immediately following would be in for some surprises were they to return to the old lecture halls today. The same professor might be holding forth. The names and dates and "facts" might sound familiar. But the old grad would soon become aware of new meanings attached to dates, altered significance given to names, and unfamiliar associations of "facts."

The changes are not primarily due to new information. It is true we have discovered, for example, that Alexander Hamilton was born a few years earlier than we thought, and we know more about the centuries of contact the white man had with the New World before Columbus. Important as they are, however, such discoveries do not account for the new look of American history. The difference arises mainly out of new readings of old evidence in the light of changed conditions by historians with new preoccupations, sensitivities, identifications, methods and moods.

Before trying to account for the changes in the historians it would be well to sample the changes in their interpretations. They are too numerous to list but most of them fall into one of four classes. One is an overhauling of historical reputations that has exalted some individuals, groups, or classes and lowered others in historical esteem and standing. A second is a general abandonment of the economic interpretation as an adequate or even acceptable account of historic movements. A third is an inclination to minimize or neglect the conflicts, contrasts, polarities, or antitheses in American history and to emphasize basic similarities, continuities and syntheses. A fourth tendency is to abandon the hunt for domestic villains to blame for our foreign wars.

The reshuffling of historical reputations can be illustrated on one level by what has happened to the prestige of the Puritans. Their stock has been going up since the nineteen-thirties but it has reached a new high in recent years. It has not been long since Puritans were pictured as a canting, bigoted, joy-killing lot of witch-burners. The revised picture is that of a humane, courageous, even pleasure-loving people with a passion for learning who are responsible for the choicest elements of our heritage. The transformation is the work of New England historians, but under their influence even Southerners strive to appreciate the sweet reasonableness of this breed.

The Founding Fathers and Constitution framers, long under suspicion of unworthy motives and crafty designs, are the beneficiaries of another trend of reinterpretation that has appreciably improved their standing. The Abolitionists, who have suffered from an unfriendly historical press for many years, now tend to be revalued according to their own estimate. Their friends, the Radical Republicans, have lost their paranoidal scowl, dropped their economic motives, and glow with goodwill. Their strivings, now that the Second Reconstruction has gained momentum, are viewed in a new light. The lot of the Negro as slave, as freedman, and as underprivileged citizen is extensively reconsidered. The lowly immigrant, favorite scapegoat of Mugwump reformers (who have been slipping in status), has moved up in historical standing. Even the business tycoon of the Gilded Age, undefended since the nineteen-twenties, has found friends in the court of history.

In the meantime other groups have been declining in prestige. Conspicuous among the losers have been individuals, parties and movements traditionally identified with the popular cause or the common man against privilege and "the interests." Roger Williams of colonial Rhode Island and Nathaniel Bacon of colonial Virginia have lost their standing as precursors of democracy. More upsetting to traditional interpretations is the revisionist attack on Andrew Jackson and his party as authentic spokesman of the common man, whether western farmer or eastern worker, against the moneyed power and the aristocracy. Recent studies have increasingly narrowed the margin of difference between the supporters of Jackson and supporters of his opponents, denied the Old Hero a monopoly on equalitarian reform, and disclosed hankerings for privilege in his own camp. It has been seriously proposed that the whole concept of Jacksonian Democracy be abandoned.

Among more recent champions of the common man, the Populists and the Bryanite Democrats have suffered most from assault and battery by revisionists. Contending that Populists had been judged too leniently by indulgent liberals, their critics have focused attention instead on the delusions, myths and foibles of the Populists and charged them with responsibility for all manner of mischief, including racism, jingoism, mobbism, and anti-intellectualism. Some make them out to be the ancestors of fascism, and undergraduates are now heard to use "Populist" as a word of comparable opprobrium. The seamy side of the progressive movement has been subjected to a similar scrutiny and the exposure of such unlovely traits as blindness to minority rights and willful perpetration of racial injustice have disarranged the halo progressives once wore securely.

The old grad who returns for a refresher course in American history will soon become aware that something else is missing, something that was once quite prominent in lectures and textbooks: the economic interpretation. Little is made of it any more. The American Revolution, whether pictured as a fight for home rule or a fight over who would rule at home, was once interpreted as a struggle for material advantage motivated by economic grievance or hope of gain. The great debate over the framing and the adoption of the Federal Constitution, so it was once thought, hung primarily over conflicts of interest between the holders of two kinds of property called "personalty" and "realty." Party battles of the Jeffersonian and Jacksonian eras resounded with clashes between "agrarians" and "capitalists," debtors and creditors, hard money and soft, anti-monopolists and bankers. That was the way "progress" was achieved. The European peasant, weighing the decision to migrate to the New World, the pioneer spying out the West, and the abolitionist crusading against slavery, all responded consciously or unconsciously to the pocket nerve.

The classic conflict and greatest tragedy of American history was said to have had at the root of it an irrepressible incompatibility between an economy of plantations and farms at the South and an economy of commerce and industry at the North. In the historiography of our subsequent wars the economic interpretation has also played a conspicuous part.

More lately, however, historians have grown increasingly impatient with all simple and deterministic interpretations, economic determinism included. They tend to ask *who* rather than *what* was responsible for an event — which individuals, groups, votes, not what vast impersonal forces. With help from psychology and sociology they look for complexity rather than simplicity in human motivation. They pursue myth and symbol and the irrational with an interest once reserved for rational economic motives.

Another change that has taken some of the simplicity, as well as much of the drama and color out of the interpretation of American history has been the tendency to tone down the contrasts, to mute the clash of ideas, to soften the differences between classes, sections and interests, and to play up basic agreements and fundamental similarities. The boldness and vividness have faded from such standard polarities as Roundheads and Cavaliers, Jeffersonians and Hamiltonians, frontier and seaboard, labor and capital, liberal and conservative. We are often reminded that such tensions were always contained within a tacitly assumed consensus. The patriots of the Revolution were really conservatives, but they rebelled to conserve John Locke's liberalism. Jefferson is better remembered these days for saying, "We are all Federalists, we are all Republicans," than for endorsing a little rebellion now and then on the ground that "The tree of liberty must be refreshed from time to time with the blood of patriots and tyrants."

Under the influence of this mood, the old themes of social justice, protest, radicalism, utopianism and violence — all of which assume conflict — tend to be neglected. Interest in the come-outer, the hot-gospeller, the agitator (abolitionist excepted), and the prophets of revolution has waned.

A striking exception to the rule of muted contrasts and low moral voltage is some of the recent historiography of the Civil War and its background of sectional conflict. This does not include the prolific chroniclers of the Blue and Gray Gun Club, who tend to bury the hatchet of ideology on the hallowed battlegrounds. But the political historians have dug up the hatchet again. Northerners complain that the Rebels have won the battle of books. Rejecting the concept of a "needless war" brought on by blunderers, and discarding the economic interpretation, which played down slavery, they have revived the moral interpretation and applied it sweepingly. They deny that there was an illiberal consensus of racism in 1860, unlimited by region or party, and define the Mason and Dixon Line as the boundary between right and wrong. Detachment is frowned upon. One is expected to choose sides, and history becomes the continuation of war by other means. As a consequence there is far less agreement over the interpretation of the Civil War today than there was a half century ago.

In the interpretation of later wars and their diplomatic history, on the other hand, there is a growing tendency to let up on the search for villains and the passing of moral judgments. This is more in line with the prevailing revision of domestic history. For a long time it seemed to be assumed that when the United States went to war some mischief of a vaguely conspiratorial sort was afoot and that blame was to be assigned among certain domestic groups, interests, or high officials. The inquiry was carried out at home rather than abroad and it was likely to be conducted in a mood of cynicism and indignation.

Ernest R. May has divided diplomatic historians into the What-Went-Wrong School and the What-Happened School. The latter and newer school does not limit its investigation to American events but looks abroad and views developments from several angles. The studies of this school are likely to be more charitable to the intentions and efforts of American officials and less likely to spot a villain. Their findings have tended to improve the reputations for conduct of foreign affairs once assigned Presidents William McKinley, Theodore Roosevelt, Woodrow Wilson and Franklin D. Roosevelt.

All in all, the last fifteen years have witnessed the most sweeping reinterpretation of American history ever attempted in so brief a period. To account for it fully would require an intellectual history of the last two decades.

The old historians began the construction of their great synthesis toward the end of the last century and the beginning of the Progressive Era. Revival of the reform impulse in the 1930's renewed the appeal of some of their views, enhanced their influence, and prolonged their sway into an era where their ideas were less relevant. Outstanding leaders of the "Progressive" or "Pragmatic" school were Charles A. Beard, Carl Becker, Vernon Louis Parrington and Frederick Jackson Turner. Men of an intellectual stature that the new generation of historians has yet to equal, they were also great individualists about whom it is difficult and dangerous to generalize.

It is probably of some significance that all four men were from the Middle West and that, by and large, their identifications were with provincial, rural America and its values. They shared a deep belief in social progress, a faith in the common man, a sympathy for the underdog against privilege, and elaborate plans for reform. The history they wrote embodied these convictions. They were themselves conscious rebels against an older generation of "scientific" history, its stance of moral neutrality, and its conservative aloofness from practical affairs and social issues.

The Progressive school believed that history could be the handmaid of reform and that it should show how progress was advanced by conflict between forces of change and forces of reaction. They therefore stressed contrast, antithesis, and conflict, particularly conflict over economic issues, and they leaned to economic interpretations. Preoccupied with domestic problems, they neglected foreign comparisons and magnified internal differences. To divert public attention to foreign adventures was to evade the real business at hand.

In the light of the Atomic Age both the present and the past looked different. The path to social progress was dark and the old history did not light it. Many of the reforms had been accomplished. An economy of abundance replaced the economy of scarcity. Economic issues lost dramatic appeal. Change was feared, not sought. The common man had supported a variety of evil causes at home and abroad. His struggles had not invariably produced progress. His motives — many of them — were neither economic nor rational, and neither were those of his superiors. Growing awareness of foreign lands and their ways made social contrasts and ideological conflicts in American history seem mild by comparison. The great contrasts were between this country and others, not between fellow Americans. Homogeneity, compromise and continuity were the central themes.

Viewing the trend in reinterpreting our history, John Higham rightly observes that "A certain tameness and amiability have crept into our view of things" and complains of "the bland history" produced thereby. Not all the new history has been bland. No friend of the New Deal can complain of tameness in the leading books on that era, nor has blandness been a conspicuous fault of histories of racial minorities, academic freedom, and civil rights. Nor is it a characteristic of many fine new biographies. The unblandness of the civil war over the Civil War has been noted.

It must be admitted, however, that the typical product of the reinterpretation does not ring with a challenge to action, open vistas from the past into the future, nor present us with a new synthesis to replace the one rejected. The main results have been negative: rooting out untenable hypotheses, discrediting loose generalizations, breaking up outmoded categories, redefining terms. This work was needed and valuable. It clears the way for more positive contributions.

The reinterpretation is not finished. It will go on responding sometimes to fads and foibles, but fundamentally to the great thirst of our time for historical meaning. The historian will have all he can do in the way of reinterpretation to satisfy that thirst, to keep history meaningful, and to sustain the relevance of the past to the present.

ALLAN NEVINS

A Conflict That Was Big with Fate

[Readers have already met Allan Nevins on page 377.]

"HERE we make Italy or die," said Garibaldi at the critical point of that conquest of Sicily which brought the unification of Italy within reach. "Here we make the United States or die," Grant might have said at Shiloh, or Meade at Gettysburg. But while the Italian war of liberation, so romantic in its incidents, so inspiring in its triumph of faith over force, was important in satisfying the passionate aspirations of a people and in giving Europe a new kingdom, much more momentous was the war that brought America a new birth of freedom and unity. In world history, the decade 1860–70 holds a luminous place. In these ten years Darwin's ideas gave all thought a new orientation; Napoleon III fell, opening the way to the French Republic; Italian nationhood changed from dream to reality; Bismarck's Germany took form from a mass of disunited states; the Canadian Dominion emerged. Most significant of all, however, was the revolutionary change in the United States.

The Civil War period, wrote James Ford Rhodes a generation later, "was an era big with fate for our country, and for the American must remain fraught with the same interest that the War of the Peloponnesus had for the ancient Greek, or the struggle between Puritan and Cavalier had for their descendants." So it has proved.

Nothing quite like the current wave of enthusiasm for Civil War subjects has previously been known in our land. Civil War

Round Tables of large membership have been formed in a score of states; less formal study groups have multiplied. Endless books refight every campaign from Bull Run to Petersburg and re-examine every general. We have a Civil War Book Club and a Civil War Quarterly.

What, after all, makes the Civil War worth our study?

Of course the Civil War is endlessly picturesque. It abounds in personal adventure: the adventure of lady spies of the Belle Boyd–Mrs. Greenhow type, of balloonists like Thaddeus Lowe and blockade runners like Pasha Hobart, of war prisoners like Henry M. Stanley and war correspondents like the frank-spoken Sylvanus Cadwallader just rescued from oblivion by the publication of his reminiscences. It abounds in opportunities for the painting of brilliant battle canvases, some of which — like Malvern Hill and that scene of masterly capture and still more masterly recapture, Fort Stedman — have been unjustly neglected. It abounds also, alas, in opportunities for blood-chilling depictions of human agony on an appalling scale, paralleling General John D. Imboden's unforgettable record of the conveyance of Lee's wounded southward the night after Gettysburg. Much is to be said for greater emphasis on the misery and loss attending the conflict. The rest, however, the adventures, the gallantry, the picturesque onset of battle, hardly touch the essence of the war.

Nor is it possible to feel an exalted respect for that study of campaigns which treats the war as a sort of gigantic chess game and the commanders as skilled or blundering chess players. From this point of view, to be sure, the conflict offers endless opportunity for debate.

Whether Halleck's advance on Corinth, one month to cover thirty miles, was prudence or folly; whether Buell's retreat into Louisville before Bragg's army was as mistaken as the frightened Northwestern Governors believed; whether Fitz-John Porter played his country false at Second Manassas; whether Meade

could have used Sedgwick's fresh Sixth Corps to cut off Lee's retreat after Pickett's charge — these and a thousand similar questions can be discussed forever. They really have the fascination of
chess problems. Dealing with a respectable element of military
study, they provide lively intellectual exercise. But they grow
increasingly jejune, and taken in detail they are petty.

What, then, are the more vital considerations which should
be kept in mind? A certain largeness of view is desirable in our
scrutiny of the four years of struggle.

It was not a strategic chess game, but a desperate life-and-death
contest between two sets of ideas and values, each determined to
sway a nation's destiny. It had few ingredients of romance, dash
and poetry; instead, it was a tremendous national tragedy, full of
blood, tears, cruelty, waste and demoralization. It was not just
"our war," a private American conflict, but a collision, the outcome of which affected weighty international interests and the
thoughts and outlook of half the globe. Looking at it in this
wise, students will not fail to discern four aspects of peculiar interest and importance.

The first is the simplest and least likely to be ignored. "Great
men," said Burke, "are the guideposts and landmarks in the state."
The enthusiasm for Civil War studies arose largely from earlier
books on leaders of the era: the volumes of Ida M. Tarbell,
Lord Charnwood, Carl Sandburg, B. P. Thomas and James G.
Randall on Lincoln, of G. F. R. Henderson on Stonewall Jackson,
Douglas Freeman on Lee, Lloyd Lewis and Liddell Hart on Sher-
man, and of Burton J. Hendrick and Gamaliel Bradford on the
civil chieftains in Washington and Richmond.

Readers rose from these works with an appetite for a larger
fare. Above all other names of the time loom two: Lincoln,
whose statesmanship was essential to Union victory, and Lee,
whose qualities of mind and character best explain why the Con-
federacy endured so long. The war was the gateway through

which these two Americans passed to immortality. The examples they set, the ideals they followed, were a priceless gift to the world. In particular, as time passes, the country is readier to emphasize Charles Eliot Norton's statement that on the whole he thought Lincoln's character the greatest single gain from the war.

The second aspect we have been slow to grasp in its entirety. Charles Francis Adams, lecturing at Oxford in 1913, spoke of "the process and consummation of a national crystallization," but even he did not fully define it. The war decided that the United States should not sliver into two, three or four fragments — for successful Southern secession might have been followed by Northwestern or Pacific secession. The long ordeal had results, however, still more important than the destruction of State's Rights ideas.

It converted the North from a sprawling, inchoate country, almost as protoplasmic in 1860 as China was in 1940, into a land at last vertebrate, organized and responsive to national leadership. The free states had to pull themselves together, enlist 2,300,000 soldiers, clothe, arm, feed and transport them, obtain more than four billion dollars by loans and taxes, and, in short, make an effort almost unprecedented in human history. In doing this, they turned themselves into a new nation.

A shrewd foreign observer, Auguste Laugel, had written of the old America: "There is a horror of all trammels, system and uniformity." But from the war effort came long trunk-line railroads, new nation-wide industries, national professional associations, national labor unions and national ideas. Parochial outlooks gave way to habits of association for common ends. The war, in thus unifying the country and in accelerating the industrial revolution, made possible the emergence of the United States as a Great Power, the equal of Britain, Germany or Russia on the world stage.

The third aspect, summed up in the word emancipation, takes on new meaning as the decades pass. Slavery by 1860 was an anachronism. Its doom had been pronounced by economic, social and moral forces. But the institution, which John Stuart Mill called "the greatest enormity which still exists among mankind," survived in other countries than the United States — in Brazil, Cuba and large areas of Asia and Africa.

Lincoln's Proclamation, reverberating around the globe, had its effect wherever serfdom, peonage or any other unjust domination of man over man persisted. It gave the war a moral import which it had at first lacked and which was felt from Bahia to Senegambia. It was the greatest single blow ever struck against the shackle and whip. In this country, as wise men foresaw, emancipation was but the beginning, and its meaning has been spelled in broader terms from generation to generation.

Finally, the Civil War, as Lincoln said plainly on the field of Gettysburg, brought a vindication of democracy in the world arena where it contended with autocratic and aristocratic principles. The Englishman Edward Dicey, talking with an Irishwoman in the North during the conflict heard her say: "This is a blessed country, sir. I think God made it for the poor." But what if it broke up in failure?

Old World privilege, declared John Bright in one of his many defenses of the Union cause, had a great stake in the defeat of the North. "Privilege has beheld an afflicting spectacle for many years past. It has beheld thirty millions of men, happy and prosperous, without emperor, without king, without the surroundings of a court, without nobles except such as are made by eminence in intellect and virtue . . . without great armies and great navies, without great debts and great taxes. Privilege has shuddered at what might happen to old Europe if the great experiment should succeed." Bright, seeing it succeed, rejoiced for all European liberals.

It is difficult to estimate the value to the world of the vindication of American democracy registered in the Emancipation
Proclamation and the scene at Appomattox. It had its immediate results in the Secord Reform Act in Great Britain and in the
stimulation of democratic impulses in France. Its remoter results,
on wider fronts, can be observed today.

Civil War study can teach us much that is profitable about the
tactics of Cedar Creek, the leadership of Jeb Stuart and the politics of the Draft Act, but in learning of such matters we should
keep in mind the larger aspects. They help to ennoble the terrible conflict. It grew out of a lamentable breakdown of statesmanship. It had many discreditable as well as heroic chapters,
and its immediate home results were sadly mixed. But when
seen in the long perspective of national and world history, it gains
in grandeur. The new republic forged in that furnace had a
strength of fiber unknown before 1860. Even in Reconstruction
times the great idealists, Lowell, Emerson (see his essay "The
Fortunes of the Republic"), Whittier, were sure its gains and
lessons would not be lost. So was Walt Whitman, uttering a challenge to those who came afterward.

"The Four Years War is over," wrote Walt, "and in the peaceful,
strong, exciting fresh occasions of today, and of the future, that
strange sad war is hurrying even now to be forgotten. The
camps, the drill, the lines of sentries, the prisons, the hospitals
(ah, the hospitals!) — all have passed away, all seem now like a
dream. A new race, a young and lusty generation, already sweeps
in with oceanic currents, obliterating the war, and all its scars, its
mounded graves, all its reminiscences of hatred, conflict, death.
So let it be obliterated. I say the life of the present and the future
makes undeniable demands upon us one and all, south, north,
east, west. To help put the United States hand in hand, in one
unbroken circle in a chant — to rouse them to the unprecedented
grandeur of the part they are to play, and are even now playing

— to the thought of their great future, and the attitude conformed to it . . ."

Historical study can be undertaken for amusement, for instruction and for inspiration. It usually blends all three — but the greatest of the three is inspiration. The Civil War seemed to ex-Capt. Oliver Wendell Holmes Jr. an abiding inspiration: "In our youth our hearts were touched with fire. It was given us to learn at the outset that life is a profound and passionate thing." In that mood we should approach the great record written in 1861–65. The significance of the conflict has thus far been understated: Its full importance to ourselves and to the world remains to be revealed; broad currents flowing down from it have still to be measured. The more we expand our view of its results, the greater will be its inspiration.

HAL BRIDGES

Roundup Time on the Western Range

At the University of Denver where he teaches history Hal Bridges is just around the corner from the old West of fact and fiction, and he has made himself something of an expert in both.

THE American West is much with us. Volumes of fiction, biography, history and legend indigenous to the spacious country along and beyond the frontier pour from trade and university presses in overwhelming numbers. One publishing house advertises a current list of nearly one hundred Western titles. Another projects a twenty-volume series dealing largely with the West. From Boston to New York to Chicago to Los Angeles the Western book is highly popular. In the Rocky Mountain region it is supreme. Bookdealers in Denver are apt to assume that when you say "Americana" you mean "Western."

Why? What explains the fascination that cowboys, Indians and frontiersmen hold for today's urban dweller? Part of the answer, of course, is that there is in this country a great tradition of Western writing. In the early nineteenth century, literate Americans read about Leatherstocking; at the start of the twentieth, about Owen Wister's Virginian and his adventures in Wyoming. Between times they shed a fast tear over Bret Harte's tales of the California mining camps and, in that interesting realm where fact meets fiction, roughed it uproariously in Nevada with Mark Twain. Current Western fiction, as written by A. B. Guthrie, Wallace Stegner, Walter Van Tilburg Clark and others, is a far cry in realism from these precursors, yet it is but a development, not something totally new.

On a more frivolous level, the Western literary heritage extends back to Deadwood Dick, Calamity Jane and the many other heroic figures of the dime novel, who spilled more blood in the decades following the Civil War than did the contending armies of North and South. The Western movie hero of today appears to be their direct descendant. Their most recent offspring is the extraordinarily popular TV gunman, who pulls his trigger with an absent-minded frown, denoting Freudian preoccupations that never troubled his grandpa.

Heading the long procession of historians of the West is Francis Parkman. His dozen volumes on the struggle that England and France waged for empire in North America during the eighteenth century called attention to the land beyond the frontier as an arena of drama and conflict and established a great tradition of writing. In Parkman's autobiographical *The Oregon Trail* (1849) he offered the unforgettable story of a proper young Bostonian who adapts so fully to Indian customs that he can serve and help eat a ceremonial feast of boiled dog.

Significantly, it was to Parkman that Theodore Roosevelt dedicated his four-volume study, "The Winning of the West." Roosevelt, to be sure, was no sympathizer with that lesser breed, the red man. Rather than boiled dogs he relished dead Indians, and he slew them in windrows as his Anglo-Saxon pioneers marched triumphantly from the Ohio Valley to the Louisiana Territory. Yet he did seek to blend true scientific research with literary vigor — "I shall try my best not to . . . make it scamp work," he wrote Henry Cabot Lodge — and by the time the last volume appeared in 1896 he had produced a landmark of Western history.

Neither Roosevelt nor Parkman, however, is the guiding force in the writing of Western history today. That honor belongs to

Frederick Jackson Turner. In 1893, in one brilliant, creative essay defining the American frontier not as a particular place but as a process of settlement through which most of the nation had passed, Turner established a permanent framework for scholarly writing about the West. Though in time his thesis encountered sharp criticism, the more important modifications of it have been affirmations rather than negations of what he wrote about the significance of the West.

Frederick L. Paxson accepted the thesis and delineated the Westward-moving frontier for readers of the nineteen twenties. In the next decade Walter Prescott Webb published his classic study of the Great Plains. More recently Henry Nash Smith has called attention to the significance of the West as it has existed in the American mind in the form of social myths and symbols.

The Western literary tradition, then, is long and viable, and today it is more meaningful to more Americans than ever before in the nation's history. Easterners are more aware of it because the western half of the country has steadily increased in importance, a fact dramatically underscored in recent years by population growth. Between 1940 and 1950 the seventeen states of the West gained 25.8 per cent in population as compared with 14.5 per cent for the entire nation.

Each year in increasing numbers a vast temporary population moves through the West, in search of scenery, a place to park, and a measure of contact however fleeting with the romantic land of symbol and myth. I refer, of course, to the great American tourist.

Earl Pomeroy in a recent history of the subject, "In Search of the Golden West," has traced the remarkable rise of Western tourism: Southern California, which had 658,594 tourists in 1928, counted 3,944,860 in 1953. In the same period visitors to Yellowstone National Park increased from 460,619 to 1,326,858. These visiting millions buy all sorts of Western books, the good along with the bad. They even buy the regional historical quarterlies. One colorful but scholarly Montana quarterly sells for a dollar on the newsstand and is said to attain a circulation of as high as 100,000 copies in the tourist season.

If the tourist often evinces interest in Western writing, this is as nothing compared to the zeal of various amateur historical groups such as, for example, the Westerners. Although the autonomous chapters of this far-flung organization often enroll professional writers, the bulk of the membership is made up of businessmen, lawyers, doctors, engineers, etc., whose common purpose is research in Western history.

The first chapter of the Westerners was organized in Chicago in 1944, the second in Denver the following year. Since then the Westerner "corrals" and "posses" have spread through the West to Los Angeles, and eastward to such remote frontier outposts as Washington, D. C., New York, Liverpool and Paris. Not only do such groups stimulate much interest in Western writing but through the books and periodicals they publish they also help to preserve local source materials that are rapidly disappearing.

Can the nation-wide interest in Western books be partially attributed to escapism? It would seem so. Escapism is doubtless an overworked concept, yet it is hard not to believe that many readers do escape from Sputniks and intercontinental missiles by vicariously saddling up and riding away to a simpler era of six-gun and tomahawk, just as half a century ago readers escaped with the Virginian from the menace of anarchists and labor unions.

Today, of course, we have more of everything — including things to escape from. Some analysts of the American mind have suggested that the "Westerns" of print and film afford our downtrodden males escape from a woman-dominated society. Even more intriguing is the idea that the American people are smitten with guilt feelings because of national inactivity in the face of pressing world problems, and therefore like to identify with a prime symbol of action like the Western hero. (Presumably the thousands who have read and watched that subtle Western study of human guilt, Walter Van Tilburg Clark's *The Ox-Bow Incident,* have been vacationing from escapism.)

If we must interpret the Western hero in terms of symbolism, I should like to suggest that we live in a time of heightened nationalistic feeling, and that the cowboy seems to be rapidly becoming our chief symbol of Americanism. He stands for a region never alienated from the rest of the nation by civil war, a region comparatively remote from the European civilization that so strongly influences the East. He is, it appears to me, beginning to eclipse Uncle Sam. When our soldiers in the last war wanted to Americanize a Korean orphan they dressed him in cowboy garb — mercifully not in an Uncle Sam suit.

National interest in the Western tradition is after all hardly separable from a much broader interest in the whole of the American past, which has within the last two decades acquired new richness of meaning in the light of international events. The American people, having survived total war and become the acknowledged leaders of the free world, are more aware today of their own history, more ready to welcome the novelists and historians who can interpret it for them. The popularity of Civil War books is part of this general interest in what has made America. So, too, with books on the West. They illuminate for us this important segment of our past. They give us, in these questing times, a renewed sense of the American potential for greatness.

JOHN A. GARRATY

How Should You Tell a Man's Story?

John Garraty is a biographer (he's also a historian at Columbia) who has set forth his ideas on the subject in The Nature of Biography *and has applied them in his lives of Henry Cabot Lodge, the elder, and of Woodrow Wilson.*

AROUND the turn of the century Gertrude Atherton, a popular lady novelist, decided to write a life of Alexander Hamilton. But her publisher discouraged her. "Nobody reads biographies," he said. Mrs. Atherton responded by writing *The Conqueror,* a novel based on Hamilton's career, which delighted a reading public no longer able to stomach the dull pomposities of Victorian biography. How strange that within a generation biographies were being published and sold in such numbers that one bemused critic suggested that anyone who could hold a pen or run a typewriter could make money writing lives. At least one author was reportedly handed a check for $5000 and a list of reference books by his publisher and put to work writing the biography of a person previously unknown to him.

Despite appearances, this violent fluctuation in the popularity of biography did not reflect any basic change in public taste. What had happened, rather, was that a host of biographers, copying the methods of romancers like Mrs. Atherton, had developed a fresh point of view toward their craft. They were writing a new kind of biography which attracted a different, and much larger, audience.

Every biographer, as he settles down at his desk, must make certain basic decisions before he begins to write. Shall he do a long "definitive" study or a brief survey? Shall he simply delineate his subject's actions, or strike out boldly and try to explain the significance of these actions? Shall he emphasize his hero's career, or stress his personality and the intimacies of his private life? In part, the biographer's decisions will depend on his philosophy of history. If, for instance, he feels that the times make the man, he will emphasize the environment and tend to show how it influenced his hero's seemingly independent judgments and decisions.

In an extreme case, he might even argue, as a sociologist once did, that Shakespeare wrote wonderful poetry because of those environmental "stimuli" that made him "the man and author he was." Of course, he will also have to consider how other biographers have treated his subject's career. Surely it will be many years before anyone will care to repeat the monumental investigations that went into D. S. Freeman's seven-volume life of Washington.

The biographer must also envision the type of reader he hopes to reach. Everyone does not turn to biography with the same end in view. One man, running his finger along the spines of a shelf of biographies, is looking for inspiration and encouragement in his struggles with life, and for him some tale of success won against great obstacles through moral fortitude will prove attractive. Another likes to personalize knowledge. Instead of a book about modern economics, he reads R. F. Harrod's life of John Maynard Keynes; instead of a history of the Civil War, he takes down J. G. Randall or Carl Sandburg on Lincoln.

Still another person seeks to be reassured that great men are no better than the rest of us, and for him there must be books like W. E. Woodward's life of Washington, devoted to the explosion of inflated reputations. There are also readers, idly curious about the private lives of the great, who want to be taken behind the scenes into boudoirs and telephone booths, as it were. Most numerous of all, perhaps, are those readers who ask only to be entertained, and nothing too "heavy," if you please. For them, please omit footnotes, and if the facts are dull, complicated, or unpleasant, alter them as neatly as possible and on with the story.

There is no single "correct" way to write biographies and no one "proper" reason for wanting to read them. Dr. Johnson was an excellent biographer who always tried to point a moral. Even in his warm and sympathetic life of Richard Savage, he contrived to use the tragedy of the poet's wasted life to educate his readers. Lytton Strachey rejected moralizing utterly, devoting his efforts to interpretation — slanted, but unfailingly interesting.

Plutarch cared little about politics, wars and great careers, preferring instead to delineate personality. "As portrait painters are more exact in the lines and features of the face, in which the character is seen, so I must be allowed to give more particular attention to the marks and indications of the souls of men," he wrote in his life of Alexander the Great. Countless scholarly biographers, on the other hand, have written careful and useful accounts of their subjects without dealing with the inner man at all.

Only the very greatest biographers are able to draw upon all these approaches. Plutarch comes close to achieving universal appeal, but James Boswell's *Life of Samuel Johnson* is the supreme example of biographical art. It is a rich mine of fact and an incomparable portrait. It contains bold interpretation, intimate gossip and a wealth of pure entertainment. But the appeal of most biographies is more limited. The serious analytical study usually cannot be fully understood unless the reader gives it his best hard thought, while the chatty memoir is, by its very nature, pretty light fluff. Alas, human nature being what it is, the latter type is more often read, if not necessarily remembered.

It was this type that restored the popularity of biography in the twenties, when the so-called "new" biography was in its heyday. Pseudo-Freudians titillated the public with jargon-filled analyses of the psyches and psychoses of great men, and debunkers flailed about wildly demolishing reputations. Imagination was substituted freely for research, fact was subordinated to effect, rumor replaced reason. "The time is coming," one critic warned in 1927, "when the biographers ain't going to the records but to the neighbors."

The result, in the hands of experts like Strachey, André Maurois and Emil Ludwig, was great fun to read. But these "new" biographers failed to treat adequately the serious side of their subjects' lives. They dealt too much with petty personal foibles and quirks, with love affairs, fancied thoughts and the superficiality of life. In time, more serious readers put these books aside and the boom collapsed. Then perhaps twenty years ago, a far more important, if less noticed, trend appeared. It was spearheaded by scholars who saw in the excesses of the "new" biographers the germ of a method that could produce books important as well as interesting, reliable as well as readable. H. F. Pringle's *Theodore Roosevelt,* published in the thirties, was a very early example of the new type, a debunking book but one based on thorough research.

S. E. Morison's biography of Columbus, *Admiral of the Ocean Sea,* pushed the budding trend along with its jaunty sailor's lingo and its freedom from the dust of closet scholarship. Morison cruised the Caribbean in Columbus' historic wake. He identified landfalls, commented shrewdly on the explorer's navigation and seamanship, used his imagination inventively, wrote vividly, dug up new facts and interpreted them wisely. He produced a brilliant and popular book, one that still sells briskly in a condensed paperback version.

Soon other writers were developing the new style further. Instead of aiming down at a large but thoughtless group of readers or up at a tiny handful of experts, they sought to be profound enough to interest the specialist and lively enough to hold the attention of the general reader. Essentially, they have taken the tricks of the "new" biographers, purged them of their deceits and applied them with patient scholarship.

The results speak for themselves. What a difference between Woodward's shallow debunking of Washington and Richard Hofstadter's reputation-busting but carefully thought-out sketches in *The American Political Tradition!* Or between any number of the early psychoanalytical biographies and Leon Edel's *Henry James: The Untried Years.*

A reader of the late F. L. Allen's *Great Pierpont Morgan* may put the book down with the feeling that he has been reading a fictional life, so smoothly is it written and so artfully constructed is its "plot." But an examination of Allen's papers in the Library of Congress reveals that his *Morgan* was based on hundreds of books, newspapers and Government reports. Careful planning and painstaking revision of a series of drafts drew from these tomes a sprightly and important biography.

Modern writers have also shown that pure imagination can play a legitimate role in the writing of lives. In the twenties biographical imagination was unbounded. If you didn't know what your hero had said at some crucial point, you simply put words in his mouth. If you discovered a good story that did not fit conveniently into its proper place in the narrative, you abandoned what one writer of that era called "exactitude" in dates.

Nowadays, however, some of our most talented biographers resort to imaginative reconstructions of a different sort. One can find new documents treating his subject's childhood. He visits the scene, studies the socio-cultural atmosphere in which the boy lived, even draws upon his observations of the antics of his own youngster.

Another — I speak here of perhaps the finest biographer of our generation, the late Benjamin P. Thomas — portrays Abraham Lincoln alone at his desk in the black of night, penning one of his deathless comments on the War and the Union. "These sentences are largely imaginative," Thomas admitted later while discussing the passage with a group of historians. "Yet I am convinced that they portray the situation accurately, and that something would have been lost . . . without the use of imagination." Thomas then described in gripping detail the reasoning that had led him to reconstruct a scene for which there was no direct evidence at all, and utterly convinced his audience that his reasoning was sound.

Where are biographers headed today? Surely no one can claim that the millennium is in sight, for there are still many clumsy, cheap, dull and empty lives being written. But the average, already high, seems to be improving. Some of the "new" biographers, now older and wiser, are putting real research into their latest books. André Maurois, as charming a stylist as ever, has succumbed to the footnote. More are likely to follow his lead.

Further prediction may be hazardous, but certain trends are evident. There will continue to be many long life-and-times biographies on the pattern of Freeman's *George Washington*. For example, multi-volumed studies of both the Roosevelts, of Wilson, Jefferson, Madison and other great Presidents are now in progress. As these appear, and as the papers of more and more of our statesmen are printed in full, many shorter lives of these men are sure to follow. The great collections of source material and the monumental biographies always need summation and interpretation.

The rise of paperbacks has also affected biography. The "quality" houses offer many first-rate scholarly lives — e.g., J. E. Neale's *Queen Elizabeth*, G. W. Allen's life of Whitman, Morris Bishop's *Ronsard*. The cheaper labels are bringing out many lives of more general appeal. (The paperback trend, by the way, should encourage particularly the writers of brief lives, since this format is poorly suited to longer volumes.)

Probably tomorrow's biographies will continue the present tendency toward raiding the social sciences for new research techniques. Of these sciences, psychology has most to offer a form of writing so intimately concerned with the actions and motives of human beings. Purged of its smugness by some of the most devastating criticism of the past two generations, the psychoanalytical biography is already making a strong comeback. At a meeting of the American Historical Association in December, 1957, Harvard's William L. Langer devoted a large part of his presidential address to a plea for the use of psychoanalytical concepts by academic historians. "If we are to retain our self-respect," Langer said, we must "believe that we can do better with the available evidence than the untrained popular biographer to whom we have so largely abandoned the field."

With blessings from such quarters, more and more scholars are likely to make use of Freud's insights in their work. The fascinating dual biography of Woodrow Wilson and Colonel House by Alexander and Juliette George shows what can and will be done in this field.

The social sciences may help biographers in other ways. The content analysis of personal documents, even of handwriting itself, can provide clues to the understanding of famous men. Anthropologists can contribute to the understanding of family relationships and their influence on personality. J. M. Burns' life of F. D. R., *Roosevelt: The Lion and the Fox,* which became a best seller by the way, illustrates how theories of the social psychology of leadership can be applied to biography. New ideas and methods are constantly becoming available.

In any case, it is unlikely that the Gertrude Athertons of the near future will be discouraged from writing biographies. Most Americans, believing with Pope that "the proper study of mankind is man," are fascinated by accounts of the actions, thoughts and feelings of their fellows. All signs indicate that a large number of biographies will continue to be written and that many of them will be the kind of lively and authoritative books that Americans will want to read.

LEON EDEL

That One May Say This Was
the Man

*[Some biographical details about the biographer Leon Edel are
on page 102.]*

A BIOGRAPHY is a record in words of something that is as mercurial
and as volatile, as compact of emotion and temperament, as the
human spirit itself. That is why Lytton Strachey spoke of the
biographical art as "the most delicate and humane of all the
branches of the art of writing." Delicate because the biographer
seeks to blow the breath of life into the inert and fragmentary
materials which survive an individual's passage on this earth.
Humane because such a process is inevitably a refining and civil-
izing process. It speaks for man's awareness of himself, his world,
his past. The dilemma of the biographer is that in seeking to
evoke the elusive flamelike spirit of man he must be neat and
orderly and logical; and the human spirit, because it is flamelike,
dances and flickers beyond order, neatness, logic.

The biographer may be as imaginative as he pleases — the
more imaginative the better — in the way in which he brings his
materials together. But he must not imagine the materials. He
must read himself into the past; but then he must read that past
into our present. He must read himself into the life he is writing;
but he must beware of re-creating that life in his own image.
He must judge the facts but not sit in judgment. He must respect the dead — but he must tell the truth.

These are large anomalies and the modern biographer does

what he can to overcome them. The old biographers had a much simpler task. They collected their data; they set it down in chronological fashion; they quoted extensively from letters and private papers, allowing the subject to speak for himself as much as possible. Boswell boasted that this was what he did for Dr. Johnson, even though he managed somehow to be busily next to, or in front of, the great doctor during much of his talk. Today, in the era of Einstein and Freud, when we have come to understand better man's symbol-creating power, things are not quite as simple for anyone who undertakes to write a life.

For one thing, the biographer must cope with twentieth-century man's acute historical sense. Boswell could boast that he did not melt down his materials and quoted from them as fully as possible. But what is the biographer of Franklin D. Roosevelt to do when he is faced with many million individual documents at Hyde Park? Or the biographer of Sir Winston Churchill, whose documents remain to be counted? By what light of theory are we to work in an era when the tape recorder and the kinescope, the gramophone and the cinema, perpetuate documents for us — the voice, the face, the actual moment — and some men even take the trouble to record their telephone conversations?

These are documents the document-collecting Boswell never dreamed of, and they may yet force biographers to work in teams. Unless, indeed, the writer of a life escapes into those comfortable centuries where there are so few documents that the very graves of the dead are opened up in the hope of finding a shred of a shred of evidence. We write Chaucer's life largely from a reading of his work and a few records dealing with the royal pensions bestowed upon him. Fancy writing someone's life today from the record of his check stubs! There seems, indeed, to be no happy middle ground. The old biographers had too few facts. We have an embarrassment of riches.

The challenge is, accordingly, all the greater. Logic — and the conditions of modern publishing — tell us that the contemporary biographer must recognize that he can seldom encompass the mountains of material available to him and that he must do the opposite of Boswell, melt them down to a sizable volume. Few lives lend themselves to the multi-volumed treatment of the Nicolay and Hay *Life of Abraham Lincoln* (ten volumes) or the Monypenny and Buckle *Disraeli* (six volumes). Synthesis must replace prolixity; rigid selection — and therefore careful interpretation — imposes itself.

The modern biographer's task accordingly becomes one of discovering the "dynamics" of the personality he is studying rather than allowing the reader to deduce that personality from documents. If he achieves a reasonable likeness, he need not fear too much that the unearthing of still more material will alter the picture he has drawn: it should add dimension to it, but not change its lineaments appreciably. After all, he has had more than enough material to permit him to reach conclusions and to paint his portrait. With this abundance of material he can select moments of high drama and find episodes to illustrate character and make for vividness. In any event, biographers, I think, must recognize that the writing of a life may not be as "scientific" or as "definitive" as we have pretended. Biography partakes of a large part of the subjective side of man; and we must remember that those who walked abroad in our time may have one appearance for us — but will seem quite different to posterity.

When we come to the writing of the lives of those who were themselves writers we encounter perhaps the greatest difficulties of all. The statesman or the soldier leaves his record in a large field of action. The life of the creative writer is often a quiet one: most of the time we hear only the scratch of the pen or the tick of the typewriter. On occasion the writer may be a Byronic personality, but more often than not he is unadventurous, and tethered to his writing desk. The problems of literary biography become linked in a large measure to the problems of literary criticism and in a deeper sense to those of psychoanalysis. For the creative writer does give himself to the world in his work; the poem is, after all, an emanation from a given poetic mind and it speaks for it, and with the poet's voice. As Yeats put it: "There is always a face behind the mask." The biographer must learn to read between the lines of the artist's work in order to recover the man — and not only as he spoke for himself but as he really was behind his word-façade. In this process the biographer turns critic as well as fact-seeker and analyst — critic not only of evidence, as all biographers have to be, but of the very texture of the works.

In undertaking to catch the mirror images of the subject, however, the literary biographer must be extremely careful not to reflect an image which is his own. Freud warned biographers against turning their subjects into paternal figures and seeking to erase all blemishes. The reverse of this is to turn the subject into a figure of hate. This usually ends in another kind of distortion and results in a debunking biography. The best way to avoid such extremes is to borrow whatever insights the psychoanalytic discipline can offer, so that the subject is seen not as all good or evil, but as a searching, erring, achieving or failing human.

Here, too, there are grave difficulties. For one thing, not all biographers are equipped to be psychoanalytical, and there can be nothing worse than an amateur psychologizer. Those who are so equipped usually go too far and reduce their subject to a clinical picture. Psychoanalysis in biography becomes a reductive process when it looks for the neurosis instead of the achievement.

Most delicate task of all is the restoring of a time-sense to the inert data, the lifeless papers piled so high on the biographer's table. Here the biographer will require all the art he can command. He must recapture old moments, old days, the very tick of the clock — and in another age. There is no way in which a biographer can completely recover lost time. He must constantly remind himself that the life he is writing did not consist of a series of facts on cards, arranged in a chronological sequence. Time for us in our daily lives is not quite so chronological. We shuttle back and forth at any given moment of the day, tissuing together widely separated moments of our experience. The modern biographer has begun to discover that a certain merging of past and present can give a rich effect of life. What he must learn to look for, it seems to me, is not only what happened in the given life but rather what everything that happened *meant* to the subject.

Ultimately the biographer paints his picture; and he can only paint it from *his* angle of vision, from *his* time and *his* relationship to the time he seeks to recover. If he has been a mere chronicler, we usually end up with one of those insufferably boring biographies in which the reader is confronted not by a palpable and breathing individual but a card index, a calendar, a date book. The biographer who respects his facts enough to evaluate and interpret them, and who presses ever to discover the life behind the facts, is the one who usually hangs before us an honest portrait which ends by being a reasonable likeness, instead of a figure of *papier-mâché*.

INDEX

Index